LAND LAW

LAND LAW

Louise Glover and Kate Campbell-Pilling

Hall and Stott Publishing Ltd
27 Witney Close
Saltford
BS31 3DX

British Library Cataloguing in Publication Data

ISBN 978 0 993336 57 7

Typeset by Style Photosetting Ltd, Mayfield, East Sussex

PREFACE

This book grew out of our writing a new course for GDL students and we are very grateful to Sue Hall and David Stott for giving us the opportunity to transform our teaching into a textbook. Our collective teaching experience encompasses teaching land law and equity and trusts to first and second year undergraduate students as well as property law and practice to professional students on our Legal Practice Course.

We have both come to teach land law after careers as practising solicitors in the commercial property sector. We know from experience that land law enables individuals and organisations to inhabit, invest in or finance property with a high degree of certainty about the outcome. Yet for many students land law remains inaccessible, over-complex and seemingly random in its application. It is frequently said with land law that it 'comes together' for many students only towards the end of the course when they are able to gain some perspective on how the detail comes together to form the whole. Some students never get to that point – either because they are not familiar enough with the detail or because they are not able to stand back to see how the detailed rules fit together to form a coherent and practical body of law.

We wanted to address these issues in our new course by giving students a broad scope to understand the general scheme of land law but also to become familiar with the source material, both statutory and case law, to grasp the detail of the rules precisely and the reasons behind them. So we have used lots of statutory and case extracts but also practical examples to see how these could be applied. We have tried to do so in a readable form, using explanations similar to those we might use in seminars, and including diagrams that we have used ourselves in teaching to make a point visually as well as verbally in the knowledge that students learn in a variety of ways. We hope that students will use this book as a starting point for further exploration and return to it to help them analyse what they have learnt.

We would also like to thank our colleagues at The University of Sheffield for their support and Sue and David at Hall & Stott Publishing for their patience throughout the writing of this book.

Louise Glover and Kate Campbell-Pilling
Sheffield
June 2017

CONTENTS

TABLE OF CASES

TABLE OF LEGISLATION

ABBREVIATIONS

AGA	authorised guarantee agreement
CML	Council of Mortgage Lenders
LA 1980	Limitation Act 1980
LCA 1972	Land Charges Act 1972
LPA 1925	Law of Property Act 1925
LPMPA 1989	Law of Property (Miscellaneous Provisions) Act 1989
LRA 2002	Land Registration Act 2002
MCOB	Mortgage Conduct of Business Rules
LTCA 1995	Landlord and Tenant (Covenants) Act 1995
TLATA 1996	Trusts of Land and Appointment of Trustees Act 1996

Introduction to Land Law

After reading this chapter, you will be able to understand:

- what is treated as land in the law of England and Wales
- the distinction between a fixture and a chattel
- what rights are recognised as being rights in the land
- the distinction between legal estates and interests and equitable interests in land
- the distinction between proprietary and personal rights
- how land can be subject to complementary and competing rights
- how human rights protection applies in the context of land.

1.1 Introduction

It is hard to overstate the importance of land to us. The Royal Institution of Chartered Surveyors (RICS) estimates that up to 70% of the world's wealth is bound up in land and real estate (RICS, April 2017). It is home to the world's citizens and the basis of mega cities and infrastructure, as well as to rural life. It is both a scarce resource requiring careful management, at risk of climate change and flooding, and a wealth-producing asset with a global investor base and favoured by sovereign wealth funds (the Abu Dhabi and Qatar Investment Funds have a combined $70 billion exposure to real estate globally). Land therefore has a 'functional and financial dimension' that other asset classes such as equities and bonds do not (RICS, *Safeguarding growth and stability in real estate and beyond*, April 2016).

It is unsurprising that this dual dimension of land is recognised by our legal system in England and Wales, as in others, by the development of a body of rules that apply specifically to land, our transactions with land and our relationship with other people in relation to land.

Many transactions relating to land are based in contract (although many are not) but land law goes further and deeper than this. Contract law is concerned about rights against an individual or individuals who have voluntarily entered into binding commitments; land law is concerned with rights considered to be so important that the law recognises them as rights in the land itself, potentially binding all future persons who come to the land, whether they wish it or not and irrespective that they are not parties to the original contract. The transmissibility of the benefit and burden of proprietary rights in land to future owners and occupiers of the land affected by the rights means that they are rights 'against the world' as well as merely rights against a particular individual.

The importance and permanence of land rights means that the law must regulate what rights will be considered proprietary, impose clear rules on when and how proprietary rights in land are created and disposed of, and develop mechanisms to resolve conflicts between competing rights and determine which existing land rights will bind a person who acquires an interest in land.

We consider it important that the law balances the rights of people who hold interests in land, and may have done so over many years, whilst enabling purchasers to buy land quickly, securely and without undue transaction cost. Our system relies on land registration to achieve this. 'Land registration ultimately aims to reduce or eliminate complexity and uncertainty in conveyancing' and provide a more efficient system (Law Commission, *Updating the Land Registration Act 2002: A Consultation Paper* (Law Com No 227, March 2016), [2.7]). Ultimately this will be fully electronic or digital although there are currently practical barriers to simultaneous completion and registration.

However, our law also recognises the validity of undocumented arrangements. In some cases this is a pragmatic response to arrangements that have operated over long periods of time (see **2.2** on adverse possession and **13.4.3** on prescription). Others are based on the conscience of the affected landowner; even before the late 1700s, it was clear that equity would step in, in certain circumstances in which it would be unconscionable to allow a landowner to insist on his or her strict legal rights (see **2.7.3**). New issues are thrown up by modern transactions such as equity release schemes in *Re North East Property Buyers Litigation* [2014] UKSC 52. Striking a balance between undocumented or unregistered rights and an efficient system of land registration is potentially devastating to individuals involved, such as former homeowners who were evicted when the equity release schemes collapsed, in some cases fraudulently. The need to respond to changes in consumer behaviour or market practice is not unique to land law; the consumer detriment in equity release schemes led to them becoming added to the list of regulated activities under s 19 of the Financial Services and Markets Act 2000, supervised by the Financial Conduct Authority. The 'functional and financial dimension' of land that we have already referred to, as well as its uniqueness and the strong emotional pull of an individual's home, mean that addressing these issues in relation to land can cause particular hardship.

We will begin by looking at the study points set out at the opening of this chapter.

1.2 What is 'land'?

The statutory definition of 'land' is set out in s 205(1)(ix) of the Law of Property Act (LPA) 1925:

'Land' includes land of any tenure, and mines and minerals, whether or not held apart from the surface, buildings or parts of buildings (whether the division is horizontal, vertical or made in any other way) and other corporeal hereditaments; also a manor, an advowson, and a rent and other incorporeal hereditaments, and an easement, right, privilege, or benefit in, over, or derived from land; … and 'mines and minerals' include any strata or seam of minerals or substances in or under any land, and powers of working and getting the same …; and 'manor' includes a lordship, and reputed manor or lordship; and 'hereditament' means any real property which on an intestacy occurring before the commencement of this Act might have devolved upon an heir;

Some of the items included in this definition of land seem quite archaic to us; for example an 'advowson' is the right to nominate a person to become minister of a church. In other cases, the concept remains relevant but the language is difficult: 'corporeal hereditaments' include physical features of the land such as buildings, plants or growing trees, whereas 'incorporeal hereditaments' include rights which have no physical form, such as a right of way over a neighbour's land or a right to take water from a spring.

The legal definition of land includes the physical land itself. This includes the subsoil beneath the land, including mines and minerals within the land, and the airspace above; the maxim was said to be that the owner of the soil also owns everything up to the sky and down to the centre of the earth (quoted in *Corbett v Hill* (1869–70) LR 9 Eq 671). Thus the invasion of a leaseholder's airspace by a sign which projected only 8 inches over the property let to him was held to be a trespass and he could obtain an injunction ordering the sign to be removed (*Kelsen v Imperial Tobacco Co (of Great Britain and Ireland) Ltd* [1957] 2 QB 334).

1.2.1 Airspace

In practice, due to the need to balance landowners' rights to use their land against the needs of the general public, rights in respect of the airspace have been limited to 'such height as is necessary for the ordinary use and enjoyment of his land and the structures upon it' (*Bernstein v Skyviews & General Ltd* [1978] QB 479 at 488, per Griffiths J). Above that height, the landowner has no greater rights than any other member of the public (*Star Energy v Bocardo* [2010] UKSC 35). A landowner cannot, therefore, prevent flights passing over his or her land at reasonable height. This also has a statutory basis in s 76(1) of the Civil Aviation Act 1982.

1.2.2 Below the ground

The owner of land owns the subsoil and strata below it. Interference by a third party will be an actionable trespass. The leading case of *Star Energy v Bocardo* [2010] UKSC 35 concerned horizontal drilling and confirmed that interference is not restricted to interfering with the owner's use and enjoyment of the land; the mere fact of boring into someone else's land, even at substantial depths, is trespass. The Supreme Court was not willing to apply the same principle as applies to airspace (namely that the surface owner would have rights over the subsoil only to such depth necessary for the ordinary use and enjoyment of the land and the structures upon it). Lord Hope stated (at [26]) that:

> It overlooks the point that, at least so far as corporeal elements such as land and the strata beneath it are concerned, the question is essentially one about ownership. As a general rule anything that can be touched or worked must be taken to belong to someone.

He accepted that there would be obviously be some practical stopping point, but noted that this would change with technological advances.

The owner of land also owns the minerals to be found within that land, subject to a number of qualifications:

(a) By statute and common law, certain valuable mines and minerals are reserved to the Crown. Examples include petroleum (Petroleum Act 1988, s 2). Statutory rights have been granted to enable organisations holding a licence from the Crown to extract those minerals. A topical and controversial example relates to 'fracking' or the extraction of shale gas (see the **topical example** below).

(b) In many cases, rights to mines and minerals have been alienated by private conveyance. It was common when selling off parts of larger estates for the seller to retain ownership of mines and minerals, together with rights to extract them.

topical example

Fracking

Fracking is the controversial method of extracting subterranean shale gas or oil. Shale gas is included in the definition of petroleum contained in s 2 of the Petroleum Gas 1988 and is therefore owned by the Crown. The Crown has the power to grant licences to extract shale gas in the UK, but until recently the licensee still had to reach agreement with all landowners concerned to drill under their land. Drilling without such consent would be trespass and could be prevented by an injunction (as in the *Kelsen* case above).

The Infrastructure Act 2015 grants a statutory right of access to drill under people's land without the need for permission from the landowner. Section 43(1) gives a right to use 'deep-level land' for the purposes of exploiting petroleum or deep geothermal energy without the landowner's permission. Deep-level land is any land at a depth of at least 300 metres below surface level (s 43(4)). The right to use may be exercised for drilling, boring, fracturing or otherwise altering the deep-level land, installing infrastructure and removing any substances.

Although landowner permission is unnecessary, landowners must be informed in advance and there will be a scheme for payments by the industry.

The Act does not give a right to use land for surface drilling sites, so fracking companies will still need to negotiate these with landowners, but they can rely on the new statutory right for bore holes passing under other land.

1.2.3 Buildings

Ownership rights in land are not limited to the surface, and they include buildings or parts of buildings on the land. Physical structures like these are known as corporeal hereditaments (this roughly translates as physical real property that is capable of being inherited by an heir of the owner).

1.2.4 Intangible rights

As well as the physical land and structures on it, the legal definition of land encompasses various rights which are connected to the land. For example, there may be a right to walk or drive over a neighbour's property in order to get access to your land. This right is known as an easement and is included within the definition of land. Intangible rights like these are described as 'incorporeal hereditaments' in the definition of land contained in s 205(1)(ix) of the LPA 1925 that you have just read.

They can be important in order to get full use or value from the land, and their status in law reflects this importance. They are considered so important that not only are they considered to be 'proprietary rights' in the land itself (rather than merely personal rights against an individual), but they are treated as if they are land in their own right. We will come to look at these in greater detail in **Chapters 13 and 14**.

1.2.5 Fixtures

When items or chattels are attached to land, they may take on the status of a fixture and become regarded in law as part of the land.

Whether an item has become a fixture depends on the intention of the original owner as ascertained from the degree of annexation and the purpose of the annexation. Of these two tests, the purpose of the annexation is the more decisive, as illustrated by Blackburn J, giving judgment in *Holland v Hodgson* (1872) LR 7 CP 328. He compared a dry stone wall which is fixed to the ground merely by its own weight, and which is part of the land. However the same stones, stored in a builder's yard and for convenience stacked in much the same way, would remain chattels. Conversely, a ship's anchor is firmly attached to the ground but only for the purpose of preventing the ship (a chattel) from drifting and is therefore a chattel itself.

The question of whether a chattel has become part of the land is important when land is sold or if a mortgagee takes possession of the land. Title to a fixture passes with the title to the land under s 62 of the LPA 1925 and therefore passes to the buyer or mortgagee in possession (unless expressly excluded in the transfer or mortgage deed). The *Holland v Hodgson* case concerned over 400 looms which were fixed to the floor of a mill to keep them steady. Following a conveyance of the mill, who had the right to them? It was found that the looms were attached to the land for the purpose of improving the land, rather than for any temporary purpose, and had become part of the land. Title to them had passed with the conveyance.

It is also important between a landlord and tenant, where a tenant attaches chattels to a property. There are special rules relating to a tenant's fixtures, allowing a tenant to remove such items at the end of the lease term, provided any damage to the property is made good (*Climie v Wood* (1868–69) LR 4 Ex 328).

In the case of *Elitestone Ltd v Morris* [1997] 1 WLR 687, Lord Lloyd approved a three-fold classification for objects brought on to land, which may be:

(a) a chattel;

(b) a fixture; or

(c) part and parcel of the land itself.

The question was whether a bungalow which rested by its own weight on concrete pillars fixed into the ground had become part of the land or remained a chattel. The House of Lords held that even though the bungalow was not fixed to the pillars, and therefore not attached to the ground other than by gravity, a house built in such a way that it could only be removed by destruction must have been intended to have become part of the land.

1.2.6 Items found in or on land

The owner of land is generally also entitled to lost items of property that are found buried in (rather than merely on) the land (*South Staffordshire Water Co v Sharman* [1896] 1 QB 44), unless they are treasure trove, in which case they belong to the Crown. The modern rules relating to treasure trove are found in the Treasure Act 1996. In his judgment in *South Staffordshire v Sharman*, Lord Russell of Killowen cited with approval at [46]–[47] Pollock and Wright, *An Essay on Possession in the Common Law* (1 January 1888):

> The possession of land carries with it in general, by our law, possession of everything which is attached to or under that land, and, in the absence of a better title elsewhere, the right to possess it also. And it makes no difference that the possessor is not aware of the thing's existence … It is free to anyone who requires a specific intention as part of a de facto possession to treat this as a positive rule of law. But it seems preferable to say that the legal possession rests on a de facto possession, constituted by the occupier's general power and intent to exclude unauthorised interference.

The rationale for this is given by Donaldson J in *Parker v British Airways Board* [1982] 1 QB 1004:

> let me know turn to another situation in respect of which the law is reasonably clear. This is that of chattels which are attached to realty (land or buildings) when they are found. If the finder is not a wrongdoer, he may have

some rights, but the occupier of the land or building will have a better title. The rational of this rule is probably either that the chattel is to be treated as an integral part of the realty as against all but the true owner and so incapable of being lost or that the 'finder' has to do something to the realty in order to get at or detach the chattel and, if he is not thereby to become a trespasser, will have to justify his actions by reference to some form of licence from the occupier. In all likely circumstances that licence will give the occupier a superior right to that of the finder.

However, chattels that are merely found *on* land (for example a lost bracelet) will not belong to the landowner or occupier unless the finder is a trespasser or the owner exercises such control over land that he has shown intention to control anything found on it (*Parker v British Airways Board*). Evidence of intention to exercise control can be express (for example putting up signs on the land requiring lost property to be handed in) or it may be implied from the circumstances (for example if the occupier accepts or is required by law to accept liability for chattels that are lost on his or her premises).

Donaldson J confirmed (at 1018) that the owner of a chattel (eg a ship, car or aircraft) would be treated as if he or she were the occupier of a building for the purposes of these rules.

1.3 What rights can exist in land?

1.3.1 Legal 'ownership' of land

In English law, we see the idea that it is not possible to 'own' land itself but instead an estate in the land. An estate in the land was described in 1573 in *Walsingham's Case* (1575) 2 Plow 547 at 555 as follows:

> An estate in the land is a time in the land, or land for a time, and there are diversities of estates which are no more than diversities of time ...

The two estates which are recognised at law under modern English law are the fee simple absolute in possession (or freehold) and the term of years absolute (or leasehold). Commonhold, which we refer to at **1.3.1.3** below, is a form of freehold estate.

1.3.1.1 The fee simple absolute in possession

This gives an indefinite right to own the land and is commonly known as the 'freehold'. It is regarded as the closest that English law gets to absolute ownership, but in theory remains an estate or a 'time in the land' even though an indefinite one. This is reflected in the fact that if the owner dies intestate without relatives then ownership will revert back to the Crown as bona vacantia or vacant goods. The Treasury Solicitor may dispose of the land, with proceeds going to the Crown.

The components of the phrase are explained as follows:

(a) a 'fee' is an estate that lasts for an indefinite period of time and is capable of being inherited (as opposed, for example, to a life interest that expires on the holder's death);

(b) 'simple' refers to a lack of restrictions as to which heirs can inherit;

(c) 'absolute' means that it is not conditional or determinable (for example, an estate granted to Nelson if he marries is conditional; an estate to which Charlie is entitled until he marries is determinable); and

(d) an estate 'in possession' allows the holder to exercise ownership rights now, rather than in the future.

1.3.1.2 The term of years absolute

This estate gives ownership for a defined period of time, which could be long or short, for example as little as a week or as long as 999 years. It is commonly known as a leasehold or as a lease or tenancy.

Under s 1(1) of the LPA 1925, the freehold and leasehold are the only two estates which are recognised as legal estates under English law:

> The only estates in land which are capable of subsisting or of being conveyed or created at law are—
>
> (a) An estate in fee simple absolute in possession; and
>
> (b) A term of years absolute.

1.3.1.3 Commonhold

Commonhold was created as a method of 'ownership' by the Commonhold and Leasehold Reform Act 2002. The new form of tenure was designed to be an alternative to leasehold tenure, appropriate for use for buildings with multiple occupiers, such as blocks of flats or a commercial office block or shopping centre. A freehold estate is registered to a commonhold association as a freehold estate in commonhold land. Individual units, such as a flat or an office unit, are disposed of as a freehold estate in the unit. The owner of each unit holds a freehold estate in the unit, and the commonhold association holds the freehold estate in the common parts (for example the common hallways or parking areas within the property). The advantage of the scheme is that the convenience of leasehold estates, in allowing positive covenants to be enforced, is retained but without the vulnerability that comes from a time limited estate. The best features of each estate are obtained: the commonhold association can require the unit holders to pay for upkeep of the common parts, and in return the unit holders can require the association to carry out maintenance works, similarly to a leasehold estate. However, the unit holder gets the benefit of an indefinite right to the unit under a freehold title, rather than one limited to a term of years (eg 99 years) as a leasehold interest would be, and removal of some of the risks of a leasehold title. The freehold titles of the commonhold association and the unit holders are each a fee simple absolute in possession within s 1(1)(a) of the LPA 1925.

Despite the advantages of commonhold and its popularity in other jurisdictions, it has not proved popular with property developers and, by early 2008, only 14 commonholds had been registered according to figures supplied by the Land Registry (Law Commission, *Easements, Covenants and Profits a Prendre* (Consultation Paper No 186), [11.4]).

1.3.2 Legal third party rights in land

As well as freehold and leasehold estates in land, English law also recognises rights or interests in land. These can be thought of as third party rights in or over land that belong to another person. Section 1(2) of the LPA 1925 states that only certain interests in land are capable of existing at law:

> The only interests or charges in or over land which are capable of subsisting or of being conveyed or created at law are—
>
> (a)   An easement, right, or privilege in or over land for an interest equivalent to an estate in fee simple absolute in possession or a term of years absolute;
>
> (b)   A rentcharge in possession issuing out of or charged on land being either perpetual or for a term of years absolute;
>
> (c)   A charge by way of legal mortgage;
>
> (d)   … and any other similar charge on land which is not created by an instrument;
>
> (e)   Rights of entry exercisable over or in respect of a legal term of years absolute, or annexed, for any purpose, to a legal rentcharge.

The most important of these rights are easements (such as the right to cross a neighbour's land to get access to your property) and mortgages. A mortgage is a device used to secure repayment of a loan. If the money is not paid back, the lender is entitled to take possession of the property and sell it, taking the money owed to it out of the sale proceeds

example

Dipak wants to build a new garage at the back of his house. In order to get to the garage from the public highway, he persuades his neighbour to grant him a right of way, with or without vehicles, over his neighbour's land. This is known as an easement. If the easement is granted for an indefinite period or for a fixed term (eg 10 years) then it is capable of being a legal easement. We know this from applying the rule set out in s 1(2)(a) of the LPA 1925 above.

Any rights in land that do not fall within s 1(1) and 1(2) of the LPA 1925 can only take effect as equitable interests in land.

1.3.3 Equitable interests in land

Equity also recognises certain interests in land which were not recognised by the common law or, now, by s 1(1) and 1(2) of the LPA 1925.

If a right in land does not fall within s 1(1) or 1(2) of the LPA 1925 then it cannot take effect as a legal estate or interest and will only take effect in equity.

Section 1(3) of the LPA 1925 states:

> All other estates, interests, and charges in or over land take effect as equitable interests.

The estates and interests set out in s 1(1) and 1(2) of the LPA 1925 may also be created in equity. Sometimes this may occur because the interest has not been created in the way that the law requires.

For example, s 52(1) of the LPA 1925 requires that a deed is used to create or transfer a legal estate or interest in land. If this formality has not been observed then equity might intervene in some circumstances. In *Walsh v Lonsdale* (1882) 21 Ch D 9, an agreement to create a lease had never been completed by deed by the parties. A lease had not been created at law. However, the contract to enter into the lease was specifically enforceable and sufficient to create an equitable lease on the same terms as the contract.

'Specific performance' means that a court will require that a contract is actually performed, rather than requiring the common law remedy of payment of damages to compensate for breach. Specific performance is an equitable remedy that is normally available in relation to land contracts as, due to the unique nature of land, damages are considered 'wholly inadequate and unjust' (*Sudbrook Trading Estate Ltd v Eggleton* [1983] 1 AC 444 at 478, per Lord Diplock).

example

If Oliver enters into a contract to sell his land to Alice and then refuses to complete the sale, Alice may be able to obtain an order of specific performance which compels the transfer of the land, rather than simply requiring Oliver to pay damages for loss that Alice incurs as a result of his refusal to honour the contract.

The equitable lease that was created in *Walsh v Lonsdale* could have existed as a legal lease if the parties had entered into a lease by deed, as they had originally intended when they entered into the contract to do so. However, equity will also recognise transactions that create equitable interests in land that have *never* been recognised by the common law or, following s 1 of the LPA 1925, are *no longer* recognised as creating legal estates or interests in land. All such rights are now categorised as 'equitable interests' in land under s 1(3) of the LPA 1925.

1.3.4 Equitable 'ownership' of land

It is possible to create rights in land that look like 'ownership' that only take effect in equity. So, for example, it is possible to own an equitable life interest which gives the right to enjoy land for the lifetime of the person holding the interest. On his or her death, the lifetime title in the property comes to an end. This is not an estate in fee simple absolute in possession as its existence is conditional on the continued life of the holder. Neither is it an estate for a term of years absolute as it is not for a fixed term (unlike, for example, a 10-year lease). As it does not fall within either of the categories above set out in s 1(1) of the LPA 1925, it cannot take effect at law but can only take effect in equity. And unlike an 'ownership' right that exists at law, it is not known as an 'estate' in land, but only as an equitable 'interest'.

As we have seen, s 1(3) of the LPA 1925 states:

> All other estates, interests, and charges in or over land take effect as equitable interests.

example

John, a retired widower with one child, Max, is the freehold owner of Beech House. He marries Judy, a divorcee with two children of her own. In his will, John wants to provide that Max will inherit his house, but that if Judy outlives John, she will have the right to live in Beech House for the rest of her life. This will take place using a trust: on John's death, the legal title to the property will pass to Max, but Judy will be granted an equitable life interest in Beech House. The legal title gives formal ownership of the property, but Judy's equitable interest gives her the right to use and occupy the property. During the period in which Judy survives John, Max's equitable interest is described as being 'in remainder'. On Judy's death, the trust comes to an end, and Max will be entitled to the full equitable interest in the property as well as to the legal title that he already holds.

1.3.5 Equitable third party rights in land

Equity also recognises certain rights in land that we would characterise as third party rights; they are rights over land that we would regard as 'belonging to' another person.

Sometimes this was because the interest was not one that the common law recognised as being an interest in land at all. The important case of *Tulk v Moxhay* [1848] 2 Ph 774 concerned restrictive covenants affecting land.

Tulk v Moxhay [1848] 2 Ph 774

case example

- A landowner named Elms promised by deed (a covenant) with his neighbour not to develop part of his land but to keep it as a garden.
- The land was later sold to a purchaser who knew of the covenant but who wished to develop the garden.
- The neighbour was able to obtain an injunction to prevent the development, even though the purchaser was not a party to the original contract.
- The Court accepted that at law the burden of a covenant did not 'run with the land' and so would not bind the purchaser.

- However, it would be 'inequitable or contrary to good conscience' for a person (Elms) who takes property at a lesser price because it is subject to a restriction to obtain full value from a third party (the purchaser) who would hold it 'unfettered' by the restriction under which it was granted. The conscience of Elms was affected and he could not hand over the property with a better title as between himself and his neighbour than he himself possessed. (Elms himself had died before any sale of the property and therefore was not at fault personally, but the principle applied to the sale by his successors.)
- The purchaser had taken the land with knowledge of the covenant and therefore had knowledge of the 'equity'. A purchaser would be bound by the covenant unless he could show that he purchased the land without notice of it.

1.3.6 No right in land at all?

Some transactions may not give rise to any right in the land at all, although they may create personal rights between two individuals. The right may be enforceable against the individual in question but will become worthless if the individual dies, becomes bankrupt or sells the property concerned. It can be very valuable to establish the existence of a proprietary right in the land that can survive these events.

King v David Allen and Sons, Billposting, Ltd [1916] 2 AC 54

case example

King, who owned a cinema, granted a right to the claimant company to display adverts on the walls of the cinema. He then granted a lease of the cinema to a third party, who refused to allow the posters to be displayed. The House of Lords confirmed that the contract granted a licence that was enforceable between King and the company only. It did not create any proprietary right in the land in favour of the company. The company was entitled to damages from King for breach of the contract but could not enforce the contract against the new tenant of the property.

1.3.6.1 'Orthodox' approach

This is the 'orthodox approach' that a contractual licence does not bind third parties. However, there are circumstances in which the courts will find that a personal arrangement like this can become binding on a new estate owner in equity. The 'conscience of the estate holder' is said to be affected so that it would be inequitable for him to refuse to honour the arrangement, creating a constructive trust.

1.3.6.2 Constructive trust

When will the conscience of the estate holder be affected? It is not enough simply for the new estate owner to buy his or her interest with notice of the personal arrangement, as it is common conveyancing practice for property to be sold 'subject to' past documents that may or may not be binding. This is to protect a seller against ongoing personal liability, rather than to impose new proprietary obligations on the purchaser and his successors where none previously existed. If the right is non-proprietary like a licence, the circumstances must also show that a *new arrangement* has arisen between the licence-holder and the new estate owner. Evidence of the new arrangement must be more than 'slender' (*Ashburn Anstalt v Arnold* [1989] Ch 1, approved and followed in a case concerning proprietary estoppel, *Lloyd v Dugdale* [2002] 2 P&CR 13). Evidence can be indirect, for example if the price is reduced to reflect the continued liability.

1.4 Law and equity

In the discussions above, we have identified a distinction between law and equity which we must now explain: what is the difference between rights that exist at law and those that exist only in equity?

Historically, equity developed to address defects in the common law. The common law was administered by the King's courts. In some cases where the common law gave no or an inadequate remedy but where 'conscience' or justice was thought to demand one, a party could bring his or her case to the King's Chancellor. Over time, this formalised into the equitable jurisdiction of the Courts of Chancery and two systems developed: common law rights were recognised and enforced by the common law courts and equitable rights by the Chancery Courts. To enforce common law or equitable rights, one had to apply to different courts, which led to conflict between the two court systems. The Judicature Acts of 1873–75 resolved this by providing that all courts could administer the law and equity.

Equity is underpinned by maxims or general principles, which are set out below.

equitable maxims

Equity will not suffer a wrong to be without a remedy

Equity follows the law

He who seeks equity must do equity

He who comes to equity must come with clean hands

Where the equities are equal the law prevails

Where the equities are equal the first in time prevails

Equity imputes an intention to fulfil an obligation

Equity regards as done that which ought to be done

Equity is equality

Equity looks to the intent rather than the form

Delay defeats equities

Equity acts in personam

Under our precedent-based system, these maxims developed into rules that may be applied as rigorously as the common law.

Although the two systems have merged, English law continues to make a distinction between law and equity. One practical effect of this is that legal and equitable rights can co-exist in the same piece of property. One meaning of the maxim that 'equity follows the law' is that property rights recognised by the common law can also exist in equity. For example, as well as legal easements, there can be equitable easements. However, equity also accepts, as rights in land, matters that are not recognised by the common law as being rights in land, such as restrictive covenants (which the common law views as essentially contractual agreements between the original contracting parties), or at all, such as rights of beneficiaries under a trust of land.

1.5 Trusts of land

Under a trust of land, the trustee holds the legal title to land on trust for a beneficiary or beneficiaries.

example

In our example above, after John's death, Max holds the legal title to the house on trust for Judy (during her lifetime) and for himself as 'remainderman'. On Judy's death, the trust comes to an end and Max holds the full equitable interest in the property as well as the legal estate.

The trustee or trustees are the legal owner(s) of the land and, if the land is registered, the registered proprietor(s). It is the trustees who have the power to sell, charge or lease the property (Trusts of Land and Appointment of Trustees Act 1996, s 6(1)). However, it is the beneficiaries who have the benefit of the use and enjoyment of the land. Trustees must act for the benefit of the beneficiaries and are under strict obligations (known as fiduciary duties) to do so. The trustees must utilise any benefit from the land (eg rent paid to the trustees under an occupational lease) for the benefit of the beneficiaries. Depending on the nature of the trust, the beneficiaries then have a right to occupy the property (Trusts of Land and Appointment of Trustees Act 1996, s 12), not the trustees.

Trusts may be created expressly but may also arise by operation of law. The law always imposes a trust of land when property is jointly owned by two or more people (LPA 1925, s 34(2)). As a result, trusts of land are very common, particularly in relation to the family home. Where land is transferred into joint names (for example a husband and wife), confusingly, the trustees and beneficiaries are the same people, who may be unaware of the legal categorisation of their relationship with the land into legal and beneficial interests under a trust. However, a trust can also arise where property is transferred into the sole name of one person but another person contributes to the purchase price or the mortgage, or where there is a common intention that the property is to be shared. In the case of *Williams & Glyn's Bank v Boland* [1981] AC 487, the family home was registered in the sole name of Mr Boland but he held it on trust for himself and his wife, as she had contributed to the purchase price.

A trust is not the only kind of equitable right, though it is an important one. Other rights like leases, easements and covenants can also exist in equity.

1.6 Proprietary rights vs personal rights

We talked at the beginning of this chapter about the difference between a proprietary right, which is a right in the land itself, and a personal right, which is a right against an individual. Many transactions give rise to both personal and proprietary rights. For example, if I enter into a contract to buy a house, I have both a personal contractual right against the seller with whom I have entered into the contract, and an equitable proprietary right in the house. This distinction can be crucial; if the seller breaches the contract by selling the land to another person, my contractual right gives me a right to seek financial compensation or damages from the seller, but my proprietary right may give me the right to have the property transferred to me in specific performance of the contract.

However, other rights may be purely personal. If the landowner breaches them, the only remedy may be against the landowner personally. That may be of little benefit if the landowner dies or has sold the land or is bankrupt.

So, how do we know whether a right is a right in land at all? A starting point could be to look at s 1(2) of the LPA 1925, which sets out legal interests in land. A right included in this list, such as an easement or mortgage, is capable not only of being a right in land but one recognised at law. However, this only gets us so far. Section 1(3) states: 'All other estates, interests, and charges in or over land take effect as equitable interests.' So clearly there are other rights that are interests or rights in land that are not listed in subsection (2). How do we identify those?

1.6.1 *National Provincial Bank v Ainsworth*

This question was addressed by the House of Lords in *National Provincial Bank Ltd v Ainsworth* [1965] AC 1175. The case concerned a claim by a wife who had been deserted by her husband to have a proprietary right in the matrimonial home. The question for the court was whether rights to cohabitation and support that existed between a husband and wife were merely personal rights between the husband and wife or also gave a proprietary right in the property. The rights existed by virtue of marriage, and were recognised in equity and enforceable against the husband by procedures contained in s 17 of Married Women's Property Act 1882 (which Act is now largely repealed). A husband could be ordered to provide a suitable dwelling house and maintenance for his wife. Mrs Ainsworth continued to live in the matrimonial home and argued that her rights as a deserted wife were not merely personal rights against her husband but proprietary rights in the marital home that took priority over a third party bank, which had lent money to her husband and held a registered charge in the property. Lord Wilberforce, dismissing her appeal, stated (at 1248):

> Before a right or an interest can be admitted into the category of property, or of a right affecting property, it must be definable, identifiable by third parties, capable in its nature of assumption by third parties, and have some degree of permanence or stability. The wife's right has none of these qualities, it is characterised by the reverse of them.

The rights were merely personal rights against the husband. They did not attach to any particular property, and the husband could satisfy his obligations by supporting her in a suitable home. The nature of a proprietary right is that it gives rights in a specific property, and Mrs Ainsworth could not establish that her rights existed in the actual matrimonial home in which she continued to live. It was possible that Mr Ainsworth might not be subject to any obligations to Mrs Ainsworth at all. The rights were also

> personal in the sense that a decision can only be reached on the basis of considerations essentially dependent on the mutual claims of husband and wife as spouses and as the result of a broad weighing of circumstances and merit. Moreover these rights are at no time definitive, they are provisional and subject to review at any time according as changes take place in the material circumstances and conduct of the parties. (per Lord Wilberforce at 1247)

1.6.2   The end of the story?

The decision in *Ainsworth* led to the Matrimonial Homes Act 1967, now contained in Part IV of the Family Law Act 1996, which extends to married couples and civil partners. A spouse or civil partner who is not a legal owner of the family home has a statutory right to occupy it, not to be excluded or evicted and, if not in occupation, the right with the leave of the court to enter and occupy the family home.

The rights are capable of binding third parties if protected by a notice on the register (in the case of registered land) (Family Law Act 1996, s 31(10)(a); Land Registration Act 2002, s 29(2)(a)(i)) or by registration of a Class F land charge (in the case of unregistered land) (Land Charges Act 1972, ss 2(7) and 4(8)). They cannot be an overriding interest (Family Law Act 1996, s 31(10)(b)) (see **5.6.2** for the overriding nature of interests of persons in actual occupation of registered land).

1.6.3   The nature of the right determines if it is proprietary

The nature of the right granted is vital. If, whether the parties intended to or not, parties create a right that is accepted as a proprietary right in the land then it will (at least in the correct conditions) create one, even if the parties are not aware that this has occurred. As Lord Hoffmann said in *Bruton v London & Quadrant Housing Trust* [2000] 1 AC 406:

> … it is the fact that the agreement is a lease which creates the proprietary interest. It is putting the cart before the horse to say that whether the agreement is a lease depends upon whether it creates a proprietary interest.

So far as the student of land law is concerned, perhaps the best answer to the question 'how do we know whether a right is a right in land at all?' is that they must become familiar through practice with the established categories of estates and rights in land – and then learn the rules that set out whether a right or purported right falls within any of those categories.

1.7 How are rights created or transferred?

1.7.1 Formalities

Because of the potential impact of proprietary rights and the need for their existence to be certain and capable of being discovered by a purchaser, there are usually formalities required for their creation and transfer. For example, the general rule is that the creation or transfer of a legal interest in land must be by deed, under s 52(1) of the LPA 1925. This means that it must be made by a document that makes it clear on its face that it is intended to be and is validly executed as a deed. For an individual, that requires it to be signed in the presence of a witness and delivered as a deed. Different formality rules apply to the creation or disposition of equitable interests (LPA 1925, s 53(1)).

1.7.2 Registration

In *Tulk v Moxhay*, it was critical that the purchaser of the garden land was aware of – to use the legal term, 'had notice of' – the restrictive covenant before he purchased title to the property. In the modern law, the covenant is likely to require registration on a public register in order to bind a purchaser:

(a) If the servient (burdened) land is registered, the restrictive covenant will be protected if it is the subject of a notice in the register (Land Registration Act 2002, ss 29(2)(a)(i) and 32(3)).

(b) If the servient land remains unregistered:

    (i) any new restrictive covenant will be void against a purchaser unless registered as a land charge under Class D(ii) (Land Charges Act 1972, s 2(5)(ii) and 4(6));

    (ii) only pre-1926 restrictive covenants affecting unregistered land continue to rely on mere notice for protection (Land Charges Act 1972, s 4(6)).

From the point of view of the person who wishes to take the benefit of an interest in land, it is very important therefore that he or she checks that all necessary steps to ensure that the interest is properly created and protected have been taken. We will look at this in greater detail in **Chapters** 3 and 5.

1.7.3 Informal acquisition

Although the general policy in land law is to require compliance with formalities and registration requirements, there are exceptions where rights can be transferred or created informally or by operation of law (such as short leases (LPA 1925, s 54) and trusts created in certain circumstances (LPA 1925, s 53(2)). We examine both the policy and the exceptions in more detail in **Chapter** 2. Similarly, those and other rights may be binding on a purchaser even though unregistered (Land Registration Act 2002, s 29(2)(a)(ii) and Sch 3), and this is covered in **Chapter** 5.

1.8 In what circumstances will rights be binding on a purchaser of land?

A person who is buying or lending money on land wants to know whether he or she will be bound by or can take advantage of rights and liabilities affecting the land. Looking again at the example of a property to which access is gained by walking or driving over the land of a neighbour, any buyer or mortgagee of the land needs to know whether they can rely on the ability to gain access to the property in this way, even if the neighbouring land is sold. In other words, has an easement been created or merely a personal licence? If it is capable of binding in this way, it is regarded as a proprietary right.

As noted above, whether a proprietary right *actually* binds in each particular case will depend on whether it has been created properly – as a general rule this means compliance with formalities – and whether mechanisms designed to communicate the right to a purchaser – as a general rule this means registration – have been satisfied. Both these general rules are subject to exceptions.

1.9 Complementary and competing interests in land

This leads on to another concept which is of paramount importance in land law. The existence of proprietary rights means that many people can have rights in one piece of land.

In many cases these are complementary because property rights can be multi-layered. It may help a student getting to grips with land law to think in terms of layers or levels of interests.

example

Eve is the freehold owner of a house (to put this in technical language she holds the fee simple absolute in possession (LPA 1925, s 1(1)(a)). Her mother Alison has contributed to the purchase price; it is not a loan or a gift, so under equitable principles (*Dyer v Dyer* (1788) 2 Cox 92) Alison has an equitable interest in the house. Eve holds the house on trust for herself and her mother, most likely in the proportions in which they have contributed. It can be helpful for students to think of both of these interests in the 'freehold ownership layer' of the property:

LEGAL ESTATE   Eve

BENEFICIAL INTERESTS   Eve and Alison

Eve's name appears on the property deeds and, if title is registered, in the proprietorship register of the title. She is the formal owner, but both Eve and Alison are entitled to the benefits of property ownership, for example, the right to live in the property (Trusts of Land and Appointment of Trustees Act 1996, s 12(1)).

Eve, as legal owner, grants a six-month assured shorthold tenancy or lease to Adam, who lives in the house. This creates a new legal estate, a term of years absolute (LPA 1925, s 1(1)(b)), which is a new layer carved out of the 'freehold ownership layer'. This new layer is a hybrid because it is both a new 'ownership layer', in this case 'ownership' of the lease, but also a third party right affecting the freehold. If the lease were longer, it would have its own registered title (leases of more than seven years on grant or transfer are registrable under s 4(1)(c)(i) and s 4(1)(a)(i) of the Land Registration Act 2002) and would also appear as a notice in the charges register of Eve's registered title (leases of three years or more can be noted on the affected title (Land Registration Act 2002, s 32 and s 33(b))).

Eve remains in possession of the freehold estate, which she continues to hold on trust for herself and Alison. Eve and Alison have now given up the right to live in the property to Adam, temporarily, for the duration of his lease. It is no longer available to the beneficiaries of the trust of land for occupation (Trusts of Land and Appointment of Trustees Act 1996, s 12(2)). However, Adam will pay rent to Eve as the legal freeholder, which Eve receives as trustee for herself and Alison, and they enjoy the right to share the rent.

We could add further layers to this; for example, part of the purchase price could have been made up of a mortgage taken out with First Bank by Eve to finance the acquisition. The property may be subject to an easement in favour of the next-door neighbour, Max, to park on the drive of the property, and it may be subject to a restrictive covenant in favour of the neighbour on the other side, Nathan, that the property may only be used for residential purposes.

These rights are capable of existing in a complementary way. In the example above, the mortgagee's consent should have been obtained (either specifically or generally in the wording of the loan agreement) to the grant of the lease to Adam. Similarly, Adam, in taking the lease, will have to observe and respect the easement and restrictive covenant rights.

However, rights can conflict. If the mortgage is unpaid and the mortgagee seeks possession, or Alison as beneficiary under the trust of land and Adam as tenant both want to occupy the property, then the law needs mechanisms to assess who has the right to do so and what rights, if any, the other people are left with. So another issue which land law has to deal with is how a person who wishes to take the benefit of a proprietary right in land can protect it, and how the law will assess the competing priorities of several people with rights in the same land.

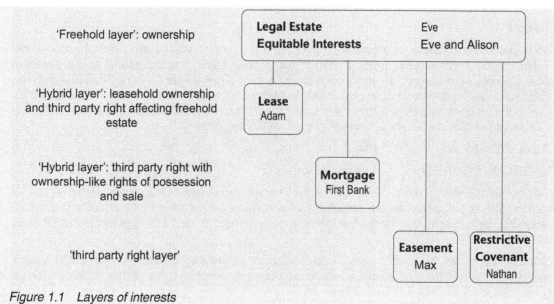

Figure 1.1 Layers of interests

We deal with this in **Chapters** 3 and 5.

1.10 Human rights

Much of this discussion has concerned rights, whether in land and therefore 'against the world' or personal rights against individuals. It is worth putting these in the context of modern understandings of rights contained in the European Convention on Human Rights, incorporated into UK law by the Human Rights Act 1998. Given that property rights can be held by any entity that is recognised in England and Wales as having legal personality, we should explain at the outset that certain articles, such as Article 1 of Protocol No 1, grant rights to natural or legal persons. And Article 34 allows Convention rights to be exercised by any person, non-governmental organisation or group of individuals. In the leading case on Article 1 of Protocol No 1, *JA Pye (Oxford) Ltd v United Kingdom* (2008) 46 EHRR 45, Application No 44302/02, the applicant was a limited company.

The two provisions that relate most closely to property rights are Article 1 of Protocol No 1 and Article 8.

1.10.1 Article 1 of Protocol No 1

Article 1 of Protocol No 1 to the European Convention on Human Rights, incorporated into UK law by the Human Rights Act 1998, provides:

Every natural or legal person is entitled to the peaceful enjoyment of his possessions. No one shall be deprived of his possessions except in the public interest and subject to the conditions provided for by law and by the general principles of international law.

The preceding provisions shall not, however, in any way impair the right of a State to enforce such laws as it deems necessary to control the use of property in accordance with the general interest or to secure the payment of taxes or other contributions or penalties.

The case of *JA Pye (Oxford) Ltd v United Kingdom* concerned adverse possession, which is a method of acquiring title informally by long usage of land without force, permission of the legal owner or stealth. The common law position is that if a squatter or trespasser on land is in possession of it for a minimum of 12 years, then the legal owner is barred from bringing an action to recover its land (Limitation Act 1980, s 15(1)). Pye was a landowner in such a situation who claimed that the loss of its land to a squatter (the Grahams) breached its rights under Article 1 of Protocol No 1. It was unsuccessful, as the Court held that the limitation period amounted to a control of the use of property, rather than a deprivation of property, and the UK Parliament's view of what was in the public interest would be respected unless manifestly without foundation. A limitation period of 12 years for actions for recovery of land pursued a legitimate aim in the public interest. (Note that in the case of registered land, different limitation provisions now apply; see 2.2.4.)

The Court stated that:

> Finding it natural that the margin of appreciation available to the legislature in implementing social and economic policies should be a wide one [the Court] will respect the legislature's judgment as to what is 'in the public interest' unless that judgment is manifestly without reasonable foundation.

The rules as to adverse possession were widely known and had been in force for many years (indeed were in force prior to the acquisition of the land by Pye), and therefore Pye was expected to be aware of them when acquiring its title to the land. Pye could have taken relatively small procedural steps to defeat the Grahams' claim; for example, if before the Grahams' claim crystallised on 12 years' adverse possession, Pye had demanded rent from the Grahams and, if refused, brought an action for recovery of the land, this would have been sufficient to defeat the Grahams' claim. The fact that very little action was needed by Pye to stop time running indicated that the provisions in the Limitation Act 1980 were proportionate between the means employed and the aims pursued.

Although the land was valuable, the value of the land could not affect the application of the principles, and the Court found that the 'fair balance' required by Article 1 of Protocol No 1 had not been breached.

1.10.2 Article 8

Article 8 of the European Convention on Human Rights, incorporated into UK law by the Human Rights Act 1998, provides:

1. Everyone has the right to respect for his private and family life, his home and his correspondence.

2. There shall be no interference by a public authority with the exercise of this right except such as is in accordance with the law and is necessary in a democratic society in the interests of national security, public safety or the economic well-being of the country, for the prevention of disorder or crime, for the protection of health or morals, or for the protection of the rights and freedoms of others.

And s 6 of the Human Rights Act 1998 states:

(1) It is unlawful for a public authority to act in a way which is incompatible with a Convention right.

(2) Subsection (1) does not apply to an act if—

(a) as the result of one or more provisions of primary legislation, the authority could not have acted differently; or

(b) in the case of one or more provisions of, or made under, primary legislation which cannot be read or given effect in a way which is compatible with the Convention rights, the authority was acting so as to give effect to or enforce those provisions.

(3) In this section 'public authority' includes—

(a) a court or tribunal, and

(b) any person certain of whose functions are functions of a public nature,

but does not include either House of Parliament or a person exercising functions in connection with proceedings in Parliament.

1.10.2.1 'Home'

The expression 'home'

> … appears to invite a down-to-earth and pragmatic consideration whether (as Lord Millett put it in *Uratemp Ventures Ltd v Collins* [2001] UKHL 43, [2002] 1 AC 301, paragraph 31) the place in question is that where a person 'lives and to which he returns and which forms the centre of his existence' since 'home' is not a legal term of art and article 8 is not directed to the protection of property interests or contractual rights (per Lord Bingham in *London Borough of Harrow v Qazi* [2003] UKHL 43 at [8]).

Whether a place is a person's home does not depend on ownership, as the European Commission on Human Rights held that

'Home' is an autonomous concept which does not depend on classification under domestic law. Whether or not a particular habitation constitutes a 'home' which attracts the protection of article 8(1) will depend on the factual circumstances, namely the existence of sufficient and continuous links. (*Buckley v United Kingdom* (1997) 23 EHRR 101, at 115, para 63)

The focus of Article 8 is very different to the focus of much of our property law, in which parties seek to assert property interests or contractual rights. Article 8 is not concerned with property rights to own or occupy property but with freedom from interference by public authorities.

1.10.2.2 'Interference'

Interference with that right must be:

(a) in accordance with the law; and

(b) necessary to satisfy some competing public interest (see the list in Article 8(2) above).

The competing public interests include protections of the rights and freedoms of others; therefore in a case where a public authority (or other public authority within the meaning of s 6 of the Human Rights Act 1998) is exercising contractual or proprietary rights to possession, it is in principle open to the occupier to raise the question whether it is proportionate to make an order for possession against him or her, and, if it is, to invite the court to take that into account when deciding what order to make (*Manchester City Council v Pinnock* [2011] 2 AC 104 and *Hounslow London Borough Council v Powell* [2011] 2 AC 186).

1.10.3 Where the landlord is a public authority

The *Pinnock* case represented, in Lord Neuberger's words, the 'resolution of a protracted inter-judicial dialogue between the House of Lords and the Strasbourg court …'. In *Pinnock* (at [49]), the Supreme Court concluded that, in the light of the ECtHR's clear and constant jurisprudence,

> if our law is to be compatible with article 8, where a court is asked to make an order for possession of a person's home at the suit of a local authority, the court must have the power to assess the proportionality of making the order, and, in making that assessment, to resolve any relevant dispute of fact.

However, the Supreme Court also made it clear at [51] and [54] that it would 'only be in "very highly exceptional cases" that it will be appropriate for the court to consider a proportionality argument' and that 'where … the local authority is entitled to possession as a matter of domestic law, there will be a very strong case for saying that making an order for possession would be proportionate'.

Lord Neuberger continued (at [52]):

> The question is always whether the eviction is a proportionate means of achieving a legitimate aim. Where a person has no right in domestic law to

remain in occupation of his home, the proportionality of making an order for possession at the suit of the local authority will be supported not merely by the fact that it would serve to vindicate the authority's ownership rights. It will also, at least normally, be supported by the fact that it would enable the authority to comply with its duties in relation to the distribution and management of its housing stock, including, for example, the fair allocation of its housing, the redevelopment of the site, the refurbishing of sub-standard accommodation, the need to move people who are in accommodation that now exceeds their needs, and the need to move vulnerable people into sheltered or warden-assisted housing. Furthermore, in many cases (such as this appeal) other cogent reasons, such as the need to remove a source of nuisance to neighbours, may support the proportionality of dispossessing the occupiers.

He went on to refer to a point raised by the Secretary of State, which was that a local authority's aim in wanting possession should be a 'given', which does not have to be explained or justified in court, so that the court will only be concerned with the occupiers' personal circumstances. In other words, the local authority need not prove that possession is justified, but that there may be particular cases where the authority may have what it believes to be particularly strong or unusual reasons for wanting possession – for example, that the property is the only occupied part of a site intended for immediate development for community housing. The authority could rely on that factor, but would have to plead it and adduce evidence to support it:

> Therefore, in virtually every case where a residential occupier has no contractual or statutory protection, and the local authority is entitled to possession as a matter of domestic law, there will be a very strong case for saying that making an order for possession would be proportionate. However, in some cases there may be factors which would tell the other way. (per Lord Neuberger)

The Supreme Court's conclusion in *Pinnock* was that proportionality should, if raised, be addressed (albeit that in the great majority of cases it could and should be summarily rejected) in every possession action against a residential occupier by a local authority or other public authority. This is because s 6(1) of the 1998 Act only applies to 'a public authority', given that the Convention is intended to protect individual rights against infringement by the State or its emanations.

1.10.4 Private landlords

In the *Pinnock* case, the Supreme Court made it clear (at [50]) that 'nothing' said in the judgment in that case was 'intended to bear on cases where the person seeking the order for possession is a private landowner', and added that it was 'preferable for this court to express no view on the issue until it arises and has to be determined'. A court is, of course, a public authority for the purposes of s 6 of the Human Rights Act 1998.

In *McDonald v McDonald* [2016] UKSC 28, the Supreme Court held that although Article 8 may be engaged when a private individual is seeking a court order for possession, it cannot be used to justify altering the private relationship between the parties. Therefore a court is not entitled to consider the proportionality of the actions under Article 8/s 6 of the Human Rights Act 1998. In *Qazi*, Lord Millett commented (obiter) (at [108]) that in a case for possession between two private individuals, the court is 'merely the forum for the determination of the civil right in dispute between the parties'.

In *McDonald*, the Court also pointed to the danger of inconsistency between judicial and non-judicial possession, as landlords have rights to exercise the self-help remedy of peaceable possession where they simply change the locks on a vacant property. In this situation, there is no recourse to court and therefore Article 8 would not be engaged (see also 11.3.3.1).

1.10.5 Equality Act 2010

An individual may also enjoy protection under the Equality Act 2010 if he or she possesses one or more of the protected characteristics specified in s 4 of the Act. These are: age, disability, gender reassignment, marriage and civil partnership, pregnancy and maternity, race, religious belief, sex and sexual orientation. The 2010 Act is designed to prevent unlawful discrimination: under s 35(1) various protections are given, including, at s 35(1)(b), that a person (A) who manages premises must not discriminate against a person (B) who occupies premises by evicting, or taking steps to evict, B from those premises.

Like the Human Rights Act 1998, the 2010 Act can be raised as a defence where the individual has no other right to remain in the property in question. The rights granted under the 2010 Act therefore go beyond establishing the existence of property rights, as stated at [55] in *Akerman-Livingstone v Aster Communities Ltd (formerly Flourish Homes Ltd)* [2015] UKSC 15:

> Section 35(1)(b) provides a particular degree of protection to a limited class of occupiers of property, who are considered by Parliament to deserve special protection. The protection concerned is founded on a desire to avoid a specific wrong in a number of fields, not just in relation to occupation of property, namely discrimination against disabled persons. (per Lord Neuberger)

The *Akerman-Livingstone* case concerned an individual with disabilities. The 2010 Act contains specific provisions relating to disability at s 15(1): a person (A) discriminates against a person (B) if A treats B unfavourably because of something arising in consequence of B's disability, and A cannot show that the treatment is a proportionate means of achieving a legitimate aim (unless A did not know and could not reasonably have been expected to know that B had the disability).

Lord Neuberger continued (at [56]) that where the occupier is disabled, the approach in *Pinnock* allowing summary judgment would not normally be appropriate as it is both:

(a) 'significantly less unlikely than in the normal run of cases that an article 8 defence might succeed'; and

(b) in relation to a claim under the 2010 Act, there are likely to be disputed facts or assessments, for example as to whether the individual suffers from a disability, whether the disability has led to the possession claim, and whether the landlord can demonstrate that eviction is a proportionate means of achieving a legitimate aim.

As stated, Mr Akerman-Livingstone was an individual with disabilities, but s 35(1) of the 2010 Act also applies to the other protected characteristics set out above.

In addition, unlike the Human Rights Act 1998, the 2010 Act applies to public and private sector landlords alike. Thus:

> … no landlord, public or private can adopt a discriminatory policy towards eviction, for example, by evicting a black person where they would not evict a white. Thus also no landlord, public or private, can evict a disabled tenant 'because of something arising in consequence of [his] disability' unless the landlord can show that this is a proportionate means of achieving a legitimate aim. (per Lady Hale at [24])

1.11 Further reading

P Birks, 'Before We Begin: Five Keys to Land Law' in s Bright and J Dewar (eds), *Land Law: Themes and Perspectives* (Oxford University Press, 1998), pp 457–86.

AM Honoré, 'Ownership' in AG Guest (ed), *Oxford Essays in Jurisprudence (First Series)* (Oxford: Clarendon Press, 1961), pp 107–47 (<http://nw18.american.edu/~dfagel/OwnershipSmaller.pdf>).

K Gray, 'Property in Thin Air' (1991) 50 CLJ 252.

S Roberts, 'More Lost than Found' (1982) 45 MLR 683.

DC Hoath, 'Some Conveyancing Implications of Finding Disputes' (1990) 54 Conv 248.

The legal definition of land is contained in s 205(i)(ix) of the Law of Property Act (LPA) 1925. It encompasses not merely the physical land itself but also a wide range of rights associated with it. These include rights above and below the land and intangible rights such as easements.

In English law it is not possible to 'own' the land but instead an 'estate' in the land. The two estates that exist at law are the fee simple absolute in possession (freehold) and term of years absolute (leasehold) (LPA 1925, s 1(1)).

Legal estates and interests are set out in s 1(1) and (2) of the LPA 1925. Section 1(3) provides that all other interests in land take effect in equity.

The distinction between law and equity also refers to the two systems recognised in our land law. Although the two systems have been merged since the Judicature Acts of 1873–75, equity continues to provide a remedy where the 'conscience' of a party is affected and where the common law may not do so.

Proprietary rights are rights in a particular asset, such as land, but may also include rights in personal property, such as jewellery. Subject to certain conditions, they are capable of being exercised 'against the world', no matter into whose hands the asset may come. Personal rights are rights against an individual, rather than against a particular asset. They may be inadequate if the individual in question is bankrupt, cannot be traced or no longer has the asset in his or her possession.

The unique and permanent nature of land means that it can be subject to multiple rights which may be complementary but which may also compete or conflict. This is reflected in the definition of land referred to above. We will look at how land law resolves these conflicts in later chapters.

Human rights protection applies in the context of land. However, it should be recognised that measures to protect the 'public interest' may be proportionate even though they affect individual rights.

1 Why are rights over land (such as a right to walk or drive over adjoining land) capable of being treated by the law as being as much a part of the land as the ground itself or buildings upon it?

2 Why does the law recognise a distinction between fixtures and chattels?

3 Why should legal systems recognise a distinction between land and other forms of property, such as shares or jewellery?

4 Why is contract law insufficient to deal with rights in land? Why does the law recognise certain rights as being 'proprietary' and capable of binding third parties?

5 What defects in the common law gave rise to equity?

6 What does equity contribute to the modern law? Why is a distinction still recognised between legal and equitable rights in land?

reflection

What is 'ownership'?

In this chapter, we have used words like 'ownership' and 'rights' as ordinary words of the English language. Some theorists have described ownership as a 'bundle of rights' or, more accurately, as rights and duties in relation to an asset that the State selects to be enforceable (see the article by Anthony Honoré in Further Reading). These would be expected to include rights to possess and use, alter or destroy property, rights to prevent others from interfering with those rights and the right to transfer this group of rights to others. The 'bundle of rights' would usually be limited by a duty not to use it for a use that is harmful to others and made subject to 'liability to execution', which means that the interest can be taken away from the owner to settle his or her debts.

What does being an estate owner mean in English law?

In *Star Energy v Bocardo* [2010] UKSC 35, the Supreme Court confirmed that an owner's right to prevent others interfering with his land was inherent in his right of ownership. Therefore horizontal drilling at substantial depths was an actionable trespass for interference with Bocardo's land regardless of whether it impacted upon the owner's use and enjoyment of the land, and it was irrelevant that he was not making any use of the land at that depth. A focus on use and enjoyment was missing the point that the question was 'essentially one about ownership. As a general rule, anything that can be touched or worked upon must belong to someone' (per Lord Hope at [26]).

What rights are granted by interests in land?

Holding an interest or third party rights in land gives specific rights which are limited by the nature of the right and any terms contained in a document granting it.

For example, the owner of dominant land benefitting from a vehicular right of way over servient land has a right of access onto the servient land both to exercise the easement and to carry out repair works that enable him or her to exercise the easement. However, he or she has no right to exclusive possession or to exclude others from the land, and, as we shall see in **Chapter 13**, a purported easement to park may be objected to if the right is so extensive that it deprives the landowner of almost all use of the land (*London & Blenheim Ltd v Ladbroke Retail Parks Ltd* [1992] 1 WLR 1278).

2

Acquisition

After reading this chapter, you will be able to understand:

- the importance of possession to title or rights in land
- how title to land can be gained by adverse possession
- what formalities are needed to create or transfer legal and equitable interests in land
- the circumstances in which rights can be created or transferred informally
- the tension between formal and informal methods of acquiring or transferring rights in land.

2.1 Possession as the basis for acquisition

Sir William Blackstone, an 18th Century Justice of the Common Pleas, the primary common law court at that time, in his *Commentaries on the Laws of England*, described possession, or occupancy as he called it, as the foundation of property:

> Occupancy is the taking possession of those things, which before belonged to nobody. This as we have seen is the true ground and foundation of all property …

This was explained more recently by Lord Millett in *London Borough of Harrow v Qazi* [2003] UKHL 43 at [87]:

> The common law protects possession as well as title. A person who is in actual possession of land is entitled to remain in peaceful enjoyment of the property without disturbance by anyone except a person with a better right to possession. It does not matter that he has no title. A squatter can maintain a claim of trespass. His want of title does not justify the authorities in searching his premises without a search warrant. He cannot be evicted save at the suit of someone with a better right to possession, and even then that person must rely on the strength of his own title and not the weakness of the squatter's.

2.2 Adverse possession

The principle of adverse possession allows a claimant who has been in factual possession of land for a minimum of 12 years with intention to possess it, to acquire a title to the land that defeats the paper title.

2.2.1 Factual possession

Factual possession requires a high degree of control and is singular – it is not possible for both the paper title owner and the person claiming adverse possession to be 'in possession' of the land at the same time, even if both are in occupation. The adverse possessor must have dispossessed the legal owner by going into ordinary possession of the land without the legal owner's licence or consent. Acts showing possession will be judged in relation to the character of the land and the manner in which a landowner might be expected to use land of that nature. For example, in *Red House Farms (Thorndon) Ltd v Catchpole* [1977] 2 EGLR 125, referred to by Slade J in *Powell v Macfarlane* (1979) 38 P&CR 452, shooting over land that was regarded as only suitable for shooting was sufficient to show possession.

2.2.2 Intention to possess

The intention of the adverse possessor was addressed by the House of Lords in the leading case of *JA Pye (Oxford) Ltd v Graham* [2003] 1 AC 419. In the words of Lord Hope of Craighead (at [71]):

> The only intention which has to be demonstrated is an intention to occupy and use the land as one's own … So I would hold that, if the evidence shows that the person was using the land in the way one would expect him to use if he were the true owner, that is enough.

It does not matter if the adverse possessor would have been willing to pay to use the land, if asked. He or she need not intend to own the land, but the would-be adverse possessor must have the intention to possess the land. Intention to possess can be demonstrated by use of the land as an owner might.

The test is a two-stage test – factual possession plus intention to possess. There is some circularity because intention to possess can be, and often is, deduced from the acts that establish factual possession.

2.2.3 Limitation Act 1980

The current rules of adverse possession are based on s 15 of the Limitation Act (LA) 1980 and, in the case of registered land, Sch 6 to the Land Registration Act (LRA) 2002. Under s 15(1) of the LA 1980, no action can be brought by a person to recover land after 12 years from the date the right of action accrued. In an action to recover possession of land, the right of action accrues on the date that the landowner was dispossessed, or his possession discontinued (LA 1980, Sch 1, para 1).

2.2.4 Land Registration Act 2002

Where land is unregistered, at the end of the limitation period of 12 years, the title of the paper owner is extinguished (LA 1980, s 17).

In the case of registered land, the position is different. There are two reasons for this: the first is that there is a State guarantee of registered title; and, secondly, the dispossessed owner is the registered proprietor of the land and will remain so until the register is altered.

Under the LRA 2002, the adverse possessor is entitled to apply to the Land Registry after 10 years' adverse possession. The 2002 Act provides for notice to be given to the registered proprietor to allow him or her to take proceedings to recover possession of the land. If he or she fails to respond to the notice, or thereafter fails to obtain possession within the period of two years from service of notice by the Land Registry, then the adverse possessor will be entitled to be registered as proprietor. The provisions are as follows:

(a) Section 15 of the LA 1980, which sets time limits in relation to recovery of land, is disapplied from registered estates, and s 17 (extinction of title on expiry of time limit) will also not apply to extinguish title to a registered estate, as the 12-year limitation period does not apply (LRA 2002, Part 9, s 96).

(b) An adverse possessor can apply to the registrar to be registered as proprietor of a registered estate in land once he or she has been in adverse possession for a period of 10 years. If the adverse possessor has been evicted after that 10-year period has been achieved, he or she must make his or her application within the six months immediately following the eviction (LRA 2002, Sch 6, para 1(1) and (2)).

(c) The registrar must give notice to the registered proprietor and the proprietor of any charge. If the estate is a registered leasehold then the proprietor of any superior estate must also be informed (LRA 2002, Sch 6, para 2).

(d) If the registered proprietor serves notice in response to the application, the applicant will only be entitled to be registered as proprietor if any of the following conditions apply. These conditions are that the applicant has an equity by estoppel or is for some other reason entitled to be registered as proprietor, or where the adverse possessor owns adjacent land and he or she (or a predecessor in title) has reasonably believed that the land to which the application relates belonged to him or her.

(e) If the application for registration is rejected, the applicant can make a further application if he or she is in adverse possession of the estate from the date of the application until the last day of the period of two years beginning with the date of its rejection. If the applicant makes that further application then he or she is entitled to be entered in the register as the new proprietor of the estate (LRA 2002, Sch 6, paras 6 and 7).

(f) If the registered proprietor fails to serve notice in response to the application, the applicant is entitled to be registered as proprietor (LRA 2002, Sch 6, para 4).

These new overlying provisions do not affect case law on whether or not an applicant is in adverse possession of the land. An applicant claiming adverse possession is not entitled to succeed under paras 4 or 7 of Sch 6 to the LRA 2002 unless he or she can satisfy the registrar on this point. The Court of Appeal confirmed in *Baxter v Mannion* [2011] 1 WLR 1594 that it is implicit in the wording of s 96 that the applicant must actually be in adverse possession for the required 10-year period. If he or she is unable to prove possession, the former registered proprietor is entitled to seek alteration of the register to correct a mistake (LRA 2002, Sch 4, paras 1 and 4).

2.2.5 *Pye* and human rights

The judgments in *Pye v Graham* showed that the House of Lords did not like the decision that it felt bound to make. Lord Bingham stated (at [427]) that, like the trial judge, his finding in favour of the Grahams as the adverse possessors was one he would 'arrive at with no enthusiasm'. His view was that whilst the rule can be justified when it applies to unregistered land as a means of ending uncertainty about ownership, the same argument does not apply to registered land. The land in dispute in the *Pye* case was registered but (as the court ruled), under s 17 of the LA 1980, Pye's title had already been extinguished by the time the new rules in the LRA 2002 came into force.

As we have seen at **1.10.1**, Pye took its case up to the Grand Chamber of the European Court of Human Rights (*JA Pye (Oxford) Ltd v United Kingdom* (2008) 46 EHRR 45) claiming an unlawful deprivation of property under Article 1 of Protocol No 1 to the European Convention on Human Rights (now contained in the Human Rights Act 1998). It was unsuccessful, as the Court found that the 'fair balance' required by Article 1 of Protocol No 1 had not been breached.

2.2.6 Legal Aid, Sentencing and Punishment of Offenders Act 2012, s 144

The 2012 Act made squatting in a residential building a criminal offence if the person enters it as a trespasser, in circumstances where he or she knows or ought to know that he or she is a trespasser and is living, or intends to live, in the building for any period.

Nevertheless, such a period of squatting can remain relevant for the purposes of gaining title by adverse possession, despite its illegality (*Best v Chief Land Registrar* [2014] EWHC 1370 (Admin)).

Because it is limited to residential buildings, the 2012 Act would not, for example, apply on similar facts to those in the *Pye* case, which concerned open grazing land.

2.3 Formalities

In practice, however, most title to land rests on title documents or registration at the Land Registry, both of which require a number of rules relating to formal requirements to be observed. We find that students of land law often struggle with the language and number of formalities for the creation and transfer of interests in land and the need for precise application of statutory provisions. In legal practice, a great deal of care is taken to ensure that formalities are complied with fully, and it is a good place for a student to learn the attention to detail that a career in the legal profession requires. Unfortunately there is no substitute for reading the actual provisions and learning the situations in which they apply. Once this hurdle is overcome, formalities are more straightforward than they initially appear, even if one can reasonably take the view that there are too many of them. We will also consider requirements to register at the Land Registry as part of the process of complying with formalities.

2.4 Stages in a typical transaction

Imagine that you are acting for a client who wishes to acquire a property, whether it is a house to live in, business premises or an investment property which the client will let out in order to receive rent. The transaction is likely to look like this:

2.4.1 Investigating title

The first question is whether the seller owns the property that he or she is purporting to sell and that he or she is entitled to sell it. This is known as having a 'good and marketable title'. You will want to know that there is no other person who can claim legal or beneficial entitlement to the property.

You will need to check if any third parties have rights over the property. For example, is there any person who has the right to occupy the property under a lease? Do the neighbours have any rights over the property, such as a right to pass over it to gain access to their land?

You will need to make sure that the purchase is done in the correct manner so that purchase monies can be paid over, secure in the knowledge that your client will be registered as owner or 'registered proprietor' of the property.

Formalities are important to these questions:

- Has the transfer deed in favour of the seller been prepared and executed as a deed?
- If a person claims to have a beneficial interest in the property, has this been properly created?
- If an occupier claims to have a right to occupy under a lease, is this a valid lease? If not, can he or she be required to vacate the property?

To answer these questions, you need to know and apply the formality rules, as well as have a good understanding of the circumstances in which English law will accept that an interest has or should be created, even if formality rules have not been complied with.

2.4.2 Contract

At exchange of contracts, all parties to the contract become bound to complete the transaction. At this stage, legal title has not passed, but parties can start to make their preparations for completion. Under standard contract terms, the risk of damage to the property (eg by fire) usually passes to the purchaser, which means that even if the property is damaged or even destroyed, the purchaser is contractually required to complete on the purchase of the property at the agreed purchase price, so he or she will want to put buildings insurance in place with effect from completion. Contracts for the sale of land are usually specifically enforceable because the unique nature of land means that money damages are not sufficient to compensate the purchaser.

Contracts for the sale of land must be in writing, must incorporate all the agreed terms of the contract and must be signed by each party to the contract, under s 2 of the Law of Property (Miscellaneous Provisions) Act (LPMPA) 1989:

> 2 **Contracts for sale etc of land to be by signed writing**
>
> (1) A contract for the sale or other disposition of an interest in land can only be made in writing and only by incorporating all the terms which the parties have expressly agreed in one document or, where contracts are exchanged, in each.
>
> (2) The terms may be incorporated in a document either by being set out in it or by reference to some other document.
>
> (3) The document incorporating the terms or, where contracts are exchanged, one of the documents incorporating them (but not necessarily the same one) must be signed by or on behalf of each party to the contract.

A purported contract that does not comply with s 2 is void. For example, if the agreement is oral or is not signed by or on behalf of any supposed party to it, it is void and does not create obligations and rights for any person.

This rule is stricter than the prior rule, which was contained in s 40 of the LPA 1925, and which allowed an oral or unsigned contract to become enforceable if it were later signed or the contract were partly performed, for example by the payment of monies due under the contract. Section 40 is now repealed but you may come across it when reading older law reports. These methods of allowing an initially void contract to become enforceable cannot occur under s 2 of the LPMPA 1989 (*United Bank of Kuwait v Sahib* [1997] Ch 107).

2.4.2.1 Use of email to form the contract

It was accepted in *Green v Ireland* [2011] EWHC 1305 (Ch) that a string of emails, with each party inserting their name at the foot of emails sent by them respectively, can constitute a signature for the purposes of s 2 of the LPMPA 1989. The email thread must still comply with the other requirements of s 2 and must incorporate all the terms of the purported contract.

2.4.2.2 Non-land contracts

Section 2 does not apply to contracts that do not dispose of land. In *Pitt v PHH Asset Management Ltd* [1994] 1 WLR 327, the parties entered into a lockout agreement, where the seller of land agreed that for a period of two weeks he would not deal with anyone other than the prospective purchaser. In fact, during that two-week period, the seller exchanged contracts to sell the property to a third party for a higher price. The disappointed prospective purchaser could sue for damages for breach of the non-s 2 compliant lockout agreement as it was not a contract for the disposition of an interest in land and therefore did not need to follow the requirements of s 2 of the LPMPA 1989.

2.4.2.3 Options

When land is being acquired for development, it is common for option agreements to be used. In a 'call' option, the purchaser can serve notice requiring the property to be sold to him or her in accordance with the terms of the option agreement. It is also possible to have a 'put' option, where the seller can serve notice requiring the purchaser to buy. In either case, the parties will enter into an option agreement signed by or on behalf of all parties. However, usually only the party exercising the option will sign the option notice triggering the obligation for sale and purchase, and the question arose whether this option notice must also be signed by both parties to comply with s 2 of the LPMPA 1989. In *Spiro v Glencrown Properties Limited* [1991] Ch 537, HC, Hoffmann J looked at the purpose of the notice which allowed a party unilaterally to activate the option and held that the only document that had to comply with s 2, and therefore had to be signed by both parties, was the option agreement itself, which was a contract conditional upon service of the option notice.

2.4.2.4 Additional terms

Difficulties can arise where the parties agree terms that are not included in the contract for sale and purchase. Section 2 requires that the written signed document (or each document where contracts are exchanged) must incorporate all the terms that the parties have expressly agreed (s 2(1)). Terms can be incorporated by being set out in the contract itself or in another document that is referred to in the contract (s 2(2)). If the signed written document does not incorporate all the terms of the disposition, it will be void under s 2.

Alternatively, the parties can choose to enter into two distinct contracts, only one of which (the contract to dispose of an interest in land) need comply with s 2. Scott LJ observed in the Court of Appeal in *Tootal Clothing Ltd v Guinea Properties Ltd* [1992] 2 EGLR 80 at 81:

If parties choose to hive off part of their composite bargain into a separate contract distinct from the written land contract that incorporates the rest of the terms, I can see nothing in section 2 that provides an answer to an action for the enforcement of the land contract, on the one hand, or of the separate contact, on the other hand. Each has become, by the contractual choice of the parties, a separate contract.

This was doubted by the Court of Appeal in *Grossman v Hooper* [2001] EWCA Civ 615 under which a property was to be transferred between a separated couple. It was agreed orally between the man (the transferor) and the woman (the transferee) that she would discharge an existing unsecured debt relating to the property when she later sold it. The correct question to ask is whether the agreement to transfer the property was conditional on the discharge of the debt. If it were, then the discharge was a term that should have been incorporated in the land contract, and the failure to incorporate it would render the land contract void under s 2. In this case, the judge had found that it was not a term of the bargain because both parties accepted that repaying the debt was the woman's obligation to fulfil; it was not mentioned in the contract because there was no disagreement between the couple. Similarly, in *North Eastern Properties v Coleman* [2010] 1 WLR 2715, a seller's obligation to pay a finder's fee was not incorporated in a series of contracts. The Court of Appeal agreed that although it was expressly agreed that the seller would pay the fee, the parties were entitled not to make this a term of the land contract, and the property sales were not intended to be conditional on payment of the finder's fee.

2.4.2.5 Effect of s 2 on certainty of contract

The case law discussed at **2.4.2.4** above demonstrates that although the purpose of s 2 is to give certainty, in a transaction where the land transfer is only one of a number of arrangements between the parties at the same time, there can be confusion about what is or is not a term of the land contract.

One could argue that *overall* the effect of s 2 is to increase certainty because if parties arrange their transactions so as to comply with it, there will be one signed document (albeit most usually in at least two counterparts each signed by one or more of the parties) that (collectively) is signed by all parties and contains or incorporates all the terms. In *some cases*, however, s 2 can lead to uncertainty as to whether there is a valid land contract, even if there is no dispute about the substance of those terms. This can enable a party to avoid the contract. The decisions in *Grossman v Hooper* and *North Eastern Properties v Coleman* make avoiding the contract less likely by accepting that not all circumstances around the contract need to be terms incorporated within it.

If a land contract is void because it fails to incorporate all relevant terms, then practical completion of the land transfer does not mean that the contract 'matures' into a valid one. The other terms remain unenforceable (*Keay v Morris Homes (West Midlands) Ltd* [2012] 1 WLR 2855).

2.4.2.6 Effect in equity of a valid contract to transfer or create a legal estate or interest in land

A valid contract to transfer or create an estate in land creates an 'estate contract'. Equity regards the purchaser as owning an equitable interest in the land from the point of exchange (*Walsh v Lonsdale* (1882) 21 Ch D 9). This is based on the maxim that 'equity looks on that as done which ought to be done' and means that, in principle, the contract will be enforceable by the equitable remedy of specific performance. The estate contract is often of short duration and ends when the legal estate is conveyed to the buyer at completion. Unless varied by the terms of the contract, during the period of the estate contract the legal owner remains entitled to enjoy the land and any income produced by it (for example if it is let out to a tenant paying rent). The owner has duties in equity to protect the interest that the buyer has taken under the contract; he or she must take reasonable care of the property and consult the buyer before making managerial decisions (*Englewood Properties v Patel* [2005] EWHC 188 (Ch)). We look in **2.7.2** at how this principle continues to apply if completion does not occur.

2.4.3 Completion

Once contracts have been exchanged, the parties can make their preparations for completion. On completion, any purchase monies will usually be paid over, the deed to transfer legal title is completed and the purchaser allowed into possession of the property. On a typical house sale, full legal and beneficial ownership will be transferred to the purchaser on completion.

2.4.3.1 Requirement to use a deed

At completion, the parties must comply with the formalities for the transfer or creation of legal title to land by using a deed. Under s 52(1) of the LPA 1925:

> All conveyances of land or of any interest therein are void for the purpose of conveying or creating a legal estate unless made by deed.

A conveyance includes any means of disposing of or creating a legal estate, other than by a will. As well as a transfer, it also includes a mortgage, a charge and a lease (LPA 1925, s 205(1)(ii)).

2.4.3.2 Exceptions

There are exceptions to this rule:

(a) Short leases for a term of three years or less can be made orally (LPA 1925, s 54(2)) (this is described in the Act as being 'by parol'). The lease must take effect in possession (in other words the tenant can take up immediate occupation of the property), at the best rent that can reasonably be obtained without taking a fine. (In this context a 'fine' is an upfront payment or premium usually at the start of the lease; see **7.3.1**.)

(b)   Any other interests in land that are purported to be made orally take effect 'at will' only, which means that they can be terminated by either party at any time (LPA 1925, s 54(1)).

2.4.3.3   Requirements of a deed

What does a deed look like?

(a)   The document must make it clear on its face that it is intended to be a deed (for example, it should be titled 'Transfer Deed') (LPMPA 1989, s 1(2)(a)).

(b)   It must be executed as a deed. For an individual this will usually mean that it is signed by the individual in the presence of a witness who him- or herself signs to confirm or attest the signature (LPMPA 1989, s 1(2)(b) and (3)(a)(i)).

(c)   It must be delivered as a deed (LPMPA 1989, s 1(3)(b)). Delivery does not mean physical delivery but an intention to be bound by the document. In *Longman v Viscount Chelsea* (1989) 58 P&CR 189, CA, signing the deed and placing it into the hands of one's solicitors was not sufficient. The intention of the landlord was that he would not be bound until his solicitors completed the deed with the tenant's solicitors, which the Court accepted as being standard conveyancing practice.

Section 1(2) and (3) of the LPMPA 1989 provides:

1   **Deeds and their execution**

(2)   An instrument shall not be a deed unless—

   (a)   it makes it clear on its face that it is intended to be a deed by the person making it or, as the case may be, by the parties to it (whether describing itself as a deed or expressing itself to be executed or signed as a deed or otherwise); and

   (b)   it is validly executed as a deed …

(3)   An instrument is validly executed as a deed by an individual if, and only if—

   (a)   it is signed—

      (i)   by him in the presence of a witness who attests the signature; or

      (ii)   at his direction and in his presence and the presence of two witnesses who each attest the signature; and

   (b)   it is delivered as a deed …

2.4.3.4   Other requirements

A maximum of four people can jointly hold a legal title to land (LPA 1925, s 32(2)). A trust will arise wherever property is transferred to two or more people. They hold the land as legal joint tenants on trust for themselves (see **6.2**). If land is transferred to more than four people, then the first four to be named on the deed who have legal capacity will become legal owners to hold on trust for themselves and all the others named.

2.4.4 Registration

We consider registration here as an additional formality as, in general, a legal estate, charge or interest will not be transferred or created until registration is complete. Registration requirements will fall into one of the following categories:

(a) title is already registered; or

(b) title is unregistered and the transaction triggers first registration of the estate being created or disposed of.

We look below (**2.4.4.2**) at the position where the legal estate which is being transferred, or out of which the charge, interest or (in the case of the grant of a lease) estate is being created, is unregistered at the time of the transaction, and, secondly, where that legal estate is already registered.

2.4.4.1 Contract

A contract to acquire or create an interest in land (such as a contract for sale and purchase of a freehold or leasehold estate or a contract for a lease) should be protected by a notice on the register (if the title in respect of which it is created is registered at the Land Registry) (LRA 2002, s 32). This will serve to protect the interest under s 29(2)(a)(i) of the LRA 2002 to ensure its priority if there are subsequent dealings with the title. A right of pre-emption (also known as a right of first refusal) is accepted as a proprietary interest in relation to registered land (LRA 2002, s 115) and can be protected by a notice. (See **Chapter 5**.)

If the relevant title is unregistered, the contract should be registered as a C(iv) land charge (Land Charges Act 1972, s 2(4)(iv)) against the name of the legal owner of the estate, which will protect the contract against a subsequent purchaser of the estate (Land Charges Act 1972, s 4(6)) and is deemed to constitute actual notice of the contract to all persons from the date of registration (LPA 1925, s 198(1)). Again, in relation to unregistered land, the definition of an estate contract expressly includes a right of pre-emption as well as a valid option to purchase (Land Charges Act 1972, s 2(4)(iv)). (See **Chapter 3**.)

In practice, this is rarely done where completion is expected to follow on promptly (most usually within 28 days of the contract date) but should be done when there is a longer completion date, for example in the case of an option agreement where exercise of the option and its completion may not take place for some time.

2.4.4.2 Completion

First registration

On most transfers of a qualifying estate in land, compulsory registration of the title at the Land Registry is required (LRA 2002, s 4(1)(a)). A qualifying estate is an unregistered freehold estate or a leasehold which, at the time of the transfer, has more than seven years to run. Compulsory first registration is triggered by a transfer on sale, as a gift, under a court order or an assent following the death of the legal owner.

The same requirement applies to the grant out of such a qualifying estate of a lease that at the time of grant has more than seven years to run, on sale, as a gift or under a court order (LRA 2002, s 4(1)(c)).

Compulsory first registration is also triggered by the grant of a first legal mortgage of a qualifying legal estate (LRA 2002, s 4(1)(g)).

The duty to register is on the responsible estate owner or his or her successor in title (LRA 2002, s 6(1)). If the registration is not made then the transfer, grant or creation becomes void in relation to the legal estate. In the case of a transfer of the freehold or a lease with more than seven years remaining, the title to the legal estate reverts to the transferor, who holds it on a bare trust for the transferee (LRA 2002, s 7(1)). In the case of the grant of a lease or a mortgage, the transaction has effect as a contract for valuable consideration to grant or create the legal estate concerned (LRA 2002, s 7(2)(b)). (See **4.5.3.2**.)

Once land is registered

Certain dispositions of a registered estate must be registered (LRA 2002, s 27) and will not take effect at law until the registration requirements are met. The most important registrable dispositions are:

- the transfer of the registered estate (this may be a freehold or leasehold estate) (LRA 2002, s 27(2)(a));
- the grant of a lease of more than seven years from the date of grant of a lease (and certain other leases) (LRA 2002, s 27(2)(b));
- the express grant of a legal easement (LRA 2002, s 27(2)(d)); and
- the grant of a legal charge (LRA 2002, s 27(2)(f)).

These dispositions will not be effective to transfer, grant or create a legal estate or interest in land until they are registered, although the disponee will obtain equitable interests on completion (*Mortgage Corpn Ltd v Nationwide Credit Corpn Ltd* [1994] Ch 49, 54 per Dillon J and confirmed to apply to ss 27 and 29 of the LRA 2002 in *Re North East Property Buyers Litigation* [2014] UKSC 52, 54, per Lord Collins).

The time between completion of a transaction and completion of any necessary registration at the Land Registry is known as the 'registration gap'. In practice, conveyancers carry out searches to protect their client's title, but the efficacy of these depend on the application to register being lodged at the appropriate Land Registry with all accompanying forms, documents and fees within the priority period that is granted by the search. In *Barclays Bank Plc v Zaroovabli* [1997] Ch 321 the dangers of late registration are shown. A couple granted a mortgage over their property to Barclays in 1988, but by some mishap no action was taken to register the charge until 1994. During that period, it created rights between the parties and took effect as an equitable interest in land rather than the legal charge that had been intended. A tenancy agreement granted to a third party after its completion but before registration of the charge took priority under Land Registry rules (at the time s 101(3) of the Land Registration Act 1925 (now repealed) applied, but the same would occur under s 29(1) of the LRA 2002). (See **5.6.1.2.**)

2.5 Trust

In the previous section we looked at a typical conveyancing transaction. Another common transaction is the creation of an express trust over land. Trusts of land are dealt with in greater detail in **Chapter 6,** but it would be useful to give a brief outline here.

The declaration of an express trust of land must comply with the formality rules in s 53(1)(b) of the LPA 1925, in that it must be in writing signed by the person able to declare the trust. If other transactions are occurring at the same time as the declaration of trust then the formalities relevant to those transactions must also be complied with.

example

If Nancy declares that she will hold her property, Seaside Villas, on trust for her children, Malo, Celeste and Rose, then she must comply with s 53(1)(b) of the LPA 1925. If she wishes to transfer Seaside Villas to Jason and herself to hold on trust for Malo, Celeste and Rose then the formalities for transfer (including registration requirements) must also be complied with.

Section 53 of the Law of Property Act 1925 provides:

> 53 **Instruments required to be in writing**
>
> (1) Subject to the provisions hereinafter contained with respect to the creation of interests in land by parol—
>
>   (a) no interest in land can be created or disposed of except by writing signed by the person creating or conveying the same, or by his agent thereunto lawfully authorised in writing, or by will, or by operation of law;
>
>   (b) a declaration of trust respecting any land or any interest therein must be manifested and proved by some writing signed by some person who is able to declare such trust or by his will;

(c) a disposition of an equitable interest or trust subsisting at the time of the disposition, must be in writing lawfully signed by the person disposing of the same, or by his agent thereunto lawfully authorised in writing or by will.

(2) This section does not affect the creation or operation of resulting, implied or constructive trusts.

Section 53(2) of the LPA 1925 excludes resulting, implied or constructive trusts from this formality requirement, and therefore they may continue to arise by operation of law if the circumstances are right (see 2.7.3).

2.6 Why are formalities important?

There are a number of reasons why formalities are important, and why they are considered particularly important in relation to land, due to its importance, scarcity and uniqueness. One reason is the idea of the extra requirements of a deed (the formality of the document and the requirement for a witness to a party's signature) acting as a 'warning flag' to the parties that the transaction carries an important legal effect. It may encourage the parties to obtain legal advice on their rights and responsibilities under the transaction and the implication of their actions. The requirement for written and signed documents also provides written evidence that a transaction has indeed taken place and, one hopes, means that the terms of the transaction are clear.

However, it is important to recognise that there are disadvantages that come with the insistence on a high level of formalities. Transaction costs are likely to be higher due to the need for legal advice. There may be situations where it is not realistic to expect such advice to be obtained, and it may be unfair to penalise informal transactions where non-compliance is as a result of ignorance, the more so if there is a risk that the party may be manipulated or taken advantage of by a better informed party.

In relation to registration, there is an additional factor, notably the aim to produce a more efficient system that reduces complexity or uncertainty by providing information on a central register, rather than by looking back through the deeds. The Law Commission called for a change in attitudes towards registration as a requirement, commenting that:

> There is a widely-held perception that it is unreasonable to expect people to register their rights over land. We find this puzzling given the overwhelming prevalence of registered title. Furthermore, the law has long required compliance with formal requirements for the transfer of interests in land and for contracts to sell or dispose of such interests. The wisdom of these requirements is not seriously questioned. We cannot see why the further step of registration should be regarded as so onerous. (Law Commission, *Land*

Registration for the Twenty-first Century: A Conveyancing Revolution (Law Com No 271, 2001)

However, the Law Commission also recognised that there are situations where 'it is neither reasonable to expect nor sensible to require any entry on the register' (ibid at 8.6). An example of this would be short leases of three years or less, similar to the exemption from use of a deed contained in s 54(2) of the LPA 1925.

2.7 Informal means of obtaining an estate or interest in land

If the parties have failed to comply with necessary formalities, it is possible that some form of interest has been created informally or by satisfying the requirements of a lesser formality (such as using a contract rather than a deed).

2.7.1 Adverse possession

We have already looked at adverse possession, which allows a person who has been in factual possession of land for a minimum of 12 years with intention to possess it, to acquire title to the land and defeat the paper or formal title.

2.7.2 Doctrine of anticipation, or, what happens if the parties fail to complete a valid deed?

In the absence of a valid deed then, unless the transaction falls into one of the exceptions to this rule (see **2.4.3.2**), the parties will have failed to transfer, create or grant a legal estate or interest in land.

Is the transaction entirely lost? This will depend on whether the parties' actions satisfy the requirements for transferring, creating or granting an equitable interest in land.

As explained at **2.4.2.6**, if a specifically enforceable contract for the transfer, creation or grant of a legal estate or interest in land has been entered into, this will act in equity to create an estate contract, under which equity regards the buyer as holding an equitable interest in the land. In the words of Jessel MR in *Walsh v Lonsdale* (1882) 21 Ch D 9:

> The tenant holds under an agreement for lease. He holds, therefore, under the same terms in equity as if a lease had been granted, it being a case in which both parties admit that relief is capable of being given by specific performance.

Note that this only applies where the contract is entered into with the legal estate owner; a contract entered into with any other person creates personal contractual rights between the contracting parties but does not create immediate equitable rights in that estate.

In *Southern Pacific Mortgages Ltd v Scott* [2014] UKSC 52, which concerned an equity release transaction, Mrs Scott sold her house for a discounted price and received in return a contractual right to continue to live there at a rent below market levels. The purchaser entered into a mortgage at completion to finance the purchase and subsequently granted Mrs Scott a two-year assured shorthold tenancy without the lender's permission. When the purchaser defaulted on the mortgage and the lender sought possession against Mrs Scott, the Supreme Court held that until such time as completion occurred, the contract created only personal rights for Mrs Scott and not equitable proprietary rights as the purchaser did not hold the legal estate in the land. By the time the purchaser held the legal estate (which 'fed' Mrs Scott's rights and turned them into equitable rights in the property), the mortgage was in existence and therefore was earlier to and had priority over Mrs Scott's rights.

Remember, of course, that for a valid contract to have been entered into, the formalities of s 2 of the LPMPA 1989 relating to a contract for disposition of an interest in land must have been complied with, as well as requirements under general contract law, such as consideration.

If the parties' dealings fall short of a valid contract (for example they are signed by the grantor only and not by both parties as required by s 2 of the LPMPA 1989), they may nevertheless comply with s 53 of the LPA 1925, which requires written documents for a declaration of trust to be signed by the person able to declare the trust (s 53(1)(b)) or for the disposition of an existing equitable interest or trust to be signed by the person making the disposition (s 53(1)(c)). However, this is not a panacea for failure to comply with formalities: for an express trust to be created under s 53(1)(b), the court must first be satisfied that the grantor intended to make a self-declaration of trust (following the principle of *Jones v Lock* (1865) 1 Ch App 25), and s 53(1)(c) only applies to a disposition of an existing equitable interest (*Kinane v Mackie Conteh* [2005] EWCA Civ 45). Therefore the disappointed party might seek instead to rely on the creation of a trust by operation of law.

2.7.3 Resulting, implied or constructive trusts

Resulting, implied or constructive trusts are exempted from formality requirements and will arise under operation of law when the circumstances that are sufficient to create them occur.

Section 2(5) of the LPMPA 1989 provides that s 2 requiring contracts to be signed does not affect the creation or operation of resulting, implied or constructive trusts. And s 53(2) of the LPA 1925 similarly provides that resulting, implied or constructive trusts do not need to be in writing signed by the person able to declare the trust under s 53(1)(b) of the LPA 1925.

2.7.3.1 Resulting trusts

A resulting trust arises to protect a person who provides funding for the purchase of an estate in land but who is not making a gift or a loan. This is a long-held principle that was already clearly established by the 1788 case of *Dyer v Dyer* (1788) 2 Cox 92, in which the Lord Chief Baron (Eyre) stated:

> The clear result of all the cases, without a single exception, is, that the trust of a legal estate, whether freehold … or leasehold; … whether in one name or several; … results to the man who advances the purchase-money.

In certain circumstances there may be a presumption that money is a gift (the presumption of advancement may apply to funding provided by a parent to a child for a property purchase – *Collier v Collier* [2002] EWCA Civ 1095) but the statement holds true as a general principle.

2.7.3.2 Constructive trust

A constructive trust may be created where parties have a common intention to share property. Sometimes the common intention is reached by an express agreement, which may be an oral agreement, between the parties. In other cases it may be inferred that the parties had a common intention from their conduct in relation to the property. The common intention is not enforceable in itself, but if it is coupled with circumstances that make it unconscionable for the owner of the property to deny the interest of the other party by asserting his or her own beneficial interest, this creates a constructive trust. A common example is in relation to the family home, where one party acts to his or her detriment on the faith of the common intention of a shared interest by contributing financially to the acquisition of the property or its improvement (*Grant v Edwards* [1986] Ch 638, CA). Constructive trusts are commonly encountered in the domestic setting and, following the decision in *Stack v Dowden* [2007] UKHL 17, the courts consider a common intention constructive trust to be a more appropriate mechanism in relation to the family home than a resulting trust in which the individual contributions of each party are totted up. This is considered in **Chapter 6**.

The principle of *Rochefoucauld v Boustead* [1897] 1 Ch 196 is that where property is transferred to a person to hold on an oral trust, lack of formality in creating the trust does not allow the transferee to claim the property as his or her own. Equity would impose a constructive trust to prevent the transferee acting unconscionably. This principle is permitted to continue under the exemption from formality requirements of constructive as well as resulting and implied trusts.

In *Bannister v Bannister* [1948] 2 All ER CA 133, the defendant sold two cottages to the plaintiff on the unwritten understanding that she would be allowed to remain in one rent free for as long as she chose. The price was reduced below market price to reflect this. The plaintiff subsequently served notice on the defendant to quit the property and, when she refused, started possession proceedings. The sale at a reduced price on the basis of the oral undertaking created a life interest in the plaintiff's favour, that would terminate if she chose to leave the property.

2.7.3.3 Use of constructive trusts or estoppel to avoid the effect of s 2 of the LPMPA 1989

Constructive trust

Section 2(5) of the LPMPA 1989 provides that s 2 does not affect the creation or operation of resulting, implied or constructive trusts. It is possible that where a purported contract is void for failure to comply with s 2, the circumstances may instead create a constructive trust. In this case, the claim will be based on that constructive trust and not the failed contract.

In *Yaxley v Gotts* [2000] Ch 162, CA, Yaxley alleged that he and Gotts had entered into an oral contract that, in return for Yaxley renovating a development property and acting as managing agent, Gotts would grant him leases of the two ground-floor flats. Yaxley carried out the works and acted as managing agent, but Gotts argued that no valid contract to transfer the flats had been created due to non-compliance with s 2. The Court of Appeal held that the circumstances were sufficient to create a constructive trust which was effective despite the lack of a valid contract. Robert Walker LJ stated:

> … the species of constructive trust based on common intention is established by what Lord Bridge in *Lloyds Bank Plc v Rosset* [1991] 1 AC 107, 132 called 'an agreement, arrangement or understanding' actually reached between the parties and relied on and acted on by the claimant. A constructive trust of that kind is closely akin to, if not indistinguishable from, proprietary estoppel. Equity enforces it because it would be unconscionable for the other party to disregard the claimant's rights. Section 2(5) expressly preserves the creation and operation of a constructive trust.

The point here is that the agreement on its own is unenforceable as it does not comply with s 2. The agreement was oral and therefore clearly did not satisfy the formality requirements of s 2. However, the agreement, although unenforceable in its own right, *together with the detriment to the claimant in acting in reliance upon it*, meant it would be unconscionable to allow the defendant to renege. In this case, the parties had worked together over many years, and Yaxley considered (and the Court held) that they had come to a 'gentleman's agreement'. The judge at first instance had held that Yaxley had the benefit of a proprietary estoppel (see **2.7.4**). Proprietary estoppel is not expressly preserved by s 2(5) but this point did not come up until appeal. The Court of Appeal held that, although the judge had not made any findings about the existence of a constructive trust, the facts that supported an estoppel claim also supported a constructive trust, which is expressly preserved under s 2(5). Yaxley was held to have a valid constructive trust over the two ground-floor flats.

Constructive trust and proprietary estoppel

Therefore if the circumstances create a constructive trust (or a constructive trust *and* proprietary estoppel), this will be valid under s 2(5). It is unclear what status a proprietary estoppel will hold if the circumstances are not sufficient to give rise to a constructive trust. In this case, there is no express saving under s 2(5). There has been some judicial comment concerning this. For example, Lord Scott took the view in *Yeoman's Row Management Ltd v Cobbe* [2008] UKHL 55 that, as proprietary estoppel did not fall in the list of exemptions in s 2(5) of the LPMPA 1989, it would be insufficient and a constructive trust would be required. However, in the reported cases where this point has arisen, the courts have been willing to hold the existence of a constructive trust as well as proprietary estoppel, and therefore the point has not been critical.

One might expect the distinction to arise in a case where a landowner stands by and allows a third party to act to his or her detriment in the mistaken belief that he or she has an interest in the land. However in *Kinane v Mackie Conteh* [2005] EWCA Civ 45, CA, in which a landowner encouraged a lender by his conduct to believe that he had a valid charge, leading the lender to make a loan, the court found that this created a constructive trust as well as an estoppel. And in *Ely v Robson* [2016] EWCA Civ 774, where the judge at first instance focussed on proprietary estoppel, the remedy for the estoppel confirmed on appeal was the imposition of a constructive trust, and therefore the point was not addressed by the Court of Appeal.

Commercial context

In *Yeoman's Row Management Ltd v Cobbe* [2008] UKHL 55, the House of Lords made clear that, in a commercial context, an oral agreement that both parties *are aware* has stopped short of a contract is unlikely to create an estoppel or a constructive trust. It cannot be said that the claimant is acting in reliance on the oral agreement that it knows to be unenforceable. Even if the court considers the behaviour of the defendant to be unconscionable, that *on its own* is an insufficient basis for allowing an estoppel or trust remedy. Cobbe was a property developer who reached agreement in principle with a property owner to buy its property. Contracts were drawn up and, as is usual, negotiations were conducted on the basis that they were 'subject to contract' and that no binding agreement would be reached until contracts were exchanged. The developer nevertheless expended time and money seeking planning permission to develop the property. Once planning permission was obtained (which increased the value of the property), the property owner withdrew from the proposed sale. The Court held that a party who incurs costs or carries out works in the hope that an agreement in principle will be honoured, or that the parties will subsequently enter into an enforceable contract, is acting speculatively. In this case the developer was entitled to a restitutionary remedy known as quantum meruit, in which the owner had to pay to the developer a sum equal to the value of the services that the developer supplied in obtaining planning permission. However, he was not entitled to a (much more valuable) share in the property.

The intentions of the parties, in the light of their awareness that the agreement remains 'subject to contract', are important here. Lord Walker stated in *Cobbe* (at [91]):

Mr Cobbe's case seems to me to fail on the simple but fundamental point that, as persons experienced in the property work, both parties knew that there was no legally binding contract, and that either was therefore free to discontinue the negotiations without legal liability – that is liability in equity as well as at law … he [Mr Cobbe] ran a commercial risk, with his eyes open, and the outcome has been unfortunate for him.

In contrast, in *Matchmore Ltd v Dowding* [2016] EWCA Civ 1233, an oral agreement for sale entered into by close friends was intended by both parties to be immediately binding, although both parties were aware of the need to sign contracts as some stage, 'at least when dealing with people who were not close friends' (at [408]). The contract was unenforceable for non-compliance with s 2 of the LPMPA 1989, but the orally agreed terms, the intention of both parties that they be binding despite this technicality, and the reliance on them by one party in making a payment in accordance with those terms created a constructive trust within the exemption created by s 2(5) of the LPMPA 1989. *Matchmore* concerned a commercial agreement; a similar decision was made in relation to domestic property in relation to a separating couple in *Ely v Robson* [2016] EWCA Civ 774. The parties were held to have intended that an oral agreement be binding, and be acted upon, although what the judge described as the 'mechanics' of putting their stated objectives into a formal agreement remained outstanding. Although unenforceable as a contract, the subsequent reliance on it by Mr Ely to his detriment created a constructive trust.

It is clear from *Cobbe*, *Matchmore* and *Ely* that the findings of fact by the judge at first instance as to what the parties' intentions were is critical. For students of land law, it is important to identify clearly the rule that the court is applying – namely that an oral understanding + an intention that it be immediately binding + a detriment arising from acting upon it can give rise to a constructive trust – before applying the rule to the given facts. Where one element of this is missing, a constructive trust will not be found. So in *Cobbe* neither party intended their oral agreement to be binding, and Mr Cobbe was well aware that he was taking a commercial risk in proceeding without a contract.

2.7.3.4 *Pallant v Morgan* equity

Constructive trusts may also be found in the commercial context. A recent example where this was explored, but not held to be a constructive trust, was the case of *Generator Developments LLP v Lidl UK GmbH* [2016] EWHC 814 (Ch). The claim was based on the principle established in *Pallant v Morgan* [1953] Ch 43 and known as the '*Pallant v Morgan* equity' that was described by Lord Scott in *Yeoman's Row Management Ltd v Cobbe* [2008] UKHL 55 at [30] as follows:

If two or more persons agree to embark on a joint venture which involves the acquisition of an identified piece of land and a subsequent exploitation of, or dealing with, the land for the purposes of the joint venture, and one of the joint venturers, with the agreement of the others who believe him to be acting for their joint purposes, makes the acquisition in his own name but subsequently seeks to retain the land for his own benefit, the court will regard him as holding the land on trust for the joint venturers. This would be either a an implied trust or a constructive trust arising from the circumstances and if, as would be likely from the facts described, the joint venturers have not agreed and cannot agree about what is to be done with the land, the land would have to be re-sold and, after discharging the expenses of its purchase and any other necessary expenses of the abortive joint venture, the net proceeds of sale divided equally between the joint venturers.

For a claim based on the '*Pallant v Morgan* equity' to succeed, there must be:

(a) a common intention or agreement between the parties before the acquisition of the property that if the property is acquired, the claimant will acquire an interest in it. It is not necessary that this intention or agreement is contractually enforceable; it may be expressly or impliedly 'subject to contract' (*Generator Developments LLP v Lidl Uk GmbH* and *Banner Homes Group plc v Luff Developments Ltd* [2000] Ch 372, CA). The agreement need not be in writing or comply with any formality requirements. In fact it is unlikely to be an enforceable contract and this is why a constructive trust remedy is sought;

(b) reliance by the claimant on the common intention or agreement to its disadvantage or to the defendant's advantage in acquiring the property. For example, the claimant relies on the agreement between the parties and takes no steps to acquire the property itself, allowing the defendant a clear run at doing so. This disadvantage to the claimant or advantage to the defendant makes it unconscionable for the defendant to go back on the agreement or understanding which allowed it to acquire the property.

A contract that is unenforceable for non-compliance with s 2 of the LPMPA 1989 may nevertheless create enforceable rights, provided the relationship between the parties in relation to the property has the necessary elements of joint venture and detriment or benefit to one party in reliance upon that joint venture (*Michael v Phillips* [2017] EWHC 614 (QB), applying *Pallant v Morgan*). It can apply in domestic or commercial cases (although the courts are likely to view the issue of whether the claimant has actually relied on any informal agreement more strictly in a commercial case, where parties are very aware that pre-contractual agreements are unenforceable). Various remedies for the equity are possible: for example in *Generator Developments* the remedy sought was rectification of a lease; in *Banner Homes* it was a beneficial interest in the property. If the parties cannot agree what should be done with a property that is the subject of a '*Pallant v Morgan*' equity, it will be sold and any profits distributed between the parties (Harman J in *Pallant v Morgan* at [50]).

2.7.4 Proprietary estoppel

Proprietary estoppel is another means by which rights in land can arise under informal arrangements. It is often claimed as an alternative to a constructive trust in the same proceedings.

The nature of proprietary estoppel was explained by Lord Scott in *Yeoman's Row Management Ltd v Cobbe* [2008] UKHL 55 at [14]:

> An 'estoppel' bars the object of it from asserting some fact or facts, or, sometimes something that is a mixture of fact and law, that stands in the way of some right claimed by the person entitled to the benefit of the estoppel. The estoppel becomes a 'proprietary' estoppel – a sub-species of a 'promissory' estoppel – if the right claimed is a proprietary right, usually a right to or over land but, in principle, equally available in relation to chattels or choses in action.

2.7.4.1 Circumstances giving rise to a claim

A claim can arise in any of the following situations:

(a) *Promise of a gift in the form of an interest or an estate in land.* If a person makes a promise of land as a gift to a person who relies on that promise and incurs expenditure as a result, then the promising party may be estopped from withdrawing the promise (*Dillwyn v Llewelyn* (1862) 4 De GF & J).

(b) *Both parties have a common expectation that one party will acquire an interest or an estate in land.* If a landowner creates or encourages an expectation that an interest in land will be created or transferred to another party at some time (either at the present time or sometime in the future), and the other party incurs expenditure on the faith of the expectation with the knowledge of the landowner and without objection by him or her, then the landowner may be estopped from denying that expectation (*Ramsden v Dyson* (1866) LR 1 HL 129, *Inwards v Baker* [1965] 2 QB 29, *Thompson v Foy* [2009] EWHC 1076 (Ch)).

(c) *One party is mistaken as to his or her rights.* If a person is mistaken as to his or her legal rights in relation to land and acts upon that mistaken belief to his or her detriment, if the other party stands by and does nothing to correct the mistaken belief, that other party may be estopped from asserting his or her strict legal rights (*Ramsden v Dyson, Wilmott v Barber* (1880) LR 15 Ch D 96, *Taylor Fashions Ltd v Liverpool Victoria Trustees Co Ltd* [1982] QB 133).

In all the categories above, for an equity to arise, the following elements are necessary – representation, reliance and detriment – making it unconscionable for the landowner to go back on his or her promise (*Gillett v Holt* [2001] Ch 210, *Yeoman's Row v Cobbe*).

2.7.4.2 Expectation

The expectation created by the promise, common expectation or mistake must be that the claimant will obtain a proprietary right. In *Yeoman's Row v Cobbe*, the expectation of a later contract was not sufficient, and Lord Scott (at [18]) quoted Oliver J in *Taylor Fashions Ltd v Liverpool Victoria Trustees Co Ltd* [1982] QB 133 (at [144]) that an expectation of a 'certain interest in land' (in that case an option to renew a lease) was required:

> [I]f A under an expectation created or encouraged by B that A shall have a certain interest in land, thereafter, on the faith of such expectation and with the knowledge of B and without objection by him, acts to his own detriment in connection with such land, a Court of Equity will compel B to give effect to such expectation.

2.7.4.3 Reliance

It is detrimental reliance that creates the estoppel. The claimant must 'show that he or she acted to his or her detriment or significantly altered his or her position in reliance on the agreement in order to give rise to a constructive trust or a proprietary estoppel' (per Bridge LJ in *Lloyds Bank Plc v Rosset* [1991] 1 AC 107 at 132).

2.7.4.4 Detriment

So what will be considered to be detriment or a 'significant change of position'? Examples include improving land belonging to the person who gave the assurance, improving your own land, purchasing new land, incurring a financial disadvantage or even a non-financial personal disadvantage, such as not taking exams which might lead to academic qualifications (*Gillett v Holt* [2001] Ch 210). When considering detriment, a court will offset benefits or advantages derived by the claimant against any alleged detriment and consider the position in the round (*Watts v Story* (1984) 124 NLJ 631, *Greasley v Cooke* [1980] 1 WLR 1306).

2.7.4.5 Satisfying the equity

The court can make an award of an appropriate remedy; there is no 'one size fits all' approach. A variety of interests can be awarded in satisfaction, or the court may award composite remedies (for example, a property interest in land and a sum of money or shares) or indeed no remedy. It has granted a proprietary estate or interest in land (including the conveyance of the freehold, grant of a lease, transfer of a share of the beneficial ownership and the award of an easement). It may grant a personal right (eg a lifetime right to occupy property).

The court has a broad discretion, but the aim is to achieve the 'minimum equity to do justice' (per Scarman LJ in *Crabb v Arun District Council* [1976] Ch 179 at 198). The aim is to fulfil the representee's expectations, but there must be proportionality between the remedy and the detriment. The court may also be mindful of the need for a 'clean break' to minimise future friction between the parties (*Pascoe v Hayward* [1979] 1 WLR 431).

2.7.4.6 Status of 'an equity' before it has been satisfied

This point is relevant in relation to proprietary estoppel because, unlike an equitable interest in land under a constructive or resulting trust, which arises by operation of law at the time that the relevant circumstances creating it exist, a proprietary estoppel is only satisfied when an order is made by the court granting an appropriate remedy. As we have seen at **2.7.4.5**, the remedy may be the grant of a proprietary right in the land but it may not be. It may be, for example, payment of a sum of money, or the court may feel that the equity has already been satisfied and award no remedy. So the question is, does the right to apply to the court for a remedy in proprietary estoppel count as a proprietary right in land *before* a court order is made? This right to apply to the court is known as 'an equity'.

The answer is yes, as confirmed by the LRA 2002, s 116(a) which provides that:

> It is hereby declared for the avoidance of doubt that, in relation to registered land, each of the following—
>
> (a) an equity by estoppel, and
>
> (b) a mere equity,
>
> has effect from the time the equity arises as an interest capable of binding successors in title (subject to the rules about the effect of dispositions on priority).

2.7.5 Priority

Trust interests and, with the clarification of s 116 of the LRA 2002, an equity that has arisen under proprietary estoppel are proprietary rights in land. We will look further in **Chapters 3** and **5** as to how interests in land can be protected against future dispositions of the land (for example the current owner sells or mortgages the land to a third party).

However, it is worth saying here that trust interests and an equity by way of proprietary estoppel may be protected in different ways:

Registered land

(a) A trust interest may not be protected by the entry of a notice on the register (LRA 2002, s 33), although if the holder is in occupation, it will be protected as an overriding interest (LRA 2002, s 29(2)(a)(ii) and Sch 3, para 2).

(b) An equity arising from estoppel may, thanks to s 116(a) of the LRA 2002, be protected by a notice on the register (LRA 2002, s 32) until the court makes an order or the case is otherwise settled. If it is not protected by a notice, it will still be protected as an overriding interest if and to the extent that the claimant is in actual occupation of the property. After a remedy in proprietary estoppel is granted by the court, the method by which it should be protected will depend on whether the remedy (if any) that is given is a proprietary right in land and, if so, whether it is a disposition that must be protected by substantive registration under s 27 of the LRA 2002 or whether a notice can be entered or, in the absence of a notice, whether it may be protected by actual occupation.

Unregistered land

(a) A trust interest falls into the residual class of interests which will bind a purchaser unless he or she is a bona fide purchaser of a legal estate for value without notice of the interest.

(b) The equity arising from an estoppel also falls into this residual class prior to any court order creating a proprietary remedy. After an order is made, the interest ordered by the court should be protected as appropriate for that interest; this will mean compulsory first registration if the order is for the transfer of a qualifying freehold or leasehold estate (LRA 2002, s 4(1)(a)(i)), the grant of a lease for a term of more than seven years (LRA 2002, s 4(1)(c)) or the grant of a first legal charge (LRA 2002, s 4(1)(g)).

reflection

What is the difference between estoppel and a constructive trust?

The two types of interest do look similar but there are important differences:

- Estoppel relies on 'representation' rather than 'common intention'.
- Estoppel creates a range of remedies and is not limited to a share of the equitable ownership.
- An interest in land is acquired by estoppel when awarded by the court, rather than, as is the case with a constructive trust, at the date of the events establishing the cause of action.

2.8 Further reading

CM Rose, 'Possession as the Origin of Property', 52 U Chi L Rev 73 (1985).

P Critchley, 'Taking formalities seriously' in s Bright and J Dewar (eds), *Land Law: Themes and Perspectives* (Oxford University Press, 1988), pp 507–28.

M Pawlowski, 'Short Leases and section 54(2) – time for a rethink? (2016) L&T Review 20(3), pp 81–83.

Lord Neuberger of Abbotsbury, 'The Stuffing of Minerva's Owl: Taxonomy and Taxidermy in Equity' (2009) 68(3) CLJ 537–49.

Law Commission, *Transfer of Land – Formalities for Contracts for Sale Etc of Land* (Report No 164, 1987)

T Boncey and F Ng, '"Common intention" constructive trusts arising from informal agreements to dispose of land' (2017) 2 Conv 146–57.

R Crozier, 'Estoppel and Elephant Traps: section 2(5) of the Law of Property (Miscellaneous Provisions) Act 1989' (2015) 3 Conv 240–44.

summary

Title to land can be acquired informally under the doctrine of adverse possession. The relevant provisions are contained in s 17 of the LA 1980 and, where land is registered, Part 9 of and Sch 6 to the LRA 2002.

However, in general, formalities are required to create or transfer interests in land. Formalities are important to warn parties that they are entering into significant transactions that will affect their rights and responsibilities and to provide evidence of a transaction and its terms. However, they add to the time and cost of transactions, and it may be unjust to penalise a party who has failed to comply with formal requirements.

A contract to create or dispose of an interest in land must comply with s 2 of the LPMPA 1989.

To create or transfer a legal interest in land:

- the estate or interest must be created or transferred by a deed (LPA 1925, s 52). There is an exception for short leases (LPA 1925, s 54(2)) which can be made orally;
- a deed must comply with s 1 of the LPMPA 1989.

To create or transfer an equitable interest in land:

- a declaration of an express trust of land must be manifested and proved in writing signed by some person who is able to declare such trust or by his or her will (LPA 1925, s 53(1)(b));
- a disposition of an already existing equitable interest or trust must be in writing signed by the person disposing of the interest or by his or her agent (lawfully authorised in writing) or by will (LPA 1925, s 53(1)(c));
- no formalities are required for the creation of resulting, implied or constructive trusts.

How can you tell if a document is a contract or a deed or neither?

Deed	Contract	Neither
The document states on its face that it is a deed, is signed by the parties and their signatures are witnessed. The deed is delivered.	All terms of the contract are contained in a document that is signed by or on behalf of the parties. If contracts are exchanged, then each party will sign an identical counterpart of the contract.	If the document does not satisfy the requirements for a contract or a deed (eg it is not signed) and it is not incorporated into a document that does satisfy the requirements, then, by itself, it does not create legal or equitable rights. You will need to consider if the surrounding circumstances are such that there are grounds to assert that rights have been created informally, for example a proprietary estoppel or a constructive, implied or resulting trust (LPA 1925, s 53(2)).
Law of Property (Miscellaneous Provisions) Act 1989, s 1	Law of Property (Miscellaneous Provisions) Act 1989, s 2	

Transactions may give rise to registration requirements under the LRA 2002, either because land is already registered (see LRA 2002, s 27) or because title is unregistered and the transaction triggers first registration of the estate being created or disposed of (see LRA 2002, s 4).

If parties fail to comply with formalities or registration requirements, then equity may provide a partial remedy under the doctrine of anticipation or if the requirements of a constructive or resulting trust or proprietary estoppel can be established.

Doctrine of anticipation	A specifically enforceable contract for the transfer, creation or grant of a legal estate or interest will act in equity.	*Walsh v Lonsdale* (1882) 21 Ch D 9
Resulting trust	Contributing funding to the purchase of an estate in land will create a resulting trust in the proportions contributed.	*Dyer v Dyer* (1788) 2 Cox 92
Constructive trust	A common intention to acquire, create or dispose of or share an estate in land acted upon by one party to his or her detriment will be enforced by equity because it is unconscionable to allow the other party to disregard his or her rights.	*Yaxley v Gotts* [2000] Ch 162
Pallant v Morgan equity	A species of constructive trust where parties have a common intention to enter a joint venture which one party acts to its detriment or the other party's advantage in relation to the acquisition of the property.	*Pallant v Morgan* [1953] Ch 43
Proprietary estoppel	A representation, common expectation or mistake as to his or her current or future proprietary rights is relied upon by one party to his or her detriment. The other party is estopped from asserting his or her full proprietary rights.	*Yeoman's Row Management Ltd v Cobbe* [2008] UKHL 55

Casper owns The Lodge, a large property with extensive grounds. His next-door neighbour Bart agrees to allow him access across his property by car for convenience.

Casper decides to convert The Lodge into flats and to let one of the flats to his friend Mary for a term of 10 years.

Sadly, Casper falls on hard times and his colleague Dhivya offers him half the current value of the property in return for a half share in it, as she thinks that the value of the property is likely to go up. Casper also agrees to sell a plot in the garden to Bart, who intends to build a small cottage on it for his retirement.

1   What formalities should Casper, Bart, Mary and Dhivya observe in entering into these transactions?

2   What registration requirements will there be under the LRA 2002?

3   If they fail to observe the correct formalities and/or registration requirements, will equity assist them?

3 Unregistered Land

After reading this chapter, you will be able to understand:

- the aim of the reduction in legal estates and interests in land contained in the Law of Property Act (LPA) 1925
- the purpose and effect on equitable interests in land of overreaching provisions contained in ss 2 and 27(2) of the LPA 1925
- the system of unregistered land in England and Wales
- how legal and equitable rights in unregistered titles to land are protected
- the risks and challenges of the conveyancing process in relation to unregistered land.

3.1 Modernisation of land law

Our current system of land law was largely shaped in 1925 when major reforms were carried out to land law to facilitate transactions involving land by making them quicker and more secure. The impetus for the reforms was that it had become difficult to buy, lease or take a mortgage over land. The unregistered land system meant that a purchaser (including a tenant or mortgagee) had to look back through the deeds, and it carried a high risk that he or she would be bound by existing interests in the land after the purchase.

This was a particular problem if buying from trustees. A purchaser (or tenant or mortgagee) could be at risk of entering into a transaction that was invalid because it was outside the trustees' powers, or that exposed him or her to the risk of interests in land of which he or she was unaware. To counteract this, the purchaser had to ensure that the trustees had power to enter into the sale. If they had no power of sale then the consent of all beneficiaries would be required. The purchaser also ran a risk that if the trustees did not have power under the trust to give a receipt discharging the property from it, and did not apply the proceeds correctly under the trust, beneficiaries could assert their beneficial title against the purchaser after completion. These difficulties required a purchaser to investigate into matters on which it could be difficult to obtain clear answers. A fuller discussion of these difficulties is given in Charles Harpum's article in the Further Reading section below.

The 1925 reforms involved five key reforming statutes. Today as land lawyers we are chiefly interested in the Law of Property Act (LPA) 1925 and (as successor to the Land Registration Act 1925, which has now been entirely repealed) the Land Registration Act (LRA) 2002.

The key reform that we are concerned with was the introduction of land registration, through which information can be found on a central register rather than looking back over title deeds, and which we shall look at in **Chapters 4** and **5**. However, there was a number of other changes designed to improve efficiency or to protect the purchaser – once he or she had done all that was reasonably required of him or her – from prior interests in the land. These apply both to registered land and those titles that remain unregistered today nearly 100 years on, and we will look now at the reduction in the number of legal estates and overreaching.

3.2 Reduction in the number of legal estates and interests

We have already seen that by s 1(1) of the LPA 1925, the number of legal estates capable of being conveyed or created at law was reduced to two:

(a) fee simple absolute in possession (the sole surviving freehold estate); and

(b) term of years absolute (the lease).

All other estates in land take effect as equitable interests (LPA 1925, s 1(3)). This means that many 'ownership' interests in land that previously would have taken effect as legal estates now take effect as equitable interests behind a trust (now defined in s 1 of the Trusts of Land and Appointment of Trustees Act 1996). An example of the kind of interest affected by the change would be the life interest awarded to Judy in our example at **1.3.4**.

We will now look more closely at the effect of this change.

In unregistered conveyancing, legal estates and interests in land 'bind the world'; that is to say that everybody who comes to land will be bound by all legal estates and interests affecting it. (The rules are different in relation to registered land, but we shall see that there are still situations in which greater protection is offered to legal estates and interests.) This brings us on to the second of our reforms: overreaching.

3.3 Overreaching

Having reduced the number of legal estates to two – freehold and leasehold – and providing that all other interests that were estates in land would now take effect as equitable interests behind a trust, the reforms provided a mechanism, known as overreaching, to enable a trustee to dispose of the land and give a clear title, free from those interests. Overreaching is the process by which trust assets can be disposed of, with the trust transferring from the asset into the cash obtained on its sale. If, subsequently, that cash is reinvested into other assets (for example another property or shares), the trust will transfer to that new asset. In other words, interests under a trust would be removed from a piece of land and transferred into an interest in the proceeds of sale. A purchaser could acquire the land safe in the knowledge that any trust interests would fall to be dealt with by the seller (who as trustee would be required to deal with the proceeds of sale in accordance with the trust) and would not bind the land in the purchaser's hands.

The purchaser benefits from a simple, quick and cheap mechanism that allows him or her confidence that he or she will not be bound by trust interests, and beneficiaries continue to benefit from the trust, albeit that it is invested in different assets. At least, that is how this is intended to work in theory; as we shall see, there are dangers if the buyer is not on his or her guard to identify a risk from trust interests or if trustees act improperly.

3.3.1 How does overreaching work?

Certain equitable interests will be overreached if there is a **conveyance** to a **purchaser** of a **legal estate in land**. In the case of beneficial interests under a trust, the conveyance must be by all the trustees (being at least two in number or a trust corporation), and any capital monies must be paid to the trustees (LPA 1925, s 2(2) and 27(2)). This is worth breaking down further:

(a) **Conveyance** means any assurance of property or interest in property by any instrument, except a will. It includes the grant of a mortgage or lease (LPA 1925, s 205(1)(ii)).

(b) The conveyance must be to a **purchaser**, which means a person who acquires an interest in or charge on the property for money or money's worth; in other words that cash or its equivalent is paid, and other consideration (such as marriage) will not count (per Rowlatt J in *Re Bateman* [1925] 2 KB 429 at 436: 'consideration in money or money's worth means that the full fair price has been paid and that nothing is left over for gift or natural love and affection or any other consideration').

(c) The purchaser must acquire a **legal estate in the land**; we know from s 1(1) of the LPA 1925 (above) that this means the freehold or a legal lease. This has been extended by s 1(4) of the LPA 1925 to include a charge by way of legal mortgage. So a purchaser of the freehold, a tenant under a lease or a bank taking a mortgage secured on the land can overreach beneficial interests under a trust of the land.

(d) Overreaching requires **two or more trustees** or a **trust corporation**. A trust corporation means the Public Trustee, an independent statutory officeholder who acts, for example, as executor or administrator of last resort for estates where the beneficiary is a vulnerable person due to his or her age or mental capacity. It will include a corporation appointed by the court to be a trustee where the trustees appointed by the settlor of a trust refuse or are unable to act.

Overreaching will also occur on a sale by personal representatives, mortgagees or by order of the court (LPA 1925, s 2(1)(iii) and (iv)), but we do not look at this here.

3.3.2 What happens to an equitable interest that has been overreached?

Overreaching means that the trust interest is removed from the land. However, the trust still exists and it transfers to the actual proceeds of sale (if there are any). The trustees hold the proceeds of sale for the beneficiaries on the terms of the trust. This is one reason why at least two trustees are required under s 2(2) of the LPA 1925 – to reduce the risk of fraud against the beneficiaries.

A purchaser can require a second trustee to be appointed if land is subject to a trust and therefore compel the seller to use the overreaching process. A purchaser cannot be required to accept a title made with the concurrence of any person entitled to an equitable interest, if a title can be made discharged from the equitable interest without such concurrence under a trust of land (LPA 1925, s 42(1)(a)).

Overreaching applies to registered and unregistered land. It is immaterial whether the purchaser was aware or not that the land that he or she has purchased was subject to a trust.

Here is an example of overreaching in practice. It comes from the facts of the case of *City of London Building Society v Flegg* [1988] AC 54.

City of London Building Society v Flegg [1988] AC 54

case example

In 1977 Mr and Mrs Flegg paid at least £18,000 towards the purchase of a property for £34,000. The daughter and her husband took out a mortgage to fund the rest of the property price. The Fleggs were aware that a mortgage of at least £15,000 would be required; in fact the daughter and her husband borrowed £20,000. The property was put into the names of the daughter and her husband, who were trustees, holding the property on trust for themselves and Mr and Mrs Flegg. Mr and Mrs Flegg were advised by their solicitor that the property should be taken in the names of all four of them; however, the Fleggs declined because they were unwilling to take any liability for payment of the mortgage.

The daughter and her husband borrowed more money (£37,000) for their own purposes, which her parents knew nothing about, and mortgaged the property to City of London Building Society. This loan was in breach of the trust. The mortgagee made no enquiries of the Fleggs.

The mortgage to City of London Building Society was a conveyance to a purchaser of a legal estate. The daughter and her husband were the two trustees. Mr and Mrs Flegg's beneficial interest in the property was shifted from the land and transferred into the capital proceeds that the daughter and son-in-law had received from the lender, and any surplus remaining once the lender had sold the property.

The Fleggs no longer held an interest in the land which could be asserted against the lender. Questions as to whether the interest in land would take priority as an overriding interest to the lender's charge were therefore irrelevant. We will look at overriding interests at **5.6**.

Discussion

The decision in the *Flegg* case as to whether Mr and Mrs Flegg's interest in land had been overreached was decided on the basis of the technical provisions of the LPA 1925. However, the effect of the decision shows a tension, that we will come across frequently in land law, as to the extent to which a just land law will protect persons who have – or think they have – property rights. This must be reconciled with the need to enable a purchaser to understand and discover all the rights that will bind him or her after completion. The weighing up of these factors was not an explicit part of the Court's decision, but there has been criticism of it on the basis that it preferred the rules that protected a purchaser who had failed to carry out proper enquiries, rather than beneficiaries who had failed to take steps that would have protected themselves. The Fleggs were left with a personal claim against their daughter and her husband for breach of trust, but, as in all cases where trustees are gone or lacking in resources to meet the claim, this personal claim on its own left the Fleggs without an effective remedy. Arguments have been raised that overreaching should never apply when a beneficiary is in occupation (see the article by Mika Oldham in Further Reading below).

From another point of view, overreaching is no more than the proper operation of a trust. Legal title to assets (whether real property, such as land, or personal property, such as shares or jewellery) is vested in the trustees who have power to sell them free from the trust and claims of beneficiaries. Trustees have obligations to obtain full market value, and the proceeds of sale are subject to the trust and subject to duties such as a duty to invest them. If the proceeds are invested into other assets, these assets too are subject to the trust. The power and responsibility of trustees is why strict fiduciary duties apply to them (see Charles Harpum's article in Further Reading and, in particular, Part I, 'The Basis of Overreaching').

3.3.3 What equitable interests can be overreached?

Overreaching applies to 'any equitable interest' affecting the estate (see the opening words of s 2(1) of the LPA 1925). Equitable interests are widely defined in s 1(8) of that Act to include all estates, interests and charges over land which are not legal estates.

Section 116 of the Land Registration Act (LRA) 2002 extends the class of equitable interests by including 'mere equities'. These are rights to bring an action to assert equitable rights (such as rights in proprietary estoppel or the right to set aside a transaction, for example as an unconscionable bargain or for misrepresentation, undue influence or lack of legal capacity). The courts have held that overreaching also applies to these interests (for proprietary estoppel, see the *Sabherwal* case (below), and for an unconscionable bargain, see *Mortgage Express v Lambert* [2016] EWCA Civ 555).

However, certain equitable interests are not capable of being overreached. These are rights such as easements, restrictive covenants and estate contracts (LPA 1925, s 2(3)). Such rights are sometimes described as commercial, as opposed to family, rights.

Robert Walker LJ in *Birmingham Midshires Mortgage Services Ltd v Sabherwal* (1999) 80 P&CR 256 referred to two decisions concerning disputes between neighbouring landowners (*Shiloh Spinners v Harding* [1973] AC 691, concerning a right of entry to enforce a covenant, and *ER Ives Investment Ltd v High* [1967] 2 QB 379, concerning an equitable easement) where the equitable rights held by one of the landowners over the land of the other were not subject to overreaching, and stated at [27] and [28]:

> Equitable interests of that character ought not to be overreached since they are rights which an adjoining owner enjoys over the land itself, regardless of its ownership from time to time.
>
> The essential distinction is ... between commercial and family interests. An equitable easement or an equitable right of entry cannot sensibly shift from the land affected by it to the proceeds of sale. An equitable interest as a tenant in common can do so, even if accompanied by the promise of a home for life, since the proceeds of sale can be used to acquire another home.

Overreaching therefore applies to equitable interests that can be described as family interests, rather than business or commercial ones. The most obvious family interest right is the trust.

Other equitable interests in land, such as an estate contract (ie the benefit of the contract to buy land), which can be seen as a commercial interest in land, cannot be overreached. The 1925 legislation dealt with these in another way, which we shall look at in 3.5.3.2.

3.3.4 Who can overreach?

As we have seen above, an equitable interest in trust property can be overreached on a sale by trustees, being at least two in number.

Overreaching of equitable interests also occurs when conveyances are entered into by mortgagees in exercise of their power of sale, by personal representatives (LPA 1925, s 2(1)(iii)) and under an order of the court (LPA 1925, s 2(1)(iv)).

3.3.5 What if there are no capital monies?

It is a requirement that the purchaser must give value, and this can be money or money's worth. For example, an exchange of land will overreach just as much as a transaction involving capital monies. The trust will attach to the land exchanged for the trust property.

In cases like *Flegg*, the trust transferred to the capital monies raised by the mortgage loan in the hands of the two legal owners, the daughter and her husband. When they dissipated these monies, they did so in breach of trust. However, overreaching still occurred in *State of India Bank v Sood* [1997] 1 All ER 169 where no capital monies were advanced; the rules relating to payment of capital monies did not limit the principle of overreaching, which will apply even where there are no capital monies involved.

3.4 Registered and unregistered land

3.4.1 Registration of title

The key change made in 1925 was to introduce a comprehensive system of registration of title to land. The modern law of land registration in England and Wales is centred in the Land Registration Act (LRA) 2002. This replaces the Land Registration Act 1925, which was repealed in full. Despite many differences, there are also some common threads between the two statutes, so students will find that, despite the repeal of the 1925 Act, case law under that Act remains good authority in many cases for the relevant provision in the LRA 2002.

3.4.2 Why was registered land introduced?

In order to answer this question, you need to understand the old system of unregistered land and the risks and challenges that it created in practice. Also, as title to some land remains unregistered today, practitioners need to use the rules relating to unregistered land, even though, in practice, many dealings with unregistered land will result in the title created or disposed of being subject to compulsory first registration and thus brought into the registered land system. We look below at how legal and equitable rights in unregistered land are protected.

3.5 Unregistered land

3.5.1 Title, priority rules and third party rights

We emphasised at 1.9 the idea that there can be several interests in the same plot of land. At many times these will be complementary but they can also compete for priority. In addition to the rights of the owner of the land, a tenant may claim the right to occupy the land, a neighbour may need to drive over the land to get access to his or her own property, and a bank may have lent money to the owner on the security of the land.

We will look first at how title is established for unregistered land and at how the competing interests of purchasers (who want to take the land free from unknown rights) and those who hold an interest in unregistered land are dealt with. There are rules that determine which of these competing interests will take priority and be effective.

We cover the unregistered land priority rules because although around 88% of the land mass in England and Wales is estimated to be registered, according to the Land Registry (Land Registry, *Annual Reports and Accounts 2015/16*, July 2016), the rest (largely rural land held by institutional landowners) remains unregistered and the rules relating to unregistered land will apply. You will see that it is necessary to clearly distinguish between the unregistered and registered land rules. We recommend that you make sure that you are clear on the rules relating to unregistered land contained in this chapter *before* you move on to **Chapters** 4 and 5 dealing with registered land.

3.5.2 How title and third party rights are investigated in unregistered land

In registered land, it is straightforward to find out who the legal owner is – he or she will be registered as proprietor of the title.

In order to put the protection of third party interests into context within the unregistered system, we need to explain how a seller proves title to unregistered land and how a buyer can check this and also verify what third party rights may affect the land that he or she wishes to acquire. Just as in **Chapter** 1, where we explained that a 'conveyance' can include a prospective tenant or a mortgagee who is taking security for a loan over the property, when we talk about a 'buyer' we are also thinking of the concerns that these individuals or organisations may have.

Imagine a typical residential transaction where a prospective buyer is seeking to purchase a home in which to live. Think about the kind of questions that the buyer will need to have answers to before he or she enters into a contract to buy the house and ultimately pay over the purchase price to complete on the acquisition.

3.5.2.1 Who is the legal owner of the land?

In unregistered land, in order to prove title, the seller has to prove that for a required period of time he or she has had complete control of the land. As stated at **2.1**, this could simply rest on possession although this is relatively unusual. In most cases, it would rest on a combination of possession and title deeds that document the right to possession. To prove this, the seller will produce title to the buyer, in the form of deeds; this is known as 'deducing title' and the process as the 'deduction of title'. Currently, for unregistered land, the seller has to produce title to the property from a conveyance (called the root conveyance) that is at least 15 years old (LPA 1925, s 44(1), as amended by the Law of Property Act 1969, s 23) as proof of the seller's ownership of the land. The root conveyance must clearly identify the land and establish title to the estate which can be traced through to the current owner. A good root therefore establishes the title of the current owner and does nothing to cast doubt on it.

As a buyer is entitled to require that the 'good root' is at least 15 years old, he or she is entitled to require to see all title deeds going back to a date at least 15 years prior to the transaction in order to establish that the seller has title. Title earlier than 15 years is likely to be required if the seller acquired the land more than 15 years ago, as the seller would be required to disclose the conveyance to him; the key thing is that, as stated above, the root must establish the seller's title. Remember that a conveyance has a broader meaning than simply a deed to complete a sale of land, and can include a mortgage, assent, disclaimer and other assurances of property if necessary (LPA 1925, s 205(1)(ii)).

As well as checking the seller's title, the buyer will also want to make sure that the estate he or she is purchasing is not burdened by undisclosed third party rights.

3.5.2.2 Do any third parties have rights in the land?

So the buyer, or his or her legal representative, should look through various deeds and carry out checks that the seller's title is good and has not been encumbered by third party interests, either legal or equitable, that would affect the buyer's enjoyment of the land. This process is also known as 'investigating' title.

To investigate title, the buyer should:

(a) review the title deeds for evidence of other rights, such as a conveyance which is subject to rights that are reserved to a third party or the grant of a deed of easements;

(b) search the land charges register;

(c) inspect the property and make reasonable enquiries.

This process is time-consuming and carries significant risk that the buyer or his or her legal representative may miss vital interests that the land was subject to, for example if deeds become lost or damaged.

3.5.3 What rights will bind the buyer after completion?

The rules for priority of interests are complex, and a buyer could be bound by interests that he or she does not know about. In particular, a buyer would be bound by all legal estates and interests existing in relation to the land whether or not he or she was aware of them. Prior to the reduction of legal estates referred to at **3.2** above, there were many more legal estates in land that a buyer could be bound by. A buyer would also be bound by all equitable interests affecting the title unless he or she was a bona fide purchaser for value without actual, constructive or imputed notice of the interest.

We will now look at the rules for establishing what rights exist in the land and whether they will bind a purchaser (which as usual can include a lender taking a mortgage or a tenant taking a lease of the land). These are summarised in **Figure 3.1** below.

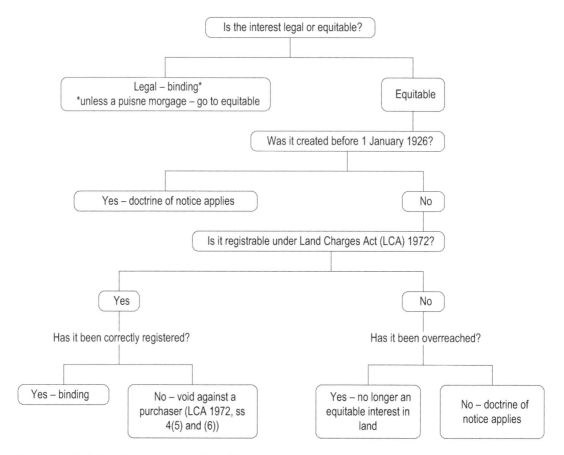

Figure 3.1 Priority of interests – unregistered land

3.5.3.1 Rule 1: Legal rights 'bind the world'

This means that legal estates and interests in the land will bind everybody who comes to the land, regardless of whether they knew about them or not.

How do you know if a right is legal?

Remember our discussion in **Chapter** 1 about legal and equitable rights in land. Legal rights are set out in s 1 of the LPA 1925.

Section 1(1) sets out legal estates or ownership of land – these are (a) the fee simple (or freehold), and (b) the term of years absolute (or leasehold):

> The only estates in land which are capable of subsisting or of being conveyed or created at law are—
>
> (a) An estate in fee simple absolute in possession; and
>
> (b) A term of years absolute.

Section 1(2) sets out legal interests or charges in land. These are interests that can be held in land belonging to another person. The most important are mortgages (where a loan of money is secured on land) and easements (such as a right of way over a neighbour's land):

> The only interests or charges in or over land which are capable of subsisting or of being conveyed or created at law are—
>
> (a) An easement, right, or privilege in or over land for an interest equivalent to an estate in fee simple absolute in possession or a term of years absolute;
>
> (b) A rentcharge in possession issuing out of or charged on land being either perpetual or for a term of years absolute;
>
> (c) A charge by way of legal mortgage;
>
> (d) … and any other similar charge on land which is not created by an instrument;
>
> (e) Rights of entry exercisable over or in respect of a legal term of years absolute, or annexed, for any purpose, to a legal rentcharge.

Under s 1(3) of the Law of Property Act 1925, all other estates, interests and charges in or over land take effect as equitable interests:

> All other estates, interests, and charges in or over land take effect as equitable interests.

The rights set out in s 1(1) and (2) of the LPA 1925 are the rights that are capable of being legal. Whether they are or not will depend on whether they have been created or registered properly. For example, if you and your neighbour agree that he will give you a legal right to drive over his land to get to your house (perhaps because you have agreed to pay him some money for this right) then the right must be granted by a deed in order to be a legal easement. In other words, it must be granted in a written document which is signed by your neighbour, and his signature must be witnessed. In some situations, granting or transferring legal estates or interests in land will trigger an obligation to register the title to the land. The grant or transfer will not take effect at law until registration is complete; if you fail to register the estate or interest, it can only take effect as an equitable interest. Formalities are also important for certain equitable interests. We looked at this in more detail in **Chapter 2**.

There are a very few exceptions to the rule that legal rights bind the world. We will look at the most important of these under the next rule.

3.5.3.2 Rule 2: Some interests must be registered

A limited scheme was introduced in 1925 under which some third party interests in land must be registered against the landowner's name. This obligation was introduced by the Land Charges Act 1925, now replaced by the Land Charges Act

(LCA) 1972. Unlike in registered land, though, the title of the landowner remains unregistered.

What interests must be registered?

There are six basic categories of land charge: A through to F. Some of these are further subdivided. You will find a full list of the charges in s 2 of the LCA 1972, but the most important interests are set out below.

Table 3.1   Categories of land charge

Class C(i)	'Puisne' or second mortgage	The first charge, Class C(i), is the exception that we mentioned earlier to the rule that all legal rights bind the world. A 'puisne' mortgage is a legal mortgage that is not protected by the lender having the title deeds in its possession. This is usually because it is a second mortgage and the first mortgagee has taken custody of the title deeds to protect its interests. The fact that a lender holds the title deeds is usually warning to a purchaser that the property is subject to a mortgage, so it makes sense to require a second mortgage to be registered to alert a purchaser to its existence too.
Class C(iii)	General equitable charge	Class C(iii) is the general equitable charge. This is a wide category which consists of all equitable charges over land, except those limited few that are excluded by the Act.
Class C(iv)	Estate contracts	Class C(iv) relates to estate contracts – in other words a contract to transfer or create a legal estate in land. This means a contract to sell the freehold or leasehold title to land or a contract to grant a lease. It also includes option agreements (LCA 1972, s 2(4)(iv)).
Class D(ii)	Restrictive covenants	Class D(ii) – restrictive covenants. It applies to restrictive covenants entered into on or after 1 January 1926 (when the original Land Charges Act came into force). A restrictive covenant is an enforceable promise by a landowner which is negative in nature, for example a promise not to build on a certain piece of land.

| Class D(iii) | Equitable easements | Class D(iii) – equitable easements created after 1 January 1926. An example of an easement is a right to walk or drive over your neighbour's land to get to your own property. (As you know, easements are capable of existing at law if granted by a legal estate owner using the right formalities – and if legal they will bind the world without the need for registration.) Equitable easements should be registered as a land charge. |
| Class F | Right to occupy family home under the Family Law Act 1996 | Class F – a spouse or a civil partner who is not on the legal title has a statutory right to occupy the family home under Part IV of the Family Law 1996. This should be registered as a Class F land charge. |

What is the effect of registration?

Registration of an interest as a land charge under the LCA 1972 is deemed to be actual notice to all persons and for all purposes (LPA 1925, s 198(1)). Any person taking an interest in the land is subject to the registered land charge.

Effect of failure to register

The effect of failure to register depends upon the type of land charge.

Class D and Class C(iv)

Unregistered Class D and Class C(iv) land charges (restrictive covenants and estate contracts) are void against a purchaser for money or money's worth of a legal estate in land. You should look at the wording of s 4(6) of the LCA 1972:

> An estate contract and a land charge of Class D created or entered into on or after 1st January 1926 shall be void as against a purchaser for money or money's worth ... of a legal estate in the land charged with it, unless the land charge is registered in the appropriate register before the completion of the purchase.

The leading case in this area is *Midland Bank Trust Co Ltd v Green* [1981] AC 513.

Midland Bank Trust Co Ltd v Green [1981] AC 513

case example

A farmer granted an option to his eldest son, Geoffrey, to purchase the family farm. The option was an estate contract and should have been registered as a Class C(iv) land charge (at the time under the previous LCA 1925; now under the LCA 1972, s 2(4)(iv)). It was never registered.

Later the son fell out with his family. The father sold the property to his wife, Evelyne, the son's mother, for £500. The market value of the property was in the region of £40,000 at this time. The son protested and tried to enforce his option. It was held to be void. Lord Wilberforce, giving the only judgment, said at 528:

> Thus the case appears to be a plain one. The 'estate contract', which by definition [now LCA 1972, s 2(4)(iv)] includes an option of purchase, was entered into after 1st January 1926; Evelyne took an interest (in fee simple) in the land 'for valuable consideration' – so was a 'purchaser': she was a purchaser for money – namely £500: the option was not registered before the completion of the purchase. It is therefore void against her.

> In my opinion this appearance is also the reality. The case is plain: the Act is clear and definite. Intended as it was to provide a simple and understandable system for the protection of title to land, it should not be read down or glossed: to do so would destroy the usefulness of the Act. Any temptation to remould the Act to meet the facts of the present case, on the supposition that it is a hard one and that justice requires it, is, for me at least, removed by the consideration that the Act itself provides a simple and effective protection for persons in Geoffrey's position – viz. – by registration.

Although the price paid by the mother was below market value, it was nevertheless for money or money's worth. The Court considered that defining money or money's worth to exclude nominal or inadequate amounts would be to rewrite the statute and was not prepared to do so. Although the mother had actual notice of the option, this was irrelevant. The legislation had clearly replaced the old doctrine of notice with a requirement of registration, and there was no room to imply a requirement of good faith on the part of the purchaser. Even if there had been, the court was not convinced that the mother had acted with an absence of good faith.

Note: although the estate contract is void against a purchaser, it remains contractually enforceable against the person who granted it (in the case of *Green*, the father). The usual remedy will be damages.

Other classes of land charge

The rules for other registrable land charges are slightly different. If unregistered, such charges will be void against a purchaser who acquires a legal or equitable interest.

Under s 4(5) of the LCA 1972, such charges:

> shall be void as against a purchaser of the land charged with it, or of any interest in such land, unless the land charge is registered in the appropriate register before the completion of the purchase

Section 17 of the LCA 1972 defines a purchaser as 'any person (including a mortgagee or lessee) who, for valuable consideration, takes any interest in land or in a charge on land'. Valuable consideration includes marriage consideration or a nominal payment.

Good faith and fraud

In *Midland Bank Trust Co Ltd v Green*, the Court was unwilling to write into the LCA 1972 an obligation on the purchaser to act in good faith. Nor was it willing to accept that a purchaser who relied on his or her rights under the LCA 1972 was not acting in good faith. However, where a transaction is in reality a sham or a fraud, we can expect that the purchaser will not be considered to be 'a purchaser' at all and therefore cannot bring him- or herself within s 4 of the LCA 1972. Although relating to registered land, in *Halifax Plc v Curry Popeck (A Firm)* [2008] EWHC 1692 (Ch), where a party acted under an alias to acquire a property that he jointly owned with another, the transfer was part of a 'fraudulent enterprise in the context of which the concept of "consideration" is entirely meaningless' (per Norris J at [43]).

Applying this reasoning to s 4 of the LCA 1972, if no meaningful consideration is provided due to fraud then the acquiring party will not be able to rely on s 4.

Exceptions

There are a few exceptional cases where the courts have held that, despite an interest created under an unregistered land charge being void for non-registration, the circumstances are such that a *separate* interest has been created that is not required to be registered and is still capable of binding a purchaser.

The purchaser may be estopped from asserting non-registration of a land charge to defeat the interest holder. A document that is unenforceable in its own right due to lack of registration as a land charge may, nevertheless, if acted upon to a person's detriment, create a proprietary estoppel. The estoppel is not a registrable interest and its priority against a purchaser will depend upon the doctrine of notice (see **3.5.3.3** below). In *ER Ives Investment Ltd v High* [1967] 2 QB 379, an equitable easement was created by an agreement for the grant of a right of way but was never completed by a formal grant. The owner of the dominant land failed to register a Class D(iii) land charge and therefore the easement was void against a purchaser for money or money's worth (LCA 1972, s 4(6)). However, the dominant owner had acted to his detriment with the acquiescence of the servient landowner by building a garage and contributing to the costs of resurfacing the yard. This created a proprietary estoppel which was outside the registration requirements of the Land Charges Act and subject to the doctrine of notice. It was therefore binding on a purchaser of the servient land who knew of the agreement.

However, an argument that an unregistered estate contract was binding on a mortgagee bank due to constructive trust or estoppel failed in *Lloyds Bank Plc v Carrick* (1997) 73 P&CR 314. Mrs Carrick, who had entered into an oral agreement to purchase the property with her brother-in-law, argued that the trust or estoppel was created by her detriment in paying the purchase price to her brother-in-law, the vendor. The Court allowed the bank's appeal, holding that a trust already arose from the estate contract which was specifically enforceable against the vendor. The payment of the price by the purchaser under that contract could not create a further constructive trust in her favour. This was not altered by the fact that the contract was void against the bank due to the purchaser's failure to register it as a C(iv) land charge. Nor was estoppel appropriate. In part this was on the same basis (namely that there was no room for estoppel in relation to a payment made under an enforceable contract). Secondly, the vendor was not seeking to resile from the position that he had led the purchaser to expect, as the contract was still enforceable against him, albeit that he was in breach of that contract for granting the mortgage. (He was also in breach of trust to the purchaser for failing to account to her for the money raised under that mortgage.) The problem was that, for non-registration, the contract was void against the bank. Nor was there any claim of estoppel binding on the bank, for it could not be unconscionable to rely on the non-registration of the contract.

It seems that the combined effect of *Ives v High* and *Carrick* is that a claim in constructive trust or estoppel can only be founded when it arises independently of any estate contract. If such a contract exists (as in *Ives v High*), any detriment must be based on a voluntary act rather than on an act done in accordance with the contract that is void against a purchaser for non-registration.

In the registered land case of *Lyus v Prowsa Developments* [1952] 1 WLR 1044, an unprotected interest was binding on a purchaser under a constructive trust that had arisen outside the land registration priority rules, where he had expressly agreed to take subject to it and paid a lower price as a result. The unprotected status of the interest was irrelevant as the purchaser's conscience was affected and he was directly bound by the trust.

in practice

Once the system of land charges was introduced, one act that a purchaser will carry out when investigating title is to make land charges searches against every legal person named in the title deeds that are deduced or disclosed, as registrations are made by reference to the owner's name rather than by the property description. As we have said, a purchaser is only entitled to investigate title back to a 'good root', which is a minimum of 15 years old. There are two practical problems with this:

Pre-root registered land charges

A land charge that is registered against an owner who is 'pre-root' and not disclosed in the deduction of title is still valid under the LCA 1972. For example, in 1980, Thomas bought The Lodge from Sara, who owned a larger property, The Hall, of which The Lodge had formed part. The conveyance reserved a restrictive covenant in favour of Sara requiring The Lodge only to be used for residential purposes, which Sara registered correctly against Thomas' name. In 1986, Thomas sold The Lodge to Mark who, in 1989, sold the property on again to Ben. When, in 2007, Ben sold the property to Shabir, Shabir received Mark's conveyance to Ben as the 'good root' of Ben's title. She carried out land charges searches against Mark and Ben's names but not against Thomas, of whom she was unaware. The earlier conveyance between Sara and Thomas was not disclosed to her as it predated the root and she did not know about the restrictive covenant. She intends to use the property for her real estate agency business. Donald, who now owns The Hall, has objected on grounds of the covenant.

The covenant is binding on Shabir under s 198 of the LCA 1972. However, s 25 of the Law of Property Act 1969 provides for Shabir to receive financial compensation from the Land Charges Registry (now operated by the Land Registry).

This problem is likely to reduce – or at least to shift into an issue of rectification and indemnity of registered titles – as more land becomes subject to compulsory registration. The Land Registry asks that on an application for first registration, *all* deeds and documents in the applicant's possession are submitted to them. One purpose is to enable pre-root title matters to be picked up.

Searching against the 'wrong' name

A key weakness of this limited system is that registration must be made against the name of the landowner. This creates immediate difficulties. Let us say that you would like to buy No 25 Acacia Avenue. If the land were registered, you could carry out a search against the property address to enable to you to see the registered title for it. If no address is available then a search can be carried out using a map. However, if the land is unregistered, you must look back on the title deeds for at least 15 years back to your good root of title – and perhaps longer – and then carry out a search against the name of each person who has held title to the land over that period. The search will reveal if any third party rights were registered as land charges against them. If you make a mistake in a name, you may not find out about registered entries, but you will still be bound by them.

In *Diligent Finance v Alleyne* (1972) 23 P&CR 346, a wife registered a land charge against her husband. His full name, as used on the conveyance to him, was Erskine Owen Alleyne. His wife registered a land charge to register her right, as his spouse, to occupy the property. This is known as a Class F land charge, as we shall see. Unfortunately she registered it against the name Erskine Alleyne and did not include his middle name. Mr Alleyne later mortgaged the property. The lender searched against his full name, which did not reveal the wife's land charge. The lender took free from the wife's interest. The court held that the name on the conveyance is to be treated as the correct form. This causes particular difficulties for a spouse who may be registering his or her spousal right of occupation (now under the Family Law Act 1996, ss 30 and 31) who may not have access to his or her spouse's title deeds. Class F land charges tend to be registered when a marriage – or civil partnership – is in the course of breaking down.

In *Standard Property Investment Plc v British Plastics Federation* (1985) 53 P&CR 25, it was held that registration should be made against the name of the estate owner in the form that the name was set out in the conveyance to him or her and not, if it is in conflict, in the form set out in his or her birth certificate.

3.5.3.3 Rule 3: Doctrine of notice

Finally, there is a residual category of equitable rights. Into it falls equitable interests which are not registrable as land charges and which either cannot or have not been overreached. It therefore includes:

(a) equitable rights (including restrictive covenants and easements) entered into before 1 January 1926 (when the original land charges legislation, the LCA 1925 (now replaced by the LCA 1972), came into force); and

(b) all equitable rights – which can have been entered into at any time – that do not fall within a registration category in s 2 of the LCA 1972. The most significant category is trust interests. It also includes an equity arising from a proprietary estoppel or the right to have a transaction set aside for a ground such as lack of legal capacity, undue influence or misrepresentation. In respect of interests falling within (b), we need first to consider whether these have been overreached by a disposition of the legal estate by two trustees (see 3.5.3.4 below).

The old doctrine of notice continues to apply to the residual categories of interests set out in (a) and (b) above. This means that a purchaser of a legal estate in the land will take priority over equitable interests in this residual category provided that he or she can show that he or she is a bona fide purchaser of a legal estate without actual, constructive or imputed notice of their existence. If the purchaser can do so then he or she will take free from the equitable rights.

A key point to make is that this is not truly a rule as to priority. It is instead a finding that the conscience of a purchaser, who, acting with good faith and without knowledge of an equitable claim on the land, purchases a legal estate in the land, is not affected by that equitable claim. He therefore buys free from it. This was stated by James LJ in *Pilcher v Rawlins* (1871–72) LR 7 Ch App 259 at 269:

> I propose simply to apply myself to the case of a purchaser for valuable consideration, without notice, obtaining, upon the occasion of his purchase, and by means of his purchase deed, some legal estate, some legal right, some legal advantage; and, according to my view of the established law of this Court, such a purchaser's plea of a purchase for valuable consideration without notice is an absolute, unqualified, unanswerable defence, and an unanswerable plea to the jurisdiction of this Court. Such a purchaser, when he has once put in that plea, may be interrogated and tested to any extent as to the valuable consideration which he has given in order to shew the *bona fides* or *mala fides* of his purchase, and also the presence or the absence of notice; but once he has gone through that ordeal, and has satisfied the terms of the plea for purchase for valuable consideration without notice, then, according to my judgment, this Court has no jurisdiction whatever to do anything more than to let him depart in possession of that legal estate, that legal right, that legal advantage which he has obtained, whatever it may be. In such a case a

purchaser is entitled to hold that which, without breach of duty, he has had conveyed to him.

There are several elements comprised in a bona fide purchase of a legal estate as a defence to a claimant asserting an equitable interest, and it is worth looking at each in detail.

Bona fide

A purchaser must act bona fide (in good faith). There is no clear statement in the case law what this might mean in addition to the absence of notice, but the requirement reinforces equity's basis in the conscience of the affected person. In the words of Lord Wilberforce in *Midland Bank Trust Co Ltd v Green* [1981] AC 513, HL at 528:

> My Lords, the character in the law known as the bona fide (good faith) purchaser for value without notice was the creation of equity. In order to affect a purchaser for value of a legal estate with some equity or equitable interest, equity fastened upon his conscience … Equity, in other words, required not only absence of notice but genuine and honest absence of notice. … But … it would be a mistake to suppose that the requirement of good faith extended only to the matter of notice … Equity still retained its interest in and power over the purchaser's conscience.

Purchaser for value

A purchaser for value must give consideration although, as seen in *Midland Bank Trust Co Ltd v Green*, it need not be the market value and can be nominal. However, it would not include the recipient of a gift, whether a lifetime gift or by will, or an adverse possessor.

Of a legal estate

As we have seen, a legal estate means a legal freehold or leasehold.

Without notice

Notice is widely defined in s 199(1) of the LPA 1925 to include actual, constructive and imputed notice:

> (1) A purchaser shall not be prejudicially affected by notice of—
>
> > (i)   any instrument or matter capable of registration under the provisions of the Land Charges Act [1972], or any enactment which it replaces, which is void or not enforceable as against him under that Act or enactment, by reason of the non-registration thereof;
> >
> > (ii) any other instrument or matter or any fact or thing unless—
> >
> > > (a) it is within his own knowledge, or would have come to his knowledge if such inquiries and inspections had been made as ought reasonably to have been made by him; or

(b) in the same transaction with respect to which a question of notice to the purchaser arises, it has come to the knowledge of his counsel, as such, or of his solicitor or other agent, as such, if such inquiries and inspections had been made as ought reasonably to have been made by the solicitor or other agent.

The provisions of subsections (1)(ii)(a) and (b) relate, respectively, to:

(a) *actual notice* – this means that the purchaser actually knew about the interest. In *Lloyd v Banks* (1867–68) LR 3 Ch App 488, Lord Cairns stated at 490:

> It must depend upon the facts of the case; but I am quite prepared to say that I think the Court would expect to find that those who alleged that [the purchaser] had knowledge of the incumbrance had made it out not by any evidence of casual conversations … but by proof that the mind of [the purchaser] has in some way been brought to an intelligent apprehension of the nature of the incumbrance which has come upon the property, so that a reasonable man, or an ordinary man of business, would act upon the information and would regulate his conduct by it …';

(b) *constructive notice* – a purchaser will be deemed to have constructive notice of an interest which, on the balance of probabilities, the purchaser would have discovered if he or she had carried out the inquiries and inspections that a prudent purchaser would reasonably be expected to make. A purchaser is expected to investigate the seller's title, carry out searches of public registers, make formal enquiries of the seller and physically inspect the property. When inspecting, a purchaser should be vigilant for signs of occupiers other than the seller and must make enquiries of any occupier (not merely the seller). The rule in *Hunt v Luck* [1902] 1 Ch 428 is that, per Vaughan Williams LJ at 433:

> if a purchaser or mortgagee has notice that the vendor or mortgagor is not in possession of the property, he must make enquiries of the person in possession – of the tenant who is in possession – and find out from him what his rights are, and, if he does not choose to do that, then whatever title he acquires as purchaser or mortgagee will be subject to the title or right of the tenant in possession.

The case concerned a tenant but the principle is wider, to encompass any occupant; and

(c) *imputed notice* – notice will be imputed to the purchaser if his or her agent, solicitor or counsel had actual or constructive notice of the interest so that they actually knew of the interest or would have known had they made the inquiries and inspections they ought reasonably to have made.

A good example of both constructive and imputed notice can be found in the case of *Kingsnorth Finance Co Ltd v Tizard* [1986] 1 WLR 783.

Kingsnorth Finance Co Ltd v Tizard [1986] 1 WLR 783

Mr Tizard was the sole legal owner of a house and land which was the matrimonial home for himself and his wife. The couple separated and it was agreed that the house would be sold and the net proceeds divided equally between them. Mrs Tizard no longer slept at the property unless Mr Tizard was away but returned for part of each day to care for the children. Mr Tizard took out a loan secured on the property with Kingsnorth Finance, describing himself as 'single' on the application. The surveyor instructed by the mortgage company visited the property, met the husband and was told by him that he and his wife were separated and that she was living elsewhere. The agent listed the occupants as the husband, son and daughter. Mr Tizard left the country with the couple's son once the loan was made, and the mortgagee sought possession. Mrs Tizard claimed an equitable interest in the property due to her contributions towards successive purchases of properties for use as a matrimonial home. The court found that, as between husband and wife, Mrs Tizard was entitled to half the equity.

The question whether the legal charge was subject to Mrs Tizard's equitable interest or not depended on whether the mortgagee was a bona fide purchaser for value of a legal estate without notice of her interest. If the mortgagee had notice of Mrs Tizard's interest, it would take subject to it. If it did not have notice, it would be able to enforce its legal charge.

Mr Tizard had described himself on his mortgagee application as single. The mortagee's agent (its valuer) was informed by Mr Tizard, when the agent inspected the property, that he was in fact married but separated, and that his wife was living nearby. The agent was under a duty to pass this knowledge on to his principal, the mortgagee, but he did not do so, and therefore this knowledge was imputed to it. The agent did inform the mortgagee that Mr Tizard had a son and daughter living with him. The mortgagee was 'prejudicially affected' (at 792H) by the information, known to its agent, that Mr Tizard was married. This put it on notice that further enquiries were necessary.

Had the enquiries been made by the mortgagee which in those circumstances ought reasonably to have been made by it, Mrs Tizard's claim to an equitable interest in the property would, in the judgment of the court, have been disclosed.

The court also considered whether the fact of Mrs Tizard's occupation was sufficient to give the mortgagee notice of her rights or whether it needed actually to be aware of her occupation? The court concluded that Mr Tizard had hidden the signs of Mrs Tizard's occupation. The court took the view that the inspection must be such as 'ought reasonably to be made' (at 794G). The court was not satisfied that a pre-arranged inspection with the vendor on a Sunday afternoon was sufficient for this. Although it did acknowledge that a pre-arranged inspection would in most cases be essential in order to view the interior, it gave no further guidance as to what would be necessary to make such an inspection 'as ought reasonably to be made', other than to state that it would 'depend on all the circumstances' (at 795B). The court did not explicitly link the inspection to the inconsistency in the information given as to Mr Tizard's marital status, but its approach implies that, in such circumstances at least, a further unannounced inspection during the week might be necessary.

We will see in **Chapter 5** that, in registered land, in a similar situation, hiding evidence of occupation may defeat an occupier's claim if his or her 'occupation would not have been obvious on a reasonably careful inspection of the land at the time of the disposition' (LRA 2002, Sch 3, para 2(c)(i)). This is an objective standard and therefore subject to the same power of the court to judge that occupation was not discovered because the inspection was inadequate.

The case report indicated what happened next; as an alternative to its claim for possession, the mortgagee had also sought an order for sale of the property. This was not heard because the mortgagee and Mrs Tizard agreed that the property would be sold, with the sale to be postponed for six months. In view of the decision as to the priority of Mrs Tizard's equitable interest in respect of half the equity in the home unencumbered by the mortgage, on sale, the net proceeds would be divided equally between the mortgagee as to one half to redeem the mortgage (with the surplus, if any, going to Mr Tizard) and, as to the other half, to Mrs Tizard. We will look at this in more detail in **Chapter 6** and at **12.4**.

3.5.3.4 Rule 4: Has the interest been overreached?

We dealt above (at **3.5.3.2**) with those interests which are required to be registered as a land charge, and which will be void if they are not registered. These interests are mainly equitable but include a legal 'puisne' or second mortgage. All these interests can loosely be termed as 'commercial' interests in land.

There are other equitable interests in land which do not fall within the classes set up in the LCA 1972 and which cannot be protected by registration as a land charge. The most important of these are the equitable rights of beneficiaries under a trust of land. These can often be thought of as 'family' interests in land. This brings us on to our fourth rule, which is a rule that you are already familiar with (see **3.3**).

Remember that beneficial interests arising under trusts are capable of being overreached if there is a conveyance (which includes a mortgage or lease) to a purchaser of a legal estate in land. The conveyance must be by at least two trustees, and any capital monies must be paid to the trustees.

Overreaching means that the trust interest is removed from the land and transferred to the proceeds of sale. The trustees hold the proceeds of sale on trust for the beneficiaries. This is why it is important that all the trustees must be involved – and that there must be at least two in number – to reduce the risk of fraud against the beneficiaries.

Overreaching applies to registered and unregistered land. There is no need for the purchaser to have notice of the trust interest.

It does not apply to all equitable interests in land. It is a valuable way of stopping 'family' interests under a trust of land from affecting purchasers by converting them into money. It does not apply to 'commercial' rights, such as easements or estate contracts, which are intended to apply despite changes in ownership of the land and which are protected by registration of land charges.

in practice

These days it is very common for the legal and beneficial title to land to be held jointly by a couple, whether they are unmarried co-habitees, married or civil partners. When one person in the couple dies, the sale will be by the sole survivor. This does not cause a problem if the couple held as beneficial joint tenants, and, by the principle of survivorship, the surviving member of the couple will hold the full equitable interest in the property. However, if the couple held as beneficial tenants in common then, in addition to the sole survivor to the legal title, other people may hold a beneficial interest in the land. This will occur if the deceased person ended or severed the equitable joint tenancy before his or her death. His or her half share will then be dealt with according to his or her will or, if there is no will, under the intestacy rules. Unless a second trustee is appointed, a purchaser or mortgagee will take subject to the interests of those unknown other people.

To avoid the need for a second trustee to be appointed every time a member of a couple dies, s 1 of the Law of Property (Joint Tenants) Act 1964 provides a solution. The sole survivor can sell as the sole beneficial owner if he sells as such in the transfer deed, provided that:

- there is no record written or endorsed on the conveyance to the couple stating that the joint tenancy has been severed; and
- no bankruptcy order has been made (or petition for bankruptcy registered under the Land Charges Act 1972) against either of the couple before the date of completion of the transfer deed by the sole survivor.

3.6 Further reading

C Harpum, 'Overreaching, Trustees' Powers and the Reform of the 1925 Legislation' (1990) 49(2) CLJ 277–333.

M Oldham, 'Estate Contracts, Constructive Trusts and Estoppels in Unregistered Land' (1997) 56(1) CLJ 32–34.

M Oldham, 'Overreaching where no Capital Monies Arise' (1997) 56(3) CLJ 494–96.

D O'Sullivan, 'The Rule in Phillips v Phillips' (2002) 118 LQR 296–323.

MP Thompson, 'The purchaser as private detective' [1986] Conv 283–87.

Sections 2 and 27(2) of the Law of Property Act 1925 provide that beneficial interests under a trust will be overreached if:

- conveyance (including mortgage or lease)
- by at least two trustees
- capital monies (if any) paid to trustees.

Investigation of an unregistered title to land:

- root conveyance
- at least 15 years old (Law of Property Act 1969, s 23)

Priority rules on a sale of unregistered land:

Legal rights – purchaser takes subject to all legal rights except:	Equitable rights – purchaser takes subject to all equitable rights except:		
certain legal rights that are void for non-registration (eg 'puisne' mortgage).	'commercial' equitable rights which are void against him or her *if* unregistered (notice of the interest is irrelevant).	'family' equitable rights *if* overreached.	unregistrable and non-overreached rights *if* he or she is a bona fide purchaser for value without notice.

Reminder of legal rights (LPA 1925, s 1):

- s 1(1) – estates (owning title to land)
    - freehold
    - leasehold
- s 1(2) – interests (holding rights over another person's land). The key ones are:
    - mortgages
    - easements
- s 1(3) – all other estates, interests and charges in or over land take effect as equitable interests
    - bona fide purchaser for value without notice

1 Liz is the owner of a large house, Grey Gables, which she purchased 10 years ago, with the help of her father who contributed £50,000 and who stays in a cottage in the grounds when he visits. Liz is seconded to the United States by her employer and decides to rent the main house. Her friend Misha agrees to rent the house and has entered into a tenancy agreement with Liz for a term of two years, the length of Liz's secondment. Misha loves the house, and he and Liz have agreed by email that if Liz wants to sell, she will give Misha first refusal to purchase the property at current market value. Misha is retired and, after moving in, took up a six-week round the world cruise. Misha's son Ben has recently lost his job, and Misha has agreed that he can move in to look after the house while he is away. Ben has been supplementing his income as a DJ, and his equipment and record collection take up a further bedroom at the house.

Liz has received an offer to buy the house from Silver Properties, a local property developer. Liz has decided to stay in the United States and has entered into a contract with Silver Properties to sell the property to it. Silver Properties has engaged a surveyor who has done a 'drive by' valuation of the property but has not inspected the interior, as it intends to demolish the house and build a modern flat development in its place.

Paula owns the adjoining property, which has the benefit of a restrictive covenant entered into in 1879, under which the then owner of Grey Gables covenanted not to use the property otherwise than as a single private residential dwelling. She and Liz also agreed five years ago to grant each other mutual rights of way over each other's properties, which they put into a document which each of them signed. Paula meant to ask her solicitor about it but has not done so.

On the assumption that title to Grey Gables is unregistered:

(a) Advise Silver Properties on what rights will be binding on it when it purchases Grey Gables.

(b) How would your answer differ if, before Liz could enter into the contract, she dies and, under her will, all her property is left to her brother Jack?

2 Can you identify the problems with unregistered conveyancing prior to 1925?

3 How did the Law of Property Act 1925 and the Land Charges Act 1972 address those problems? Do they do it effectively?

Registration of Title

4.1 Introduction

It is estimated that almost 88% of land in England and Wales is now registered, in almost 24.5 million titles (Land Registry, *Annual Reports and Accounts 2015/16*, July 2016). The same report states that in the last two years, approximately 1% of the land mass of England and Wales has been registered in a new title every six months. The system is required to be robust, dealing in 2015/16 with over 30 million applications, ranging from requests for information and official searches to applications to change the register.

4.2 Registration of title

The registered land system sought to avoid the problems relating to dealings with unregistered land (that we saw in **Chapter 3**) by creating a register that was a 'mirror image' of the state of the title to the land, and thereby reducing the time it took to investigate title and the risk of deeds being destroyed or lost and, most importantly, enabling a buyer to proceed with confidence that he or she was aware of any matters affecting the title to the property that would bind him or her after completion.

4.3 The principal objectives of a system of registered land

> The fundamental aim of [the Land Registration Act (LRA) 2002] is that … the register should be a complete and accurate reflection of the state of the title of the land at any given time, so that it is possible to investigate title to land online, with the absolute minimum of additional enquiries and inspections. (Law Commission, *Land Registration for the Twenty-First Century: A Conveyancing Revolution* (Law Com No 271), Part I, para 1.5)

4.4 The overall scheme of registered land in England and Wales

There are some key principles under which the system of registered land operates. These are known variously as the mirror, curtain and insurance or indemnity principles.

key principles

The **mirror principle** is that the register should be like a mirror. All rights that affect the land should be reflected or visible in it.

The **curtain principle** is that rights that will not affect a purchaser should be kept off the register.

The **insurance or indemnity principle** is that purchasers can rely on the register. The register is conclusive and is backed up by a State guarantee under which compensation is paid for loss due to a mistake or correction of the register.

We now look at those principles in more detail.

4.5 Mirror principle

The stated purpose of land registration is that 'the register should be a complete and accurate reflection of the state of the title of land at any given time' (Law Com No 271).

4.5.1 Conclusiveness of the register

A purchaser can search the register (which is open for public inspection) and establish the current registered proprietor of the land. The person registered as proprietor can be taken at face value as being entitled to be so registered, without examining the document which gave rise to his or her registration (LRA 2002, s 58, which we look at in greater detail at 4.7.1 below).

4.5.2 Powers of the owner

The registered proprietor can exercise all the powers of an owner in relation to the title (LRA 2002, s 24). These include the power to make a disposition of almost any kind permitted by the general law, for example by selling, leasing or mortgaging the land, or perhaps by entering into a restrictive covenant or an easement with a neighbour (LRA 2002, s 23). This means that a prospective purchaser, tenant or mortgagee of the land can deal in confidence with the individual(s) or legal entity named as registered proprietor. This position is backed up by the system of indemnity or State guarantee that we look at in 4.7.4 below.

4.5.3 How the mirror principle is upheld on first registration

When unregistered land comes into registration for the first time, either because one of the events set out in s 4 of the LRA 2002 that trigger compulsory registration has occurred (for example the land has been sold), or when the owner decides voluntarily to register his or her land holdings (s 3 of the Act), then all title deeds that the applicant has or that he or she has a right to require the holder to produce must be sent to the Land Registry (Land Registration Rules 2003, r 24(1)(c)). Applicants are instructed to 'resist the temptation to edit the deed package' to include only a recent root of title and subsequent conveyances (Land Registry Practice Guide 1, para 4.4.4). When registering the title, the Land Registry will enter encumbrances that are disclosed on to the register, and old documents may contain definitive details of, for example, old covenants, easements or other matters that should go on the register.

In addition, it is recognised that not all rights that affect land are documented. There may be rights that could be binding on third parties that have arisen informally, such as the exercise of an informal right of way over a long period of time, creating an easement by prescription. Such a right will be binding on the registered proprietor even though it does not appear on the title deeds. This is described as an interest that overrides first registration, or an overriding interest.

Table 4.1   Overriding interests

What overrides first registration?	A lease granted for a term not exceeding seven years from the date of grant (subject to exceptions)	This is wider than the list of interests that will override a disposition of registered land after land has come into the registration system.
	An interest belonging to a person in actual occupation, so far as relating to land of which he or she is in actual occupation	
	A legal easement or profit a prendre	
	A customary right	
	A public right	Compare LRA 2002, Sch 1 with LRA 2002, Sch 3.
	A local land charge	
	Various rights relating to mines and minerals	

The LRA 2002 Act aims to get such rights entered on the register, and the registrar may enter a notice on the register in respect of any overriding interest that is disclosed (Land Registration Rules 2003, r 28(4)). A person making an application for first registration (usually the solicitor or conveyancer of the person entitled to be registered as proprietor) is required to disclose to the Land Registry such overriding interests (with certain exceptions) when making the application for first registration (Land Registration Rules 2003, r 28(1)), using form DI.

If squatters are on any part of the property, this must also be disclosed. Adverse possession rights which have been, or are in the course of being, acquired under the Limitation Act 1980 will be investigated by the Land Registry before it completes the registration of title to the property.

4.5.3.1 Events set out in s 4 of the LRA 2002 that trigger compulsory registration

The LRA 2002 does not impose a mandatory requirement to register all land, but seeks to bring land into registration when there is a dealing with it of some kind. This is, after all, when a landowner is likely to take legal advice and to be aware of an obligation to register.

Title must be registered when land is transferred, whether that transfer is on sale, as a gift or to satisfy a court order or other circumstances (LRA 2002, s 4(1)(a)).

If a lease of more than seven years is granted (s 4(1)(c)(i)) or an existing lease with more than seven years left to run is transferred (s 4(1)(a)) – again whether on sale, gift, court order or otherwise – then the estate that is created or disposed of is subject to compulsory registration. In other words, the newly granted or transferred leasehold estate must be registered. There is no *obligation* to register the freehold or superior leasehold estate out of which it is granted (although this may be done voluntarily; see **4.5.3.3** below).

Some leases not exceeding seven years are required to be registered on grant because they are future leases that will take effect in possession after three months from grant or where certain provisions of the Housing Act 1985 apply (s 4(1)(b), (d) and (e)).

The grant of a first legal mortgage will also trigger first registration of the qualifying legal estate on which it is granted (s 4(1)(g)). This may be the freehold or a lease which has more than seven years to run. The same applies if a new trustee is appointed of land held in trust (s 4(1)(aa)).

The categories can be amended or added to by the Secretary of State by order.

4.5.3.2 Effect of failing to register when first registration is compulsory

The duty to register falls to the responsible estate owner, or his or her successor in title, during the period of two months beginning with the date on which the relevant event occurs (LRA 2002, s 6(1) and (4)). The registrar has the power to extend the period if he or she is satisfied that there is good reason for doing so (s 6(4) and (5)).

However, if registration is not made within the two-month period or any extension that is granted, then the transfer, grant or creation will become void as regards the legal estate (s 7(1)).

Although void in respect of the legal estate, the transferee or grantee would have some protection by equitable rights. In the case of a transfer of a qualifying estate, the current registered owner will continue to hold the legal title but on bare trust for the transferee. If the transfer was to reflect the appointment of a new trustee then that will fail and the legal title will continue to be vested in the outgoing trustee and subject to the existing trust. In the remaining cases mentioned above, the grant or creation would take effect as a contract made for valuable consideration to grant or create the legal estate concerned (s 7(2)). Specific performance would generally be available for such a contract, which would therefore itself create an equitable interest in land (*Walsh v Lonsdale* (1882) 21 Ch D 9).

An unprotected equitable interest is, however, vulnerable to the risk of losing priority to a third party, and therefore the transferee or grantee who fails to register within the two-month time period risks losing his or her proprietary rights. We look at priorities in more detail in **Chapter 5**.

As the transfer, grant or creation is void as regards the legal estate, the legal estate may need to be re-transferred, re-granted or re-created. The transfer*ee* or grant*ee* or, in the case of a mortgage the mortgag*or*, will be responsible for the other parties' costs in doing so and must indemnify them against other liabilities reasonably incurred as a result of the failure to register (s 8).

4.5.3.3 Voluntary first registration

As well as requiring registration in the situations set out above, the registrar also encourages estate owners in unregistered land to register their title voluntarily. This may be done at any time by the person in whom an unregistered freehold estate or an unregistered leasehold estate of more than seven years is vested (or who is entitled to have it vested in them) (LRA 2002, s 3(2)).

Why might an owner decide voluntarily to register his or her land holdings?

There are a number of advantages in voluntarily registering one's landholding. Commercially, it can tidy up a complex unregistered estate and, if a disposal is planned, help matters to go smoothly. Legally, it enables the estate owner to benefit from some of the protections that registered land can give, in particular, protection against adverse possession under the new procedure set out in Sch 6 to the LRA 2002. This requires notice of an adverse possession claim to be given to the registered proprietor allowing him or her a period of two years in which to take possession proceedings against the adverse possessor. This offers a benefit over the rules under s 15 of the Limitation Act 1980, which provide that such an action will be barred automatically after 12 years have passed without need for notice to the estate owner.

in practice

Registered title – what it looks like – property, proprietorship and charges registers

The Land Registry will register the land with one of the following classes of title:

- absolute freehold title –the best class of title and will be granted if 'the registrar is of the opinion that the person's title to the estate is such as a willing buyer could properly be advised by a competent professional adviser to accept' (LRA 2002, s 9(2));
- absolute leasehold title –the best class of leasehold title and one that will be granted if the test set out above is met and the registrar approves the landlord's title to grant the lease (LRA 2002, s 10(2));
- good leasehold title – granted if the test set out above is met but the registrar has not approved the landlord's title (LRA 2002, s 10(3));
- qualified title – granted if the registrar is of the opinion that the person's title to the estate is limited or subject to reservations (LRA 2002, s 9(4) or 10(5)); or
- possessory title – granted if the registrar is of the opinion that the person is in actual possession of the land (or receiving rents in respect of it) but he or she cannot show sufficient paper title to be registered with another class of title (LRA 2002, s 9(5) or 10(6)).

The registrar records on the register of title (kept at the Land Registry) the title awarded and all other relevant information relating to the property of which he or she is aware (including all the rights and interests benefiting the property (the pluses) and all the rights and interests to which it is subject (the minuses)). There is a separate register of title at the Land Registry for every registered title in England and Wales. There used to be a card index system but now the register is computerised. Since 1990, the register has been open to public inspection (Land Registration Act 1988).

The register of title is in three parts:

(1) Property register

The property register:

- describes the land;
- specifies the estate for which the land is held;
- refers to a map or plan of the land (the filed plan); and
- specifies what interests the land benefits from, eg easements and restrictive covenants for the benefit of the land (the pluses).

Usually the map or plan is stated to be for identification only.

(2) Proprietorship register

This states:

- the grade of title awarded (ie absolute, possessory, qualified, or good leasehold);
- the name, address and description of the registered proprietor;
- certain entries made which affect his or her right to deal with the land (restrictions).

(3) Charges register

The charges register contains entries concerning rights adverse to the land, eg mortgages, easements or restrictive covenants in favour of neighbouring land, and notices protecting rights over the land (the minuses).

All incumbrances that were formerly entered against the estate owner as land charges under the LCA 1972 are entered against the title; as are any incumbrances, such as pre-1926 restrictive covenants, that formerly depended upon the equitable doctrine of notice to be binding.

4.5.4 How the mirror principle is upheld on subsequent dealings with the land

Once land is registered, the mirror principle requires that all dealings affecting it are reflected on the register. This is achieved two key ways.

4.5.4.1 Registrable dispositions

This rather grand term includes a transfer of registered freehold or leasehold land (LRA 2002, s 27(2)(a)), the grant of a lease for a term of more than seven years from the date of grant and certain other leases (s 27(2)(b)), the express grant or reservation of a legal easement (s 27(2)(d)) and the grant of a legal charge (s 27(2)(f)).

There are others but these are the key dispositions that a student of land law needs to be aware of, and their treatment under the LRA 2002 reflects their importance.

These transactions must be 'completed by registration' (s 27(2)). This means as follows:

(a) Once registered, the transaction takes effect at law and creates legal rights in the disponee.

(b) If the registrable disposition has been made for valuable consideration (this excludes marriage consideration or a nominal consideration in money – s 132(1)) then once registered it will enjoy a special priority. It will take priority over any existing disposition whose priority is not protected at the time of registration. We look at this in greater detail at **5.3** below.

(c) However, until this occurs, the transaction will not take effect at law (LRA 2002, s 27(1)). In legal terms this means that the rights created by such a transaction will be merely equitable until completed by registration and, as they have not been presented at the Land Registry, they will take effect as unprotected equitable interests. Under the priority rule contained in s 29(1), they are at risk of losing priority to certain later transactions. In practical terms, a purchaser who fails to register his or her purchase risks losing his or her land.

There is therefore a powerful incentive for a person taking a registrable disposition of registered land to ensure that it is entered on the register.

4.5.4.2 Other rights in land

Notices (LRA 2002, ss 32–39)

Other rights in land that fall short of being a registrable disposition can nevertheless be entered on the register by applying to the registrar for an entry of a notice in the register (LRA 2002, s 34). A notice is an entry in the register in respect of the burden of an interest affecting a registered estate or charge (s 32(1)).

A notice may be an agreed notice or, where this is not possible, entered as a unilateral notice. Agreed notices can only be entered with the consent of the registered proprietor (or a person entitled to be registered as proprietor) or if the registrar is satisfied that the interest is valid. In contrast, unilateral notices do not have the consent of the registered proprietor, and the Land Registry will serve notice of them on the registered proprietor, who has the ability to apply for cancellation of a unilateral notice if he or she objects to the registration. Documents in support of an application for a notice (of either sort) will usually be available for the public to inspect and receive an official copy of (s 66(1)) but, if of a personal or commercially sensitive nature, it is possible to apply to have them exempted from this general right.

The registrar also has the power to enter a notice if it appears to him or her that a registered estate is subject to an unregistered interest which is capable of being registered as a notice (s 37).

Once entered on the register as a notice (whether agreed, unilateral or on the instigation of the registrar), an interest is protected against later registrable dispositions under the special priority rule contained in s 29(1). This gives protection against subsequent dispositions to the interest that is the subject of the notice whilst it is on the register. A unilateral notice is vulnerable to being removed if the registered proprietor objects, and, if this occurs, the protected status of the interest concerned will be lost.

There are certain interests in respect of which a notice cannot be registered. These include:

(a) an interest under a trust of land (s 33(a)(i));
(b) a leasehold estate which is granted for a term of years of three years or less from the date of grant and is not otherwise required to be registered (s 33(b)).

Due to their short term, it is considered impractical to require short leases to be registered, and they are protected in a different way (see **5.6.1** below). An interest under a trust of land is expected to be dealt with under the overreaching provisions that we have already seen, and it may be more appropriate to make another kind of entry on the register, a restriction, in respect of the trust.

Restrictions (LRA 2002, s 40–47)

A restriction is an entry in the register regulating the circumstances in which a disposition of a registered estate or charge may be entered on the register (LRA 2002, s 40(1)). In particular, it may prohibit the making of an entry in respect of any disposition, or a disposition of a particular kind, unless notice is given to a particular person or their consent is obtained or unless ordered by the court or the registrar. The prohibition may be for an indefinite period of time or a specified period or until a specified event occurs (s 40(2) and (3)).

In order to secure that interests which are capable of being overreached on a disposition of a registered estate are overreached, the registrar has powers to enter a restriction on the title:

(a) The registrar *must* do so when entering two or more persons in the register as the proprietor of a registered estate (s 44(1)).

(b) The registrar *may* do so at any time when it appear to him or her necessary or desirable to do so (s 42(1)(b)).

The court also has the power to order entry of a restriction (s 46(1)).

A restriction requires that a certain process is followed when an application is made for entry of a disposition on the register, and before it can be so registered unless disapplied by the registrar (ss 40(1) and 41(2)). It does not give direct protection for an interest under s 29(1) in the way that entry of a notice does, and it is not appropriate for use where a notice could be entered (ss 42(2) and 46(2)). However, it does give an indirect form of protection by preventing the registration of a subsequent disposition for value – which would have the effect of postponing the priority of a third party interest – until the circumstances required by the restriction have occurred.

There are standard form restrictions which cover many common circumstances. For example, the standard form of restriction that the registrar is required to enter when two or more persons are registered as a proprietor and therefore a trust exists (which cannot be entered as a notice (s 33(a)(i))) is designed to secure that overreaching occurs in relation to that trust interest:

> **Form A**
>
> No disposition by a sole proprietor of the registered estate (except a trust corporation) under which capital money arises is to be registered unless authorised by an order of the court.

In the case of an express trust, it may be appropriate to require that no disposition can be made unless it is certified to be authorised under the trust deed, and there is a standard form restriction to achieve this too. There are also standard form restrictions relating to charity or club land, settled land, land in respect of which a trustee in bankruptcy has been appointed or which is subject to a charging, freezing, restraint or interim receiving order, and so on. Another standard form restriction, designed to protect a registered chargee, requires that no entry can be made in respect of a disposition without a written consent by the proprietor of a specified registered charge affecting the estate (*Guidance Note 19: Notices, restrictions and protection of third party interests in the register*, HM Land Registry, updated 6 April 2017).

4.5.5 'Cracks' in the mirror

The mirror principle famously has 'cracks' in it. If a right is binding on a registered title but does not appear on the title register, then this is a crack – or distortion – in the mirror. The LRA 2002 itself contains two 'cracks' in the mirror – rectification and overriding interests. We look at these in greater detail at 4.7.3 and 5.6 below.

4.5.6 The prudent purchaser

A note of caution about the mirror principle. Even if the LRA 2002 were altered to remove overriding interests and the right to seek rectification as 'cracks in the mirror', a prudent purchaser would still need to carry out other searches, enquiries and inspections of the land:

Other searches and enquiries

We are discussing rights that affect title to the property, but a prudent purchaser will need to carry out further searches to discover other issues. For example, searches are routinely carried out to discover whether the property is in a flood zone or may be affected by environmental contamination. A purchaser (or his conveyancer) will also carry out a local search with the local authority to discover whether access to the property can be obtained directly from a publicly adopted highway, or whether a private right of way is required, and whether the buildings on the property and their use have been authorised under planning laws.

So the idea is not that a purchaser will never need to carry out additional checks as well as looking at the title register, but that the register should, so far as practicable, be the only source required for matters of *title*.

Inspections

A purchaser will also need to carry out a physical inspection of the property. This is not just to check that the property is suitable for his or her needs and that he or she is willing to buy it, or in order to enable an assessment of its value to be carried out for his or her mortgage lender. It is also to check that there are no rights that are apparent on inspection that may have been acquired or be in the course of being acquired against the property.

A purchaser will wish to check that there is no one other than the vendor who is in occupation of or using the property who may hold rights that are binding on the purchaser. As well as overriding interests that are discussed at **5.6**, a purchaser will want to check that there are no squatters on the property who may have acquired rights in the property under the Limitation Act 1980. Adverse possession is discussed at **2.2**. Although changes have been made in Sch 6 to the LRA 2002 to give much greater protection to the registered proprietor of land, the risk of adverse possession means that a purchaser should always inspect property that he or she is in the course of acquiring.

4.6 Curtain principle

The curtain principle is that only interests that bind a purchaser should be entered on the register. Those that do not affect him or her should be kept off the register. This primarily means trust interests. Under s 33 of the LRA 2002, no notice can be put on the register in respect of an interest under a trust of land; this is the curtain that sweeps such interests from sight.

The intention is that such interests should be overreached, and swept off the land and into the proceeds of sale. Take a look again at **3.3** to revisit overreaching if you need to. A purchaser can overreach trust interests if he or she deals with two trustees. In that case the purchaser will take free from the trust interest and need not be concerned about it. As we have seen at **4.5.4.2**, the registrar has both an obligation and a power to enter restrictions in order to secure that interests which are capable of being overreached on a disposition of a registered estate are overreached.

So far, so good. However, the danger for a purchaser comes if he or she is dealing with a sole owner of the land where there is no indication on the register that a trust exists. The purchaser may be unaware of the trust's existence (for example that another person contributed to the purchase price and has an interest in the land under a constructive or resulting trust). If the purchaser fails to overreach the trust – because he or she buys from only one trustee – the purchaser will be bound by the trust interest if the beneficiary is in actual occupation of the land. The landmark case that established this interpretation of the land registration rules was *Williams & Glyn's Bank v Boland* [1981] AC 487. It was decided under the Land Registration Act 1925, which has now been fully repealed and replaced by the LRA 2002, but the result would be the same under the 2002 Act (s 29(2)(a)(ii) and Sch 3, para 2).

4.7 Insurance or indemnity principle

The insurance or indemnity principle is that purchasers can rely on the register. The register is conclusive and is backed up by a State guarantee under which compensation is paid for loss due to a mistake or correction of the register. It is essential so that people are willing to rely on the register. The relevant provisions are contained in Sch 8 to the LRA 2002.

4.7.1 Conclusiveness of the register

Section 58 of the LRA 2002 states that once a person is registered as the proprietor of a legal estate, it will be deemed to be vested in him or her as a result of the registration, even if it would not otherwise be vested in him or her. If, for example, a person is registered as proprietor on the basis of a forged transfer, the effect of s 58 is to confirm that the legal estate vests in the transferee on completion of his or her registration as proprietor. The same would not occur in unregistered land, where the principle of *nemo dat quod non habet* (which translates as 'no one can give what he does not have') means that a forged transfer cannot give good title. This means that the effect of a forged transfer in registered and unregistered land is different.

Let us look at an example. A is the owner-occupier of a property. B, a fraudster, manages to sell the property to C, an innocent purchaser. What are the effects of this fraudulent transfer in unregistered and registered land?

Table 4.2   Effect of fraudulent transfer in unregistered and registered land

Unregistered land	Registered land
In unregistered land, B cannot give good title, so the original owner, A, retains his or her ownership. C would be left without the property and out of pocket, unless he or she is able to trace and sue B for the purchase monies.	In registered land, A would be described as the registered proprietor in possession. The effect of s 58 is that registration of C as registered proprietor, even under a forged transfer, is to vest legal title to the estate in C. What does this mean for A? This is a problem that the courts have struggled with.

Let us look at how our original owner, A, would be treated in registered land. After uncertainty, the law has recently been clarified in *Swift 1st Ltd v Chief Land Registrar* [2015] EWCA Civ 330.

Table 4.3   Effect of fraudulent transfer in registered land under old law and current law

Old law	Current law
In an attempt to protect A, the Court of Appeal held in *Malory Enterprises Ltd v Cheshire Homes (UK) Ltd* [2002] Ch 216 that a fraudulent transfer was effective to transfer the **legal title** to an innocent purchaser but that the **beneficial title** remained with the innocent prior-registered proprietor. This case was decided under the now repealed Land Registration Act 1925, but the principle was considered to be the same under s 58 of the LRA 2002. It was followed in the case of *Fitzwilliam v Richall Holdings Services* [2013] EWHC 86 (Ch), which applied s 58.	In *Swift 1st Ltd v Chief Land Registrar* [2015] EWCA Civ 330, the Court of Appeal decided that this part of the decision in *Malory Enterprises Ltd v Cheshire Homes (UK) Ltd*, namely that beneficial ownership did not pass under a fraudulent transfer of registered land, was *per incuriam*. *Per incuriam* translates as 'through lack of care', meaning that judgment was made without reference to a contradictory statute or binding authority, and is therefore wrongly decided. Section 58 means that on registration as proprietor, full title (legal and equitable) is vested in the innocent purchaser, C.
The effect of this rule was that although legal title was guaranteed by the State and protected by an indemnity, equitable title was not. If C is bare trustee for A, he can be compelled to transfer the property back to A or to be the subject of an alteration to the register that has the same effect, without the benefit of being entitled to State compensation for his or her loss. This would mean that the State guarantee of title is of little, if any, value. This rule was much criticised by legal commentators for bypassing the State guarantee for registered land.	This decision has been met with approval by many legal commentators. It is not the end of the story under the LRA 2002, however. We now need to consider how provisions of the Act dealing with alteration of the register and indemnity (the State guarantee) work.

4.7.2 Alterations to the register

The registrar has the ability to alter the register under the LRA 2002, Sch 4, para 5. The courts also have the right to order an alteration to be made (Sch 4, para 2). The rights are broadly similar and apply to:

(a) correcting a mistake;

(b) bringing the register up to date;

(c) giving effect to any estate, right or interest excepted from the effect of registration.

The registrar has an additional power to alter the register for the purpose of removing a superfluous entry (Sch 4, para 5(d)).

4.7.3 Rectification of the register

Rectification is a limited class of alterations which involves the correction of a mistake and prejudicially affects the title of a registered proprietor (Sch 4, para 1). Protection is given to a proprietor in possession of his or her land. Rectification cannot be made against a proprietor in relation to land in his or her possession unless he or she has by fraud or lack of proper care caused or substantially contributed to the mistake, or it would for any other reason be unjust for the alteration not to be made (Sch 4, para 6).

Unless and until the register is altered, the register can be relied upon at face value. If the registrar and the courts have power to make the alteration, they must do so unless there are exceptional circumstances that justify them not doing so (Sch 4, paras 3(3) and 6(3)).

Let us see how this would apply to our scenario.

example

In our example, A was the owner-occupier of a property that was fraudulently sold by B to an innocent purchaser, C.

We have already explained that under s 58 of the LRA 2002, when C is registered as proprietor, the legal estate (which following *Swift* means an undivided legal and beneficial title to the property) is deemed vested in him.

A has the right to seek an alteration to the register. He may do so by applying to the registrar or to the courts. A's application would be that registration of C as proprietor of the estate was a mistake as it was based on a forged transfer.

The alteration that A seeks would be classed as a rectification, as it involves the correction of a mistake and prejudicially affects the title of a registered proprietor, C.

Under paras 3(2) and 6(2) of Sch 4, no alteration affecting the title of the proprietor of a registered estate to land may be made without the proprietor's consent in relation to land in his or her possession unless:

(a) he or she has by fraud or lack of proper care caused or substantially contributed to the mistake; or

(b) it would for any other reason be unjust for the alteration not to be made.

If neither (a) nor (b) above apply then, if C is in possession of the land and does not consent, no rectification will be made. C will remain registered proprietor. In our example, we described A as an owner-occupier, which means that C cannot be in possession. In this case, the registrar or the court would be obliged to make the rectification unless there are exceptional circumstances that justify not doing so.

However, we are not at the end of the story yet. If an alteration is classed as a rectification (in other words it involves the correction of a mistake and prejudicially affects the title of a registered proprietor) then, if an application for rectification is granted or refused, the disappointed party can seek an indemnity under the State guarantee contained in Sch 8 to the LRA 2002.

No indemnity is payable for alterations that are not classed as rectification (for example because they do not prejudicially affect the title of a registered proprietor). In a case of alteration not involving rectification, the registrar does have a discretion to pay costs (Sch 4, para 9) but not to indemnify against substantive loss.

4.7.4 State guarantee

Let us look at the State guarantee of registered title to explain how this works and protects a disappointed party:

Under Sch 8 to the LRA 2002:

1. *Entitlement*

   (1) A person is entitled to be indemnified by the registrar if he suffers loss by reason of—

   (a) rectification of the register,

   (b) a mistake whose correction would involve rectification of the register,

   (c) a mistake in an official search,

   (d) a mistake in an official copy,

   (e) a mistake in a document kept by the registrar which is not an original and is referred to in the register,

   (f) the loss or destruction of a document lodged at the registry for inspection or safe custody,

   (g) a mistake in the cautions register, or

   (h) failure by the registrar to perform his duty under section 50.

   (2) For the purposes of sub-paragraph (1)(a)—

...

(b) the proprietor of a registered estate or charge claiming in good faith under a forged disposition is, where the register is rectified, to be regarded as having suffered loss by reason of such rectification as if the disposition had not been forged.

(3) No indemnity under sub-paragraph (1)(b) is payable until a decision has been made about whether to alter the register for the purpose of correcting the mistake; and the loss suffered by reason of the mistake is to be determined in the light of that decision.

5. *Claimant's fraud or lack of care*

(1) No indemnity is payable under this Schedule on account of any loss suffered by a claimant—

(a) wholly or partly as a result of his own fraud, or

(b) wholly as a result of his own lack of proper care.

...

In *Swift 1st Ltd v Chief Land Registrar* [2015] EWCA Civ 330, a mortgage lender was the victim of fraud in accepting a fraudulently signed charge. On the basis of the charge, it made a loan to the fraudster. When no repayments were made, the mortgage lender pursued the registered proprietor, whom it believed to be its borrower, for possession. The registered proprietor was able to defend this action and to have his title rectified to remove the fraudulent charge. The mortgage lender then obtained an indemnity under Sch 8 in respect of the outstanding loan monies. The ground was para 1(1)(a), namely that Swift had suffered loss by reason of rectification of the register by removal of its charge. The registrar's appeal against the payment of the indemnity was dismissed.

The policy of the LRA 2002 Act is that it is *registration* that creates a proprietor's right to a registered estate or charge, and not the document on which that registration is based. If registration is based on a forged disposition and is subsequently rectified against the proprietor of a registered estate or charge who is claiming in good faith, then the proprietor is regarded as having suffered loss by reason of the rectification as if the disposition had not been forged (para 1(2)(b)). This sub-paragraph was inserted into the 2002 Act to prevent an argument that the claimant's loss is in fact due to his or her reliance on a forged document, rather than the rectification of the register to undo the registration that has been innocently made on the back of that forged document.

Where an indemnity is payable in respect of the loss of an estate, interest or charge, the value of the estate will not be regarded as exceeding (in the case of rectification) its value immediately before rectification and, in the case of a mistake for which no rectification is made, its value at the time when the mistake which caused the loss was made (para 6(a) and (b)). There are also provisions regarding payment of costs (para 3) and time limits for the registrar's liability to pay an indemnity (six years from the time when the claimant knows (or but for his or her own default might have known) of the existence of his of her claim (para 8(a) and (b))).

4.7.5 The relationship between rectification, the State guarantee and overriding interests

4.7.5.1 No indemnity for rectification giving effect to an overriding interest

The *Swift* case also touched on another complication seen in rectification cases, namely whether an indemnity is available where the register is rectified to give effect to an interest that falls within the class of overriding interests set out in Sch 3 to the LRA 2002. We look at overriding interests in greater detail at 5.6.

The issue in relation to rectification is that all registered estates are subject to overriding interests. At first registration, registration as proprietor of a freehold or leasehold estate with absolute title is subject to (as well as to other matters) the unregistered interests which override first registration, which are set out in Sch 1 to the Act (LRA 2002, ss 11(4)(b) and 12(4)(c)). On disposition of a registered estate, the basic rule is that the priority of an interest affecting a registered estate is not affected by a disposition of the estate (LRA 2002, s 28). Even the special rule contained in s 29 of the LRA 2002, which gives special protection to a purchaser of a legal estate, retains priority against that purchaser for unregistered interests listed in Sch 3 to the Act as overriding registrable dispositions. The bottom line is that a registered proprietor is always subject to unregistered overriding interests that are binding upon him or her.

If the register is rectified to make an entry on the register in respect of a previously unregistered but overriding interest, then the position of the registered proprietor has not changed. It may appear to have changed because there is a new entry on the register to which he or she is subject, but the truth of the matter is that the interest was binding when it was an unregistered overriding interest, and it remains binding upon him or her now that it is protected by the making of an entry in the register. The registered proprietor therefore has not suffered loss by reason of the rectification, and therefore no indemnity is payable under Sch 8, para 1(1)(a).

This principle was seen at work in the case of *Re Chowood's Registered Land* [1933] Ch 574, Ch D. The case was heard under s 83 of the Land Registration Act 1925, but the same principle applies under the LRA 2002, Sch 8, para 1(1)(a) and (b), where an indemnity is payable by the registrar to a person who suffers loss by reason of a rectification of the register, or by reason of a mistake whose correction would involve rectification but a decision is made not to rectify. In *Re Chowood*, the purchaser of land's title was rectified to exclude strips of land to which a neighbour, Lyall, had gained title by adverse possession. Lyall's rights were binding on Chowood as overriding interests. Rectification to remove the strips of land from Chowood's title did not put him in any worse position than prior to the decision to rectify. No indemnity was payable because Chowood's loss was due to the overriding nature of Lyall's rights, rather than the rectification.

This principle may be of wider application than to a case like *Re Chowood*, where Lyall had an existing proprietary right (adverse possession) coupled with actual occupation. Like its predecessor clause under the 1925 Act (s 70(1)(g)), Sch 3, para 2 elevates any proprietary right in land to an overriding interest when coupled with actual occupation of that land. The Court of Appeal held in *Malory Enterprises Ltd v Cheshire Homes (UK) Ltd* [2002] Ch 216 that a right to seek rectification was a proprietary right in land. That point was not challenged in the *Swift* appeal. If a right to seek rectification is a proprietory right then, whenever a person who successfully seeks rectification is also in actual occupation, that person has an overriding interest under the LRA 2002, Sch 3, para 2 (due to his or her occupation coupled with his or her right to rectify). This means that an indemnity could be refused in any case where a decision to rectify benefits an individual in actual occupation of the property. The defeated party who is not in occupation and who loses his or her rights in the property may also not qualify for an indemnity because that loss is classed as due to the overriding nature of his or her opponent's rights.

The categorisation of a right to seek rectification as a proprietary right remains good law but has been criticised. When coupled with actual occupation, it creates an unnecessary overriding interest in the party seeking rectification. Overriding interests are a means to allow a party with unregistered rights to retain priority. A party seeking rectification does not need an overriding interest because he or she has rights under Sch 4 which, if accepted by the registrar, will lead to alteration of the register regardless of existing priorities. There is no need for the right to seek rectification to be a proprietary right in addition to the rights given in Sch 4. The schemes of rectification and indemnity set out in Schs 4 and 8 of LRA 2002 are complete on their own. Converting the right to seek rectification into a proprietary right, and, in consequence, bringing in the overriding interest rules where a party is seeking rectification, distorts the indemnity provisions in Sch 8. It introduces a random factor to the indemnity process whereby an indemnity will not be available to the disappointed party if the party achieving rectification happens to be in actual occupation.

The Law Commission agrees, and in its 2016 consultation, *Updating the Land Registration Act 2002: A Consultation Paper* (Consultation Paper No 227), proposes that the statutory right to seek rectification should not be capable of being an overriding interest. The benefit, it states, is to ensure that 'all questions of indefeasibility will be answered by reference to the statutory criteria that have been devised specifically to determine the appropriate outcome of such cases' (para 1.44).

4.7.5.2 Exception for fraud

One point worth noting is the exception to this rule in cases of fraud. As stated above, under Sch 8, para 1(2)(b), the proprietor of a registered estate or charge who claims in good faith under a forged disposition is, where the register is rectified, regarded as suffering loss due to the rectification rather than the forgery. This reverses the decision in *Attorney-General v Odell* [1906] 2 Ch 47 that rectification to remove a forged document causes no loss because the person claiming the benefit of the document never had good title as he or she could not derive title from a forged, and therefore void, disposition.

In *Swift*, which concerned the fraudulent grant of a mortgage, the innocent registered proprietor remained in actual occupation of the property. The registrar's appeal against the indemnity required the court to make a choice between holding that there was no loss due to rectification because the rectification recognised an overriding interest (following *Re Chowood*) or that the loss was due to rectification despite the forgery (applying Sch 8, para 1(2)(b)). The Court preferred to rely on Sch 8, para 1(2)(b), stating that much clearer wording would be needed to refuse an indemnity in cases of fraud using the *Re Chowood* principle.

There is therefore an exception to the principle that no indemnity is payable for a rectification to recognise an overriding interest, where the party seeking indemnity has relied in good faith on a forged disposition. Whilst this statutory loophole helped the mortgagee in *Swift*, in principle it is an unsatisfactory way of dealing with the problem, as it creates a distinction between the right to an indemnity where there is a forged disposition and other grounds.

in practice

In its Consultation Paper No 227 (see above), the Law Commission notes that whilst rectification often arises in cases that do not involve fraud, the leading cases interpreting rectification under the LRA 2002 have all arisen in the context of fraud, and between 2008–09 and 2013–14, in all but one year at least half the total amount paid out by the Land Registry in indemnity payments had been in cases involving fraud.

4.7.5.3 Land law reform – 2017 onwards?

The Law Commission, in Consultation Paper No 227, has recommended that the right to seek rectification should not be an overriding interest and therefore should not affect the ability to obtain an indemnity for loss arising from that rectification. This would not affect the inability to claim an indemnity where the rectification recognises an overriding interest based on another form of proprietary right (eg adverse possession or an unregistered estate contract) plus actual occupation (or indeed any other form of overriding interest).

In the consultation, the Law Commission set out four objectives that need to be achieved in relation to the indefeasibility question:

(1) The legislation should provide clarity.

(2) There should be a point when finality is provided so that the registered proprietor knows that his or her title is indefeasible.

(3) The rules must 'enable fact-sensitivity to determine which party gets the land and which receives an indemnity'.

(4) The register must be reliable, which, the Law Commission states, means that 'an adequate indemnity must be available to the party (or parties) who lose out because the register was wrong'.

The Law Commission proposes a 10-year 'long stop' so that, after this period, rectification of the register should generally cease to be available. There would be exceptions where the person whose name was mistakenly removed or omitted from the register remained in possession or where the registered proprietor caused or contributed to the mistake by fraud or lack of proper care. Even after the long stop, it would still be possible for a party to seek an indemnity.

The Commission also proposes that a chargee should not be able to oppose rectification of the register but would only be able to claim an indemnity, reflecting the fact that a chargee's interest is purely financial in nature.

In relation to the indemnity, the Commission asks whether a cap on recovery under the indemnity should be imposed. An argument that it raises in favour of doing so is that

> while the Land Registry carries the risk of transactions once they are entered on the register, Land Registry is not best placed to detect fraud. Those who may be better placed – such as conveyancers and mortgage lenders – may not be incentivised to develop best practice because they will not necessarily bear the cost. (at para 148)

The Commission also seeks views on how identity fraud (eg a fraudster impersonates the registered proprietor in order to sell or mortgage registered land) could be better detected and prevented.

Two other key features are that where a registered proprietor's name is removed (or omitted) by mistake, the law should prioritise returning the land to him or her. However, the Commission also wishes to retain the current protection given to a registered proprietor who is in possession. In its words, 'English law has long seen possession as an indication of who most needs or values land in the context of indefeasibility questions' (para 1.43(2)). These two aims may well conflict with each other.

4.8 Electronic conveyancing – the future?

The purpose of the LRA 2002 was described by the Law Commission as a 'bold and striking one. It is to create the necessary legal framework in which registered conveyancing can be conducted electronically.' It heralded the changes as bringing about an 'unprecedented conveyancing revolution'. We will see that it has fallen short of this objective, as electronic conveyancing in the form envisaged by the Act has not come to pass and was put on hold by the Land Registry in 2011.

However, there is no doubt that the Land Registry has adopted technological change: 94% of its applications are made electronically using its Business e-services portal, with the remaining applications that are made on paper scanned on receipt so as to be treated in the same way.

The Law Commission's Consultation Paper No 227 aims to look at the experience of the LRA 2002 and then make changes, in the main quite technical changes, in the light of it. One area that it acknowledges is that the predictions for e-conveyancing have not come about in practice, and it takes the view that the immediate goal is not simultaneous completion and registration (even if that remains a longer term aspiration) but to phase out paper-based conveyancing.

The Government has also consulted on moving Land Registry operations into the private sector (Department for Business, Innovation and Skills, *Consultation on moving Land Registry operations into the private sector* (March 2016)). The proposed privatisation appears to be on pause, but no final statement has been made by the Government of its intentions.

4.9 Further reading

G Owen and D Cahill, 'Overreaching – getting the balance right' (2017) 1 Conv 2017 26–44.

R Smith, 'Forgeries and Indemnity in Land Registration' (2015) 74(3) CLJ 401–05.

P Milne, 'Guarantee of title and void dispositions: work in progress' (2015) 4 Conv 356–65.

Law Commission, *Updating the Land Registration Act 2002: A Consultation Paper* (Consultation Paper No 227, 2016) and *Land Registration for the 21st Century: A Conveyancing Revolution* (Law Com No 271, 2001).

The three guiding principles are the mirror, curtain and insurance or indemnity principles.

The mirror principle means that the register is an accurate and conclusive reflection of ownership of title and relevant interests in the land. It relies on registration of rights. See the LRA 2002, s 4 (when title must be registered), s 27 (dispositions required to be registered) and s 32 (nature and effect of notices). If interests exist that cannot or need not be registered then the register does not give an accurate picture of the title to the land. In our registered land system, overriding interests and rectification act as 'cracks' in the mirror.

The curtain principle means that the purchaser of land is not concerned with matters behind the entries on the register, such as trusts affecting the land, and is not concerned with whether the beneficiaries' interests under the trust are satisfied after the sale. The curtain principle is supported by the overreaching mechanism (LRA 2002, ss 2 and 27(2)) and undermined by overriding interests (LRA 2002, s 29(2)(a)(ii) and Sch 3). The interaction between these two principles is explained in *City of London Building Society v Flegg* [1988] AC 54.

The insurance or indemnity principle means that the accuracy of the register is guaranteed, and if it is found to be inaccurate, it will altered or rectified. Any persons affected by alteration/rectification (or by the decision not to do so) should be paid a sum in compensation.

1   Explain your understanding of the mirror, curtain and insurance principles and the legislation that enacts them.

2   How can 'cracks' in the mirror be justified? What other principles are relevant in addition to the objective to achieve an efficient system of land registration? Are there any cases that illustrate to you the importance of the 'cracks'?

3   Explain how a person who is in possession of land is protected under the Land Registration Act 2002 by reference to overriding interests and rectification.

4   Do you agree with the Land Registry's proposals for reform of the rectification provisions set out in its Consultation Paper No 227?

Registered Land Priority Rules

After reading this chapter, you will be able to:

- identify and apply the priority rules relating to registered land
- understand how to protect an interest affecting registered land
- understand how and why unregistered interests still have a relevance to registered land due to their overriding status
- analyse the aims of land registration and evaluate the extent to which these have been achieved
- evaluate recent proposals for reform of the Land Registration Act 2002
- identify the main differences between registered and unregistered land.

5.1 Introduction

As we have discussed in **Chapter 4** above, the aim of land registration is that 'the register should be a complete and accurate reflection of the state of the title of land at any given time' (Law Com No 271, at para 1.5). However, this is not the end of the story. We also need a mechanism to determine what should go on the register and how priorities between conflicting interests should be resolved.

For example, a purchaser of a house arrives with his removal van to move in and finds another individual, not the owner from whom he has just bought the property, living there. We know from ss 23 and 24 of the Land Registration Act (LRA) 2002 that the registered proprietor has the rights of an owner to sell the land, but what does this mean and what is the status of the occupier? Who has priority between the purchaser and the occupier?

All systems of land law, whether registered or not, need a mechanism to find an answer to this question. In England and Wales, the continued existence of unregistered land means that we have two operational systems for doing so. It is vital that a student of land law understands this and draws in their mind a clear dividing line to distinguish between our registered and unregistered priority rules. If land is unregistered, the unregistered priority rules that we have already looked at apply. As a dealing with unregistered land will almost certainly trigger first registration of the estate in land that is created or disposed of, the rules applying on first registration will then be applied in addition. However, if land is registered, only the registered land priority rules apply and we examine these in this chapter.

5.2 Basic rule

The basic rule is that an interest which is created first takes priority over an interest that is created later. This rules applies whether or not either of those interests have been entered on the register.

Under s 28 of the LRA 2002:

(1) Except as provided by sections 29 and 30, the priority of an interest affecting a registered estate or charge is not affected by a disposition of the estate or charge.

(2) It makes no difference for the purposes of this section whether the interest or disposition is registered.

For example, a landowner, Lillian, enters into a contract to sell her property to Hugh. If she later agrees to sell it to Sarah, then under the basic rule, the contract with Hugh will take priority over the later contract with Sarah. This will be the case even if Sarah enters a notice on the register to protect her contract and Hugh does not. The application of this rule was demonstrated in *Halifax Plc v Curry Popeck (A Firm)* [2008] EWHC 1692 (Ch), a complex case involving mortgage fraud. In deciding the priority of two charges (which in respect of the property in question had taken effect as equitable rather than legal charges due to the fraud), the basic rule set out in s 28 applied, which meant that the first in time retained its priority. In effect, this preserves the old equitable rule that 'where the equities are equal, the first in time prevails'.

5.3 Special priority rule

However, the basic rule is trumped by the special rule contained in s 29(1) of the LRA 2002, which gives a special priority to registrable dispositions. A registrable disposition of a registered estate made for valuable consideration will take priority over all existing interests affecting the estate, unless the priority of the interest is protected at the time of registration of the registrable disposition. A registrable disposition includes a transfer of a registered freehold or leasehold estate, grant of a lease of more than seven years, express grant of a legal easement and grant of a legal charge (LRA 2002, s 27(2)) (see **4.5.4.1**).

Valuable consideration is defined in s 132(1) of the LRA 2002 as not including marriage consideration or a nominal consideration in money. There is no further definition in the LRA 2002, but in *Midland Bank Trust Co Ltd v Green* [1981] AC 513, Lord Wilberforce stated (at 531) that valuable consideration was 'a term of art which precludes any enquiry as to adequacy' and continued that, 'Valuable consideration requires no definition: it is an expression denoting an advantage conferred or a detriment suffered.' He went on (at 532) that, '"Nominal consideration" and a "nominal sum" in the law appear to me, as terms of art, to refer to a sum or consideration which can be mentioned as consideration but is not necessarily paid.' A purchaser who provides valuable consideration will provide some value but it need not be market value; however, purely nominal consideration such as £1 or 'a peppercorn' will not count.

Under s 29 of the LRA 2002 (effect of registered dispositions: estates):

(1) If a registrable disposition of a registered estate is made for valuable consideration, completion of the disposition by registration has the effect of postponing to the interest under the disposition any interest affecting the estate immediately before the disposition whose priority is not protected at the time of registration.

(2) For the purposes of subsection (1), the priority of an interest is protected—

(a) in any case, if the interest—

(i) is a registered charge or the subject of a notice in the register,

(ii) falls within any of the paragraphs of Schedule 3, or

(iii) appears from the register to be excepted from the effect of registration, and

(b) in the case of a disposition of a leasehold estate, if the burden of the interest is incident to the estate.

(3) Subsection (2)(a)(ii) does not apply to an interest which has been the subject of a notice in the register at any time since the coming into force of this section.

(4) Where the grant of a leasehold estate in land out of a registered estate does not involve a registrable disposition, this section has effect as if—

(a) the grant involved such a disposition, and

(b) the disposition were registered at the time of the grant.

This means that a buyer of registered land (or a bank lending money against a mortgage of it or a tenant taking a lease of it) will take free of all earlier interests in land unless the priority of that interest has been protected.

To take our earlier example, where Lillian had entered into a contract to sell the land to Hugh but then entered into a later contract to sell the land to Sarah, if the second contract is completed, that is, Sarah pays the purchase price and the landowner completes a deed which transfers the title to her which Sarah registers at the Land Registry, then Sarah will buy the land free from Hugh's contract unless Hugh's contract has been protected.

This is the mirror principle in action and it is the key to understanding how land registration works.

The special priority rule also benefits short leases: s 29(4) of the LRA 2002 provides that where the grant of a leasehold estate in land out of a registered estate does not involve a registrable disposition, s 29 will take effect as if the grant involved such a disposition and the disposition were registered at the time of grant.

5.4 Interplay between ss 28 and 29 of the LRA 2002

The interplay between ss 28 and 29 of the LRA 2002 was shown in the case of *Halifax Plc v Curry Popeck (A Firm)* [2008] EWHC 1692 (Ch), which we have already looked at briefly. The case concerned two mortgages, both intended to be full legal mortgages. This would have been achieved if they had been properly protected under s 29 of the LRA 2002 by substantive registration at the Land Registry under s 27 of the LRA 2002. However, due to the fraud, or incompetence of the conveyancer in question, neither charge was registered. A couple of fraudsters took out a loan with Halifax Plc which was expected to be registered over their bungalow. However, it was only registered over a much less valuable strip of land. It was accepted that an estoppel in favour of Halifax had arisen due to the assurances by the proprietors that it would acquire a charge over the bungalow, on which it had acted in reliance by making the loan. The fraudster couple then transferred the property to one of them acting under an assumed name, 'John Sinclair'. John Sinclair granted a mortgage to the Bank of Scotland but, again, security was only granted over the less valuable strip. The Bank of Scotland obtained a charging order against John Sinclair when repayments were not made. Both banks therefore claimed an equitable charge over the bungalow. Halifax's equitable charge was the earlier and therefore, under the basic rule contained in s 28 of the LRA 2002, took priority.

The Bank of Scotland then argued that the transfer to 'John Sinclair' (ie one of the fraudsters) invoked s 29 of the LRA 2002. As the equitable charge created by estoppel in favour of Halifax had not been entered on the register, it was not protected under s 29 and therefore John Sinclair took free of it when he took the transfer. This, it was argued, would mean that Halifax's earlier charge no longer bound the land, and Halifax's only claims could be a personal claim against the fraudsters or in negligence against their solicitors. The charging order in favour of the Bank of Scotland that was subsequently created would have priority because it was created out of John Sinclair's unencumbered estate. This argument was rejected, as the transfer to John Sinclair had not been made for valuable consideration, and indeed, given the fraudulent nature of the scheme, the concept of value was meaningless in the transaction. The Bank of Scotland therefore could not rely on the s 29 special priority rule which would allow John Sinclair to take free from all unprotected prior interests, and Halifax took priority under the s 28 basic rule that earlier transactions retain their priority.

Our next question, therefore, is how can an interest be protected for the purposes of the special priority rule contained in s 29 of the LRA 2002?

5.5 Protection of earlier interests

An interest will be protected if it is a registered charge or is the subject of a notice on the register (LRA 2002, s 29(2)(a)(i)).

In our example, Hugh's contract should be protected by registering a notice on the register, under s 32 of the LRA 2002. If it is, then Sarah will buy the land subject to his contract to purchase and may be required to transfer the land to him, even if the price that has been agreed under his contract is less than the price that Sarah paid.

A registered charge or an interest that is the subject of a notice on the register will be visible on the face of the register. This is consistent with the mirror principle.

An interest will also be protected if it falls within any of the paragraphs of Sch 3 to the LRA 2002 (LRA 2002, s 29(2)(a)(ii)). These are unregistered interests that are binding on a purchaser even though they are not on the register. The overriding status that is given to these interests is sometimes described as a 'crack' in the mirror.

5.6 Overriding interests

Overriding interests are unregistered interests that are binding on a purchaser even though they are not on the register.

There are currently nine categories, which reduced from 16 on 12 October 2013 when certain transitional provisions under the Act came to an end. Of these nine, the most important are the first three:

(a) short legal leases (seven years or less);

(b) interests of persons in actual occupation; and

(c) easements.

If Hugh is in actual occupation of the land (he may be living there for example) then, as before, Sarah will buy the land subject to his contract to purchase and may be required to transfer the land to him, even if the price that has been agreed under his contract is less than the price that Sarah paid. However, in this case, his contract was not discoverable from the register, and Sarah will only find out about it if she inspects the property and asks further questions. This is why overriding interests can be a controversial issue.

5.6.1 Short legal leases (seven years or less) (LRA 2002, Sch 3, para 1)

A leasehold estate in land granted for a term not exceeding seven years from the date of grant is an overriding interest under the LRA 2002, Sch 3, para 1. There are some exceptions to this rule (see para 1(a) and (b)), for example short leases that are required to be registered on grant because they will take effect in possession after three months from grant.

5.6.1.1 Legal leases

The reference to a 'leasehold estate' means that only legal leases fall into the category of overriding interest under Sch 3, para 1. In practice, this is not usually an issue because of the exemption from formalities for short legal leases under s 54(2) of the Law of Property Act (LPA) 1925, which provides that leases taking effect in possession for a term not exceeding three years (whether or not the tenant has power to extend the term) at the best rent that can be reasonably obtained without taking a fine can be made orally ('by parol'). A legal lease for a term of three years or less can be made by deed, by contract or by no formalities at all, simply the taking up of possession and payment of rent (this is known as a periodic tenancy and its term is the length of the rental period).

A lease for a term of more than three years must be made by deed (LPA 1925, s 52(1)).

5.6.1.2 Overriding nature of short leases

A legal lease is overriding automatically in its own right. This principle can be seen as a survivor of the rule in unregistered land that legal estates and interests bind the world (see **3.5.3.1**). This no longer applies to other legal estates and interests that are required to be registered to attain legal status and protection and which will not operate at law until the relevant registration requirements are met (LRA 2002, s 27(1)). However, because it is not considered reasonable or desirable to require short leases to be registered – it is not worth the time, cost and trouble - the old unregistered land rule is, in effect if not in name, preserved by Sch 3, para 1.

Although decided under the similar rules existing under s 70(1)(k) of the now repealed Land Registration Act (LRA) 1925, *Barclays Bank Plc v Zaroovabli* [1997] Ch 321 (considered at **2.4.4.2**) shows this principle in action. Note, however, that in order to grant a legal lease, the landlord must him- or herself hold a legal estate in the land; therefore if a person contracts to buy a property and agrees prior to completion to grant a lease to a prospective tenant, the lease is not granted at law until completion of the property purchase. If the purchase is with the aid of a mortgage, there is no moment in time (or *scintilla temporis*) between the completion of the purchase and the grant of the mortgage in which the legal lease can take effect and take priority over the mortgage as an overriding interest (*Coventry Permanent Building Society v Jones* [1991] 1 All ER 951, cited with approval by Lady Hale in *Re North East Property Buyers Litigation* [2014] UKSC 52). Where the purchaser already holds the legal estate, a lease granted before the mortgage will keep priority as an overriding interest under Sch 3, para 1, and even, in the unusual circumstances of *Zaroovabli*, a lease granted after the mortgage would take priority under s 29(4) of the LRA 2002 and retain it under Sch 3, para 1 as an overriding interest if the mortgagee delays in registering its rights, such that it holds merely an equitable interest in the property at the time of lease grant and loses the benefit of its priority period (see **2.4.4.2** for an explanation of the priority period).

5.6.1.3 Other methods of protecting leases

A lease granted for a term of three years or less cannot be the subject of a notice on the register and is only protected as an overriding interest.

A lease granted for more than three years but not more than seven years is capable of being the subject of a notice on the register, as it does not fall within the excluded interests in s 33 of the LRA 2002. If it is not entered as a notice, it will nevertheless override under Sch 3, para 1.

Such leases will fall to be dealt with under the registered land system if they affect a registered estate; in other words if the superior estate out of which they are granted is itself registered. (Note that if the superior estate is unregistered then such leases will be subject to the unregistered land rules. As we have said at 3.5.3.1, legal estates and interests in unregistered land bind the world.)

A lease granted for more than seven years is required to be substantively registered with its own title number, whether the legal estate out of which it is granted is registered (LRA 2002, s 27(2)(b)) or unregistered (LRA 2002, s 4(1)(c)). If the superior legal estate is registered, a notice of the lease will be entered automatically against the superior title at the same time that the leasehold title is registered.

5.6.1.4 Equitable leases

If an equitable lease is created (for example under the doctrine of anticipation in *Walsh v Lonsdale* (1882) 21 Ch D 9), it is not overriding under Sch 3, para 1. An equitable lease of any length of term should be protected by entry of a notice on the register (LRA 2002, s 32). However, if the tenant is in actual occupation then it will be protected as an overriding interest under Sch 3, para 2.

5.6.2 Interests of persons in actual occupation (LRA 2002, Sch 3, para 2)

The category of overriding interests that has caused, and continues to cause, the most difficulty is contained in Sch 3, para 2, which provides that an interest belonging at the time of the disposition to a person in actual occupation, so far as relating to land of which he or she is in actual occupation, will override a registrable disposition, subject to certain exceptions. A similar provision applied in s 70(1)(g) of the LRA 1925, which is now repealed; much of the case law decided under the 1925 Act remains good law, but this overriding interest has been tightened up in the LRA 2002 and students should exercise some caution. It is worth reviewing Sch 3, para 2 in some detail.

5.6.2.1 'An interest …'

The person claiming an overriding interest under Sch 3, para 2 must have an interest in the land. The overriding interest is made up of an interest in the land belonging to a person in actual occupation. In other words:

interest in land + actual occupation = overriding interest

We shall see as we go through Sch 3, para 2 that this simple formula is hedged with other criteria and qualifications, but this is a good starting point. An unregistered interest held by a person who is not in occupation of the land is an unprotected interest in the land and will be 'postponed' to – or, in less statutory language, defeated by – a person taking a disposition that takes advantage of the special priority rule in s 29 of the LRA 2002.

A person who is in actual occupation but who has no interest in the land (eg a lodger or licensee) has no interest capable of holding priority against anyone.

What kind of interest will be benefitted by this? The short answer is any proprietary right in the land (see our earlier discussion about proprietary rights at 1.6).

Once it is established that the person seeking to rely on Sch 3, para 2 holds a proprietary right in the land then, under the magic of Sch 3, para 2, it is capable of being raised to overriding status. This applies even if the right could and should have been protected by registration, either substantively under s 27(1) of the LRA 2002 (for example a lease of more than seven years) or as a notice under s 34 of the LRA 2002 (for example an estate contract to purchase the property).

5.6.2.2 '… belonging at the time of the disposition …'

The interest must exist at the time of the disposition. *Thompson v Foy* [2009] EWHC 1076 (Ch) confirms that this means that the interest relied upon by the person seeking to assert an overriding interest must be in existence at the date of actual completion of the registrable disposition in question. This means the date of completion of the transfer, grant of the lease, legal charge or whatever relevant disposition under s 27(2) has been entered into, and not merely the date that such a disposition operates at law because it has been completed by registration (LRA 2002, s 27(1)). Section 27(2) refers to a transfer (s 27(2)(a)) or grant of a term of years absolute (s 27(2)(b)) or grant of a legal charge (s 27(2)(f)) and so on, and not their completion by registration. The ultimate goal of e-conveyancing is that completion and registration will be simultaneous, but at present there is a 'registration gap' between the time at which a disposition occurs and the later time or indeed date at which it is registered. *Thompson v Foy* confirms that the interest must already exist at the time at which the disposition occurs, and it is accepted that this is the correct time as a matter of practical realities because it is at this point that the purchaser, tenant or mortgagee will be paying over the purchase price, rent or loan proceeds.

The practical effect of this is that it is more or less impossible for a person who obtains rights in a transaction funded by a lender who is taking security over the property at completion to obtain an overriding interest against that mortgagee.

Putative rights in the land

There are some quite technical issues here concerning when a contractual right becomes a right in the land, rather than merely a personal right between two individuals. Remember that the essence of a proprietary right (also known as a right *in rem* or a right in the land itself) is that it can be enforced against the land itself (provided it is protected under the priority rules that we are now discussing). A contractual or personal right (a right *in personam*) can be enforced against an individual.

A proprietary right must be held in specific property, as we have already seen from Lord Wilberforce's judgment in *National Provincial Bank Ltd v Ainsworth* [1965] AC 1175 at 1248:

> Before a right or an interest can be admitted into the category of property, it must be definable, identifiable by third parties, capable in its nature of assumption by third parties and have some degree of permanence and stability.

The requirement that the interest be in specified property was also relevant in *Abbey National Building Society v Cann* [1991] 1 AC 56. Abbey National lent money for the acquisition of a house, 7 Hillview, which was intended to be occupied by the purchaser, George Cann, and also his mother and the man whom she subsequently married. The facts were that Mrs Cann's son George was the sole legal owner of a property, 30 Island Road, to which Mrs Cann, his mother, had contributed to the purchase price. George contracted to sell that property and to use the proceeds, including the proportion that belonged in equity to his mother, and topped up with the new mortgage from Abbey National, to purchase 7 Hillview as a new home for them. When, following completion of the purchase of 7 Hillview, the son subsequently defaulted on the mortgage and the lender sought possession, the mother claimed an overriding interest due to her equitable interest in and occupation of the property.

The Court considered whether Mrs Cann held an interest in 7 Hillview 'at the time of the disposition', namely at the time of the grant of the legal charge. (*Cann* was decided under the now repealed LRA 1925 but *Thompson v Foy* confirms that the same position would be arrived at by reading Sch 3, para 2 with s 27(2)(f) of the LRA 2002.)

On the principles in *Walsh v Lonsdale*, from exchange of contracts to purchase 7 Hillview, George held an equitable interest in the property. But what of Mrs Cann? Up until the point of completion of the sale of 30 Island Road, Mrs Cann held a beneficial interest under the trust affecting their existing home. (At the time, it was a trust for sale; now, under the Trusts of Land and Appointment of Trustees Act 1996, it would be a trust of land.) But what was the status of her rights in 7 Hillman Road?

Lord Oliver in the House of Lords looked in more detail at the question of Mrs Cann's interest in 7 Hillview.

Pre-acquisition

Unlike her son George, Mrs Cann was not a party to the contract. She expected to hold a beneficial interest in the property on acquisition and a right to occupy it.

Lord Oliver held that at the stage prior to its acquisition, she had only a personal right against George. As he put it:

> One can perhaps test it in this way. If prior to acquisition of 7, Hillview, George Cann had been able to complete the sale of 30 Island Road, and had absconded with the proceeds, financing the purchase of 7, Hillview entirely by means of a mortgage advance, could his mother have claimed any interest in that property?

His answer was that Mrs Cann would have no beneficial interest based on contribution to the purchase price (although she may have had a right of occupation by estoppel based on his promise to accommodate her and her having, in reliance on that promise, vacated 30 Island Road to enable that sale to be completed).

Acquisition

Lord Oliver also rejected the idea that there was a *scintilla temporis* or a brief moment of time between George Cann's purchase and the creation of the mortgage that partially funded it, in which Mrs Cann's estoppel claim could be '"fed" by the acquisition of the legal estate so as to become binding on and take priority over the interest of the chargee'. He felt that this was a 'legal artifice' that 'flies in the face of reality'. The acquisition of the legal estate and the creation of the charge were simultaneous and 'indissolubly bound together'.

Implied acceptance of the charge

Even had Lord Oliver found for Mrs Cann on either of the grounds above and accepted that she had a beneficial interest in the property, he accepted the reasoning of Dillon LJ in the Court of Appeal that Mrs Cann knew that there was a shortfall between the value of the new property and what George Cann could afford to pay. The Court of Appeal inferred that she left it to George to raise the funds any way that he could, and, therefore, even if she had an interest that would otherwise have had priority over Abbey National, she could not take priority over the mortgagee where she had impliedly given authority to George to raise funds on the security of the property.

Re North East Property Buyers Litigation [2014] UKSC 52

Similar reasoning was applied by the Supreme Court in this litigation, which concerned the rights of homeowners who had sold their properties under a purported equity release scheme. In a properly structured equity release scheme, an elderly home owner can free up or 'release' equity in his or her home while continuing to live there for the rest of his or her life. The homeowner sells his or her property to a financial company and simultaneously enters into a lifetime lease or express trust deed. However, in the cases held together here, although the homeowner was promised a lifetime right to continue living there after the sale, in practice he or she was granted only a two-year assured shorthold tenancy. The buyer did not disclose the grant of the tenancy to the mortgage lender funding the purchase, and the buyer was in breach of the lender's mortgage conditions. The seller claimed that the promise by the buyer created a constructive trust or proprietary estoppel in his or her favour which was a proprietary right in the land (LRA 2002, s 116) and, due to the seller's actual occupation of the property, binding on the mortgagee as an overriding interest (LRA 2002, s 29 and Sch 3, para 2).

The Supreme Court held that prior to completion of its purchase, the buyer could only create personal rights, rather than proprietary ones. When completion occurred, this 'fed the estoppel' to create a proprietary right in the seller. However, by then the purchase and mortgage had been created simultaneously, and therefore the seller's proprietary right was not one that was in existence prior to the disposition (ie the actual completion of the mortgage). As Lady Hale put it at [114]–[116]:

> It has been accepted that, at least in the standard case where completion and mortgage take place virtually simultaneously and the mortgage is granted to secure borrowings without which the purchase would not have taken place, completion and mortgage are one indivisible transaction and there is no scintilla temporis between them. We have been invited to distinguish *Cann* [referring to *Abbey National Building Society v Cann* [1991] 1 AC 56] and not to bury it … The conveyance vests the legal estate in the purchaser who instantly mortgages it to the lender. All the purchaser ever acquires is the equity of redemption.

There was some disquiet in the Supreme Court about the application of this principle to the facts in *Re North East Property Buyers Litigation*. Lady Hale, with whom Lords Wilson and Reed agreed, made the point that the facts of the case differed from *Cann* in that whereas Mrs Cann was aware, at least implicitly, that her son would need to mortgage the property in order to raise the rest of the purchase price, Mrs Scott (the vendor in occupation) did not know that the purchaser proposed to mortgage her home, nor that the mortgage would prohibit the granting of the tenancy which she had been promised. 'Thus in no sense is this a "tripartite" transaction, to which vendor, purchaser and lender are all party' (at [119]). She continued at [122]:

> This case has been decided on the simple basis that the purchaser of land cannot create a proprietary interest in the land, which is capable of being an overriding interest, until his contract has been completed. If all the purchaser ever acquires is an equity of redemption, he cannot create an interest which is inconsistent with the terms of his mortgage. I confess to some uneasiness about even that conclusion, for two reasons. First, *Cann* was not a case in which the vendor had been deceived in any way or been made promises which the purchaser could not keep. Should there not come a point when a vendor who has been tricked out of her property can assert her rights even against a subsequent purchaser or mortagee? Second, *Cann* was not a case in which the

lenders could be accused of acting irresponsibly in any way. Should there not come a point when the claims of lenders who have failed to heed the obvious warning signs that would have told them that this borrower was not a good risk are postponed to those of vendors who have been made promises that the borrowers cannot keep? Innocence is a comparative concept. There ought to be some middle way between the 'all or nothing' approach of the present law. I am glad, therefore, that the Law Commission have included a wide-ranging review of the 2002 Act in their recently announced Twelfth Programme of Law Reform (2014, Law Com No 354), which is to include the impact of fraud.

The review of land registration announced in Law Com No 354 has been carried out under Law Com No 227; for more on Law Com No 227, see **4.7.5** and **4.8**.

5.6.2.3 ... to a person in actual occupation ...

Meaning of actual occupation

The starting point on this is the key authority of *Williams & Glyn's Bank v Boland* [1981] AC 487. Lord Wilberforce explains (at 504) that 'the words "actual occupation" are ordinary words of plain English and should be interpreted as such'. The word 'actual' emphasises that physical presence is required, not merely an entitlement in law to be there.

However, the principle has to deal with the myriad of circumstances that can exist, for example, where building works are being carried out or a person is absent temporarily.

Nature or condition of the property

When considering whether a person is in actual occupation, the state of the property is relevant. A number of cases have been concerned with the position when a property is not being used as a residence because renovation or rebuilding works are being carried out and the property is not in a habitable state. When such building works are being carried out, the question is whether the presence of an individual on the property is evidence of his or her actual occupation *at that time* or merely evidence that the individual intends to go into occupation when the building is ready.

Where a property is undergoing renovation works, it can be capable of actual occupation while the works are carried out and before anyone has started to live in the building. This point was considered by the Court of Appeal in *Lloyds Bank Plc v Rosset* [1989] 1 Ch 350 (the case was subsequently appealed to the House of Lords ([1991] 1 AC 107)). A husband and wife agreed to purchase a property in a semi-derelict condition. The vendors allowed them to enter the property to undertake renovation work before exchange. The Court of Appeal held that the carrying out of works could in principle constitute actual occupation even though no one was residing in the property. Nicholls LJ said at 377F:

I can see no reason, in principle or in practice, why a semi-derelict house such as Vincent Farmhouse should not be capable of actual occupation whilst the works proceed and before anyone has started to live in the building.

The test set out by Nicholls LJ in *Rosset*, as followed by and in the words of Ramsay J in *Thomas v Clydesdale Bank Plc (t/a Yorkshire Bank)* [2010] EWHC 2755 (QB) at [33], was whether a claimant's presence on the property, and that of his or her agent, is 'of the nature, and to the extent, that one would expect of an occupier having regard to the then state of the property in the state of renovation for residential use'.

Does the interest holder need to be physically present?

An interest holder can be in actual occupation even though he or she is not physically present him- or herself, provided that there is presence on his or her behalf. In *Abbey National Building Society v Cann* [1991] 1 AC 56, where a mother claimed actual occupation relying on the presence at the property of her son and future husband to enable her carpets to be laid, Lord Oliver (at 93F) stated:

> It does not necessarily, I think, involve the personal presence of the person claiming to occupy. A caretaker or the representative of a company can occupy, I should have thought, on behalf of the employer.

And Nicholls LJ in *Rosset* (at 377F) said:

> I can detect nothing in the context in which the expression 'actual occupation' is used in paragraph (g) to suggest that the physical presence of an employee or agent cannot be regarded as the presence of the employer or principal when determining whether the employer or principal is in actual occupation.

However, actual occupation by a licensee (who is not a representative of the interest holder and who occupies in his or her own right) does not count as actual occupation by the licensor (*Strand Securities v Caswell* [1985] Ch 958 per Lord Denning MR at 981).

Timing of actual occupation

We have already looked in 5.6.2.2 at the date on which the interest in the property must exist. We must also consider – as a separate point – at what date must the person claiming an overriding interest under Sch 3, para 2 be in actual occupation.

Under the repealed LRA 1925, the person claiming the overriding interest had to have been in actual occupation at the time of creation or transfer of the legal estate. This meant the date of completion of the transaction and not the date of registration (*Abbey National Building Society v Cann*). This avoids a 'conveyancing absurdity' (per Lord Oliver at 83) that a mortgagee can make all the proper enquiries at completion and advance the mortgage money, and yet be bound by a party taking up occupation in the period after actual completion but before registration of the charge.

In *Thompson v Foy* [2009] EWHC 1076 (Ch), Lewison J affirmed that this remained the position under the LRA 2002. He went on to question whether the impact of s 27(1) meant that the person claiming an overriding interest must also be in actual occupation at the date of registration as, under s 27(1), a disposition of a registered estate that is required to be completed by registration (ie a transfer, mortgage or lease) will not operate at law until so registered.

'Permanence and continuity'

In *Abbey National Building Society v Cann* [1991] 1 AC 56, on the day of completion of the purchase of 7 Hillview, Mrs Cann's son George was allowed by the vendor to gain access to the property before completion had occurred to allow carpet-layers to attend to lay the mother's carpets. Her furniture began to be unloaded and taken in. Mrs Cann asserted that her equitable interest in the property was overriding on Abbey National due to her actual occupation of the property. Her claim to occupy was based on the carpet-laying and unloading of furniture during a period of roughly 35 minutes prior to actual completion of the purchase and mortgage. Lord Oliver (in the House of Lords at 93F) accepted the judge's finding of fact that these actions were 'no more than the preparatory steps leading to the assumption of actual residential occupation on or after completion'. He continued:

> It is, perhaps, dangerous to suggest any test for what is essentially a question of fact, for 'occupation' is a concept which may have different connotations according to the nature and purpose of the property which is claimed to be occupied ... it does in my judgment, involve some degree of permanence and continuity which would rule out mere fleeting presence.

Mere presence on the property, even if coupled with an intention to take up occupation, is not sufficient to show current actual occupation.

The dangers of setting out a test for what constitutes 'actual occupation' were alluded to by Mummery J in *Link Lending Ltd v Bustard* [2010] EWCA Civ 424, in which the interest holder had once lived at the property but had been taken in psychiatric care. The question arose whether she was in actual occupation. Mummery LJ (at [27]) confirmed that the construction of the provisions as to actual occupation contained in s 70(1)(g) of the LRA 1925 remained binding when interpreting Sch 3 to the LRA 2002. Mummery J also commented on the 'trend of the cases', in avoiding a single test for actual occupation, to list factors which may have a bearing:

> The trend of the cases shows that the courts are reluctant to lay down, or even suggest, a single test for determining whether a person is in actual occupation. The decisions on statutory construction identify the factors that have to be weighed by the judge on this issue. The degree of permanence and continuity of the person concerned, the intentions and wishes of that person, the length of absence from the property and the reason for it and the nature of the

property and personal circumstances of the person are among the relevant factors.

Such a list increases the flexibility that judges can exercise in a particular case but also increases the difficulty of predicting whether, on a set of facts that differ from straightforward residential use, an individual claiming an overriding interest under Sch 3, para 2 will be held to be in actual occupation.

In *Chhokar v Chhokar* [1984] FLR 313, actual occupation continued during the wife's absence in hospital to give birth to her baby and was manifested by the presence of her belongings in the house. In *Stockholm Finance Ltd v Garden Holdings Inc* [1995] NPC 162 a claimant who was absent for 14 months, leaving belongings in the property, was held not to be in actual occupation. In a judgment that demonstrates the difficulty of comparing cases with different facts, Robert Walker J said:

> Whether a person's intermittent presence at a house which is fully furnished, and ready for almost immediate use, should be seen as continuous occupation marked (but not interrupted) by occasional absences, or whether it should be seen as a pattern of alternating periods of presence and absence, is a matter of perception which defies deep analysis. Not only the length of any absence, but also the reason for it, may be material (a holiday or a business trip may be easier to reconcile with continuing and unbroken occupation than a move to a second home, even though the duration of the absence is the same in each case). But there must come a point at which a person's absence from his house is so prolonged that the notion of his continuing to be in actual occupation of it becomes insupportable.

In *Link Lending Ltd v Bustard*, an absence of a year, whilst detained against her will under the Mental Health Act 1983, with regular visits to the property, the presence of her belongings there and her determination to return when permitted to do so, was not considered to have reached the point at which continuing occupation was considered insupportable, and Ms Bustard was held to be continuing in actual occupation.

Relevance of subjective intention of interest holder

Let us look in more detail at the relevance of the intention of the person claiming an overriding interest and his or her wishes to reside permanently at the property.

The mere presence of some of the claimant's furniture will not usually count as actual occupation (*Strand Securities v Caswell* [1985] Ch 958, per Russell LJ at 984). However, if accompanied by a continuing intention to occupy, it may do so (*Hoggett v Hoggett* (1980) 39 P&CR 121, per Sir David Cairns at 127).

In *Link Lending Ltd v Bustard*, Ms Bustard suffered from mental illness and was hospitalised on a number of occasions. She transferred her property to a third party, Mrs Hussein, but continued to live in the property when not in hospital. Ms

Bustard was sectioned under the Mental Health Act 1983 in January 2007 and was detained at a residential care home. In 2008, Mrs Hussein took out a loan on the security of the property and charged the property to Link Lending. Mrs Hussein defaulted and Link Lending took possession proceedings. Ms Bustard successfully set the transfer aside on the ground of undue influence. Her right to do so was an equity in the property (often described as a 'mere equity'), recognised by s 116 of the LRA 2002 as a proprietary right in land and, therefore, an interest in land that would be protected against Link Lending under s 29(2)(a)(ii) of the LRA 2002 if she were in actual occupation at the date of creation of Link Lending's charge.

Could Ms Bustard be said to be in actual occupation despite her hospitalisation? She was not physically present on the date of registration of the charge and had not been resident there for the previous year. Her absence was involuntary; she was incapable of living safely at the property and was prevented from leaving the psychiatric hospital by powers exercised under the 1983 Act. Her furniture and personal effects remained in the property, and she was permitted supervised visits to the property about once a week to visit and to check her post. She paid for regular outgoings in relation to the property. It was known that it was her desire to live there again. HHJ Walton in the Newcastle County Court (*Link Lending v Hussein* [2010] 1 P&CR DG6, [45]) found that

> She genuinely wanted to return home even though prevented from doing so by an order under the Mental Health Act ... She was visiting the property, admittedly supervised, precisely because she still considered it her home. She was trying to return there when she made her applications to the Mental Health Tribunals. No-one ever, that I can see, took a final and irrevocable decision that she would not eventually be permitted to return there to live. In my judgment she still occupied the house even though she was for the time being resident elsewhere ... I accept ... that while Mrs Bustard was not physically present on the land her occupation was manifested and accompanied by a continuing intention to occupy.

On appeal, Link Lending relied on the facts that Ms Bustard was not physically present in the property at the date the charge was registered and had not lived in the property for the previous year. It argued that, after a year in residential care, Ms Bustard's occupation ceased to have the quality of 'permanence and continuity' and that her connection with the property was no longer one of actual occupation.

In the Court of Appeal, Mummery LJ noted (at [29] and [30]) that

> The decisions of the courts on the different facts of other cases have been cited against his [the judge's] conclusion but they do not demonstrate that he was wrong. The assistance given in the authorities is in clarifying the legal principles, exploring the range of decisions available to the court and identifying the factors to which weight should be given.

The judge at first instance was justified in ruling:

at the conclusion of a careful and detailed judgment, that Ms Bustard was a person in actual occupation of the Property. His conclusion was supported by evidence of a sufficient degree of continuity and permanence of occupation, of involuntary residence elsewhere, which was satisfactorily explained by objective reasons and of a persistent intention to return home when possible as manifested by her regular visits to the Property.

5.6.2.4 '... so far as relating to land of which he is in actual occupation ...'

An occupier's rights will be protected in respect of land which he or she actually occupies. If his or her rights also extend to other registered land that he or she does not occupy, then his or her unregistered rights will be unprotected in respect of that other land. This reverses the decision in *Ferrishurst Ltd v Wallcite Ltd* [1999] Ch 355, which allowed a tenant who occupied only part of a registered title over which he held an option, to claim an overriding interest that protected his rights over the whole registered title. The Law Commission put forward two arguments forward in support of this change in the law: first, the difficulty for a purchaser who may need to investigate whether a person who holds rights in his or her land is in actual occupation of other land within the same registered title, which runs counter to the principle that investigation of title to land should be made simpler, quicker and cheaper by allowing the purchaser to rely on the register, and, secondly, the principle that it is reasonable to expect a person who holds rights in land to register those rights (Law Com No 271 (2001), para 8.58).

5.6.2.5 Exception 'for an interest of a person of whom inquiry is made before the disposition and who failed to disclose the right when he could reasonably have been expected to do so' (Sch 3, para 2(b))

A purchaser is expected to act as a prudent purchaser. If he or she does so, he or she should be protected against overriding interests. An interest will not override if an inquiry is made of the interest holder before the disposition and he or she fails to disclose the right when he or she could reasonably have been expected to do so. An example of this occurred in *Mortgage Express v Lambert* [2016] EWCA Civ 555, where a vulnerable seller sold her leasehold flat to two buyers at an undervalue. It was agreed that she would be able to continue living in the property indefinitely for a rent. The sale documentation was silent about the lease and provided that the seller would give vacant possession. The two buyers entered into a mortgage and subsequently failed to pay the mortgage. When the mortgagee sought possession, the seller sought to set the sale aside as an unconscionable bargain. The judge held that she would be entitled to have the transaction set aside against the buyers but not against the mortgagee. Her appeal to uphold the priority of her rights against the mortgagee failed on a number of grounds, but the Court of Appeal made reference to the fact that inquiry was made of the seller and that she did not disclose the existence of the lease.

Lewison LJ accepted (at [41]) that the seller could not reasonably have been expected to have 'attached the label "unconscionable bargain" to the right that she now claims'. However, she could reasonably have been expected to have disclosed that she was not giving vacant possession and that the buyers would be bound by the tenancy that she had agreed to take. In consequence, her claim to an overriding interest would have fallen within the exception contained in para 2(b), had it not already failed due to overreaching (see 3.3).

Students should be aware that conveyancing practice may not be helpful to the potential overriding interest holder here. The making of an enquiry may not be fully understood by the lay person, who is likely to be heavily dependent on his or her solicitor to explain what is happening and its significance. In *Lambert*, the enquiry was made by the seller being asked to complete an 'Overriding Interests Questionnaire', in which she was asked to complete details of the 'rights of persons in occupation', and in which she made no disclosure of the lease to be granted to her. The seller also signed a contract agreeing that vacant possession would be given on completion. In requisitions on title, the seller's solicitor confirmed that there was no change in the information previously given, and in the transfer deed, the seller gave a full title guarantee. This includes a presumption that the seller is disposing of the whole of her interest and that she will do all she reasonably can to give the title that she purports to give. The seller's solicitor did advise the seller that she was selling at a considerable undervalue but did not follow up when the seller mentioned an arrangement for a tenancy. The judge was critical of the seller's solicitor's failure to follow up about the leaseback, and the Court of Appeal endorsed his view.

5.6.2.6 'Obvious on a reasonably careful inspection' (Sch 3, para 2(c)(i))

This new requirement, imposed expressly in the LRA 2002, was considered for the first time in a reported decision in *Thomas v Clydesdale Bank Plc (t/a Yorkshire Bank)* [2010] EWHC 2755 (QB). What will amount to a 'reasonably careful inspection'? Ramsey J stated that is it the 'visible signs of occupation which have to be obvious on inspection':

> [38] … In my judgment the concept of inspection strongly suggests that what has to be obvious is the relevant visible signs of occupation upon which a person who asserts an interest by actual occupation relies. It is clear … that, in order to determine whether somebody is in actual occupation it is necessary to determine not only matters which would require enquiry to ascertain them. That includes such things as the permanence and continuity of the presence of the person concerned, the intentions and wishes of that person and the personal circumstances of the person concerned.
>
> [39] An inspection which only required something to be visible might show that somebody was staying at the property but without enquiry it would not be known whether they were there for an hour, a day, a month, or had some more permanent continuous presence to give rise to the required occupation.
>
> [40] I find it difficult to read into the objective phrase 'reasonably careful inspection' a requirement that the person inspecting would have any

particular knowledge or that, in the absence of any express provision, the term 'inspection' would also require the person inspecting to make reasonable enquiries. On that basis, it is the visible signs of occupation which have to be obvious on inspection.

5.6.2.7 'Actual knowledge' of the interest (para 2(c)(ii))

In this paragraph, the focus switches from visible signs of the *occupation* to actual knowledge of the *interest*. This distinction is important. Again, this was considered for the first time in a reported case in *Thomas v Clydesdale Bank*. Ramsey J held (at [48]) that

> the question of actual knowledge under paragraph 2(c)(ii) has to be construed in the context of the type of interest which is being dealt with. Where an interest belongs to somebody in actual occupation, very often the scope and extent of that interest will depend on the legal analysis of a number of facts and will rarely be ascertainable from a legal document.

He held that the person seeking to deny the overriding interest (in this case the bank) would have actual knowledge of the interest if it has actual knowledge of the facts which give rise to the alleged interest. There is no need for the interest to be recorded in a deed that is submitted to the bank for the bank to have actual knowledge of the interest. This meant that a credit memorandum submitted by a bank employee a year before the loan agreement was entered into, which stated that Ms Thomas would be selling a house to release £100,000 to reduce the debt, could be sufficient to show that the bank had actual knowledge of the facts giving rise to the alleged interest of Ms Thomas.

5.6.2.8 Reflection on the interest + actual occupation overriding interest

Priority between a purchaser (which as you know by now includes a tenant or a mortgagee) and the holder of an unregistered interest that may be overriding is an area where concepts of land law conflict and clash in a manner that has practical consequences. In *Link Lending Ltd v Bustard*, Mummery LJ explained that '[i]n human terms the appeal is about which of two innocent parties duped by a dishonest third party will lose out'. In other cases there may be no fraud involved but still a high cost for the losing party who may lose his or her home and/or his or her money.

Look again at Mummery LJ's words on the test for actual occupation:

> The trend of the cases shows that the courts are reluctant to lay down, or even suggest, a single test for determining whether a person is in actual occupation. The decisions on statutory construction identify the factors that have to be weighed by the judge on this issue. The degree of permanence and continuity of the person concerned, the intentions and wishes of that person, the length of absence from the property and the reason for it and the nature of the

property and personal circumstances of the person are among the relevant factors.

Compare these with the words of Wilberforce LJ in *Williams & Glyn's Bank v Boland* [1981] AC 487 at 504 that:

> In the case of registered land, it is the fact of occupation that matters. If there is actual occupation, and the occupier has rights, the purchaser takes subject to them. If not, he does not. No further element is material.

The words 'actual occupation', he continued, '… are ordinary words of plain English, and should, in my opinion, be interpreted as such'.

Wilberforce LJ was dealing with a case in which there was physical presence (the wives in the two cases heard together on appeal both lived in the properties). What then of a case where the interest holder is not present?

Lewison J, developing the concept of actual occupation, accepted, albeit obiter, in *Thompson v Foy* [2009] EWHC 1076 (Ch) (at [127]), that where a person is not physically present at the property at the relevant date, his or her occupation can be manifested by the presence of his or her possessions at the property, together with a continuing intention to return.

There are a number of implications of this, both practical and conceptual. In practical terms:

- It is difficult to predict whether a person who is not physically present at the property but retains possessions there would be found to be in actual occupation. The decision will be dependent, not merely upon physical evidence, but also on the subjective intention of the interest holder and his or her own personal facts and circumstances. This makes investigation of title more difficult before the event and is likely to encourage the risk and cost of litigation after the transaction has completed.

- A purchaser must therefore be alive to any possessions found at the property. If there are visible signs of occupation then a purchaser must be prepared to make enquiries – possibly extensive enquiries – in order to satisfy him- or herself whether there is a risk of continuing priority of an interest holder after the transaction. In *Link Lending Ltd v Bustard*, a 'drive-by' inspection was carried out by a surveyor who noted signs of occupation. Once these signs are noted, in a case like *Link Lending*, it may not be possible for a purchaser to satisfy him- or herself on the facts, and therefore he or she should only proceed once steps to remove the priority of the interest are taken or should not proceed at all.

Steps that could be taken would be to overreach the interest by requiring capital monies to be paid to two trustees (see 3.3). This would satisfy in the case of interests under a trust that are overreachable (LPA 1925, s 2(2)) but not if, for example, Mrs Bustard's interest had been under an estate contract or an equitable easement (see LPA 1925, s 2(3) for equitable interests that are not overreachable). Conveyancing practice would be to require the interest holder to consent to the transaction and (to avoid the risk that this consent be set aside) after receiving independent legal advice.

However, in conceptual terms, the issues that flow from these practical difficulties are just as important. Remember the words of the Law Commission when introducing the changes now encapsulated in the LRA 2002:

> The fundamental aim of [the Land Registration Act 2002] is that ... the register should be a complete and accurate reflection of the state of the title of the land at any given time, so that it is possible to investigate title to land online, with the absolute minimum of additional enquiries and inspections. (Law Commission, *Land Registration for the Twenty-First Century: A Conveyancing Revolution* (Law Com No 271), Part I, para 1.5)

In order to achieve this objective, 'the categories of overriding interests will have to be very significantly reduced in scope' (at para 1.8(2)) and, accordingly, at para 1.14

> the range of overriding interests will be significantly restricted in their scope: the ambit of particular categories of overriding interests will be narrowed, some categories will be abolished altogether and others will be phased out after 10 years.

Christopher Bevan argues (see his article in Further Reading below) that the trend identified by Mummery LJ is contrary to the necessary direction of travel for land registration and the intentions behind and purpose of the LRA 2002. Rather than accepting the narrowing in the scope, recent cases on Sch 3, para 2 blow it wide open by accepting evidence of subjective intention and personal circumstances.

5.6.2.9 Justification for overriding interests

The Law Commission was clear that: 'The guiding principle on which it proceeds is that interests should be overriding only where it is unreasonable to expect them to be protected in the register.' And:

> [I]t is unreasonable to expect all encumbrancers to register their rights, particularly where those rights arise informally, under (say) a constructive trust or by estoppel. The law pragmatically recognises that some rights can be created informally, and to require their registration would defeat the sound policy that underlies their recognition. Furthermore, when people occupy land they are often unlikely to appreciate the need to take the formal step of registering any rights that they have in it. They will probably regard their occupation as the only necessary protection. The retention of this category of overriding interest is justified ... because this is a very clear case where protection against purchasers is needed, but where it is 'not reasonable to expect or not sensible to require any entry on the register'. (Law Com No 254, para 5.61).

One can argue that Ms Bustard's interest was precisely one which it is unreasonable to expect to be protected on the register. Due to her severe medical condition, she had no recollection of the transaction with Mrs Hussein and only discovered the possession proceedings when she visited the property and found a letter from Link Lending's solicitors addressed to Mrs Hussein. However, this is not the statutory test – the statutory test is whether the person both holds an interest in the land and is in actual occupation.

5.6.3   Easements (LRA 2002, Sch 3, para 3)

Schedule 3, para 3(1) provides that a legal easement or profit a prendre will be an overriding interest. There is an exception for an easement or profit a prendre which at the time of the disposition:

(a)   is not within the actual knowledge of the person to whom the disposition is made, and

(b)   would not have been obvious on a reasonably careful inspection of the land over which the easement or profit is exerciseable.

Sub-paragraph (2) provides that the exception will not apply if the person entitled to the easement or profit proves that it has been exercised in the period of one year ending with the disposition.

The exception also does not apply if the easement or profit has been registered under Part I of the Commons Act 2006.

The purpose of Sch 3, para 3 is to continue to keep the overriding nature of legal easements that arise informally, whether by prescription or implied grant. From the coming into force of the LRA 2002, an expressly granted legal easement must be completed by registration under s 27(2)(d) in order to operate at law. Schedule 3, para 3 excludes equitable easements, which must be protected by a notice (LRA 2002, s 32) in order to be protected under the special priority rule in s 29(2).

However, because of the importance of easements, whether a right of way, emergency escape or drainage, to the continuing use of dominant land benefitting from the easement, transitional provisions contained in Sch 12, para 9 apply to any easement or profit a prendre which was an overriding interest in relation to a registered estate immediately before the coming into force of Sch 3, but which would not fall within para 3 of that Schedule if created after the coming into force of that Schedule. In such a case, Sch 3 shall have effect as if the interest were not excluded from the Schedule. In other words, any easement or profit that was an overriding interest prior to the LRA 2002 will continue to override under the new Act, even if it does not fall within Sch 3, para 3. This will include certain equitable easements that benefit a person in actual possession of land (*Celsteel Ltd v Alton House Holdings Ltd* [1985] 1 WLR 204) and easements that fail under any of the exceptions in para 3 (namely that they are not obvious on a reasonable inspection, not within the actual knowledge of the person to whom a disposition is made and cannot be proven to have been used within the year ending with the day of the disposition). Unlike other transitional provisions in the Act, this saving for easements and profits is not limited in time and will continue indefinitely.

5.7 Comparison between registered and unregistered land priority rules

In the introduction to this chapter, we referred to a 'clear dividing line' between registered and unregistered land priority rules, which we illustrate here:

Table 5.1   Comparison between registered and unregistered land priority rules

Registered land	Unregistered land
Proprietary right	Proprietary right
Basic rule	Legal interests – bind the world
	Exception for 'puisne' mortgage
Special priority rule	Registrable equitable interests and legal 'puisne' mortgage
	Land Charges Act 1972
Is it a protected interest?	Non-registrable equitable interests
	Doctrine of notice
Overreaching	Overreaching

Rules do not cross over the clear dividing line. If the registered land rules apply, do not throw in the doctrine of notice just in case.

However, you have probably noticed that there are some common themes running through unregistered and registered land priority rules. This is unsurprising as they both have to deal with the same issues, such as the occupier who has unregistered proprietary rights. The rules do not always result in the same conclusion, as, famously, is shown by the case of *Midland Bank Trust Co Ltd v Green* [1981] AC 513, where an estate contract over unregistered land was void for non-registration as a Class C(iv) land charge but, if the estate had been registered, would have been overriding as an interest belonging to a person in actual occupation. But despite this, the common themes are worthy of analysis:

- Compare the special priority rule for registrable dispositions with the unregistered land rule that legal interests bind the world. Although registration requirements must be met under s 27 of the LRA 2002 in relation to registered land, both give special privileges to important dealings with legal estates or interests in land.

- Both systems give special protection to those who have paid for an interest in land. Although dealing with different types of interest, see the requirement for valuable consideration under the special priority rule contained in s 29(1) of the LRA 2002, enabling a purchaser of registered land to take free from unprotected interests, and compare this to the concept of the bona fide purchaser for value without notice in unregistered land.

- Both give qualified protection to a person who is in occupation of land as an overriding interest (in registered land) and under the doctrine of notice (unregistered land). In each case, protection is vulnerable to a purchaser who makes the appropriate inspections and enquiries but is unable to discover the existence of the occupier or his or her interest.

5.8 Further reading

M Dixon, 'Priority, overreaching and surprises under the Land Registration Act 2002' (2017) 133 (Apr) LQR 173–77.

C Bevan, 'Overriding and over-extended? Actual occupation: a call to orthodoxy' [2016] Conv 104–17.

B Bogusz, 'Defining the scope of actual occupation under the LRA 2002: some recent judicial clarification' [2011] 4 Conv 268–84.

N Jackson, 'Title by registration and concealed overriding interests: the cause and effect of antipathy to documentary proof' (2003) 119 (Oct) LQR 660–91.

M Dixon, 'Mortgages, co-owners and priority: some basics' [2016] 2 Conv 81–83.

summary

Protection of earlier interests

Basic rule – s 28 of the Land Registration Act (LRA) 2002 provides that an earlier interest takes priority over an interest that is created later, whether or not the interests are registered.

This is subject to a 'special rule' for registrable dispositions – s 29(1) of the LRA 2002.

If a a key transaction (set out in s 27 of the LRA 2002 as registrable dispositions) affecting a registered estate is made for valuable consideration, completion of the disposition by registration has the effect of postponing to the interest under the disposition any interest affecting the estate immediately before the disposition whose priority is not protected at the time of registration. The priority of an interest will be protected if it is a registered charge, the subject of a notice on the register or an overriding interest.

Overriding interests are listed within Sch 3 to the LRA 2002, of which the key provisions are found in paras 1, 2 and 3, with para 2, the rights of a person in actual occupation, causing the most difficulty in case law. An interest holder who is in actual occupation can lose his or her overriding status if his or her occupation is not obvious on a reasonably careful inspection or is not disclosed on inquiry (if he or she could reasonably be expected to so disclose).

1 Look again at the problem scenario concerning Liz and her property Grey Gables in the 'Test your knowledge' section in **Chapter 3**. Answer the question on the basis that Liz's title to Grey Gables is registered.

2 Read **5.6.2.8** (Reflection on the interest + actual occupation overriding interest). Do you consider that the meaning of the statutory test has been – or should be – manipulated from its original purpose to deal with hard or deserving cases? What balance should be struck between doing justice in individual cases and the efficient operation of the land register? Is your analysis changed by the view of the World Bank that a 'well-designed land administration system … makes it possible for the property market to exist and to operate' (quoted in *Updating the Land Registration Act 2002: A Consultation Paper* (Law Com Consultation Paper No 227, 2016)).

chapter 6

Co-ownership and Trusts of Land

After reading this chapter, you will be able to:

- understand the differing ways in which land can be co-owned
- identify when a trust of land arises
- distinguish between a joint tenancy and a tenancy in common in equity
- identify and apply the rules by which a joint tenancy in equity may be severed
- understand and apply the rights granted to a beneficiary by the Trusts of Land and Appointment of Trustees Act (TLATA)1996
- understand and apply how the TLATA 1996 resolves disputes with beneficiaries and trustees.

6.1   What is co-ownership?

Co-ownership occurs when more than one party owns property. A typical example is where a husband and wife purchase their home. You probably remember that equity follows the common law, so there are two titles involved in co-ownership: the legal title and the equitable title. You will also probably recognise this as a trust.

In our example, the husband and wife both own the legal title and are also both beneficially entitled to the land. Following the Trusts of Land and Appointment of Trustees Act (TLATA) 1996, this immediately creates what is called a trust of land. We will look at this in more detail later in this chapter. The diagram below shows that the husband and the wife both own the legal and equitable titles:

Legal title: H W	
	This is a trust
Equitable title: H W	

The Law of Property Act (LPA) 1925 provides that the legal title can only be held as a joint tenancy and effectively that the equitable title can be held either as a joint tenancy or as a tenancy in common. Look at s 36(2) (emphasis added):

36   Joint tenancies

(2) *No severance of a joint tenancy of a legal estate,* so as *to create a tenancy in common* in land, *shall be permissible,* whether by operation of law or otherwise, but *this subsection does not affect* the right of a joint tenant to

release his interest to the other joint tenants, or *the right to sever a joint tenancy in an equitable interest* whether or not the legal estate is vested in the joint tenants:

Provided that, where a legal estate (not being settled land) is vested in joint tenants beneficially, and any tenant desires to sever the joint tenancy in equity, he shall give to the other joint tenants a notice in writing of such desire or do such other acts or things as would, in the case of personal estate, have been effectual to sever the tenancy in equity, and thereupon the land shall be held in trust on terms which would have been requisite for giving effect to the beneficial interests if there had been an actual severance.

Note that although this section refers to a tenancy, it does not mean a lease but refers to the ownership between the husband and the wife and comes from the historical way of describing a person's interest in land.

6.2 Joint tenancy

A joint tenancy is where the co-owners all own the property as a whole.

Legal title: H   W   (joint tenants)

Equitable title: H   W   (joint tenants)

They do not have distinct shares but are all entitled to the whole property. Survivorship applies to a joint tenancy so that if one joint tenant dies, he or she ceases to be a joint tenant and the remaining joint tenants continue to own the whole property. In this example, H and W purchase their marital home. H later dies, so W is the sole owner of the property, and if she sells it, she will be entitled to the whole sale proceeds. Even if H made a will leaving a share in the property to another person, W would still be the sole owner. It was famously said that a joint tenant's interest in the property passed to the surviving joint tenant as his dying breath left his body. Although somewhat gruesome, this is a reminder of how survivorship operates. The diagram below shows how the ownership would then look:

Legal title: W   (sole owner)

Equitable title: W   (sole beneficiary)

W then becomes the sole owner of the property and can deal with it as she wishes. If H had left his interest in the property to another person in his will, this would be ineffective and not affect W's ownership of the property; remember the dying breath!

6.3 Tenancy in common at equity

The first important thing to remember is that, following the LPA 1925, it is no longer possible to own the legal title as a tenancy in common, so when we are talking about a tenancy in common, it can only be of the equitable title. See s 1(6) and s 34 of the LPA 1925, set out below.

A tenancy in common is where the co-owners have separate shares in the equitable title of the property; this does not mean that they own only part of the property though, which is why it is referred to as being held in undivided shares. A tenant in common can deal with his or her interest in the property; this is his or her beneficial share in it. He or she can sell or transfer this interest in the property and can leave it to another person in his or her will. The beneficial undivided shares do not have to be equal, and if the co-owners are contributing different amounts to the purchase price of a property, their shares often reflect this. For example, if A contributes 75% of the purchase price and B contributes 25% of the purchase price, they could decide to hold the equitable title as tenants in common with A holding a 75% share and B holding a 25% share. The diagram below shows this. When they sell the property, A will receive 75% of the sale proceeds and B will receive 25% of the sale proceeds.

Legal title: A   B   (joint tenants)

Equitable title: A 75%   B 25%   (tenants in common)

6.4 What was the problem with co-ownership and how did the Law of Property Act 1925 help?

In order to understand the reasoning behind the changes to co-ownership made in the LPA 1925, we need to look at co-ownership before 1925.

Imagine that Alan, a farmer, has eight children. When Alan dies, he leaves his farm to his children in equal shares, so each child inherits a 1/8th share. In order for a purchaser to buy this house, he or she would have to deal with eight owners. Now imagine that two of Alan's children die, leaving their share to their own two children, who each have a 1/16th share. A purchaser would then have to deal with 12 owners; they may not all be available to sign the necessary paperwork or they may not all agree to the sale. This meant that property became very difficult to sell and transfer. The LPA 1925 sought to address this problem in two ways in s 1(6) and s 34(2):

Section 1(6) of the LPA 1925 states that

> A legal estate is not capable of subsisting or of being created in an undivided share in land or of being held by an infant.

This contains three important points:

(a) The legal title can only be held as a joint tenancy and not in undivided shares (ie not as a tenancy in common).

(b) It does not refer to the equitable title, which means that it is still possible to hold this in undivided shares (ie as a tenancy in common).

(c) A minor cannot hold property.

Section 34(2) of the LPA 1925 states:

> Where, after the commencement of this Act, land is expressed to be conveyed to any persons in undivided shares and those persons are of full age, the conveyance shall (notwithstanding anything to the contrary in this Act) operate as if the land had been expressed to be conveyed to the grantees, or, if there are more than four grantees, to the first four named in the conveyance, as joint tenants …

This contains two important points:

(a) It puts a statutory limit of four on the number of co-owners of land that there can be in law. If a conveyance attempts to transfer land to more than four owners, this section applies and only the first four adults named will be registered as the owners of the legal title. Remember, under s 1(6), that a minor cannot hold property. As all the legal owners have to sign the conveyance, this means that a maximum of four will ever have to sign it, and it makes it easier to transfer the property.

(b) Those first four owners will hold the legal title as joint tenants, even if the conveyance referred to undivided shares, ie tenants in common. In such a case the legal title would be held as a joint tenancy, and the equitable title would be a tenancy in common reflecting the shares referred to in the conveyance.

You should also note s 2(2) and s 27 of the LPA 1925, which state that provided a purchaser pays the purchase money to at least two trustees, any equitable rights under a trust will be overreached and the purchaser will take free of these.

Now we can look at how these changes helped with the problems with the sale of Alan's farm. First, when Alan dies, the property will be transferred to the first four named children in the conveyance (provided they are not a minor), say B, C, D and E. These four will hold the property on trust for themselves and the remaining children. We have seen this in s 1(6) and s 34(2) of the LPA 1925.

> **Legal title:** B C D E (joint tenants)

> **Equitable title:** B C D E F G H I (could be joint tenants or tenants in common)

Secondly, if one of the two children who dies and leaves his share to his own children is B, this would mean that C, D and E continue to hold the legal title to the property.

> **Legal title:** C D E (joint tenants)

If the property is sold, the purchaser would have to deal with C, D and E, as the legal owners. It is more straightforward. Remember the rule of survivorship. Note also that when B dies, another one of the children does not automatically become a legal owner as they are protected by the trust. In this situation you do not have to have four people holding the legal title; that is just the maximum number.

Thirdly, provided the purchaser pays the purchase money to at least two trustees, he or she does not have to be concerned with the other children's and grandchildren's interests in the property as he or she will have overreached their interests. Remember s 2(2) and s 27 of the LPA 1925.

This may seem unfair as the other children and grandchildren now have no rights in the property, but this is because the LPA 1925 saw property as an investment and that the real interest was in the sale proceeds, not the property itself. The children and grandchildren will have their respective shares in the sale proceeds. We will look at this idea again later in this chapter, as the TLATA 1996 changed this position.

6.5 Joint tenancy or tenancy in common of the equitable title?

As s 1(6) of the LPA 1925 provides that where there is co-ownership, the legal title can only be held as a joint tenancy, it is always clear how that title will be held. But how do you determine the way the equitable title is held? To answer this you must consider the following points.

6.5.1 The four unities

In order for the equitable title to be held as a joint tenancy, the four unities need to be present. The acronym PITT can be useful. Let us look at these unities in more detail:

- Possession – unity of possession is the most important one as, without this, there is no co-ownership. It means that all owners have the same rights to possess and own the whole property.
- Interest – unity of interest means that the owners must have the same rights over the property, for example one owner cannot have the right to the freehold estate and another owner the right to the leasehold estate.
- Time – unity of time means that the rights of the owners must be created at the same time.
- Title – unity of title means that the owners must have received their right to the property from the same document.

So if all four unities are present, the owners may hold the equitable title as joint tenants. Remember that unity of possession is always required with co-ownership, and if it is not present then there cannot be co-ownership. If any of the other unities (interest, time or title) are missing then the owners cannot hold the equitable title as joint tenants but must hold the equitable title as tenants in common.

You must be clear then that a tenancy in common in equity does not need to have these three unities; it may have them but it only needs to have unity of possession to ensure co-ownership.

6.5.2 Express indication in the document

If the four unities are present, we can move on to consider whether the document transferring the property to the owners expressly created a joint tenancy or a tenancy in common. Words such as 'jointly' or 'as joint tenants' are clear indicators of a joint tenancy. Words such as 'in equal shares', 'equally', 'to be divided between' or 'as tenants in common' are clear indicators of a tenancy in common. These words show that the owners are to have separate shares in the property (but, as we have seen, these will be undivided shares).

6.5.3 Presumptions

If the four unities are present, but there is no clear wording in the document, you need to consider the usual presumption that equity follows the law, and therefore the owners will be holding the equitable title as joint tenants. If the owners purchase the property by contributing unequal shares of the purchase price then equity will presume that they wish to hold a share of the property which is proportionate to their contribution. In such a case it will be presumed that the owners hold the equitable title as tenants in common. Equity will also make such a presumption in business arrangements, such as where business partners buy a business property together. This should make sense, as one partner is likely to want his or her family, rather than the other partner, to inherit the property.

6.5.4 Help from the Land Registry?

The Land Registry has developed standardised forms for property transfers. If you want to transfer the whole of the land, for example, you must use form TR1 (the complete form is available on the Land Registry website). Set out below is an extract from the form (section 10), and you can see that it requires the new owners to declare how they are holding the property. This should prevent any argument later on.

---

10   Declaration of trust. The transferee is more than one person and
☐   they are to hold the property on trust for themselves as joint tenants
☐   they are to hold the property on trust for themselves as tenants in common in equal shares
☐   they are to hold the property on trust:

If only it were that simple. Even if this section has been completed, the Land Registry will not record the detail of the shares, but merely enter a restriction reflecting that the equitable title to the property is held, for example, as a tenancy in common. The owners must have the good sense to retain a copy of their transfer/declaration of trust giving this information.

Moreover, the Land Registry will still register applications where the box has not been completed at all. In the case of *Stack v Dowden* [2007] UKHL 17, Baroness Hale urged the Land Registry to review its practice on this. However, in their article (see Further Reading below), Mark Pawlowski and James Brown carried out a survey of practitioners' experiences of current Land Registry practices and found that

> When asked the question 'Does the Land Registry in your district insist on completion of the "Declaration of Trust" (Panel 10) in the TR1/FR1/TP1 (or alternatively execution of a separate declaration of trust) before it registers co-purchasers as joint legal proprietors', of the 40 responses received, 63 per cent replied 'no' to this question. Of those that replied in this way, the majority stated that the local Land Registry would, in the absence of a declaration of trust, assume a tenancy in common and automatically enter a restriction to that effect. In some cases, the local registry would also respond by letter allowing the omission to be rectified (free of charge) provided a contrary intention was received within 14 days.

The authors refer to Alan Moran's comments (see Further Reading):

> [Moran] rightly observes [that] the potential for further litigation of the kind exemplified by *Stack* will continue so long as completion of Panel 10 is seen as discretionary by many land registries throughout the country. The Form A restriction (requiring at least two trustees to give a valid receipt for capital money) may suggest a tenancy in common, but it does not by itself constitute

a declaration of trust nor does it assist in drawing any inferences as to the parties' common intention regarding their beneficial ownership.

6.5.5 No express declaration of trust

This issue has been considered in several important cases. Let us start with the case of *Stack v Dowden* [2007] UKHL 17. The main facts and findings of the case are set out below to aid your understanding, before we consider the way the House of Lords reached its decision.

Table 6.1   Facts in Stack v Dowden

Mr Stack contributed 35% of the purchase price	Ms Dowden contributed 65% of the purchase price
The purchase was registered in the usual way at the Land Registry, but there was no express declaration of trust setting out how the parties owned their equitable interests. The property was held in joint names and the parties lived there for approximately 20 years. The relationship then broke down.	
Mr Stack claimed a 50% share as the property was owned in joint names.	Ms Dowden claimed a share equal to the 65% she had initially contributed to the purchase price.
The judge at first instance upheld Mr Stack's claim.	
The case was heard by the Court of Appeal and then the House of Lords, which granted Ms Dowden a 65% share and Mr Stack a 35% share.	

Baroness Hale gave the leading judgment and noted, first, that had there been an express declaration of trust, there would have been no dispute and that would have been conclusive as to how the parties held their shares. She emphasised the need to complete the appropriate box on the Land Registry form (see above).

However, as there was no express declaration, there would be a strong presumption that equity follows the law. As Mr Stack and Ms Dowden held the property as joint tenants at law, equity would follow this and they would also hold the equitable title as joint tenants. Baroness Hale (at [58]) stated that 'a conveyance into joint names indicates both legal and beneficial joint tenancy, unless and until the contrary is proved'.

Baroness Hale explained that, in order to depart from this presumption, the burden is on the party claiming not to have equal shares to show this. She noted (at [56]) that 'the onus is upon the person seeking to show that the beneficial ownership is different from the legal ownership'. In her judgment she made it clear that cases such as this would be 'very unusual' but gave guidance on what the court would take into account when determining that the presumption had been rebutted. Although there is no substitute for reading the full judgment, we have set out an extract below:

> 69. In law, 'context is everything' and the domestic context is very different from the commercial world. Each case will turn on its own facts. Many more factors than financial contributions may be relevant to divining the parties' true intentions. These include: any advice or discussions at the time of the transfer which cast light upon their intentions then; the reasons why the home was acquired in their joint names; the reasons why (if it be the case) the survivor was authorised to give a receipt for the capital moneys; the purpose for which the home was acquired; the nature of the parties' relationship; whether they had children for whom they both had responsibility to provide a home; how the purchase was financed, both initially and subsequently; how the parties arranged their finances, whether separately or together or a bit of both; how they discharged the outgoings on the property and their other household expenses. When a couple are joint owners of the home and jointly liable for the mortgage, the inferences to be drawn from who pays for what may be very different from the inferences to be drawn when only one is owner of the home. The arithmetical calculation of how much was paid by each is also likely to be less important. It will be easier to draw the inference that they intended that each should contribute as much to the household as they reasonably could and that they would share the eventual benefit or burden equally. The parties' individual characters and personalities may also be a factor in deciding where their true intentions lay. In the cohabitation context, mercenary considerations may be more to the fore than they would be in marriage, but it should not be assumed that they always take pride of place over natural love and affection. At the end of the day, having taken all this into account, cases in which the joint legal owners are to be taken to have intended that their beneficial interests should be different from their legal interests will be very unusual.
>
> 70. This is not, of course, an exhaustive list. There may also be reason to conclude that, whatever the parties' intentions at the outset, these have now changed. An example might be where one party has financed (or constructed himself) an extension or substantial improvement to the property, so that what they have now is significantly different from what they had then.

Note, though, that the first paragraph confirms that domestic cases are very different from commercial ones. In *Laskar v Laskar* [2008] EWCA Civ 347, a mother and daughter had jointly purchased a property as an investment, not as a joint home. Lord Neuberger held that where the property was purchased as an investment, it was inappropriate to apply the presumption of joint ownership, despite the relationship between these purchasers which, when actually examined, was as business investors. See also *Erlam v Rahman* [2016] EWHC 111 (Ch).

Let us return to *Stack v Dowden*. Ms Dowden demonstrated to the court that the parties had kept their finances strictly separate, such as by having separate bank accounts and separate responsibilities for household expenses. The unequal contribution to the purchase price was also a weighty factor. Baroness Hale stated (emphasis added):

> 92. This is, therefore, a very unusual case. There cannot be many unmarried couples who have lived together for as long as this, who have had four children together, and whose affairs have been kept as rigidly separate as this couple's affairs were kept. *This is all strongly indicative that they did not intend their shares*, even in the property which was put into both their names, *to be equal* (still less that they intended a beneficial joint tenancy with the right of survivorship should one of them die before it was severed). Before the Court of Appeal, Ms Dowden contended for a 65% share and in my view she has made good her case for that.

Baroness Hale also referred to Lord Hoffmann's 'ambulatory constructive trust', which he used to describe the parties' changing intentions over time, and noted that the parties' interests must be the same; they cannot intend to rely on survivorship if one of them dies whilst they are still in a relationship, but at the same time intend a tenancy in common should they separate, and further dictate the share allocation in the event of an acrimonious separation.

The Court found that the parties' intention was not to share the interests in the property equally and awarded Ms Dowden a 65% share. This approach was the Court trying to quantify the shares the parties themselves intended to hold, looking at their course of conduct.

It is interesting to note that Lord Neuberger (in the minority) disagreed with this approach. He agreed with the starting presumption that the equitable title follows the legal title, but then saw that this was rebuttable by evidence of different financial contributions to the purchase price. He noted that equity had consistently used the resulting trust as a means of addressing such situations, and that it was wrong and against precedent to use fairness to impute the parties' intentions regarding beneficial ownership which could not be evidenced from their own conduct. He went on:

> 141. ... I am unconvinced that the original ownership of the beneficial interest could normally be altered merely by the way in which the parties conduct their personal and day-to-day financial affairs. I do not see how the facts that they have lived together for a long time, have been in a loving relationship, have children, operated a joint bank account, and shared the outgoings of the household, including in respect of use and occupation of the home, can, of themselves, indicate an intention to equalise their originally unequal shares any more than they would indicate an intention to equalise their shares on acquisition, as discussed earlier. So, too, the facts that they both earn and share the home-making, or that one party has a well-paid job and the other is

the home-maker, seem to me to be irrelevant at least on their own. Even the fact that one party pays all the outgoings and the other does nothing would not seem to me to justify any adjustment to the original ownership of the beneficial interest (subject to the possible exception of mortgage repayments).

142. In many cases, these points may result in an outcome which would seem unfair at least to some people. However (unless and until the legislature decides otherwise) fairness is not the guiding principle as Baroness Hale says, and, at least without legislative directions, it would be a very subjective and uncertain guide. Further, it is always important to bear in mind the need for clarity and certainty.

Stack v Dowden did create uncertainty as to whether the court could impose the division it deemed fair, or whether it was restricted to inferring the intention of the parties.

The issue was then considered in *Jones v Kernott* [2011] UKSC 53. In this case, again, an unmarried couple purchased a house, with Ms Jones contributing a sum to the purchase price. There was no express declaration of trust when the purchase was registered. The couple occupied the property, Mr Kernott paid for and carried out works to increase the value of the property, but the household expenses were shared equally. The couple separated in 1993, after which time Ms Jones was solely responsible for the household expenses. Some 12 years later Mr Kernott claimed a half share in the property.

The Court used this opportunity to clarify the principles of *Stack v Dowden*. It

- affirmed the presumption that the beneficial interests follow the legal estate;
- held that this can be rebutted by the parties' contrary intention;
- held that it was for the court to find the common intention of the parties as to what shares they should each hold;
- held that the court could look at the whole course of the parties' conduct;
- held that the court could impute an intention if it could not ascertain the common intention of the parties; and
- stated that each case will turn on its own facts.

The extract from Lord Walker and Baroness Hale's judgment neatly sets out the position:

51. In summary, therefore, the following are the principles applicable in a case such as this, where a family home is bought in the joint names of a cohabiting couple who are both responsible for any mortgage, but without any express declaration of their beneficial interests.

(1) The starting point is that equity follows the law and they are joint tenants both in law and in equity.

(2) That presumption can be displaced by showing (a) that the parties had a different common intention at the time when they acquired the home, or (b)

that they later formed the common intention that their respective shares would change.

(3) Their common intention is to be deduced objectively from their conduct: 'the relevant intention of each party is the intention which was reasonably understood by the other party to be manifested by that party's words and conduct notwithstanding that he did not consciously formulate that intention in his own mind or even acted with some different intention which he did not communicate to the other party' (Lord Diplock in *Gissing v Gissing* [1971] AC 886, 906). Examples of the sort of evidence which might be relevant to drawing such inferences are given in *Stack v Dowden*, at para 69.

(4) In those cases where it is clear either (a) that the parties did not intend joint tenancy at the outset, or (b) had changed their original intention, but it is not possible to ascertain by direct evidence or by inference what their actual intention was as to the shares in which they would own the property, 'the answer is that each is entitled to that share which the court considers fair having regard to the whole course of dealing between them in relation to the property': Chadwick LJ in *Oxley v Hiscock* [2005] Fam 211, para 69. In our judgment, 'the whole course of dealing … in relation to the property' should be given a broad meaning, enabling a similar range of factors to be taken into account as may be relevant to ascertaining the parties' actual intentions.

(5) Each case will turn on its own facts. Financial contributions are relevant but there are many other factors which may enable the court to decide what shares were either intended (as in case (3)) or fair (as in case (4)).

On the facts of *Jones v Kernott*, the Court felt able to find an inferred common intention so did not need to impute the intention, and on this basis the Court awarded a 90% share to Ms Jones and a 10% share to Mr Kernott.

This was further considered in the case of *Barnes v Phillips* [2015] EWCA Civ 1056 where, in 1996, the couple had purchased the property in joint names. In 2005, Mr Barnes experienced financial problems and the couple mortgaged the property. A large proportion of this money was used by Mr Barnes to ease his financial position. The couple separated later that year. The Court found that when the property was originally purchased, the parties had intended to hold it as joint tenants. However, following the allocation of the remortgage monies, the Court found that there was a common intention to change their interests, and this was further supported by the fact that, from the time of the separation shortly after the remortgage, Ms Philips had been solely responsible for the mortgage repayments on the property. However, the Court could not find a common intention as to the percentage split, so it was entitled to impute this intention. It awarded Ms Philips an 85% share and Mr Barnes a 15% share.

You may recall Baroness Hale referring to these cases as being unusual; it could be argued that this is not the case at all!

6.5.6 Ambulatory constructive trust

Described by Lord Hoffmann during the course of argument in *Stack v Dowden*, this is an interesting legal concept (it was also referred to in *Jones v Kernott*). The case noted that beneficial interests can subsequently change, but the ambulatory constructive trust goes further than this and means that the parties' interests may continue to change over time in light of circumstances until they need to be quantified. This raises the question of how far can this ambulatory trust go? It is easy to see the change where there is a major event but harder in usual everyday life. What is the position if there is a minor change in financial contributions? Can there be multiple events changing the parties' interests? Is it almost necessary to create a chart showing the parties' interests over time? Can, in fact, one joint owner have his or her interest effectively extinguished over time? How does this trust sit with third parties when the co-owners' interests can be ever-changing?

6.5.7 Resulting and constructive trusts

The above cases deal with issues arising when the property is co-owned. Let us now consider the position when the property is registered in the name of one sole owner. There are many cases that involve a claim by another party that he or she is entitled to a beneficial share in a property where the property is registered in the name of a sole owner.

6.5.7.1 Resulting trust

This form of trust arises where, for example, A purchases the property for £100,000 and is registered as the sole owner but B had contributed £50,000 to the purchase price. B is seen as having a beneficial interest in the property and a resulting trust is produced (see *Dyer v Dyer* (1788) 2 Cox 92). You can see that the resulting trust is based on the parties' presumed intention when the property was purchased and looks to their initial contributions to the purchase price as evidence of this. In our example the beneficial interests are likely to be shared equally.

However, *Stack v Dowden* marked a shift in the court's approach to this situation, which has moved away from resulting trusts, looking at the initial contributions, to looking at the parties' intentions in the context of a constructive trust. In her judgment (at [60]), Baroness Hale stated that

> The presumption of resulting trust is not a rule of law ... the law has indeed moved on in response to changing social and economic conditions. The search is to ascertain the parties' shared intentions, actual, inferred or imputed, with respect to the property in the light of their whole course of conduct in relation to it.

Note, though, that resulting trusts are still important and appropriately argued in a commercial purchase (see *Laskar v Laskar* above).

6.5.7.2 Constructive trust (known as a common intention constructive trust)

A common intention constructive trust has been much used in family home cases and, following the shift away from resulting trusts, becomes more important.

Step 1 – Acquisition

In order to gain a beneficial interest, the claimant must show that this constructive trust has arisen. In *Lloyds Bank Plc v Rosset* [1991] 1 AC 107, Lord Bridge set out the circumstances in which a constructive trust arises. He gave two scenarios:

The family home is registered in the sole name of one of the parties (often the man), but he effectively holds it on trust for himself and the woman because of:

(a) an express agreement which one party acted or relied upon to their detriment (see *Eves v Eves* [1975] 1 WLR 1338 and *Oxley v Hiscock* [2005] Fam 211, CA). In *Oxley v Hiscock*, the property was held solely in Mr Hiscock's name, but both parties had contributed to the purchase price, then to the upkeep and improvement of the property from joint funds, and at some point they had discussed that each would have a beneficial share in the property. The Court held that this fell into the first of Lord Bridge's categories; or

(b) implied agreement and reliance shown by the parties' conduct or intention. This has been interpreted narrowly, and indeed Lord Bridge in *Lloyds Bank Plc v Rosset* stated that only a contribution to the purchase price or to mortgage payments would qualify. The case of *Geary v Rankine* [2012] EWCA Civ 555 held that wider conduct can be taken into account but still referred to domestic duties and contributions to utility bills as not being enough to give an interest.

Step 2 – Quantification

This step now establishes the proportion of the parties' respective interests. But how is this to be done? In *Oxley v Hiscock*, Chadwick LJ concluded that the court must decide what is fair, looking at the whole course of dealing between the parties. In *Stack v Dowden*, Baroness Hale considered the approach taken by Chadwick LJ and commented that 'Oxley v Hiscock has been hailed by Gray and Gray [*Elements of Land Law*, 4th edn, p 931, para 10.138] as "an important breakthrough"'. The passage quoted is very similar to the view of the Law Commission in *Sharing Homes, A Discussion Paper* (Law Com No 278), para 4.27, on the quantification of beneficial entitlement:

> If the question really is one of the parties' 'common intention', we believe that there is much to be said for adopting what has been called a 'holistic approach' to quantification, undertaking a survey of the whole course of dealing between the parties and taking account of all conduct which throws light on the question what shares were intended.

That may be the preferable way of expressing what is essentially the same thought, for two reasons. First, it emphasises that the search is still for the result which reflects what the parties must, in the light of their conduct, be taken to have intended. Secondly, therefore, it does not enable the court to abandon that search in favour of the result which the court itself considers fair.

Does this signal a move away from fairness? In *Graham-York v York* [2015] EWCA Civ 72, the Court considered the parties' respective financial contributions. It appeared to limit the consideration to factors specifically relevant to the property; in effect this meant financial contributions and not the wider interpretation of the whole course of dealing of the parties advocated by *Stack v Dowden*, which specifically referred to financial and non-financial matters. It can been argued that this approach is some way off the 'more practical, down-to-earth, fact-based approach' that Lord Hope proposed in *Stack v Dowden*.

6.5.8 Reform

As we have seen, the law is badly in need of reform in this area. The Law Commission published *Cohabitation: The Financial Consequences of Relationship Breakdown* (Law Com No 307) in 2007, which Lord Walker referred to in his judgment in *Stack v Dowden*, noting that Parliament may 'recast the law in this area'. The need was clear then. The Law Commission proposed that qualifying cohabitants would be able to obtain financial relief if they separated. In its Executive Summary at para 1.19, it explained:

> In broad terms, the scheme would seek to ensure that the pluses and minuses of the relationship were fairly shared between the couple. The applicant would have to show that the respondent retained a benefit, or that the applicant had a continuing economic disadvantage, as a result of contributions made to the relationship. The value of any award would depend on the extent of the retained benefit or continuing economic disadvantage. The court would have discretion to grant such financial relief as might be appropriate to deal with these matters, and in doing so would be required to give first consideration to the welfare of any dependent children.

In 2011 the Government announced that it would not be taking the recommendations for reform forward during that parliamentary term.

Resolution 'an organisation of 6,500 family lawyers and other professionals in England and Wales, who believe in a constructive, non-confrontational approach to family law matters' and which also campaigns for improvements to the family justice system, has a manifesto calling for basic legal rights for couples who live together and then separate.

Private Members' Bills have been introduced on several occasions, but perhaps '"Common law marriage" and cohabitation' (Briefing Paper 03372, 9 March 2017), which provides general information about how the law applies to cohabitants, the number of cohabiting couples, and the Law Commission's proposals for reform, shows that the much-needed parliamentary scrutiny and reform may be on the horizon.

6.6 Severing a joint tenancy in equity

Remember that when we are considering severing a joint tenancy, we are only concerned with the equitable title, as we have identified, in the discussions above, that where there is co-ownership, the legal title can only ever be held as a joint tenancy. Look again at s 36(2) of the LPA 1925 which prevents the severance of a legal joint tenancy:

> No severance of a joint tenancy of a legal estate, so as to create a tenancy in common in land, shall be permissible, whether by operation of law or otherwise …

6.6.1 How can you sever a joint tenancy in equity?

A co-ownership may start as a joint tenancy, but then the parties may wish to change this to a tenancy in common, for example if a relationship breaks down and the parties no longer wish one of them to benefit in the event of the other's death. The LPA 1925 does not prevent tenancies in common in equity, so the joint tenancy of the equitable title can be severed to become a tenancy in common of the equitable title.

There are four main possible methods of severance. The first three, set out below, are common law methods and were propounded by Page-Wood VC in *Williams v Hensman* (1861) 1 J&H 546, 557. This case still has significance today in relation to the severance of joint tenancies in equity. These methods are now enshrined in law in s 36(2) of the LPA 1925. The section added a fourth method which we will also consider below:

36 Joint tenancies

(2) No severance of a joint tenancy of a legal estate, so as to create a tenancy in common in land, shall be permissible, whether by operation of law or otherwise, but this subsection does not affect the right of a joint tenant to release his interest to the other joint tenants, or the right to sever a joint tenancy in an equitable interest whether or not the legal estate is vested in the joint tenants:

Provided that, where a legal estate (not being settled land) is vested in joint tenants beneficially, and any tenant desires to sever the joint tenancy in equity, he shall give to the other joint tenants a notice in writing of such desire or do such other acts or things as would, in the case of personal estate, have been effectual to sever the tenancy in equity, and thereupon the land shall be held in trust on terms which would have been requisite for giving effect to the beneficial interests if there had been an actual severance.

6.6.1.1 An act operating on the share of one of the joint tenants

A joint tenancy in equity will be severed if one of the joint tenants goes bankrupt or transfers, mortgages, leases or enters into an enforceable contract to sell his or her beneficial interest during his or her lifetime. It is an action that shows that the co-owner believes that he or she has a share in the property, and he or she does something with that share, such as transfer it to someone else. By doing something with the share, it shows that he or she no longer believes that all the co-owners own the whole property together, but that they have separate shares of it.

Note that this act must happen during the transferor's lifetime. Remember that leaving his or her share in his or her will does not sever a joint tenancy because the will only becomes effective on his or her death. At this point he or she has no interest to pass, as the right of survivorship will have taken effect and transferred that interest to the surviving joint tenant(s).

Imagine there are three co-owners, Aurora, Baljinder and Cate, holding as joint tenants at law and in equity. Aurora then transfers her beneficial interest to Daniel in writing. This transfer will operate to sever the joint tenancy in equity, and Daniel will now become a tenant in common with Baljinder and Cate. Remember, though, that Baljinder and Cate will remain joint tenants as they have not taken any act to sever their joint tenancy. You should also have realised that unity of title is no longer present, as Daniel will have received his interest in the property from a different document at a different time from that of Baljinder and Cate.

To aid your understanding, the diagram below sets out this scenario and shows the shares that the parties will hold. Remember that shares are only appropriate for tenants in common.

Legal title: A B C Joint tenants who hold on trust for A, B and C who also have equitable interests.

Equitable title: A B C Joint tenants

A transfers her beneficial interest to D

Legal title: A B C Joint tenants who hold on trust for A, B and D who have equitable interests. Remember A only transferred her beneficial interest; she did nothing to affect the legal title.

Equitable title: Joint tenants B C $\frac{2}{3}$ Tenant in common D $\frac{1}{3}$

Section 53(1)(c) of the LPA 1925 states that the sale or disposition of an equitable interest must be in writing and signed by the person disposing of the interest, so in the above example A must have transferred her beneficial interest to D by a written document which A signed. Do not forget this formality.

6.6.1.2 Mutual agreement

A joint tenancy in equity will be severed if all the joint tenants mutually agree to sever. The difficulty arises when this agreement is not express but inferred. In *Burgess v Rawnsley* [1975] 1 Ch 429, Mr Honick and Mrs Rawnsley became friendly and subsequently bought the property where Mr Honick had rented the ground floor. The purchase was in joint names, and the conveyance stated that they held the property on trust for themselves as 'joint tenants'. Some months after the purchase, Mr Honick and Mrs Rawnsley seemed to agree between themselves that she would sell her share in the property to him. Mrs Rawnsley later changed her mind and asked for a higher price, but this was not agreed before Mr Honick died. Mrs Rawnsley argued that survivorship applied and the property belonged to her solely, whereas Mr Honick's daughter argued that the joint tenancy had been severed by their mutual agreement and therefore that Mr Honick's share should pass to his estate. This case was heard in the Court of Appeal, and two of the judges (Browne LJ and Sir John Pennycuick) reluctantly agreed the finding of the previous county court judge that the agreement to sell amounted to severance by mutual agreement and could not be set aside. The Court therefore held that Mrs Rawnsley held the property on trust for herself and Mr Honick's daughter in equal shares. This case highlights an evidential uncertainty in using this ground as, although the agreement has to be mutual, ie agreed by all the parties, it does not have to be in writing. The judgment of Browne LJ discusses the issues with the oral agreement between the parties.

Contrast that case with *Gore and Snell v Carpenter* (1993) 60 P&CR 456. Mrs Snell and Mr Gore were the executors of Mr Carpenter's will and Mrs Carpenter was his widow. Before Mr Carpenter died, the couple had decided to divorce and were in settlement negotiations regarding the two properties they owned. Severance of the joint tenancies was raised as part of these negotiations. The court held that although there may have been an agreement in principle between the parties, both parties had reserved the right to further negotiate the point, and there had been no action by either of them to show that they believed that the properties were no longer held as joint tenancies. Talk of severance in the negotiations did not constitute actual severance. The properties were still held as joint tenancies.

6.6.1.3 Course of dealing/mutual conduct

This is where the conduct of the joint tenants shows a clear intention that the joint tenancy is to be severed, but there has been no express or implied agreement to sever. A unilateral statement by one joint tenant to the other(s) will not constitute a severance by this method.

6.6.1.4 Section 36(2) written notice

This section allows one joint tenant to serve written notice on all the other joint tenants of his or her desire to sever the joint tenancy. There are several important points to note from this.

First, it is a unilateral act and the other joint tenants do not need to consent or take any action.

Secondly, although there is no prescribed form for the notice, it must be in writing and clearly state the desire to sever.

Thirdly, this desire must be immediate. It cannot be at a time in the future. This has caused difficulties. In *Harris v Goddard* [1983] 1 WLR 1203, it was held that severance had not taken place where, in the divorce petition, the wife had asked the court to make such order as it saw fit regarding the matrimonial property. Similarly, in *Gore and Snell v Carpenter*, severance had not taken place when it was referred to in an offer to the other party but never agreed to. However, in *Re Draper's Conveyance* [1969] 1 Ch 486, where the wife applied for an order for sale of the matrimonial property with the sale proceeds be divided equally, the court held that this was effective severance. It also held that the wife had been acting on her own share (see **6.6.1.1** above). The more recent case of *Quigley v Masterton* [2011] EWHC 2529 reaffirmed *Harris v Goddard* and *Re Draper's Conveyance*. When the wife applied to the court for the matrimonial property to be sold and the proceeds split equally, this was held to have been a notice of severance.

Fourthly, the notice must be served (or deemed to have been served) on all the other joint tenants. This also causes difficulties and we must now think about notice provisions. Consider s 196 of the LPA 1925 below (emphasis added):

(1) Any notice required or authorised to be served or given by this Act shall be *in writing.*

...

(3) Any notice required or authorised by this Act to be served shall be *sufficiently served if it is left at the last-known place of abode or business* in the United Kingdom of the lessee, lessor, mortgagee, mortgagor, or other person to be served, or, in case of a notice required or authorised to be served on a lessee or mortgagor, is affixed or left for him on the land or any house or building comprised in the lease or mortgage, or, in case of a mining lease, is left for the lessee at the office or counting-house of the mine.

(4) Any notice required or authorised by this Act to be served shall also be *sufficiently served, if it is sent by post in a registered letter addressed to* the lessee, lessor, mortgagee, mortgagor, or other person to be served, *by name, at the aforesaid place of abode or business, office, or counting-house, and if that letter is not returned by the postal operator* (within the meaning of Part 3 of the Postal Services Act 2011) concerned *undelivered;* and that *service shall be deemed to be made at the time at which the registered letter would in the ordinary course be delivered.*

So if a notice is addressed to the recipient's residence or place of business and posted by registered post or recorded delivery and the notice is not returned undelivered, it is deemed to have been served when the letter would normally be delivered. Cases have been decided on this point.

Kinch v Bullard [1999] 1 WLR 423 (Ch) concerned a wife who wished to divorce her husband. She instructed her solicitors to sever their beneficial joint tenancy; they prepared the notice and posted it by first class post. Whilst the letter was in the postal system, the husband suffered a heart attack, and the wife, realising that she would survive her husband, destroyed the letter when it arrived at their home. The husband died shortly afterwards having never seen the letter. His executors claimed that severance had taken place. The wife disputed this and claimed the full beneficial entitlement to the property. The court held that, under s 196(3), service had taken place when the letter had been posted through the letter box, as it had been left at the last known place of abode, and therefore severance had taken place. In his judgment. Lord Neuberger even briefly considered the position if the notice had been eaten by the dog!

Re 88 Berkeley Rd NW9 [1971] Ch 648 concerned two ladies who shared a home. When Miss Eldridge announced her forthcoming marriage, Miss Goodwin was advised to sever their beneficial joint tenancy. She instructed her solicitors accordingly, and they duly prepared the notice and posted it by recorded delivery to their home. The notice arrived when Miss Eldridge was out at work, as she usually was when the post arrived, and Miss Goodwin signed for the delivery. Miss Goodwin died shortly afterwards. Miss Eldridge argued that she had never seen the notice and that severance had not been effected. The court had to consider the service of notice provisions and held, with regret, that notice had been sufficiently served under s 196(4) and that the beneficial joint tenancy had indeed been severed.

6.6.2 Can a will ever sever the joint tenancy of the equitable title?

The easy answer to this is no. A will cannot sever a joint tenancy. Remember that the interest passes with the dying breath.

6.6.3 What is the effect on the joint tenancy of the legal title when the joint tenancy of the equitable title is severed and it becomes a tenancy in common?

The easy answer to this is nothing. It has no effect and the co-owners continue to hold the legal title as joint tenants. The diagrams below show this:

Before severance

Legal title: A B both own the whole	Joint tenants

Equitable title: A B both entitled to the whole	Joint tenants

After severance

Legal title: A   B   both own the whole   Joint tenants

Equitable title: A $\frac{1}{2}$ B $\frac{1}{2}$ Tenants in common

Remember that the parties could mutually agree a different split of the shares

For the sake of completeness, you should know that severance of a joint tenancy in equity can also be carried out by:

- a court order where the court settlement contradicts holding as joint tenants;
- unlawful killing so that a joint tenant cannot benefit by taking the life of the other joint tenant to become solely entitled to the property; and
- merging of interests, which is rare and need not concern you at this stage.

6.7   Some history: the trust for sale and the doctrine of conversion

When the LPA 1925 tried to deal with the problem of many owners of land frustrating the selling and buying of property, the use of property was different. The Act needed to make sure that property was alienable, but it also needed to protect those who had a beneficial interest in it. At that time, property was seen as an asset rather than as a family home, and so ownership by use of a trust allowed this asset to be managed by the trustees but gave the necessary protection to those with a beneficial interest. Then, most co-owners held the legal title as trustees for the benefit of other people. In reality, the benefit was often for families, but their interest was seen to be in the income from the asset and/or its value rather than in the asset itself, and there was no automatic right to live in the property.

6.7.1   Trust for sale

Under the 1925 Act, when co-owners, such as a husband and wife, bought a property for their own enjoyment, it automatically created a trust, which was known as a trust for sale.

Legal title: H   W   Joint tenants   Trustees

Equitable title: H   W   Joint tenants/tenants in common   Beneficiaries

The point of this trust was the ability to sell the property and invest the sale proceeds. These proceeds would then be held on trust for those with the beneficial interest in the trust. You can see that this is not the intention of someone buying a family home and not what H and W (above) might have intended. The 1925 Act, however, gave trustees the right to postpone this sale and this was quite common, particularly in the case of a family home. Naturally this seems very artificial to us today. H and W probably did not even realise that, as trustees, they were postponing their sale.

6.7.2 Doctrine of conversion

As we have seen, the beneficial interest in property held in a trust for sale is in the sale proceeds, ie money, not the property itself. This created the doctrine of conversion, which provided that the beneficial interest was in the sale proceeds (personal property), rather than in the property itself (real property). The result of this was a need for careful drafting in a will, for example. Imagine that Joanna died and in her will left her real property to Keith and her personal property to Musa. Any property Joanna owned which was subject to a trust for sale would be seen as being personal property – remember that the purpose of the trust for sale is to sell the property. This would mean that Musa would inherit the beneficial interest in the property. This is probably not what Joanna would have intended.

6.8 Trusts of Land and Appointment of Trustees Act 1996

You will have realised that a trust for sale was an artificial way to hold a property and that it does not fit with the way we may want to buy a property today. If a husband and wife buy their home together, they generally do not buy it with the intention of selling it and investing the sale proceeds to benefit themselves. They buy it as a family home and, importantly, they want the right to live there.

In fact this concept had already been recognised by the courts. In *Bull v Bull* [1955] 1 All ER 253, Lord Denning held that the doctrine of conversion did not prevent beneficiaries acquiring a right of occupation where the property had been bought for the beneficiaries to live in. This judgment was followed in subsequent cases and affirmed in *Williams & Glyn's Bank v Boland* [1981] AC 487. It was time for statute to recognise the modern purpose of co-ownership.

6.8.1 Section 1 – Trust of land

The Trusts of Land and Appointment of Trustees Act (TLATA) 1996 acknowledged that the trust for sale did not reflect modern living and introduced the trust of land. Section 1(1)(a) of the TLATA 1996 defines a trust of land as meaning any trust of property which consists of or includes land. Note that is it not limited to just land so, for example, could include both land and money. Section 5 of the TLATA 1996 provides that if a trust for sale is implied by statute, it will become a trust of land.

You can still expressly create a trust for sale but it will be governed by the TLATA 1996. Section 4 implies a right to postpone the sale for an indefinite period regardless of what the document creating the trust says, and it provides that such a right cannot be excluded from the trust for sale.

6.8.2 Section 3 – Abolition of the doctrine of conversion

Section 3 of the TLATA 1996 abolished the doctrine of conversion and states that land is not to be regarded as personal property. A beneficiary will have an interest in the property rather than in the sale proceeds (ie the money). The exception to this is where there is a trust created by a will and the testator died before the coming into force of the TLATA 1996, as it is assumed that his or her will was written with his or her understanding of land as personal property.

6.8.3 Section 6 – General powers of trustees

This is an important section (emphasis added):

> (1) *For the purposes of exercising their functions as trustees*, the trustees of land *have* in relation to the land subject to the trust *all the powers of an absolute owner*.

So in relation to the trust of land, the trustees have all the powers of an absolute owner. They can sell, lease or mortgage the land, purchase land for investment or for occupation by a beneficiary or indeed for any other reason. This is subject to the terms of the trust document which, under s 8, can restrict or exclude such powers. When exercising their powers under the TLATA 1996, the trustees must (as must all trustees) have regard to the rights of the beneficiaries (s 6(5)).

Note s 6(2), which empowers the trustees to transfer the land to beneficiaries of full age and full capacity who have an absolute right to the land. The beneficiaries would then hold the legal title and the trustees would cease to be trustees. Indeed the case may be that the trustees demand that the beneficiaries take a transfer of the property. Of course if there were two or more beneficiaries, a new trust would be created with the beneficiaries wearing two hats, one as beneficiary and the other as trustee.

Section 9 permits the trustees to delegate their powers, and note s 9A:

> (1) The duty of care under section 1 of the Trustee Act 2000 applies to trustees of land in deciding whether to delegate any of their functions under section 9.

This duty of care is to 'exercise such care and skill as is reasonable in the circumstances' (Trustee Act 2000, s 1).

The trustees must act unanimously.

6.8.4 Section 11 – Consultation with beneficiaries

Before we consider this section, you should note that it only applies to trusts coming into force after the commencement of the Act, and, similarly, where a will creates a trust of land, this section will only apply to that trust of land if the will was made after the commencement of the Act.

11 Consultation with beneficiaries

(1) The trustees of land shall in the exercise of any function relating to land subject to the trust—

(a) so far as practicable, consult the beneficiaries of full age and beneficially entitled to an interest in possession in the land, and

(b) so far as consistent with the general interest of the trust, give effect to the wishes of those beneficiaries, or (in case of dispute) of the majority (according to the value of their combined interests).

You can see that the duty of the trustees to consult with beneficiaries extends only to 'so far as practicable' and only to 'beneficiaries of full age and beneficially entitled to an interest in possession in the land'. The effect of the beneficiaries' wishes will depend on their consistency with the general interest of the trust (see s 11(1)(b)). Therefore the beneficiaries cannot dictate what will happen, as it is up to the trustees to determine the general interests of the trust.

6.8.5 Section 12 – Right to occupy

Section 12 is an important provision as it recognises the modern reason for buying a family home and gives beneficiaries who are entitled to an interest in possession (not in remainder) a right to occupy the land at any time if:

- the purpose of the trust included making it available for beneficiaries; or
- the land is available for such occupation.

There are several points to note here:

- The right applies if the beneficiary has an interest in possession, for example if the land is held on trust for X for life, then remainder to Y. It is X who has the right to occupy, with his or her interest vested in possession. Y only has an interest in remainder or in reversion.

- If the land has been acquired for investments purposes, say to produce an income for the beneficiary from rent from the property, then there is no right to occupy.

- The land must be available – if it has been leased then it will not be available for the beneficiary to occupy.

- Under s 12(2), if the land is not available or is unsuitable for occupation then there is no such right. This raises the question as to what is unsuitable. The Act gives no further guidance on this, but in *Chan v Leung* [2002] EWCA Civ 1075 Parker LJ explained that:

  4. There is no statutory definition or guidance as to what is meant by 'unsuitable' in this context, and it would be rash indeed to attempt an exhaustive definition or explanation of its meaning. In the context of the present case it is, I think, enough to say that 'suitability' for this purpose must involve a consideration not only of the general nature and physical

characteristics of the particular property but also a consideration of the personal characteristics, circumstances and requirements of the particular beneficiary. This much is, I think, clear from the fact that the statutory expression is not simply 'unsuitable for occupation' but 'unsuitable for occupation by him', that is to say by the particular beneficiary.

The right to occupy is also subject to the provisions of s 13 of the TLATA 1996, which we will now look at.

6.8.6 Section 13 – Exclusion and restriction of right to occupy

Section 13 is actually quite straightforward, and a good starting point would be to read the section itself:

13 Exclusion and restriction of right to occupy

(1) Where two or more beneficiaries are (or apart from this subsection would be) entitled under section 12 to occupy land, the trustees of land may exclude or restrict the entitlement of any one or more (but not all) of them.

(2) Trustees may not under subsection (1)—

    (a) unreasonably exclude any beneficiary's entitlement to occupy land, or

    (b) restrict any such entitlement to an unreasonable extent.

(3) The trustees of land may from time to time impose reasonable conditions on any beneficiary in relation to his occupation of land by reason of his entitlement under section 12.

(4) The matters to which trustees are to have regard in exercising the powers conferred by this section include—

    (a) the intentions of the person or persons (if any) who created the trust,

    (b) the purposes for which the land is held, and

    (c) the circumstances and wishes of each of the beneficiaries who is (or apart from any previous exercise by the trustees of those powers would be) entitled to occupy the land under section 12.

(5) The conditions which may be imposed on a beneficiary under subsection (3) include, in particular, conditions requiring him—

    (a) to pay any outgoings or expenses in respect of the land, or

    (b) to assume any other obligation in relation to the land or to any activity which is or is proposed to be conducted there.

(6) Where the entitlement of any beneficiary to occupy land under section 12 has been excluded or restricted, the conditions which may be imposed on any other beneficiary under subsection (3) include, in particular, conditions requiring him to—

      (a)   make payments by way of compensation to the beneficiary whose entitlement has been excluded or restricted, or

      (b)   forgo any payment or other benefit to which he would otherwise be entitled under the trust so as to benefit that beneficiary.

  (7)   The powers conferred on trustees by this section may not be exercised—

      (a)   so as prevent any person who is in occupation of land (whether or not by reason of an entitlement under section 12) from continuing to occupy the land, or

      (b)   in a manner likely to result in any such person ceasing to occupy the land,

unless he consents or the court has given approval.

  (8)   The matters to which the court is to have regard in determining whether to give approval under subsection (7) include the matters mentioned in subsection (4)(a) to (c).

You can see from this that s 13(1) provides that where there are two (or more) beneficiaries who are entitled to occupy the land, if the trustees act reasonably they can exclude or restrict the occupation of one or more (but not all) of the beneficiaries.

Section 13(5) allows the trustees to impose reasonable conditions relating to the beneficiary's occupation. It states that these conditions include requiring the beneficiary to pay any outgoings or expenses in respect of the land or assume any other obligation in relation to the land or any activity which is carried on there. Practically this could mean requiring the beneficiary to pay the council tax and utility bills for the property.

You will appreciate that a beneficiary being excluded from a property that he or she has a right to occupy is a harsh order. Section 13(6) deals with such beneficiaries who have been excluded or restricted. It allows the trustees to require beneficiaries who are occupying the land by the right in s 12 either to make compensation payments to the excluded/restricted beneficiary or to forgo a payment or benefit so as to benefit that other beneficiary. You can see that this subsection tries to balance the situation.

Under s 13(4), when exercising their powers, the trustees must have regard to:

• the intentions of the person(s) who created the trust;

• the purposes for which the land is held; and

• the circumstances and wishes of each of the beneficiaries who is entitled to occupy the land under this section.

There are further limitations on the powers of the trustees in s 13(7). The trustees cannot force a beneficiary who is already occupying to leave if that beneficiary refuses to leave.

6.8.7   Section 14 – Applications for order

This is an extremely useful and important section to help resolve disputes between co-owners.

As you can imagine, disputes relating to co-owned property are not unusual. An obvious example is a family home where the personal relationship between the two trustees breaks down. Consider the trustees as husband and wife; W wants to sell the property but H does not. Section 14 provides that any person who is a trustee of land or has an interest in property which is the subject of a trust can apply to the court for an order to settle their dispute.

You will note that the wording is wide and allows anyone with an interest in the property to make an application. This is not limited to the beneficiaries and would, for example, include a trustee in bankruptcy.

The court's powers are wide. It can make any order relating to the exercise of the trustees' functions or declaring the nature or extent of a person's interest in the trust property. Examples of this would be an order removing the need for the trustees to consult a beneficiary, or the example above where W wants to sell the property but H does not.

However, s 14(3) prevents the court ordering the appointment or removal of trustees.

The court clearly has wide powers under this section, and s 15 gives guidance on matters the court should consider when deciding on the application.

6.8.8   Section 15 – Matters relevant in determining applications

Again this section is straightforward, so let us start by setting it out:

> 15   Matters relevant in determining applications
>
> (1)   The matters to which the court is to have regard in determining an application for an order under section 14 include—
>
> > (a)   the intentions of the person or persons (if any) who created the trust,
> >
> > (b)   the purposes for which the property subject to the trust is held,
> >
> > (c)   the welfare of any minor who occupies or might reasonably be expected to occupy any land subject to the trust as his home, and
> >
> > (d)   the interests of any secured creditor of any beneficiary.

This should be an easy subsection to interpret and apply. But that is not the end of the story, as there is another important matter the court can consider. This fifth matter is contained in s 15(2) and s 15(3):

> (2)   In the case of an application relating to the exercise in relation to any land of the powers conferred on the trustees by section 13, the matters to which the court is to have regard also include the circumstances and

wishes of each of the beneficiaries who is (or apart from any previous exercise by the trustees of those powers would be) entitled to occupy the land under section 12.

(3) In the case of any other application, other than one relating to the exercise of the power mentioned in section 6(2), the matters to which the court is to have regard also include the circumstances and wishes of any beneficiaries of full age and entitled to an interest in possession in property subject to the trust or (in case of dispute) of the majority (according to the value of their combined interests).

Taking s 15(2) first, it states that where the court is considering an application in relation to the powers under s 13 (Exclusion and restriction of right to occupy), the court can also consider the circumstances and wishes of each beneficiary entitled to occupy the land under s 12.

Section 15(3) then relates to any other type of application and states that the court can also consider the matter of the circumstances and wishes of any beneficiaries of full age and entitled to an interest in possession in the trust property or, if there is a dispute between them, the majority of the beneficiaries according to the value of their combined interests.

It is important to note that the section states the matters '*include* the circumstances and wishes …', so they are not limited to those listed. The court can take other factors into account if applicable.

Let us apply this now to an example.

example

Aidan transfers one of his properties, known as The Homestead, to his two sons Ben and Caleb jointly for the purposes of it being a family home for them and their families. You should already be able to identify that a trust of land arises and know how to analyse how they hold property.

Ben is married and has no children. Caleb is divorced and has two children, Daniel aged 21 who now lives in Canada, and Eve aged 14 who is still at school. Eve and Caleb live in The Homestead. Ben lives in another part of the UK and wants to sell The Homestead so that he can fund a round the world trip. Caleb and Eve want to continue living there.

Aidan
(as a family home for you and your families)

Ben   Caleb

Daniel (21)   Eve (14)

First let us look at s 14. Under this section, in fact Ben is both a trustee and has an interest in the property, so he can make an application to the court for an order. The court will look at the matters in s 15 when determining the application:

(a)   s 15(1)(a) – the intentions of the person or persons (if any) who created the trust. Here Aidan created the trust for the purpose of a family home for his sons and their families. It is clear that selling The Homestead would not meet his intentions.

(b)   s 15(1)(b) – the purposes for which the property subject to the trust is held. Again, Aidan was quite clear that the purpose was as a family home for his sons and their families.

(c)   s 15(1)(c) – the welfare of any minor who occupies or might reasonably be expected to occupy any land subject to the trust as his home. Remember that a minor is a person under the age of 18. Eve is 14 years old, falls into this definition and so her welfare should be taken into account. She and her father want to continue living in the property.

Section 15(3) is also helpful here, as it refers to the circumstances and wishes of any beneficiaries who are of full age and entitled to an interest in possession in the property. Again this will give weight to Caleb's argument that the property should not be sold. The reference to the majority is of no help here as there are only two owners who disagree.

In this example it is likely that, having applied the matters in s 15, the court would not order a sale of the property. In practical terms and subject to finances, you could advise Caleb to buy out Ben and become the sole owner.

Let us take that example further and imagine that Aidan had three sons, Ben, Caleb and Frank. Frank also lives in The Homestead and wants to continue living there.

Aidan

(as a family home for you and your families)

Ben   Caleb   Frank

Daniel (21)   Eve (14)

Now the reference to the majority in s 15(3) is very useful as the court can have regard to the circumstances of and wishes of beneficiaries who are of full age and entitled to an interest in possession or, if there is a dispute, the wishes of the majority which is calculated according to the value of their combined interests. Imagine that Caleb and Frank want to keep The Homestead and only Ben wants to sell. You can see that as all three owners have equal interests, Caleb and Frank will have the majority and again it is unlikely that the court will order the property to be sold.

The final subsection of s 15 is also very important. Again let us start by reading the subsection itself:

(4)   This section does not apply to an application if section 335A of the Insolvency Act 1986 (which is inserted by Schedule 3 and relates to applications by a trustee of a bankrupt) applies to it.

So s 15 does not apply to an application if s 335A of the Insolvency Act 1986 applies to it. When you look at s 335A, you will see that it refers to applications made by a trustee in bankruptcy of a co-owner for an order for sale of the co-owned trust property.

335A Rights under trusts of land

(1)   Any application by a trustee of a bankrupt's estate under section 14 of the Trusts of Land and Appointment of Trustees Act 1996 (powers of court

in relation to trusts of land) for an order under that section for the sale of land shall be made to the court having jurisdiction in relation to the bankruptcy.

(2) On such an application the court shall make such order as it thinks just and reasonable having regard to—

(a) the interests of the bankrupt's creditors,

(b) where the application is made in respect of land which includes a dwelling house which is or has been the home of the bankrupt or the bankrupt's spouse or civil partner or former spouse or former civil partner—

(i) the conduct of the spouse, civil partner, former spouse or former civil partner, so far as contributing to the bankruptcy,

(ii) the needs and financial resources of the spouse, civil partner, former spouse or former civil partner, and

(iii) the needs of any children; and

(c) all the circumstances of the case other than the needs of the bankrupt.

You will see, again, that the matters the court has to have regard to are clearly set out. Do not overlook the sting in the tail in s 335A(3) though (emphasis added):

(3) Where such an application is made after the end of the period of one year beginning with the first vesting under Chapter IV of this Part of the bankrupt's estate in a trustee, *the court shall assume, unless the circumstances of the case are exceptional, that the interests of the bankrupt's creditors outweigh all other considerations.*

The effect of this is that, after the one year, the interests of the creditors will outweigh all other considerations unless those considerations are exceptional. You should be able to see that the trustee in bankruptcy is likely to wait for a year and then apply for the sale. The courts have firmly upheld this, and examples of exceptional circumstances are few and far between. In *Re Citro (Domenico) (A Bankrupt)* [1991] Ch 142, Nourse LJ said:

What then are exceptional circumstances? As the cases show, it is not uncommon for a wife with young children to be faced with eviction in circumstances where the realisation of her beneficial interest will not produce enough to buy a comparable home in the same neighbourhood, or indeed elsewhere. And, if she has to move elsewhere, there may be problems over schooling and so forth. Such circumstances, while engendering a natural sympathy in all who hear of them, cannot be described as exceptional. They are the melancholy consequences of debt and improvidence with which every civilised society has been familiar.

Subsequently, courts have held that a relapse of paranoid schizophrenia would need only postpone the sale for a year (*Re Ravel* [1998] 2 FLR 718) and that the tests being applied by the courts using this section were compatible with human rights legislation (*Ford v Alexander* [2012] EWHC 266 (Ch)).

6.8.9 Section 2 – Settlements

For the sake of completeness you should know that s 2 of the TLATA 1996 provides that no new settlements can be created after the Act came into force on 1 January 1997. Settlements created before then are still governed by the Settled Land Act 1925, but such settlements are beyond the scope of this book.

6.9 Further reading

P Luther, '*Williams v Hensman* and the uses of history' (1995) 15(2) Legal Studies 219–35.

NP Gravells, 'Severance of a joint tenancy: a land law "whodunnit?"' (2012) 71(1) Cambridge Law Journal 42–44.

A Hayward, 'Common intention constructive trusts and the role of imputation in theory and practice' (2016) 3 Conveyancer and Property Lawyer 233–42.

M Pawlowski and J Brown, 'Joint purchasers and the presumption of joint beneficial ownership - a matter of informed choice? (2013) 27(1) Trust Law International 3–17.

S Pascoe, 'Section 15 of the Trusts of Land and Appointment of Trustees Act 1996 – a change in the law?'[2000] Conveyancer and Property Lawyer 315–28.

M Dixon, 'To sell or not to sell: that is the question. The irony of the Trusts of Land and Appointment of Trustees Act 1996' (2011) 70(3) Cambridge Law Journal 579–606.

A Moran, 'Anything to Declare? Express Declaration of Trust on Land Registry Form TR1: The Doubts Raised in *Stack v Dowden*' [2007] Conv 364.

Where there is co-ownership, the only way the legal title can be held is as a joint tenancy.

A trust of land arises when two or more people purchase property. There are two titles involved in co-ownership, the legal title and the equitable title.

The equitable title can be held as a joint tenancy or as a tenancy in common.

The key features of a joint tenancy are that all owners own the whole property, there are no shares and the right of survivorship applies. This means that when the joint tenant dies, his or her interest in the property automatically passes to the remaining joint tenant(s).

The key features of a tenancy in common are that the owners hold undivided shares and the right of survivorship does not apply: when one owner dies, his or her share in the property will pass under his or her will or through the intestacy rules.

There are four ways a joint tenancy in equity can be severed to become a tenancy in common:

- an act operating on the share of one of the joint tenants;
- mutual agreement;
- course of dealing/mutual conduct; or
- written notice under s 36(2) of the LPA 1925.

The TLATA 1996 created the trust of land. Under such a trust, a beneficiary has a right to occupy the property.

Section 11 provides that, as far as practicable, trustees must consult with the beneficiaries. Anyone with an interest under a trust of land can apply for a court order to settle a dispute between trustees and/or beneficiaries under s 14. Section 15 sets out what the court has to consider, and s 335A of the Insolvency Act 1986 sets out what the court has to consider if the application is made by a trustee in bankruptcy.

Some years ago, Hector transferred his large country house, Fairlight, to his three children, Celeste (aged 24), Alexandra (aged 20) and Pedro (aged 10) jointly to use and enjoy themselves and as a family home in the future. Three years ago, Celeste wrote to Alexandra and Pedro saying that she was now holding her share in Fairlight for herself and her partner Sarah.

Sadly Celeste has now died. She had just made a new will in which she left all her real property to the local hospice and all her personal property to the local homeless shelter.

Sarah wants to sell Fairlight as it brings back too many memories, Alexandra and Pedro still live there and are against the sale. Pedro is adamant that he will celebrate his upcoming 16th birthday at Fairlight.

1   Explain who has equitable interests in Fairlight and how they hold such interests.

2   Where will Celeste's share in Fairlight go?

3   Imagine that Celeste had wished to sever her tenancy with Sarah. What are the different ways she could have done this?

4   If Celeste had successfully severed, who would inherit her interest under her will?

5   How would your answer differ if her will had been written in 1992?

6   Who is entitled to bring an application to the court asking for Fairlight to be sold?

7   What will the court consider when making this application?

8   How would your answer change if the person making the application was Alexandra's trustee in bankruptcy?

9   If Fairlight is sold, who should sign the legal transfer?

chapter 7

Use of Leases, Lease Characteristics, Formalities, Licences and Forms of Lease

After reading this chapter, you will be able to:
- explain why a lease is used
- identify the essential characteristics of a lease
- understand the formalities required for the creation of different forms of lease
- distinguish between a lease and a licence
- identify different forms of lease.

7.1 What is a lease?

A lease is a proprietary interest in land and one of the two legal estates in land set by s 1(1)(b) of the Law of Property Act (LPA) 1925:

> 1 **Legal estates and equitable interests**
> (1) The only estates in land which are capable of subsisting or of being conveyed or created at law are—
> (a) An estate in fee simple absolute in possession;
> (b) A term of years absolute.

You can see from this that the technical term for a leasehold interest in land is a term of years absolute.

So a lease is one of the two legal estates recognised in law. You should note, though, that s 4 and s 27 of the Land Registration Act (LRA) 2002 state that if the lease is granted for a term of more than seven years, that lease will not take effect at law until it has been properly registered.

7.1.1 Terminology

Let us imagine that Lorelei buys the freehold estate of a property. She does not wish to occupy that property; in fact it is a shop unit and she would like to use it as an investment so that it brings in revenue.

Thomas would like to start a new business selling shoes. He needs a shop unit to open this business but does not have enough money to buy the freehold of such a property.

Lorelei and Thomas agree that he will rent this shop unit. Lorelei becomes the landlord (or she could be known as the lessor; it is the same) and she grants the lease to Thomas for three years (this is known as the term of the lease). The technical term for the grant of the lease is a demise and so the shop unit can be known as the demised premises. Thomas becomes the tenant (or the lessee; again it means the same).

At the end of the three-year term (ignoring for now any other legislation), Thomas will have to leave the property and Lorelei can lease the property to someone else. Lorelei has what is called the reversion, as the property reverts to her at the end of the term.

L (landlord/lessor)

↓

T (tenant/lessee)

If Lorelei sold the shop unit to Rowan, Rowan's purchase would be subject to Thomas's lease. It is now usual to refer to Rowan as the landlord, even though he did not grant the lease. He would be the owner of the freehold and Thomas would pay the rent to him. Lorelei would no longer be the landlord.

L (landlord/lessor) ➡ Rowan (new landlord/lessor)

↓

T (tenant/lessee)

Assignment

Imagine that Thomas then falls ill and does not know when he will be able to return to his business. He has various options open to him but we will concentrate on the main two. Subject to the provisions in the lease, he can transfer his lease to someone else, or he can remain as the tenant and he can grant a lease to someone else.

In the first option, Thomas transfers his lease to Austin. This is called an assignment of the lease. Thomas is the assignor and Austin is the assignee. Austin then becomes the tenant and is subject to the rights and obligations in the lease. Thomas is no longer the tenant. In **Chapter 8** we will consider what liabilities under the lease Thomas may still have and how Austin becomes subject to the lease.

L (landlord/lessor)

↓

T (tenant/lessee now known as the assignor) ➡ A (assignee/new tenant)

Sublease

In the second option, Thomas remains the tenant but grants a sublease to Simon; obviously this cannot be for any longer than remains of Thomas's original three-year term. Thomas's lease is usually then referred to as the head lease and Simon's lease the sublease.

L (landlord/lessor/head landlord)

⬇ (original lease/head lease)

T (tenant/lessee, also Simon's landlord)

⬇ (sublease)

S (subtenant/underlessee)

Note that this chapter uses the terms 'lease' and 'tenancy' interchangeably.

7.1.2 So why use a lease?

Let us look at some examples. Take a commercial lease of a shop: here the tenant may not have the financial resources to buy the freehold of the property, and/or it may be a new venture and the tenant wants to see if it will be successful, or the tenant may need to be flexible so that the business can move to more appropriate property as it grows. The rent payable will be determined by market conditions: what a landlord wants to charge and what a tenant is willing to pay. A typical example of this is a lease of a florist's shop on the high street for a term of three years at an annual rent of £12,000. It is easy to see why a lease is so useful in such circumstances.

Now let us think about a lease granted for a term of 999 years. In reality this is virtually identical to a fee simple, so why would the landlord choose to grant a lease rather than sell the freehold? One important reason is that it is much easier to enforce covenants in a lease. We will consider this later in **Chapter 8**. Perhaps the landlord owns many properties in the area and is keen to retain control over the uses of the properties. Where such a long term is granted, it is a valuable right. It is the right to occupy that property for 999 years. The landlord will charge a premium for the grant of this lease, and this will be determined by the market, ie what a landlord wants to charge and what a tenant is willing to pay for such a right. It may help the student to see this as similar in nature to the sale and purchase of a freehold. However, the lease will also reserve a nominal rent which is payable in addition to the premium. A typical example of this is a lease of a residential apartment for 999 years for a premium of £400,000 with an annual rent of £50.

Perhaps a more difficult example is a house with a lease granted for a term of 99 years. Again there will be a premium and a nominal rent but it is harder to see why a lease would be used. In such a case, perhaps the landlord envisages redeveloping at some distant point in the future or has other neighbouring properties in the area and is keen to have some control over the appearance of the area by imposing covenants, which are easier to enforce in a lease than a freehold.

The final example is likely to be familiar to you. Take a student who is studying at a university for a year; he or she is unlikely to have the desire or financial resources to purchase a property and so will enter into a short-term residential lease. This usually takes the form of an assured shorthold tenancy agreement, which as you will be aware does not entail a premium but regular payments of rent. Such tenancies are beyond the scope of this book

7.2 Essential characteristics of a lease

Street v Mountford [1985] AC 809 is the authoritative case on the essential characteristics of a lease.

Mr Street entered into a written agreement with Mrs Mountford giving her the right to occupy some furnished rooms. The document itself was only short and is set out within Lord Templeman's judgment. It is useful to read it, so it is set out below.

> 'I Mrs. Wendy Mountford agree to take from the owner Roger Street the single furnished room number 5 and 6 at 5 St. Clements Gardens, Boscombe, Bournemouth, commencing 7 March 1983 at a licence fee of £37 per week.
>
> I understand that the right to occupy the above room is conditional on the strict observance of the following rules:
>
> 1. No paraffin stoves, or other than the supplied form of heating, is allowed in the room.
>
> 2. No one but the above-named person may occupy or sleep in the room without prior permission, and this personal licence is not assignable.
>
> 3. The owner (or his agent) has the right at all times to enter the room to inspect its condition, read and collect money from meters, carry out maintenance works, install or replace furniture or for any other reasonable purpose.
>
> 4. All rooms must be kept in a clean and tidy condition.
>
> 5. All damage and breakages must be paid for or replaced at once. An initial deposit equivalent to 2 weeks' licence fee will be refunded on termination of the licence subject to deduction for all damage or other breakages or arrears of licence fee, or retention towards the cost of any necessary possession proceedings.
>
> 6. No nuisance or annoyance to be caused to the other occupiers. In particular, all music played after midnight to be kept low so as not to disturb occupiers of other rooms.
>
> 7. No children or pets allowed under any circumstances whatsoever.

8. Prompt payment of the licence fee must be made every Monday in advance without fail.

9. If the licence fee or any part of it shall be seven days in arrear or if the occupier shall be in breach of any of the other terms of this agreement or if (except by arrangement) the room is left vacant or unoccupied, the owner may re-enter the room and this licence shall then immediately be terminated (without prejudice to all other rights and remedies of the owner).

10. This licence may be terminated by 14 days' written notice given to the occupier at any time by the owner or his agent, or by the same notice by the occupier to the owner or his agent.

Occupier's signature

Owner/agent's signature

Date 7th March 1983

I understand and accept that a licence in the above form does not and is not intended to give me a tenancy protected under the Rent Acts.

Occupier's signature.'

You can clearly see that the agreement refers to itself as a licence, and at the end Mrs Mountford agrees that it is not a tenancy. Mrs Mountford later asserted that this was a tenancy so that she had the benefit of the protection of the Rent Acts. The detail of these Acts are beyond the scope of this book, but it is enough to know that they gave tenants important protection and so it was in an occupier's interest to have a tenancy. A licensee would not have such protection.

In fact Mr Street conceded that Mrs Mountford did have exclusive possession but argued that her occupation was as a licensee, because the intention of the parties was that the rights of occupation were personal, and not as a tenant. In his judgment, Lord Templeman disagreed and explained that both parties were free to negotiate the terms of the contract but that, once agreed, the legal consequences could only be determined by the effect of the agreement. He stated that

> If the agreement satisfied all the requirements of a tenancy, then the agreement produced a tenancy and the parties cannot alter the effect of the agreement by insisting they only created a licence.

He went on to note, famously, that

> the manufacture of a five pronged implement for manual digging results in a fork even if the manufacturer, unfamiliar with the English language, insists he intended to make and has made a spade.

It was an important decision as the Court confirmed that the intention of the parties does not determine the legal nature of the agreement they enter into.

In his judgment, Lord Templeman set out three characteristics of a lease:

- exclusive possession;

- certainty of term; and
- for a rent or other consideration (but see 7.2.3 below).

Section 52 of the LPA 1925 adds a further requirement that the creation of the lease comply with the correct formalities.

7.2.1 What does exclusive possession mean?

Regardless of what is said in *Street v Mountford*, it is too simplistic to look at the basic fact of occupation. It is necessary to look at the terms on which occupation is taken to see whether there is true exclusive possession.

Exclusive possession means that the tenant has control over anyone who enters the premises and can exclude anyone, including the landlord. If someone occupying property does not have exclusive possession, he or she can only claim a licence, which is a mere personal right. A tenancy can bring important protection rights, so there have been many cases considering whether or not occupation amounts to exclusive possession. Let us look at some of these:

Examples where occupation *does not* amount to exclusive possession
- In *Westminster City Council v Clarke* [1992] 2 AC 288, the council ran a hostel for homeless men. The occupants could be moved from one room to another by the council and required to share such rooms. The council also had rules governing the occupation of the rooms, such as a curfew and restrictions on visitors. The court held that there was no exclusive possession.
- *Shell-Mex v Manchester Garages* [1971] 1 WLR 612 concerned the use of a petrol station, but the agreement was called a licence and referred to the landowner's rights of possession and control of the property regarding its layout. The court held that these rights were inconsistent with a tenancy, and the agreement was indeed a licence.
- *Marcou v De Silvesa* (1986) 52 P&CR 2 and *Huwyler v Ruddy* (1995) 28 HLR 550 both concerned the provision of services, such as cleaning. Even though those services could be minimal, or in fact no longer provided, it was the landlord's ability to enter the property at any time that prevented the occupier enjoying exclusive possession. Contrast this with *Vandersteen v Agius* (below).
- *Lugana v Service Hotels* [1969] 2 Ch 209 and *Brillouet v Landless* (1996) 28 HLR 836 concerned occupation of a furnished room and a hotel room. The court held that exclusive occupation, such as of a furnished room, did not amount to exclusive possession. Nor did the occupation of a hotel room. This is an important point to note – that exclusive occupation is not the same as exclusive possession.
- In *Street v Mountford* a clear distinction was drawn between a tenant and a lodger. A lodger is a person who receives services or attendance from the landlord, and therefore the landlord has to retain possession to supply these services or attendance. The landlord has unrestricted access and can enter the

property at will. Accordingly, a lodger cannot have exclusive possession and so cannot have a tenancy.

- *AG Securities v Vaughan* [1990] 1 AC 417 was heard with the case of *Antoniades v Villiers*, which is discussed below. In the *AG Securities* case, four people entered into four separate agreements made on different dates to occupy a room each in a four-bedroom flat, in common with the other three who were granted a similar right. The agreements were for the same length of time but the rent was for different amounts. The court held that each occupant was a licensee rather than a tenant. Its reasoning was that the four agreements were independent of the other. One occupant would have signed without another signing, and the agreement granted a right to share the flat with others without exclusive possession. Contrast this with *Antoniades v Villiers* (below).

Examples where occupation *does* amount to exclusive possession

- *Aslan v Murphy* [1990] 1 WLR 766 concerned an occupant who exclusively occupied a basement flat. The written agreement stated that he was not granted exclusive possession but had a licence to use the room in common with other licensees, and that he had to vacate the room for 90 minutes each day. The owner also retained a key to the flat. The court held that although the agreement was not a pretence or a sham, regard had to be had to the true bargain made between the parties. This was that the occupant was entitled to exclusive possession and this was what he had been granted. The requirement to share the room was a pretence. Lord Donaldson noted that the owner retaining a key to the property did not prevent the agreement being a lease, but that it would depend on the reason for the key being retained.

- *Antoniades v Villiers* [1990] 1 AC 417 concerned a man and his girlfriend whom the landlord knew were living together as such. Each entered into a separate agreement but at the same time. It allowed them to occupy a one-bedroom flat but stated that the agreement was a licence and did not confer exclusive possession. In fact the agreement stated that their occupation was subject to the landlord's ability to allow others to use the flat. The court held that the agreements were interdependent and should be read together as a single agreement; one would not have entered into their agreement without the other. The reservation by the landlord to allow others to occupy the flat was a pretence to avoid protection offered to a tenancy, and the intention had been to grant them exclusive possession.

- *Vandersteen v Agius* (1992) 65 P&CR 266 dealt with an agreement which reserved a right for the landlord to enter the property for occasional inspections and to perform agreed cleaning services, which were at an additional separate cost to the tenant. The court held that this was a tenancy with exclusive possession, as the right of entry reserved was inconsistent with a landlord being able to enter the property at will, and the cleaning services were outside the landlord and tenant relationship in this case. Contrast this with *Marcou v De Silvesa* and *Huwyler v Ruddy* above.

Exclusive possession but not a tenancy

It is important to note, though, that exclusive possession does not automatically mean that the occupation is a tenancy. In his judgment in *Street v Mountford*, Lord Templeman laid out situations where a person can have exclusive possession but only a licence, not a lease. Think about examples of where this could be the case and then consider the situations below:

- *No intention to create a legal relationship*. In *Heslop v Burns* [1974] 1 WLR 1241, feeling sympathy for a couple, a property owner allowed them to live in one of his properties. The court held that there had never been any intention that the owner was excluding himself from his own property, and only a licence had ever been granted.

- *An act of kindness*. In *Marcroft Wagons Ltd v Smith* [1951] 2 KB 496 the mother, who was the tenant, died and the landlord allowed her daughter to remain living at the property for six months, accepting rent from her but refusing to accept her as the tenant. The court held that there was no intention to create a tenancy; it was kindness on the part of the landlord.

- *A service occupancy*. This was referred to in *Street v Mountford* and has been affirmed by cases such as *Norris v Checksfield* [1991] 1 WLR 1241, where the court held that an employee's right to exclusive possession did not necessarily create a tenancy if the employee was genuinely required to occupy the property for the better performance of his duties.

A non-proprietary lease

In *Bruton v London & Quadrant Housing Trust* [2000] 1 AC 406, the Court dealt with an unusual situation. The case caused controversy in the world of land lawyers when it was decided, so it needs short mention here. The facts were that the housing trust was granted a licence, not a lease, by the local authority. The local authority did not actually have the power to grant a lease. The trust in turn granted licences to homeless people. That licence stated that the trust held the property on licence from the local authority and, in turn, granted a weekly licence to Mr Bruton. Mr Bruton argued that as he had been granted a term, enjoyed exclusive possession and was paying a weekly fee, he had actually been granted a lease. The court agreed with him and held that, despite the housing trust having no legal estate from which to grant a lease, nevertheless it had indeed done just that.

It has been acknowledged that this lease cannot bind a third party so it is an unusual lease, often called a non-proprietary lease, but there are still obligations and duties that can be enforced between the parties as they are in a landlord and tenant relationship.

7.2.2 What is certainty of term?

Both the commencement (the start) of the term of the lease and the duration (the length) of the term of the lease must be clear. If they are not the lease will be void.

The maximum duration of the term must be certain at the date of commencement. The case of *Lace v Chantler* [1944] KB 368, CA famously held that a lease 'for the duration of the war' was void as no one had any idea when the war would end.

This was the clear common law position but *Ashburn Anstalt v Arnold* [1989] Ch 1 started a departure from this. In this case the court held that a lease which would end when the tenant gave a quarter's notice to the landlord was sufficiently certain because it was certain how the lease could be ended. This case was criticised as it could not be predicted when the lease would end as it was unknown when the tenant would give notice.

Prudential Assurance Co Ltd v London Residuary Body [1992] 2 AC 386 halted this line of thinking and overruled the case. Lord Templeman stated that a landlord and a tenant cannot create an uncertain term. Although in agreement, the House of Lords noted that following this rule in this particular case had produced an unsatisfactory result for the parties to the case. Nevertheless, it was held that one of the essential characteristics of a lease remained certainty of duration.

This was again tested in the case of *Mexfield Housing Co-operative Ltd v Berrisford* [2011] UKSC 52. In this case Mrs Berrisford was granted a monthly tenancy of her property, which she could determine by giving one month's notice. The landlord could only terminate the tenancy on certain grounds, such as failure to pay rent. Clearly this was not a certain term. The Supreme Court, however, managed to protect Mrs Berrisford by using an old common law rule that a lease with a rent or premium being paid with an uncertain term is converted into a lease for life. The court then relied on s 149(6) of the LPA 1925, which applies only to individuals (not companies), where a lease for life takes effect as a lease for 90 years. Therefore Mrs Berrisford had a lease for 90 years which could only be determined by notice from Mrs Berrisford or on one of the given grounds, which in this case had not occurred. This came as a surprise to the landlord!

7.2.3 For a rent or other consideration?

Although *Street v Mountford* seemed to state that rent was an essential characteristic of a lease, it is now agreed that this is not the case. The case of *Ashburn Anstalt v Arnold* held that Lord Templeman had not laid down a principle of 'no rent, no lease', as that was contrary to s 205 of the LPA 1925 which defines a term of years as 'whether or not at a rent', and that it was also inconsistent with the case of *Radaich v Smith* (1959) 101 CLR 209 which he expressly approved. Therefore rent is not necessary for the creation of a tenancy.

It is important to note, though, that in order for a written agreement to be enforceable, it must have been granted for some consideration. A deed does not require this. In reality most leases will be granted for some consideration, and remember that consideration does not have to be monetary.

7.3 Formalities

There are three kinds of formalities for a lease, which we will look at in turn:

- legal leases arising by express grant;
- legal leases arising by operation of law; and
- equitable leases arising by virtue of a contract or an informal grant.

7.3.1 Express grant

The grant of a lease for a fixed term of more than three years must be by deed (LPA 1925, s 52(1)). Remember that this means that the document should be clear on its face that it is intended to be a deed, is validly executed as a deed and is delivered as a deed under s 1 of the Law of Property (Miscellaneous Provisions) Act (LPMPA) 1989. There is a further hurdle for a lease to become legal if the term is for more than seven years as, under s 4 or s 27 of the LRA 2002, it must be registered to be recognised at law.

This is straightforward but consider s 52(2)(d) of the LPA 1925, which provides that a lease does not have to be by deed if it is not required by law to be in writing. Now look at s 54(2) of the LPA 1925, which states:

> (2) Nothing in the foregoing provisions of this Part of this Act shall affect the creation by parol of leases taking effect in possession for a term not exceeding three years (whether or not the lessee is given power to extend the term) at the best rent which can be reasonably obtained without taking a fine.

This means that a lease for a term not exceeding three years may be created in writing (not by deed) or by an oral agreement.

There are certain requirements that must *all* be satisfied though under s 54(2):

(a) The lease must take effect in possession, so the lease must begin at the date of the grant and not at a date in the future.
(b) The lease must be for a term not exceeding three years.
(c) The lease must be at the best rent which can reasonably be obtained without taking a fine or premium. This raises a question as to what is the best rent? The case of *Fitzkriston LLP v Panayi* [2008] EWCA Civ 283 held that the best rent is the market rent.

7.3.2 By operation of law

Periodic tenancies arise by operation of law. We will consider how they are formed and how the period is calculated at **7.5.2** below.

7.3.3 Equitable leases

Let us first remind ourselves of s 2 of the LPMPA 1989:

2   Contracts for sale etc of land to be made by signed writing

(1) A contract for the sale or other disposition of an interest in land can only be made in writing and only by incorporating all the terms which the parties have expressly agreed in one document or, where contracts are exchanged, in each.

(2) The terms may be incorporated in a document either by being set out in it or by reference to some other document.

(3) The document incorporating the terms or, where contracts are exchanged, one of the documents incorporating them (but not necessarily the same one) must be signed by or on behalf of each party to the contract.

So a contract for the sale of land or other disposition must therefore be in writing, incorporate all the terms and be signed by or on behalf of each party. This is important in the creation of equitable leases.

7.3.3.1   How are equitable leases created?

There are two ways.

Contract to create a lease

Let us imagine that Rory wants to take a lease from Sabeena, but he wants Sabeena to carry out some works to the property before he takes the lease. Sabeena is happy to do this as she is keen for Rory to become the tenant. Sabeena is going to expend money on these works, so she wants to be sure that Rory will enter into the lease once she has done so. The usual way to give her this security is for them to enter into what is called an agreement for lease. This is a document where the parties agree to enter into the lease once conditions are satisfied or on a certain date. It is a contractual agreement, and the form of lease is usually attached to that agreement so that there is no later argument as to its form. This is a contract for the creation of an interest in land and should comply with s 2 of the LPMPA 1989.

A contract relating to land is long established as one where equity will grant the remedy of specific performance. As we have seen, land is seen as unique, and equity views this as the appropriate remedy. Therefore if the contract to grant the lease/agreement for lease is not carried out, the court will order it to be completed. It is often said that a contract to create a lease is as good as a lease. From the discussions above, you should be able to identify that a contract to create a lease can be turned into an equitable lease, but we will consider below if an equitable lease is as good as a legal lease.

The creation of an equitable lease in this way was famously considered in the case of *Walsh v Lonsdale* (1882) 21 Ch D 9. Here a landlord and a tenant had entered into a contract for a lease of a mill for seven years, and the tenant had been allowed to take possession following the contract but before the actual lease had been completed. The parties then omitted to complete the formal deed needed to create the legal lease. In the contract, the rent clause stated that, under the lease, the rent was to be payable in advance at the start of each year. The landlord claimed the rent in advance, but the tenant claimed that there was no legal lease as there was no deed, so rent could be payable in arrears.

The court held that the landlord could claim the rent in advance as the contract had created an equitable lease. This was enforceable between the parties and the terms would follow those in the contract. The court used the equitable principle, 'equity looks on that as done which ought to be done', and so held that equity would treat the situation as if there were a lease in existence. This would be an equitable lease.

A lease in writing but not made by deed

As you will recall, a legal lease must be made by deed. However, if a lease is not made by deed but does comply with the requirements of s 2 of the LPMPA 1989, then rather than a legal lease it will be an equitable lease.

7.3.3.2 Is an equitable lease as good as a legal lease?

There are important differences. First, remember that the parties are dependent on the availability of specific performance. Equitable remedies are discretionary, and remember the maxim that you must come to equity with clean hands. The court will only grant the remedy if you are free of improper conduct.

A legal lease will simply bind third parties but this is not the case with an equitable lease. Whether the equitable lease will bind a third party will depend on whether or not the lease has been registered, in the case of unregistered land as a Class C(iv) land charge estate contract, or in registered land on the charges register. In registered land it may also take effect as an overriding interest but only if the tenant is in actual occupation.

7.4 Why do we need to distinguish between a lease and a licence?

Leases are an estate or interest in land. They are freely alienable, so can be given away, sold or left by will. A licence on the other hand is a personal right to the licensee and cannot be assigned.

Leases are proprietary property rights, so in principle they bind third party purchasers of the landlord's reversion. Licences generally do not bind purchasers of the land over which the licence is exercisable other than in exceptional circumstances.

Leases are generally subject to legislation protecting tenants' rights, such as the Rent Acts and the Landlord and Tenant Act 1954. This protection can be extremely valuable to the tenant. Licences are usually outside the scope of such legislation.

It has been famously said that a lease gives a stake in the land whereas, from *Errington v Errington* [1952] 1 KB 290, a licence is a 'personal privilege'.

7.5 Types of lease

There are two main types of lease: fixed-term leases and periodic tenancies.

7.5.1 Fixed-term leases

This is quite straightforward and is the standard form of tenancy. As the name suggests, it is a lease where the exact duration is fixed at the beginning of the lease and can be for any period, as long as it is certain.

7.5.2 Periodic tenancies

A periodic tenancy can continue indefinitely and can run from, say, week to week, month to month, or quarter to quarter. It will end when the appropriate length of notice has been given by one party to the other. The length of the tenancy is determined according to the basis on which the rent is calculated. For example, if the rent is payable weekly, it will be a weekly periodic tenancy. If the rent is referred to as £1,200 per annum, payable by 12 equal monthly payments of £100, then it will be a yearly periodic tenancy.

At first it is difficult to see how this does not infringe the rule that the term of the lease must be certain. How does one know at the start of a periodic tenancy when it will end? This was considered in the case of *Prudential Assurance Co Ltd v London Residuary Body* [1992] 2 AC 386, where the court favoured the explanation of a periodic tenancy as a lease for one period which goes on renewing itself automatically.

The notice period to end such a tenancy is usually one full period expiring at the end of a completed period, but the parties can agree a shorter time. The exception is for yearly tenancies when, unless the parties agree otherwise, the notice period is six months expiring at the end of a completed period (ie a year).

You should also be aware of two further types of tenancy.

7.5.3 Tenancies at will and tenancies at sufferance

A tenancy at will is created by the will of the parties and can be terminated by either party without prior notice. The party simply terminates the tenancy by withdrawing his or her will. It will also terminate when either party assigns or dies. Such tenancies are uncertain and offer no protection or certainty to tenants who could be required to vacate the property at any time. An example of when they are used is when a landlord allows a tenant into occupation of the property before the formal lease has been granted. This is not common though, and, in such a situation, there is always the danger that if the tenant then starts to pay rent on a regular basis, the tenancy at will becomes a periodic tenancy. This possibility has been limited by the case of *Javad v Aquil* [1991] 1 All ER 243, where it was held that the tenant had not acquired a periodic tenancy as the lease negotiations had been continuing.

A tenancy at sufferance arises when the tenant's lease has expired, and he or she does not vacate the property but unlawfully remains in occupation of the property without the landlord's express agreement or disagreement. Again if the tenant starts paying rent on a regular basis, this occupation will be converted into a periodic tenancy.

A landlord would usually be advised to avoid both such situations, as if the occupancy becomes a periodic tenancy, various statutes such as the Housing Acts, the Rent Acts and the Landlord and Tenant Act 1954, Part II will then provide that tenancy with forms of statutory protection regarding ending the lease, which may prevent the landlord from dealing with the property as he or she wishes.

Specific residential tenancies created under the Rent Acts or Housing Acts and the treatment of business tenancies under the Landlord and Tenant Act 1954, Part II are outside the scope of this book.

7.6 Further reading

P Williams, 'Exclusively yours – a look back at Street v Mountford' (2014) 18(3) Landlord & Tenant Review 92–95.

I Williams, 'The certainty of term requirement in leases: nothing lasts forever' (2015) 74(3) Cambridge Law Journal 592–609.

P Clark, 'Licence to lease?' (2015) 6 Conveyancer and Property Lawyer 474–79.

M Pawlowski, 'Short leases and section 54(2) – time for a rethink?' (2016) 20(3) Landlord & Tenant Review 81–83.

M Walsh, 'An English (leasehold) reformation?' (2015) Estates Gazette 1511, 108.

M Pawlowski, 'Joint owners, severance and the family home' (2016) 46 Family Law 1238–41.

summary

A lease can be used for a variety of reasons. A lease allows a landlord a great deal of control over the property. The freehold is usually owned by the landlord as an investment. A tenant often takes a lease as he or she does not want to purchase the freehold him- or herself.

They key case is *Street v Mountford* [1985] AC 809. Following this, there are two essential characteristics of a lease: exclusive possession and certainly of term. Remember that s 52 of the LPA 1925 requires the correct formalities.

A lease is a proprietary interest in land. It is one of the legal estates created by s 1 of the LPA 1925. In principle it will bind third parties. It is alienable. A licence is a personal right and is not alienable.

There are two main types of lease: fixed-term leases and periodic tenancies.

Pam owns Silverbrook House. It is a five-storey block of flats with one flat on each floor. The following events take place.

Pam agrees that John can use Flat 1 until she finds a more suitable tenant. He pays an initial lump sum of £600 but then after a few months starts paying £200 to Pam each month. This has been going on for several months now.

Pam and Enid (a hairdresser) signed a written document allowing Enid to use Flat 2 for a term of 12 years.

Flat 3 is occupied by Rob and Constance. It is a small one-bedroom flat. They all signed a document called 'Licence of Flat 3' which set out the term, the rent and also provided that Pam could introduce other occupiers into the flat at any time.

During a telephone conversation between Pam and Aftab, Pam agreed that Aftab could occupy Flat 4 for a term of two years at an annual rent of £2,400. Aftab moved in on the same day.

Earlier this year, Pam and Hilda signed a contract for a lease of Flat 5 for a term of six years at an annual rent of £2,500. The contract stated that the lease would be in a form which was agreed by the parties and attached to the contact. This lease stated that Hilda would repair the wooden window frames and that Pam would repair the external door of the flat. Unfortunately Pam then went on holiday and the parties never actually completed the lease.

1 Explain the nature of the occupation of each flat. Give statutory or case authority for your answers where appropriate.

2 Can Hilda enforce the repairing covenant against Pam? What does she need to demonstrate herself?

Privity of Contract and Privity of Estate, Enforceability of Covenants and the Landlord and Tenant (Covenants) Act 1995

After reading this chapter, you will be able to:

- understand the concept of privity of contract and privity of estate
- understand enforceability of covenants
- understand and apply the effect of the Landlord and Tenant (Covenants) Act 1995.

8.1 Privity of contract and privity of estate

Let us return to our example of Lorelei, the landlord, granting a lease to Thomas, the tenant.

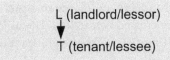

L (landlord/lessor)

T (tenant/lessee)

The lease is a contractual agreement between them, so they have privity of contract and all the covenants in the lease will be enforceable between them. They both signed the lease and agreed to be bound by the covenants in it.

They also have privity of estate as they are in a direct landlord and tenant relationship. If Thomas breaches one of the covenants in the lease, Lorelei will simply sue him for breach of contract. She also has remedies through the privity of estate relationship but usually does not need to rely on these. Similarly, Thomas can sue Lorelei if she breaches her covenants under the lease.

As you are aware, subject to the terms of the lease, a tenant can assign the lease to an assignee. So now let us return to the situation where Thomas assigns the lease to Austin.

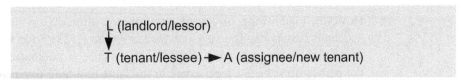

L (landlord/lessor)

T (tenant/lessee) ➤ A (assignee/new tenant)

If you assign a lease, how will the assignee be bound by the covenants? There is no privity of contract as Lorelei did not enter into the lease with Austin. Austin has taken a transfer of the existing lease which was originally granted by Lorelei to Thomas. Clearly, Lorelei as the landlord needs to be able to enforce the covenants in the lease against Austin. Subject to rules we will consider below, she is able to do this because they have privity of estate.

Privity of estate governs the relationship between a current landlord and a current tenant. Can you can see that privity of estate is a means by which covenants in a lease may be enforced between individuals who do not have a direct contractual relationship? The phrase 'privity of estate' recognises the existence of a relationship between the landlord and the tenant which, though not contractual, nevertheless creates obligations arising from the tenure that has been granted. In theory this means that Lorelei can take action against Austin if he breaches the covenants in the lease.

Whilst it is often a tenant who breaches a covenant in the lease, as we will consider later in this chapter, leases also contain covenants by landlords.

8.2 Enforceability of covenants

1 January 1996 is a date to commit to memory when considering leases, as it marks a dramatic change in the enforceability of covenants in leases. This is the date that the Landlord and Tenant (Covenants) Act (LTCA) 1995 came into force. Lawyers refer to leases created before that date as 'old leases' and leases granted after that date as 'new leases'. It makes a significant difference whether a lease is an old lease or a new one.

Let us consider the position pre-1996 first.

8.2.1 Old leases – granted before 1 January 1996

Where the landlord and tenant have entered into a lease for a term of years, the tenant is liable to perform the covenants in that lease for the entire term. This applies even if the tenant has assigned the lease. This may appear a harsh rule, but remember that the tenant agreed to this when he signed the lease, and the lease is a contractual agreement.

But what is the position of the assignee if the tenant assigns the lease? Although the landlord can sue the tenant for breach of contract, what relationship do the landlord and the assignee have? You will have realised that, as they are in a landlord and tenant relationship, they have privity of estate.

However, establishing privity of estate is not sufficient on its own to enforce leasehold covenants. The very old *Spencer's Case* (1583) 5 Co Rep 16a provided that, for the leasehold covenant to bind an assignee or purchaser of the reversion, the parties must have a legal estate in the land, and only covenants which touch and concern the land will be binding. So provided these two conditions are met, the covenants in the lease, positive or restrictive, will bind an assignee or purchaser of the reversion. This is crucial in privity of estate and effectively makes leasehold workable, even though, as you should realise, it is completely against contractual principles by binding persons who were not parties to the original lease.

Let us look at each element in turn:

8.2.1.1 Legal lease

This is straightforward and means that an equitable lease would not satisfy this condition.

8.2.1.2 Touch and concern the land

This is a difficult test to clearly define, but in practice the courts have not found it hard to determine which covenants do and do not touch and concern the land.

Examples of covenants that *do* touch and concern the land
- Tenant covenants to pay rent, to repair the property or not to assign or sublet without the landlord's consent.
- Landlord covenants, such as to repair or insure the property, to give quiet possession or not to develop adjoining land.

Examples of covenants that *do not* touch and concern the land
- Tenant covenants to perform a personal service to the landlord.
- Landlord covenants to pay for chattels which were not fixtures at the end of the lease.

As we have seen, covenants that are personal to the parties will not satisfy the test of touching and concerning the land.

8.2.1.3 Old leases – example

Let us return to our practical examples:

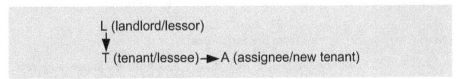

If Austin breaches a covenant in the lease, provided he took a legal lease and the covenant touches and concerns the land, Lorelei can take action against Austin even though he was not an original party to the lease. This is due to privity of estate, as Lorelei and Austin are in a direct landlord and tenant relationship. Remember that this is an old lease and Lorelei could also sue Thomas for this breach, even though the breach was committed by Austin.

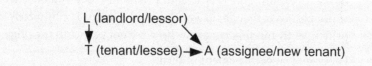

Indemnity from assignee to assignor

It is worth noting here that both common law (*Moule v Garrett* (1871–72) LR 7 Ex 101) and statute (Law of Property Act (LPA) 1925, s 77(1)) imply an indemnity to Thomas from Austin. This means that effectively Austin gives a promise to Thomas that he will observe and perform the covenants in the lease, and if he breaches them he will indemnify Thomas against any costs Thomas incurs as a result of this breach. So if Thomas paid money to Lorelei in respect of the breach, he could recover this money from Austin. This was meant to provide some protection to Thomas so that if Lorelei sued him for Austin's breach after he assigned the lease, he could seek redress from Austin. The problem with this should be clear. If Lorelei is bringing an action against Thomas, it is likely to be because it is not worth her bringing one against Austin. If Austin has no assets, his indemnity to Thomas is worthless.

8.2.2 New leases – granted on or after 1 January 1996

The LTCA 1995 applies to any lease, legal or equitable, created on or after 1 January 1996:

> 5   **Tenant released from covenants on assignment of tenancy**
>
> (1)   This section applies where a tenant assigns premises demised to him under a tenancy.
>
> (2)   If the tenant assigns the whole of the premises demised to him, he—
>
>> (a)   is released from the tenant covenants of the tenancy, and
>>
>> (b)   ceases to be entitled to the benefit of the landlord covenants of the tenancy,
>
> as from the assignment.

You should realise that this is a complete change and reverses the previous position. Now, once a tenant assigns a lease, he or she is no longer bound by the tenant covenants in the lease. Looking again at our example:

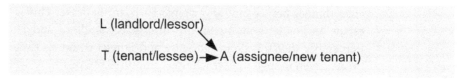

There is now no relationship between Lorelei and Thomas. This is despite their contractual agreement as the Act removed this privity of contract after the assignment.

8.2.2.1 Section 3 attaches the benefit and burden of covenants to the property

Let us look at the first three subsections of s 3 in turn (emphasis added):

> 3 **Transmission of benefit and burden of covenants**
>
> (1) The *benefit and burden of all landlord and tenant covenants* of a tenancy—
>
>   (a) shall be *annexed* and incident *to the* whole, and to each and every part, of the *premises* demised by the tenancy and of the reversion in them, and
>
>   (b) shall in accordance with this section *pass on an assignment* of the whole or any part of those premises *or of the reversion* in them.

The test of whether the covenant touches and concerns the land is no longer applicable, as s 3 clearly states that the benefit and burden of the covenant is annexed to the land.

> (2) Where the assignment is by the tenant under the tenancy, then as from the assignment the *assignee*—
>
>   (a) *becomes bound by the tenant covenants* of the tenancy except to the extent that—
>
>   (i) immediately before the assignment they did not bind the assignor, or
>
>   (ii) they fall to be complied with in relation to any demised premises not comprised in the assignment; and
>
>   (b) becomes entitled to the benefit of the landlord covenants of the tenancy except to the extent that they fall to be complied with in relation to any such premises.

So now if Austin breaches the lease, Lorelei can only sue Austin; she cannot bring an action against Thomas as he is no longer liable under the tenant covenants. Note, though, that s 3(6) states that this does not apply to personal covenants, but, other than this, the covenants in the lease will no longer bind Thomas but become attached to the property.

> (3) Where the assignment is by the landlord under the tenancy, then as from the assignment the *assignee*—
>
>   (a) *becomes bound by the landlord covenants* of the tenancy except to the extent that—
>
>   (i) immediately before the assignment they did not bind the assignor, or
>
>   (ii) they fall to be complied with in relation to any demised premises not comprised in the assignment; and
>
>   (b) becomes entitled to the benefit of the tenant covenants of the tenancy except to the extent that they fall to be complied with in relation to any such premises.

This similarly applies to a landlord who transfers the reversion; the new landlord is bound by the covenants in the lease. See **8.3.3** below for whether the original landlord is still bound.

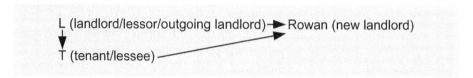

If Rowan breaches one of the landlord covenants then Thomas can bring an action against him, and, as the new owner of the reversion, Rowan will be bound by those covenants.

From these examples you should have realised that both landlords and tenants can transfer their interests. The lease can be assigned by the tenant, and the reversion subject to the lease can be sold by the landlord.

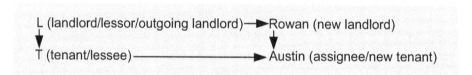

Now we have a situation where both the original landlord and the original tenant have transferred their interests. If Austin or Rowan breaches a term of the lease, one may bring an action against the other. Thomas is now out of the picture in terms of liability for breach of covenant, and Lorelei can apply to become so too, as we will consider at **8.3.3** below.

8.2.2.2 Excluded assignments

Section 11 provides that assignments referred to in the LTCA 1995 as excluded assignments do not release the tenant from liability. Examples of such assignments are where the tenant assigns the lease in breach of a clause within the lease, or where the tenant dies. Similarly, where the landlord carries out such an excluded assignment, for example the reversion being vested in his personal representative on his or her death, there will be no release. In such case, the tenant or the landlord, as the case may be, remains liable on his or her covenants until the next assignment. This follows the principle of the length of the liability under an authorised guarantee agreement (see **8.3.1**).

8.3 Some comfort for landlords

This change in liability brought great concern to landlords. Imagine a situation where Thomas no longer wants his lease. Under the LTCA 1995, he could assign the lease to Austin, knowing that Austin does not have the money to meet the rent payments and that he will default on these. When he does, and the landlord brings an action against Austin, Austin will be unable to pay. The landlord may then decide to end the lease due to this breach. The landlord will have no right to take any action against Thomas. Can you see how unscrupulous tenants could use this method as a way of getting out of a lease?

8.3.1 Authorised guarantee agreements (AGAs)

Section 16 of the LTCA 1995 sought to bring comfort to landlords. It provided that where a landlord had to consent to an assignment, a landlord could require an assignor to guarantee his or her immediate assignee. As this guarantee was permitted by the Act, it was termed an 'authorised guarantee agreement' or AGA.

Section 16 provides as follows:

16 **Tenant guaranteeing performance of covenant by assignee**

(1) Where on an assignment a tenant is to any extent released from a tenant covenant of a tenancy by virtue of this Act ('the relevant covenant'), nothing in this Act (and in particular section 25) shall preclude him from entering into an authorised guarantee agreement with respect to the performance of that covenant by the assignee.

(2) For the purposes of this section an agreement is an authorised guarantee agreement if—

(a) under it the tenant guarantees the performance of the relevant covenant to any extent by the assignee; and

(b) it is entered into in the circumstances set out in subsection (3); and

(c) its provisions conform with subsections (4) and (5).

(3) Those circumstances are as follows—

(a) by virtue of a covenant against assignment (whether absolute or qualified) the assignment cannot be effected without the consent of the landlord under the tenancy or some other person;

(b) any such consent is given subject to a condition (lawfully imposed) that the tenant is to enter into an agreement guaranteeing the performance of the covenant by the assignee; and

(c) the agreement is entered into by the tenant in pursuance of that condition.

(4) An agreement is not an authorised guarantee agreement to the extent that it purports—

(a) to impose on the tenant any requirement to guarantee in any way the performance of the relevant covenant by any person other than the assignee; or

(b) to impose on the tenant any liability, restriction or other requirement (of whatever nature) in relation to any time after the assignee is released from that covenant by virtue of this Act.

(5) Subject to subsection (4), an authorised guarantee agreement may—

(a) impose on the tenant any liability as sole or principal debtor in respect of any obligation owed by the assignee under the relevant covenant;

(b) impose on the tenant liabilities as guarantor in respect of the assignee's performance of that covenant which are no more onerous than those to which he would be subject in the event of his being liable as sole or principal debtor in respect of any obligation owed by the assignee under that covenant;

(c) require the tenant, in the event of the tenancy assigned by him being disclaimed, to enter into a new tenancy of the premises comprised in the assignment—

   (i) whose term expires not later than the term of the tenancy assigned by the tenant, and

   (ii) whose tenant covenants are no more onerous than those of that tenancy;

(d) make provision incidental or supplementary to any provision made by virtue of any of paragraphs (a) to (c).

Let us apply this ability to require an AGA.

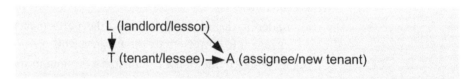

If the lease between Lorelei and Thomas requires Lorelei to consent to an assignment, she can require Thomas to guarantee that Austin will observe and perform the covenants in the lease. Thomas will give an AGA. If Austin does breach a covenant, Lorelei can bring an action against Austin or against Thomas under his AGA. You should be able to see that this is, in fact, a similar position to that existing before the LTCA 1995.

However, see how it changes when Austin himself assigns the lease to Helen.

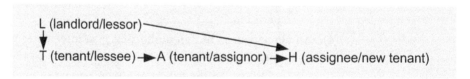

As we know, the lease requires Lorelei's consent to an assignment, so she can require Austin to guarantee Helen. At this point Thomas's liability ends. If Helen fails to perform the covenants, Lorelei can bring an action against Helen or Austin (under his AGA) but not against Thomas. Remember that the LTCA 1995 can only require a tenant to guarantee his or her *immediate* assignee.

8.3.2 How do existing guarantors and an AGA sit together?

In *Good Harvest Partnership LLP v Centaur Services Ltd* [2010] EWHC 330 (Ch), the court had to consider whether the guarantor for an assigning tenant could be required to directly guarantee the assignee, or whether such a requirement fell foul of s 25 of the LTCA 1995, which provides that an agreement is void if it restricts the operation of the Act. The court held that the guarantor could not be required to guarantee the assignee, but the assignor could be required to enter into an AGA and the guarantor would still be required to guarantee the assignor's performance under that. This has been referred to as a guarantee of an authorised guarantee agreement, a GAGA!

This decision was approved in the case of *K/S Victoria Street v House of Fraser (Stores Management) Ltd* [2011] EWCA Civ 904 which considered the effect of s 24(2), which effectively releases a guarantor from ongoing liability when the tenant it is guaranteeing lawfully assigns the lease. Lord Neuberger stated that there

> appears to be nothing inconsistent with section 24(2) if the assignor's guarantor is required to guarantee the assignor's liability under the AGA: the guarantor is released to precisely the same extent as the assigning tenant.

In the discussions above, we have identified the logic in this. If the landlord required a guarantor for the tenant in the first place, it stands to reason that the landlord will want that guarantee to continue when the tenant still has potential liability under an AGA.

8.3.3 Is a landlord bound after transferring the reversion?

You may find it strange to know that the answer to this is yes, but the LTCA 1995 provides a procedure for a landlord to be released from liability. Section 6 allows a landlord to apply to the tenant to be released from the landlord covenants. Section 8 sets out the procedure by which the landlord can serve a notice on the tenant before or up to four weeks after the transfer of the reversion. If the tenant does not object within four weeks, or makes an objection to the court and the court declares the release to be reasonable, the landlord is released from his or her covenants.

8.4 Subleases

Finally we should also consider subleases here. You will remember this scenario from **Chapter 7**:

L (landlord/lessor)

⬇ (original lease/head lease)

T (tenant/lessee/also S's landlord)

⬇ (sublease)

S (subtenant/underlessee)

Hopefully you will now see that there is privity of contract between the landlord, Lorelei, and the tenant, Thomas, but not between the Lorelei and the subtenant, Simon. Simon will have privity of contract with Thomas, who granted him the sublease.

If Simon commits an act which is in breach of the lease between Lorelei and Thomas, in an old lease Lorelei would bring action against Thomas. For this reason, the sublease provisions usually referred to or mirrored the ones in the head lease. In a new lease, s 3(5) of the LTCA 1995 provides that the landlord can take direct action against the subtenant as the occupier of the land for a breach of a sublease covenant. Accordingly Lorelei could deal directly with Simon.

8.5 Further reading

P Walter, 'The Landlord and Tenant (Covenants) Act 1995: a legislative folly' [1996] Conveyancer and Property Lawyer 432–40.

P Clark, '20 years on – the 1995 Act' (2015) 3 Conveyancer and Property Lawyer 191–98.

M Pawlowski, 'Law reform - a plea for implementation' (2012) 16(2) Landlord & Tenant Review 47–49.

R Crozier and I Dulmeer, 'Guarantor lease assignments – staring into the void?' (2017) 21(2) Landlord & Tenant Review 54–57.

Privity of contract is the contractual relationship between the original landlord and the original tenant. Both parties can rely on their contractual rights against each other. Privity of estate is the relationship between the current landlord and the current tenant. This allows parties who did not contract directly with each other to enforce covenants against each other.

For leases granted before the LTCA 1995 came into force on 1 January 1996, the original tenant was liable for the covenants in the lease for the entire term, even if he or she assigned the lease.

For leases granted after the LTCA 1995 came into force on 1 January 1996, the tenant is only liable whilst he or she is actually the tenant. If the tenant lawfully assigns the lease, he or she is no longer liable. However, the Act allows a landlord to require the outgoing tenant to enter into an authorised guarantee agreement, which means that the tenant effectively guarantees his or her immediate assignee. This will last only until the assignee assigns the lease.

Let us again use the scenario where Pam owns Silverbrook House. It is a five-storey block of flats with one flat on each floor, but we will only consider Flat 2 here. The following events take place:

Pam and Enid (a hairdresser) enter a lease of Flat 2 for a term of 12 years. Enid agreed to redecorate the interior of the flat every three years and to cut Pam's hair every month. Last month, in accordance with the terms of the lease, Enid assigned the lease to Janet. Janet is refusing to redecorate the interior of the flat and to cut Pam's hair.

1 Is Janet obliged to comply with both the covenants? Give an answer for leases beginning both before and after 1 January 1996.

2 If Enid assigned the lease after 1 January 1996, what document is Pam likely to have required her to enter into? Why? How would your answer differ if the lease had been granted and assigned before 1 January 1996?

3 Imagine that James acted as a guarantor for Enid. Could Pam require him to guarantee Janet? Refer to appropriate legislation and cases in your answer.

4 If Pam sold the building tomorrow, what should she do to ensure she is not still bound by any covenants?

Lease Clauses, Breaches and Ending a Lease

After reading this chapter, you will be able to:

- understand the main clauses of a lease
- identify and apply remedies for breach of a leasehold covenant
- explain how a lease can be ended.

9.1   Lease structure and clauses

Now let us consider the form of a lease and some typical clauses that a lease will contain. Although there is brief mention of residential leases in places, this section primarily concentrates on commercial leases.

in practice

The Code for Leasing Business Premises in England and Wales 2007 refers to itself as 'the result of collaboration between commercial property professionals and industry bodies representing both owners (Landlords) and occupiers (Tenants)'. It states that it 'aims to promote fairness in commercial leases, and recognises a need to increase awareness of property issues, especially among small businesses, ensuring that occupiers of business premises have the information necessary to negotiate the best deal available to them'.

You should appreciate that the Code is voluntary, and many landlords will not desire to enter into leases complying with the Code, but it can be used as a negotiating tool when the lease itself is being negotiated.

Remember that the lease is a contract between the landlord and the tenant. When the lease is granted, it is in a form that has been negotiated between and agreed by the landlord and the tenant. The lease will contain various clauses, and most commercial leases created today are long documents. The form of the lease can vary from landlord to landlord, but ultimately most leases will contain the main clauses referred to in this chapter.

As long as you understand the clause itself, it does not matter in what order the clauses are arranged in the lease, but a typical lease might follow the order below:

Table 9.1   Clauses in a typical lease

Clause	Explanation
Parties	Details of the landlord, the tenant and any guarantor.
Parcels	Describes the extent of the property and reserves rights to the landlord and grants rights to the tenant.
Demise	The actual grant of the lease.
Term	The length of the lease.
Rent	Payments from the tenant to the landlord for the use of the property.
Rent review	The ability to change the rent at certain points in the lease.
Tenant's covenants	Covenants by the tenant. These will usually be extensive and can form the main part of the lease.
Landlord's covenants	Covenants by the landlord. These will usually be much shorter than the tenant covenants.
Provisos	Provisions the lease is made subject to, for example the landlord's right to take the lease back if the tenant breaches a covenant.
Schedules	These often contain a detailed description of the property, rights granted to the tenant and rights reserved to the landlord.
	They may also include the form of an authorised guarantee agreement (see **8.3.1**).

Let us consider these clauses in more detail.

9.1.1 Parties

This should be a straightforward start, with the clause giving the details of both the landlord and the tenant. In practice, a landlord will want to ensure that the tenant has what is called a good strength of covenant. This means that it will be able to pay the rent and observe and perform the covenants under the lease.

in practice

A newly formed company, for example, may not be able to evidence strength of covenant, so the landlord may decide to insist that the tenant provide a guarantor. The guarantor will then guarantee the tenant's obligations under the lease, so that if the tenant defaults, the landlord can seek redress from the guarantor. An alternative to a guarantor is a rent deposit deed, which you may be familiar with in the context of a student tenancy, where the landlord requires a rent deposit or a bond to hold in case of damage to the property.

9.1.2 Parcels

This clause describes the extent of the property being let to the tenant. The lease may refer to a separate definition in a schedule, but the lease must contain a full description of the property. For instance, does it include the walls, the foundations or the roof? It is also very important to have a plan if it is a lease of part of a building.

The landlord's fixtures are usually included in the property so fall within the definition of the property. The tenant's fixtures are not included so the lease must reflect that. This is important as the definition of the property will link into the repairing obligations, which we will consider at 9.1.7.1.

Rights granted and reserved

Such rights may be set out in a separate schedule but will be referred to under this head. Examples of rights the landlord may grant to the tenant are a right of way over part of the landlord's retained property, or free passage of services through the landlord's retained property for the benefit of the property.

Examples of rights the landlord may reserve are rights of way over a rear yard, a right of entry to inspect the state of repair of the property, or free passage of services through the property for the benefit of the landlord's retained property.

9.1.3 Demise

This is the actual grant of the lease where the landlord creates the legal estate and gives the tenant the right of exclusive possession.

9.1.4 Term

Most leases granted in such a form will have a specified duration. The term of the lease will be stated and the date this term will commence is also stated. Remember that this is an essential characteristic of a lease.

9.1.5 Rent

As you will also recall from *Ashburn Anstalt v Arnold* [1989] Ch 1, rent is not an essential requirement for a lease, but most landlords will require that the rent is expressly reserved. The rent must be certain. The exact figure does not have to be stated in the lease provided the means by which it is calculated is clear, for example the rent could relate to the turnover of a business.

9.1.6 Rent review

This allows the landlord to ensure that the rent continues to be at the market rent for that property during the term. The rent is usually reviewed every three or five years, but the frequency will be specified in lease. There are different types of rent review clauses, such as fixed increases, increases linked to the retail prices index, and increases on the basis of the open market value of the property during the term of the lease. Open market rent review is the most common review in commercial leases and aims to ensure that the rent payable reflects the rent payable for such a property in the market at the time of the review. The complexities of rent review are outside the scope of this book, and you should refer to a detailed landlord and tenant text for a full commentary on this.

9.1.7 Tenant's covenants

9.1.7.1 Repair

Responsibility for repair is the most common source of dispute between the landlord and the tenant. Some repairing obligations are implied by statute but they are of little practical importance; therefore it is important that the parties' repairing obligations are set out in detail as covenants in the lease. It is normal to expect the tenant to covenant to repair the property, which is why it is so important to clearly define the extent of the property so that the tenant knows exactly what it is obliged to repair and can ensure that it is happy with this obligation. In residential leases, implied covenants, either by common law or statute, regarding repair are imposed on the landlord. There are no such statutory implied obligations in commercial leases.

Commercial leases usually place the burden of repair of the property on the tenant. This raises the question of how far does that burden extend. In *Proudfoot v Hart* (1890) 25 QBD 42, Lopes LJ considered the meaning of 'good tenantable repair' and held that the tenant's obligation was to put and keep the property in 'such repair as, having regard to the age, character, and locality of the house, would make it reasonably fit for the occupation of a reasonably-minded tenant of the class who would be likely to take it'. It is important to note the word 'keep', as this was held to mean that the tenant has to *put* the property into repair (crucially this applies even if the property was in disrepair at the start of the lease) and then keep the property free of disrepair (see *Payne v Haine* (1847) 16 M&W 541).

In order for a landlord to require a tenant to carry out repair works, the landlord must show that the property condition has deteriorated (*Post Office v Aquarius Properties Limited* [1987] 1 All ER 1055). A distinction has been drawn between repairing the property and improving it (see *Morcom v Campbell-Johnson* [1955] 3 All ER 264).

A tenant should carefully consider the repairing covenant that it is entering into.

9.1.7.2 Alienation

This means the tenant dealing with the lease, for example assigning it, granting an underlease or sharing possession. Unless the lease contains some restriction, the tenant is free to deal with its leasehold interest in any way it wishes. A landlord is likely to want to have control over the tenant's dealings; remember that the landlord is keen to protect its investment.

Types of covenant

The lease may contain an *absolute* covenant prohibiting the tenant from any form of alienation. This does not stop the tenant from asking the landlord for consent to deal with the property, but it does mean that the landlord can act unreasonably in making its decision.

However, it is more likely that the landlord will want to allow some forms of alienation but will want to have some control over the tenant's dealings. As we have identified, this is because the landlord's interest in the property is valued on the strength of the tenant's covenants, in particular the payment of rent. If the tenant has good financial standing then that will maintain the value of the landlord's interest. If the tenant assigns the lease to an assignee with less financial standing, the value of the landlord's interest is likely to reduce.

The lease is likely to contain a *qualified covenant* so that the tenant cannot deal with the property without the landlord's consent. In reality there is no check on the landlord here either, as under the lease the landlord does not have to act reasonably in giving or refusing permission, so this is little better than an absolute covenant. Fortunately, in several important circumstances, statute has intervened (as we will see below).

In most leases, it is often stated that the landlord cannot unreasonably withhold consent, and this is called a *fully qualified covenant*.

In the case of dealings with the property, s 19(1)(a) of the Landlord and Tenant Act 1927 is very helpful to the tenant (emphasis added):

19   **Provisions as to covenants not to assign, etc without licence or consent**

(1)   In *all leases* whether made before or after the commencement of this Act *containing a covenant condition or agreement against assigning, underletting, charging or parting with the possession of demised premises or any part thereof without licence or consent,* such covenant condition or

agreement shall, notwithstanding any express provision to the contrary, be deemed to be subject—

(a) to a proviso to the effect that *such licence or consent is not to be unreasonably withheld*, but this proviso does not preclude the right of the landlord to require payment of a reasonable sum in respect of any legal or other expenses incurred in connection with such licence or consent; …

So the effect of this section is that, in the case of such dealings, a qualified covenant will automatically be turned into a fully qualified covenant. This gives more protection to the tenant. Remember that it has no effect on an absolute covenant though. We will look at s 19(1)(a) in more detail below.

There is further protection for the tenant in s 1(3) of the Landlord and Tenant Act 1988:

(3) Where there is served on the person who may consent to a proposed transaction a written application by the tenant for consent to the transaction, he owes a duty to the tenant within a reasonable time—

(a) to give consent, except in a case where it is reasonable not to give consent,

(b) to serve on the tenant written notice of his decision whether or not to give consent specifying in addition—

(i) if the consent is given subject to conditions, the conditions,

(ii) if the consent is withheld, the reasons for withholding it.

This strengthens the position of the tenant seeking consent to assign or sublet the lease as it provides that, where the lease contains a fully qualified covenant against alienation (be it expressly or by statute), when the tenant makes an application for consent, the landlord has a duty within a reasonable time to give consent unless reasonable not to and to serve a written decision notice on the tenant. It is interesting to note that, under s 1(4), giving consent subject to an unreasonable condition does not satisfy this duty.

The burden on proving reasonableness is on the landlord. If the landlord breaches this statutory duty, the tenant can bring an action in tort against the landlord for damages pursuant to s 4. In *Design Progression Ltd v Thurloe Properties Ltd* [2004] EWHC 324 (Ch), the court not only ordered damages as compensation but also as a punitive measure in light of the landlord's conduct where it had sought personally to benefit from the situation.

In the case of *No 1 West India Quay (Residential) Ltd v East Tower Apartments Ltd* [2016] EWHC 502 (Ch), the tenant sought declarations that the landlord had unreasonably withheld consent and delayed consent to assign. As part of considering the application, the landlord had required the tenant to comply with certain conditions, including paying the landlord's costs of dealing with the applications. These costs were £1,250 for each of the three applications. The court held that this condition was unreasonable in light of the work involved by the landlord in considering the applications. Other conditions, such as requiring bank references for the assignees and inspection for breach of covenants, were reasonable. It is also an important to note though that, as the tenant had not served the application for consent correctly in accordance with the lease provisions, the delay claimed by the tenant did not fall within the protection given by the Act.

What is a reasonable time?

The Act does not specify this, so it has been up to the courts to determine it. In *Norwich Union Life Insurance Society v Shopmoor Ltd* [1999] 1 WLR 531, the judge said that a landlord should deal with the application 'expeditiously' and 'at the earliest sensible moment'.

In *Go West Ltd v Spigarolo and Another* [2003] EWCA Civ 17, Munby J stated that reasonable time 'will sometimes have to be measured in weeks rather than days; but even in complicated cases, it should in my view be measured in weeks rather than months'.

Contrast this with the case of *E.ON UK Plc v Gilesports Ltd* [2012] EWHC 2172 (Ch), which held that that 11 days was not an unreasonable time.

in practice

The lesson for landlords here is to carefully consider the financial consequences of delaying/refusing consent unreasonably, and to operate procedures to ensure applications are dealt with quickly and in accordance with the Act.

So when can the landlord refuse consent?

Remember that s 19(1)(a) of the Landlord and Tenant Act 1927 converts a qualified covenant into a fully qualified covenant so that the landlord cannot unreasonably withhold consent to a dealing with the property. The question is what is unreasonable?

The Act does not say, and again it is for the court to decide. A landlord could insert a clause into the lease stating that it will not withhold consent to assignment or subletting to a respectable and responsible person. In such a case, the landlord cannot then refuse on other grounds if the assignee is indeed a responsible and respectable person.

The case of *International Drilling Fluids Ltd v Louisville Investments (Uxbridge) Ltd* [1986] Ch 513 laid down guidelines on the issue of landlord reasonableness, which are set out below, but these were further considered and generally approved in the case of *Ashworth Frazer Ltd v Gloucester City Council* [2001] UKHL 59, where the court held that principles 2, 3 and 6 should be overriding (emphasis added):

(1) The purpose of a qualified covenant is to protect a landlord from having its premises used/occupied in an undesirable way or by an undesirable tenant.

(2) *The landlord cannot refuse consent to an assignment on grounds unrelated to the landlord and tenant relationship in regard to the subject matter of the lease.*

(3) *The landlord does not have to prove that the conclusions which led it to refuse consent were justified if the same would have been reached by a reasonable man in such circumstances.*

(4) The landlord may reasonably refuse consent on the grounds of the assignee's purpose even if that is not prohibited by the lease.

(5) Whilst the landlord need only usually consider its own relevant interests, there may be cases where there is such disproportion between the benefit to the landlord and the detriment to the tenant that withholding consent is unreasonable.

(6) *Subject to the above conditions, whether or not the consent is being unreasonably withheld by the landlord is a question of fact in each case depending on the circumstances of the matter. The onus of showing that the landlord acted reasonably is on the shoulders of the landlord.*

Section 19(1A) of the Landlord and Tenant Act 1927

This subsection was inserted by the Landlord and Tenant (Covenants) Act 1995. It only applies to:

- qualified covenants relating to assignments; and
- leases granted on or after 1 January 1996.

19 Provisions as to covenants not to assign, etc without licence or consent

(1A) Where the landlord and the tenant under a qualifying lease have entered into an agreement specifying for the purposes of this subsection—

(a) any *circumstances* in which the landlord may withhold his licence or consent to an assignment of the demised premises or any part of them, or

(b) any *conditions* subject to which any such licence or consent may be granted,

then the landlord—

(i) *shall not be regarded as unreasonably withholding his licence or consent* to any such assignment if he withholds it on the ground (and it is the case) that any such circumstances exist, and

(ii) if he gives any such licence or consent subject to any such conditions, shall not be regarded as giving it subject to unreasonable conditions;

and section 1 of the Landlord and Tenant Act 1988 (qualified duty to consent to assignment etc) shall have effect subject to the provisions of this subsection.

(1B) Subsection (1A) of this section applies to such an agreement as is mentioned in that subsection—

(a)   whether it is contained in the lease or not, and

(b)   whether it is made at the time when the lease is granted or at any other time falling before the application for the landlord's licence or consent is made.

(1C) Subsection (1A) shall not, however, apply to any such agreement to the extent that any circumstances or conditions specified in it are framed by reference to any matter falling to be determined by the landlord or by any other person for the purposes of the agreement, unless under the terms of the agreement—

(a)   that person's power to determine that matter is required to be exercised reasonably, or

(b)   the tenant is given an unrestricted right to have any such determination reviewed by a person independent of both landlord and tenant whose identity is ascertainable by reference to the agreement,

and in the latter case the agreement provides for the determination made by any such independent person on the review to be conclusive as to the matter in question.

Section 19(1A) allows the landlord to stipulate, in the lease, conditions which need to be satisfied or circumstances which must exist before the landlord will give consent to the assignment (see emphasis added).

Accordingly, if the landlord withholds consent on one or more of those conditions or circumstances stated in the lease, the landlord will be deemed not to be withholding consent unreasonably (see emphasis added).

If the landlord withholds on other grounds then s 19(1)(a) will apply. As we have seen, the effect of s 19(1A) is to reduce the protection given by s 19(1)(a).

Conditions and circumstances

It is up to the parties to decide what conditions and circumstances are inserted into the lease during the lease negotiation process, but s 19(1C) anticipated:

(a)   those that can be factually or objectively verified, for example an assignee has to have a certain level of pre-tax profits or has to provide guarantors, or, most commonly, the assignor has to enter into an authorised guarantee agreement (see **8.3.1**), although remember the limitations on what an existing guarantor can be asked to guarantee (see **8.3.2**);

(b)   those where a judgement has to be made as to whether or not they have been satisfied. To be a valid condition or circumstance, if the landlord is to make the determination, the landlord must agree to make a reasonable determination. Alternatively an independent third party can make the determination. For example, the assignee has to be of no less financial standing than the assignor.

What can a tenant do if it believes that consent is being unreasonably withheld?

The tenant could assign the lease in the belief that the landlord is unreasonably withholding consent. In such a case, the tenant would not be breaching the covenant. This can be a dangerous course of action, though, as if it is then held that the landlord was acting reasonably, the tenant will have breached the alienation covenant, and the remedies discussed below, such as forfeiture, will be available to the landlord.

If the tenant assigns in breach of the covenant, the assignment will be an excluded one under s 11 of the Landlord and Tenant (Covenants) Act 1995 (see **8.2.2.2**). Therefore the tenant is not released from the tenant covenants in the lease and remains liable.

The tenant could seek a court declaration that consent is being withheld unreasonably. This is a safer course of action, but it brings with it the inevitable cost and time issues which may effectively end the proposed assignment.

Licence to assign

The landlord's consent is usually given in a document called a licence, which will expressly permit the dealing.

in practice

As you may now appreciate, applications for consent to dealings with the property are an area of common dispute between a landlord and a tenant. In an attempt to help the process, a group of property professionals have produced a Protocol for Applications for Consent to Assign or Sublet, which is available at <www.propertyprotocols.co.uk>. It will be interesting to see how widely it is adopted and used in practice in the coming years.

9.1.7.3 User

The landlord will want to protect its investment, maintain rental values, avoid damaging the reputation of the property and any adjoining property and ensure, if the landlord has a development, that it keeps a good tenant mix. Therefore a landlord needs control over the tenant's use of the property.

The lease is likely to provide for a permitted use. This can be widely drafted, for example permitting the property to be used as a shop or offices, or by reference to a use class from the Town and Country Planning (Use Classes) Order 1987 (as amended), or more narrowly, for example, permitting the property to be used only as a shoe shop.

Just as we considered in connection with alienation, there can be an absolute covenant so that the tenant cannot change the use at all, a qualified covenant so that the tenant cannot change the use without the landlord's consent, or a fully qualified covenant so that the tenant cannot change the use without the landlord's consent but the landlord's consent cannot be unreasonably withheld.

9.1.8 Landlord's covenants

9.1.8.1 Quiet enjoyment

Most leases contain a covenant for quiet enjoyment but, if not, one is implied (see *Budd-Scott v Daniell* [1902] 2 KB). This means that if the tenant pays the rent and performs all the covenants in the lease, the tenant can physically enjoy the benefit of the property without the landlord or anyone claiming under it adversely affecting that enjoyment.

An example of this is illustrated by the case of *Timothy Taylor Ltd v Mayfair House Corp* [2016] EWHC 1075 (Ch). Here, the tenant was a high-class art gallery which leased a ground-floor property from the landlord. The landlord planned to carry out works to the upper floors of the building, and showed the tenant a sketch of how the scaffolding could be erected to leave the gallery front open and visible. In fact the scaffolding was erected in such a way as to encase the gallery, so that it appeared to be part of the building site. In addition, a hoist used to lift materials from the ground floor to the upper floors was located in front of the entrance to the gallery, and the front was often obstructed by delivery lorries for the building works. The tenant also complained of high noise levels. The court held that even though the landlord had reserved a right to carry out these works in the lease, the landlord had not taken reasonable steps to minimise disturbance to the tenant or liaised with the tenant as to the effect of the works and whether they could be mitigated. The covenant for quiet enjoyment had been breached and the court awarded damages.

9.1.8.2 Non-derogation from grant

This goes hand in hand with the landlord's covenant for quiet enjoyment and effectively means that the landlord cannot give with one hand and take away with the other. If not contained in an express covenant, it will be implied into the lease.

The classic case of *Harmer v Jumbil (Nigeria) Tin Areas Ltd* [1921] 1 Ch 200 dealt with this issue. Here the tenant leased land to store explosives in accordance with an appropriate licence which the landlord was aware of. The landlord later let the adjoining site to a mineral extraction company which erected buildings on that site in contravention of the explosives licence. The court held that the lease implied an obligation on the landlord not to do anything to violate that licence, and therefore there had been a derogation from grant. The court granted an injunction to prevent the building and the works on the adjoining land continuing.

9.1.8.3 Repair

In a commercial lease, this is only likely to be present where there is a lease of part of a building and the landlord will carry out repairs to the structure and the exterior of the building the property forms part of. The tenant will usually be responsible for the repair of the interior and non-structural part of the property. In reality, the landlord will effectively pass the cost of these repairs on to the tenant through a service charge provided for in the lease.

In short-term residential leases, there are statutorily implied terms on the landlord as to repairing obligations (deriving from Landlord and Tenant Act 1985) but the detail of these is beyond the scope of this book.

9.1.9 Provisos

These are conditions which affect the existence of the lease. Probably the most important one is forfeiture.

9.1.9.1 Forfeiture

Forfeiture is the right of the landlord to re-enter the property and end the lease following a breach of a tenant's covenant. This is an important right for a landlord to be able to exercise, and, if the right of re-entry is expressly reserved in the lease, it is a legal interest under s 1(2)(e) of the Law of Property Act 1925. Much more unusually, it is also automatically available where the lease has been drafted so that there is a condition that the term will only continue if the tenant observes its obligations (see *Doe d Henniker v Watt* (1828) 8 B&C 308). This is largely an academic point as leases are usually drafted to include an express re-entry clause.

Interestingly though, in an equitable lease, this right is implied as an equitable right of re-entry.

Although a breach of a tenant's covenant can trigger the exercise of this right, it is up to the landlord whether to waive the breach and allow the lease to continue, or to re-enter the property and forfeit the lease.

What is waiving the breach of covenant?

The landlord can waive the breach by knowing about it but still allowing the lease to continue and recognising its existence to the tenant. The case of *Van Haarlam v Kasner* (1992) 64 P&CR 214 held that the landlord had waived the right to forfeit the lease when he continued to demand and accept rent when he was aware of the tenant's arrest and subsequent conviction for breaching the Official Secrets Act, the actions of which were a breach of the tenant's covenants not to use the property for an illegal use.

Forfeiture for non-payment of rent

The landlord must make a formal demand, but this is usually dealt with by the lease stating that the rent does not need to be formally demanded by the landlord.

How does the landlord re-enter the property and forfeit the lease?

There are two methods of re-entering the property:

(a) peaceable re-entry (*Aglionby v Cohen* [1955] 1 QB 558). This is a difficult option as the landlord must be convinced that the tenant has left or will freely leave the property. It is a minefield for landlords to ensure that they are not falling foul of various statutes regarding re-entry, and most landlords will avoid using this method. This method is not allowed in residential property leases without a possession order pursuant to the Protection from Eviction Act 1977, and residential landlords trying to peaceably re-enter may face criminal prosecution (Criminal Law Act 1977, s 6); and

(b) applying for a court order. Generally landlords will use this option.

Relief from forfeiture for non-payment of rent

You should also be aware that forfeiture is not necessarily the end of the lease. The tenant can apply to the court for relief from forfeiture. If the court grants this, the lease will continue. Lord Mansfield, in the old case of *Goodright d. Walter v Davids* (1778) 98 ER 1371, stated that 'Cases of forfeiture are not favoured in law …', and this can still be seen today.

Relief from forfeiture claims should only be brought in the High Court in exceptional circumstances.

High Court

If the landlord forfeits by peaceable re-entry, the tenant can apply to the court for relief but it is not granted automatically. The tenant will need to pay the rent arrears and the landlord's costs of the forfeiture. This should usually be made within six months. In the case of *Pineport v Grangeglen* [2016] EWHC 1318 (Ch), though, the court held that, in light of the circumstances, a period of 14 months before the tenant applied for relief was acceptable.

If the landlord forfeits by court action, under s 38 of the Senior Courts Act 1981 the High Court has the power to grant relief and, where a tenant pays the arrears and landlord's costs, will usually grant relief.

Sections 210 and 212 of the Common Law Procedure Act 1852 provide that where there are six or more months of arrears, if the tenant pays the arrears and costs within six months of the forfeiture the court can grant relief. After this six-month period has elapsed, the tenant is 'barred and foreclosed from relief or remedy in law or equity' pursuant to s 210.

If there are less than six months of arrears then the time limit to apply for relief is not applicable, and the tenant can apply for relief at any time, although the court tends to use the six months rule from the Common Law Procedure Act 1852 as a guide for considering applications.

County Court

If the landlord forfeits by peaceable re-entry, the tenant can apply to the court for relief within six months of the forfeiture.

Under s 138(2) of the County Courts Act 1984, the tenant has an automatic right to relief from forfeiture if the tenant pays the arrears and the landlord's costs of the forfeiture five clear days before the hearing.

Under s 138(3) of the County Courts Act 1984, if the tenant fails to do this and the court is satisfied to make an order of possession in favour of the landlord, the effect of this order is suspended for at least four weeks and, again, if the tenant pays these sums before the order becomes effective, relief from forfeiture is automatically granted.

Under s 138(9A) of the County Courts Act 1984, even where the landlord has been granted the order and retaken possession, the tenant has a right to apply for relief within six months.

Forfeiture for other breaches of covenant

Before the landlord can forfeit the lease for a breach other than non-payment of rent, the landlord must serve a notice under s 146 of the Law of Property Act 1925, so you will see why this is known as a section 146 notice. If the landlord does not serve such a notice, the action then taken will be unenforceable.

The section 146 notice must state:

- the breach;
- if it is capable of being remedied, the remedy that must be carried out within a reasonable time; and
- if the landlord so requires, that compensation is payable by the tenant.

There is wide case law on whether a breach is remediable, but mostly breaches should be remediable. In the case of *Akici v LR Butlin Ltd* [2006] 1 WLR 201, Lord Neuberger stated his view that

> it seems to me that the proper approach to the question of whether or not a breach is capable of remedy should be practical rather than technical. … In principle I would have thought that the great majority of breaches of covenant should be capable of remedy …

In the case of *Savva v Hussein* (1997) 73 P&CR 150, the court held that a negative covenant not to erect signs which had been breached was capable of remedy. The courts have consistently held, however, that a breach of a covenant not to assign the property is incapable of remedy. In *Scala House & District Property Co v Forbes* [1974] QB 575, the lease contained a covenant not to assign or sublet without the landlord's consent. A tenant subsequently sublet without this required consent, and the Court held that the breach was by its nature incapable of remedy. In his judgment James LJ stated:

The breach of this class of covenant is a once-and-for-all breach; whatever events follow the breach they cannot wipe the slate clean, the breach remains. I conclude that a breach of this covenant is incapable of remedy ...

If the tenant fails to comply with the notice, the landlord may then forfeit the lease in the same way as for non-payment of rent: by peaceable re-entry or applying for a court order.

Relief from forfeiture for other breaches of covenant

As with forfeiture for non-payment of rent, forfeiture for other breaches of covenant is not necessarily the end of the lease.

Section 146(2) of the Law of Property Act 1925 sets out the court's discretion to grant relief:

> **146 Restrictions on and relief against forfeiture of leases and underleases**
>
> (2) Where a lessor is proceeding, by action or otherwise, to enforce such a right of re-entry or forfeiture, the lessee may, in the lessor's action, if any, or in any action brought by himself, apply to the court for relief; and the court may grant or refuse relief, as the court, having regard to the proceedings and conduct of the parties under the foregoing provisions of this section, and to all the other circumstances, thinks fit; and in case of relief may grant it on such terms, if any, as to costs, expenses, damages, compensation, penalty, or otherwise, including the granting of an injunction to restrain any like breach in the future, as the court, in the circumstances of each case, thinks fit.

If the breach has been remedied, and taking into account the circumstances of the case, the courts generally try to grant relief (see *Cremin v Barjack Properties Ltd* [1985] 1 EGLR 30) and have resisted setting anything other than broad principles on the exercise of their discretion to grant relief. The cases of *Magnic Ltd v Ul-Hassan* [2015] EWCA Civ 224 and *Freifield v West Kensington Court Ltd* [2015] EWCA Civ 806 discussed factors the court may consider when hearing an application for relief.

However, there are differences in when the tenant can apply for relief for breaches of other covenants.

If the landlord is granted a court order, the tenant can only apply for relief up to the time when the landlord re-enters the property (see *Packwood Transport Ltd v Beauchamp Place Limited* (1977) 3 P&CR 112). Therefore the tenant cannot apply for relief after the landlord has re-entered (see *Billson v Residential Apartments Ltd* [1992] AC 623).

If the landlord re-enters peaceably, the tenant can seek relief after this (again see *Billson v Residential Apartments Ltd*) but the court will consider the tenant's delay in making the relief application.

What is the effect of forfeiture on a sublease?

Under common law, for example the judgment in *Great Western Railway Company v Smith* [1875] G 64, if the landlord forfeits the head lease, the sublease will automatically end. Clearly this is potentially unfair on the subtenant, so s 146(4) of the Law of Property Act 1925 allows the court discretion to grant relief to a subtenant. If granted, the sublease will continue, with the landlord and the subtenant now in a direct relationship. The subtenant should be wary as to whether it will then be liable to remedy the original breach.

in practice

Generally forfeiture is only used in commercial leases. If is often a last resort for the landlord; as we have seen, this is because it ends the lease. Whether a landlord will want to do this will depend on the market conditions. If the property can easily be let to another tenant, a landlord may wish to forfeit and carefully select a new tenant, knowing that it will be able to observe and perform the covenants under the lease. If the market conditions are slow and re-letting the property will be difficult, the landlord may be reluctant to end the lease and have an empty property. Remember that a property is an investment for a landlord; the landlord wants it to give a good return.

Forfeiture of residential tenancies

Forfeiture of residential tenancies is governed by various statutes, such as the Rent Act 1977 and the Housing Acts 1985 and 1988 – which one is applicable will depend on the type of residential tenancy. Detail of this is beyond the scope of this book.

Reform?

The Law Commission's consultation paper, *Termination of Tenancies for Tenant Default* (Law Com CP No 174, 2004), which led to the Law Commission's report of the same name (Law Com No 303, 2006), stated 'that the law of forfeiture is complex, it lacks coherence, and it can lead to injustice'. The report proposed that the law of forfeiture should be abolished and replaced by a new statutory scheme. As part of the report, it sets out a draft bill covering matters such as a new concept of 'tenant default', setting out the circumstances a landlord can terminate a tenancy, requiring the landlord to give a written warning to the tenant, and inserting a statutory right of re-entry. You will appreciate that this was some time ago, and no further action has yet been taken to address these issues.

9.1.10 Schedules

These are usually quite straightforward and may contain a full description of the property – remember how important this is as it will relate to the tenant's repairing obligations. Rights granted to the tenant and reserved to the landlord may also be set out in a schedule. Another common schedule is one setting out the form the authorised guarantee agreement (or AGA) will take if the lease is assigned. There is then no argument as to the clauses/contents of the AGA when the assignor is asked to enter into it on an assignment.

9.2 Remedies for breach of covenant

9.2.1 Breach of tenant covenants

The first point for a landlord to consider is who to act against. Although the tenant is in breach, there may be a guarantor or former tenant acting as a guarantor under an authorised guarantee agreement, or the original tenant under an old lease could also be liable. The landlord may also be holding a rent deposit deed that monies could be withdrawn from. Let us consider different types of breach.

9.2.1.1 Breach of covenant to pay rent

Section 19 of the Limitation Act 1980 provides that no action may be brought after six years from the date on which the arrears became due.

To recover rent arrears, the landlord may:

(a) bring a court action;

(b) commence insolvency proceedings against the tenant (bankruptcy for an individual and liquidation for a company) in the hope that this urges the tenant into paying. There is a commercial risk with this though as, if the tenant then becomes insolvent/bankrupt, the landlord will rank as an unsecured creditor and face the likely possibility of not recovering all the money owed by the tenant;

(c) use the Commercial Rent Arrears Recovery (CRAR) procedure, contained in Part 3 of the Tribunals, Courts and Enforcement Act 2007. This is a complex process which replaced the ancient remedy of distress, where a landlord could seize the tenant's goods and sell them to recover monies owed. CRAR sets out a strict procedure which must be followed to enable the landlord to sell the tenant's goods in order to recover rent owed. It uses a very narrow definition of rent and, for example, will not allow the recovery of a service charge or repair costs. Arguably the procedure reduces the benefit of this method for a landlord;

(d) serve notice on a subtenant to pay rent directly to the head landlord. Again this strategy has been weakened by the Tribunals, Courts and Enforcement Act 2007, as s 81 provides that 14 clear days must expire before the payments need to be made. It also uses the very narrow definition of rent. The danger is that in such time the subtenant will have already paid the tenant, and the landlord will have to wait until the next rent payment is due for it to be paid to the landlord, rather than the tenant; or

(e) forfeit the lease (see **9.1.9.1**).

Finally you should note that for all leases (ie old or new leases), before being able to proceed against a former tenant or a guarantor of a former tenant, the landlord must serve on it a default notice pursuant to s 17 of the Landlord and Tenant (Covenants) Act 1995. If the former tenant/guarantor of the former tenant makes this payment then s 19 allows it to call for what is known as an overriding lease. If an assignor gives an authorised guarantee agreement (AGA), it can also call for an overriding lease. An overriding lease will effectively slot in between the landlord and the tenant (see below) and give the payee some control over the situation, as it can take steps to end the newly formed sublease.

L

⬇

Payee (former tenant/guarantor of former tenant/assignee under AGA)

⬇

Subtenant (defaulting tenant)

9.2.1.2 Breach of repairing covenant

Damages

The landlord could claim damages. The maximum amount claimed cannot exceed the amount by which the value of the reversion has been diminished owing to the breach (Landlord and Tenant 1927, s 18). However, if the lease was granted for a term of seven years or more and has at least three years of the term remaining, there is a further hurdle for the landlord in order to be able to sue for damages or forfeit the lease. Section 1 of the Leasehold Property (Repairs) Act 1938 provides (emphasis added):

1 **Restriction on enforcement of repairing covenants in long leases of small houses**

   (1) *Where a lessor serves on a lessee* under subsection (1) of section one hundred and forty-six of the Law of Property Act, 1925, *a notice that relates to a breach of a covenant or agreement to keep or put in repair* during the currency of the lease all or any of the property comprised in the lease, *and at the date of the service of the notice three years or more of the term of the lease remain unexpired, the lessee may within twenty-eight days from that date serve on the lessor a counter-notice to the effect that he claims the benefit of this Act.*

   ...

   (3) Where a counter-notice is served by a lessee under this section, then, notwithstanding anything in any enactment or rule of law, no proceedings, by action or otherwise, shall be taken by the lessor for the enforcement of any right of re-entry or forfeiture under any proviso or stipulation in the lease for breach of the covenant or agreement in

question, or for damages for breach thereof, otherwise than with the leave of the court.

This provides that the landlord must serve the section 146 notice, but it must also contain a statement informing the tenant that it has a right to serve a counter-notice within 28 days claiming the benefit of the Act. If the tenant does so, the landlord cannot proceed with the damages claim or forfeiture without leave of the court. To obtain this leave, under s 1(5) the landlord must prove:

(a) that the immediate remedying of the breach is needed to prevent substantial diminution in the value of the reversion, or that has already happened;

(b) that the immediate remedying of the breach is needed to comply with any act or bylaw, etc;

(c) where the tenant does not occupy the whole property, that immediate remedying of the breach is needed for the interests of the other occupiers;

(d) that the breach can be immediately remedied at a smaller expense than the expense that would be involved if the work was postponed; or

(e) special circumstances which, in the opinion of the court, render it just and equitable to grant leave.

Section 1(6) allows the court to impose terms and conditions on either party as it sees fit.

Self-help

The landlord could use the remedy of self-help if it is expressly reserved in the lease, as it usually is. This allows the landlord to enter the property, carry out the necessary repairs and then charge that cost to the tenant. This sum is then seen as a debt due to the landlord. The advantage of this method is that the sum is simply seen as a debt and is not caught by the restrictions on the level of damages or the need to serve a section 146 notice. This type of action was upheld by the important case of *Jervis v Harris* [1996] Ch 195 which gives its name to such a clause.

Specific performance

The landlord could apply for an order of specific performance. The case of *Rainbow Estates Ltd v Tokenhold Ltd* [1999] Ch 64 held that specific performance could be used to enforce a tenant's repairing covenant where damages were not an adequate remedy. It did note, though, that the other remedies available to landlords meant that it would rarely be an appropriate remedy unless there were unusual circumstances warranting it, as was the case here.

Forfeiture of the lease (see 9.1.9.1)

9.2.1.3 Breaches of other covenants

The remedies above are open to the landlord for other breaches, so the landlord could:

(a) claim damages. The aim of such damages is to put the landlord in the position it would have been but for the breach, assessed on a contractual basis and usually the amount by which the reversion has reduced in value. You may be aware of the rule from *Hadley v Baxendale* (1854) 9 Exch 341 that 'damages recoverable for a breach of contract should be such as might fairly and reasonably be considered as arising naturally from the breach or might reasonably be supposed to have been in the contemplation of the parties at the time the contract was made';

(b) obtain an injunction in some circumstances. Clearly this is a discretionary equitable remedy and will either be an injunction prohibiting the breach of a covenant or a mandatory injunction requiring the tenant to perform a covenant;

(c) apply for an order of specific performance, although not for a covenant requiring the tenant to keep open a retail property; see *Co-operative Insurance Society Ltd v Argyll Stores (Holdings) Ltd* [1998] AC 1, HL, where the Court refused to order a supermarket to comply with a covenant in its lease obliging it to keep open and trade; or

(d) forfeit the lease (see **9.1.9.1**).

9.2.2 Breach of landlord covenants

If the landlord is in breach of an express covenant contained in the lease, the tenant's usual remedy is to claim damages. Damages will be assessed on the difference between the tenant's interest in the property with the covenant performed and the interest in the property with the covenant not performed (see *Calabar Properties Ltd v Stitcher* [1984] 1 WLR 287). The option of pursing specific performance or an injunction is also available to the tenant (see below).

9.2.2.1 Examples of specific breaches and their remedy

If the landlord breaches the covenant of *quiet enjoyment*, the tenant's remedy is to claim damages, as in *Timothy Taylor Ltd v Mayfair House Corp* [2016] EWHC 1075 (Ch), or apply for an injunction.

If the landlord breaches the covenant of *non-derogation from grant*, the tenant's remedy is to claim damages or apply for an injunction, as in *Harmer v Jumbil (Nigeria) Tin Areas Ltd* [1921] 1 Ch 200.

There are various remedies available to a tenant for a breach of the landlord's *repairing obligation*:

(a) The tenant may claim damages, but it may be that damages are not an appropriate remedy so the option of pursing specific performance (see *Joyce v Liverpool City Council* [1996] QB 252) or an injunction is also available to the tenant (see *Peninsular Maritime Ltd v Padseal Ltd* [1981] 2 EGLR 43).

(b) Subject to complying with certain conditions, the tenant can carry out the repair works and reclaim the cost from the landlord by deducting it from rent payments. This is known as self-help (see *Lee-Parker v Izzet* [1971] 1 WLR 1688).

(c) The tenant may claim specific performance (see above).

(d) A receiver may be appointed, who will collect the rent and manage the property in accordance with the terms of the lease. Section 37 of the Senior Courts Act 1981 gives the court power to make this appointment, and see *Daiches v Bluelake Investments Ltd* [1985] 2 EGLR 67.

9.3 The end of the lease

So how does a lease come to an end?

9.3.1 Effluxion of term

This is where the fixed term of the lease simply comes to an end.

9.3.2 Notice to quit

This is used to end a periodic tenancy. Remember that the notice period must equal one rent period payment and expire at the end of a period (see **7.5.2**). The exception is for a yearly periodic tenancy where only six months' notice needs to be given. You should note, though, that there are additional rules relating to ending residential and commercial tenancies which enjoy statutory protection, for example under the Housing Act 1988 or the Landlord and Tenant Act 1954, Part II, but the detail of these is outside the scope of this book.

9.3.3 Operation of an option to determine or break clause

This allows either or both the parties to the lease to end it earlier than the end of the fixed term. The lease will usually provide for a notice to be served and may attach conditions to the exercise of this break.

9.3.4 Surrender

This is where the landlord and the tenant both agree that the lease will end before the end of the fixed term. It can be agreed in a formal surrender deed, but often a surrender is effected by operation of law. The classic situation is where the tenant hands the keys back to the landlord and, crucially, the landlord accepts them as a surrender of the lease. The conduct of both the landlord and the tenant must be an unequivocal acceptance that the lease is ending. It cannot be a unilateral act; remember that a lease is a contract. The recent case of *Padwick Properties Ltd v Punj Lloyd Ltd* [2016] EWHC (Ch) demonstrated this as, although the administrators of the tenant returned the keys to the landlord, the landlord expressly accepted them for security reasons. In fact the landlord then went on to change the locks to secure the property and market the property for rent with vacant possession. The court considered this but held that, as the keys had not been accepted as a surrender and no new lease had actually been granted, the lease had not been surrendered and was still in existence.

9.3.5 Merger

Merger is where the leasehold and the freehold title are owned by the same person; an example of this would be where the tenant purchases the landlord's freehold and the lease merges into this superior title. In the case of *Barrett and Others v Morgan* [2000] 2 WLR 284, Lord Millett referred to 'the principle that a person cannot at the same time be both landlord and tenant of the same premises'.

9.3.6 Forfeiture (see 9.1.9.1 above)

9.3.7 Disclaimer

Disclaimer is where, for example, a trustee in bankruptcy or liquidator declares the lease to be onerous property and disclaims the lease under s 178 and s 315 of the Insolvency Act 1986. It may help the student to remember that such a lease is not an asset but an onerous obligation, as it is likely to contain covenants to pay rent and repair etc. The trustee in bankruptcy or liquidator will want to end this ongoing liability and can end the lease by disclaiming it.

9.3.8 Frustration

Frustration is where an event beyond the control of either party renders the lease useless or changes the circumstances so that one party would not have entered into it. It used to be believed that this rule did not apply to leases, but *National Carriers v Panalpina* [1981] AC 675 held that this was not the case and that it could be applied.

9.3.9 Repudiation

Repudiation is where there is such a serious breach of a covenant by one party that the other party can treat the lease as being terminated. This is rare in the case of leases (see *Nynehead Developments v RH Fibreboard Containers Ltd* [1999] 1 EGLR 87).

9.4 Further reading

M Pawlowski, 'Law reform – a plea for implementation' (2012) 16(2) Landlord & Tenant Review 47–49.

P Clark, 'A model lease?' (2015) 4 Conveyancer and Property Lawyer 291–300.

M Walsh, 'An English (leasehold) reformation?' [2015] Estates Gazette 1511, 108.

K Dunn, 'Food for thought on forfeiture' [2016] Estates Gazette 1642, 86–87.

summary

Although each lease is different, the main clauses will usually be present.

Examples of important covenants from the perspective of both the landlord and the tenant are repair and alienation.

The options available to the landlord when the tenant breaches a covenant depend on the type of covenant breached. An important remedy is forfeiture which is governed by complex rules that must be followed.

There are fewer options available to a tenant when the landlord breaches a covenant.

There are nine ways a lease can be ended. Some are in accordance with the agreed lease terms but others are more contentious.

test your knowledge

Let us again use the scenario of Pam owning Silverbrook House. It is a five-storey block of flats with one flat on each floor. The following events take place.

Pam and John formalise his use of Flat 1, agreeing that they will enter into a commercial lease for a term of 10 years at an annual rent of £10,000. Pam wants John to be responsible for keeping the property in good repair.

Pam and Enid (a hairdresser) have entered into a lease of Flat 2 for Enid's business for a term of 12 years. Enid agreed to redecorate the interior of the flat every three years and to cut Pam's hair every month. Last month, in accordance with the terms of the lease, Enid assigned the lease to Janet.

Flat 3 is now empty, Andrew is going to take a lease of this for his estate agent's office. He is concerned, though, that Pam plans to carry out refurbishment works to the top floor of Silverbrook House and that these works will affect his business.

1   Identify clauses (other than repair) that Pam's solicitor should draft in the lease of Flat 1. Briefly explain what each clause will contain.

2   How should the repairing covenant in the lease of Flat 1 be drafted?

3   The lease of Flat 2 provides that Pam must consent to any assignment. Pam does not like the look of the proposed assignee; does she have to agree to the assignment? Can she just ignore the request and hope that the assignee loses interest in the property? Refer to statute and cases in your answer.

4   Would your answer to question 3 differ if the alienation clause in the lease referred to s 19(1A) of the Landlord and Tenant Act 1927?

5   What protection would be offered to Andrew?

6   What action can Pam take for breach of the repairing covenant in the lease of Flat 2? How would your answer differ if the breach was for non-payment of rent?

7   How could the various leases end?

chapter 10

Mortgages: Concept, Creation and Protection

After reading this chapter, you will be able to understand:

- the concept of a mortgage or charge
- terminology commonly used in relation to a mortgage or charge
- how to create and protect legal and equitable mortgages
- what priority is enjoyed by a legal or equitable mortgage.

10.1 Introduction

For many students, mortgages are most easily understood in the context of housing and as a means of financing the family home. The dual 'functional and financial dimension' of land (RICS, April 2016) that we referred to in **Chapter 1** is particularly acutely drawn in relation to mortgages of residential property. The inevitable tensions between the power of a mortgage lender to enforce its security, and protection for a mortgagor who may be losing his or her most significant asset and the family home as well, indicate the need to analyse mortgage law on its social impact as well as its efficiency and clarity. See, for example, N Elphicke, *Save 100,000 homes from repossession*, Centre for Policy Studies, February 2009.

Moreover:

(a) Housing more generally, including social housing, the rented sector and the absence of housing, including legal duties of local authorities to homeless people, makes up a broader topic that is rarely touched on in any depth, if at all, in traditional land law courses and remains a topic of more specialist study.

(b) In addition to the role that mortgages play in financing home acquisition, mortgages over residential property (in the case of small and medium enterprises) and commercial property (in the case of larger enterprises) are important sources of funding for business. Nicholls LJ referred in *RBS Plc v Etridge (No 2)* [2001] UKHL 44 at [34] to bank finance as 'by far the most important source of external capital for small businesses with fewer than ten employees. These businesses comprise about 95% of all businesses in the country, responsible for nearly one-third of all employment. Finance raised by second mortgages on the principal's home is a significant source of capital for the start-up of small businesses.'

(c) Mortgages have also spawned other financial products, such as securitisation, in which the income stream from mortgage repayments is bundled up and sold to investors; the securitisation of US sub-prime mortgages was a contributor to the 2008/09 financial crisis. See 'The return of securitisation: Back from the dead', *The Economist*, 11 January 2014 and 'Europe's securitisation market remains stunted', *The Economist*, 23 February 2017.

(d) Residential property is commonly used as an investment vehicle by individuals in the form of buy-to-let property, student housing and so on. The private rented sector in the UK increased from 9.4% of the housing stock in 2000 to 19% of a considerably larger housing stock in 2014; the number of privately rented units increasing by almost 125% over a 15-year period (K Scanlon and C Whitehead, 'The Profile of UK Private Landlords', CML Research, December 2016).

(e) Students may also want to consider wider issues around home ownership and wealth. One useful source is the Joseph Rowntree Foundation Paper, 'Home-ownership and the distribution of personal wealth', published in September 2010 and available at <www.jrf.org.uk>. The availability of mortgage finance, which has expanded from the 1980s onwards in the UK, has had a mixed effect. As one academic quoted in the Paper notes: 'In one sense the liberalisation of mortgage finance was socially progressive and helped to widen access to housing finance ... [but] has been undermined by its impact on house prices, which in turn have narrowed access to home-ownership, while housing market instability has sharpened the risks associated with home-ownership by making future price trends uncertain.' (M Stephens, 'Mortgage market deregulation and its consequences' (2007) 22(2) Housing Studies 201–20).

(f) Black letter law is only one source of the 'rules' around mortgages and mortgage finance. Financial services have been regulated in a variety of ways, depending on whether a mortgage is a first or second charge and whether it is over the borrower's home or not. The Financial Conduct Authority (formerly the Financial Services Authority) regulates first mortgages to homeowners under the Financial Services and Markets Act 2000 and the Mortgage Conduct of Business Rules (MCOB), which are based around the duty to treat customers fairly. Second mortgages were regulated under the Consumer Credit Acts, now also regulated by the FCA and which are being brought into line with the regime for first mortgages, with some modification. The Mortgage Credit Directive (MCD) came into force on 21 March 2016 and introduced an EU-wide framework of conduct rules for mortgage firms which will apply to first and second mortgages and consumer buy-to-let mortgages.

(g) In addition to the tension between the rights of mortgagees and protection given to mortgagors that we have already referred to, there is a tension between the rights of secured and unsecured creditors. Put simply, in an insolvency situation, assets that are 'reserved' by the taking of security in favour of a particular creditor or creditors are not available to ordinary or unsecured creditors, at least until the secured creditors have been repaid in full. For a discussion of this tension in the corporate context, see J Zhao and S Wen, 'The legitimacy of unsecured creditor protection through the lens of corporate social responsibility' (2013) 8 JBL 868–98.

With all this in mind, we turn to look in greater detail at what we mean by a mortgage.

10.2 What is a mortgage?

A mortgage is one of the most important interests in land. In the case of *Santley v Wilde* [1899] 2 Ch 474 it was defined by Lindley LJ (at 474) as:

> a conveyance of land or an assignment of chattels as a security for the payment of a debt or the discharge of some other obligation for which it is given. This is the idea of a mortgage: and the security is redeemable on the payment or discharge of such a debt or obligation, any provision to the contrary notwithstanding.

The difference between secured and unsecured debts is at the heart of the law of mortgages. A mortgage is a means of securing a debt. It is a contract and, most importantly, it is also a proprietary interest in the land of the borrower – in other words it gives rights in and to the property itself and not merely personal rights to sue the borrower. It is a form of security interest in land which guarantees the amount of a loan made so that the lender has confidence it will be able to recover the money loaned. Under a mortgage, property is used as security for a loan and, once the loan has been repaid or redeemed, the property is no longer affected. If the borrower repays the money then the mortgage will be released from the security. But if the borrower does not repay the money, the lender can take possession of and sell the property, take what is owed to it and any costs associated from the proceeds of sale before returning any balance to any other secured lender and, finally, the borrower.

An important consequence of this is that, until all lenders that have security over the property have been paid back, funds raised on sale of the asset are not available for the borrower or for any other creditors (also called unsecured creditors) that he or she may have. So the existence of security over the borrower's assets reduces the pool from which other, unsecured creditors will be paid and may mean that they recover less for each pound that is owed to them.

example

Clare's house is worth £500,000 and is subject to a mortgage in favour of National Bank on which £400,000 is outstanding. She has other debts of £500,000. Who will get what?

National Bank can take possession and sell the property, using the proceeds to repay the debt to it in full. Assuming no costs, National Bank must return the balance of £100,000 to Clare or – more likely in this scenario – her trustee in bankruptcy who will distribute the money amongst all her remaining creditors. Unless Clare has other assets, those creditors will only receive an amount equivalent to 20 pence for every pound that is owed to them. This shows us some of the tensions in mortgage law, not only between the mortgagee and the mortgagor but between secured and unsecured creditors.

10.3 Terminology

Let us think about the terminology now and the common situation of a person acquiring a freehold property and needing to borrow money to fund this purchase. As soon as he or she has purchased the freehold, the purchaser grants a mortgage to the lender. It is the purchaser, the person borrowing the money, who grants the mortgage so he or she is the 'mortgagor'. The lender was granted the mortgage in return for lending the money, so it is the 'mortgagee'.

Table 10.1   Terminology

Mortgagor – also known as:	**Mortgagee** – also known as:
The person granting the mortgage, or the grantor	The person to whom the mortgage is granted, or the grantee
The borrower	The lender
The debtor	The secured creditor
The property or home owner	The bank

The mortgagee has a proprietary interest in the land subject to the mortgagor's equity of redemption. This phrase refers to the bundle of rights that the mortgagor holds in the property that is subject to the mortgage. It includes the right to redeem the mortgage, which is the right of the borrower to repay the loan and have the mortgage discharged.

The legal right to redeem is the contractual right held by the borrower to repay the mortgage (plus interests and costs) and to have the mortgage discharged. At common law, a date for redemption was specified in the mortgage deed or agreement. The borrower has no right to redeem before that date (*Brown v Cole* (1845) 14 Sim 427) and, at common law, no right to do so once it has passed. Due to the harshness of this rule, equity will continue to allow a borrower to redeem after the legal date for redemption has passed. This equitable right to redeem becomes effective once the contractual date has passed and the legal right to redeem has been lost. In consequence, the contractual date has become largely unimportant other than as the date on which the mortgage money has become due in order for the mortgagee's power of sale to arise under s 101(1)(i) of the Law of Property Act (LPA) 1925. This contractual date is traditionally specified as six months from the date of grant of the mortgage.

10.4 'Once a mortgage always a mortgage'

Any term of the mortgage which purports to exclude the borrower's right to redeem is void as being inconsistent with the nature of a mortgage.

Returning to the case of *Santley v Wilde* [1899] 2 Ch 474, and Lindley MR (at 475):

> Any provision inserted to prevent redemption on payment or performance of the debt or obligation for which the security was given is what is meant by a clog or fetter on the equity of redemption and is therefore void. It follows from this, that 'once a mortgage always a mortgage'... A 'clog' or 'fetter' is something which is inconsistent with the idea of 'security': a clog or fetter is in the nature of a repugnant condition ... If I give a mortgage on a condition that I shall not redeem, that is a repugnant condition.

Examples of arrangements that have been held to be a clog or fetter on the equity of redemption – and therefore void – include:

(a) agreements to postpone or delay redemption until the possibility of redemption becomes illusory (for example *Fairclough v Swan Brewery Ltd* [1912] AC 565 where postponement of the right to redeem a mortgage of a 20-year lease until six weeks before the lease was due to expire was void because 'for all practical purposes this mortgage is irredeemable', but see also *Knightsbridge Estates v Byrne* [1940] AC 613 where a postponement for 40 years between parties of equal bargaining strength was not oppressive);

(b) terms which prevent redemption, such as an option by the mortgagee to purchase the mortgaged property (see *Samuel v Jarrah Timber and Wood Paving Corporation Ltd* [1904] AC 323 where such an option was unenforceable). See also cases where a separate transaction for the mortgagee to purchase the mortgaged property is upheld (*Alec Lobb (Garages) Ltd v Total Oil* [1985] 1 All ER 303); the court will look at the substance of the transaction to decide whether the nature of the agreement as a whole is a mortgage to secure the repayment of money (*Warnborough Ltd v Garmite* [2003] EWCA Civ 1544); and

(c) terms by which the mortgagee seeks to obtain a collateral advantage or benefit in return for the loan, in addition to a normal rate of interest. A common example is a 'solus tie' under which a brewery tenant is lent money by the brewery to finance his or her property lease and is tied to buying alcohol from the brewery. During the life of the mortgage, such a benefit is valid in principle but will be void if oppressive or unconscionable. Any benefit that is claimed after the mortgage has been redeemed is likely to be void as a 'fetter' or 'clog' as all terms of the mortgage should fall away once the mortgage is redeemed. A collateral benefit can be valid if it is an independent transaction (*C&G Kreglinger v New Patagonia Meat and Cold Storage Co Ltd* [1914] AC 25).

Abnormal interest rates can be struck down if oppressive and unconscionable (see *Cityland and Property (Holdings) Ltd v Dabrah* [1967] 2 All ER 489) but a high rate can be justified if bargained for between the parties (see *Multiservice Bookbinding Ltd v Marden* [1978] 2 All ER 489). See also the comments concerning regulation of mortgage business in the introduction to this chapter.

10.5 How to create and protect a legal mortgage

Mortgages today are almost always created by a charge by deed expressed to be by way of legal mortgage.

10.5.1 Obsolete methods of creating charges

Before the LPA 1925, a mortgage would mean that the mortgagor would convey the property to the mortgagee subject to the mortgagor's right to redeem the mortgage. This meant the right to repay the debt and have the property conveyed back to the borrower free from the mortgage. Although the title to the property was transferred to the mortgagee, in practice the mortgagor was allowed to retain possession of the property. The right to redeem was on a set date, and if the loan and interest were paid on that date, the mortgagee would re-convey the property to the mortgagor. There were difficulties with this.

10.5.2 Some history

If we look again at the extract from *Santley v Wilde* (emphasis added):

> a *conveyance* of land… as a *security* for the payment of a debt or the discharge of some other obligation for which it is given. This is the idea of a mortgage: and the security is *redeemable* on the payment or discharge of such a debt or obligation …

Before 1925 the borrower literally transferred the property to the lender. In other words, he or she conveyed full title to the property. The conveyance was subject to a proviso for redemption. If the loan was paid back with appropriate interest on a named date, the mortgagee was obliged to re-convey the title to the mortgagor. This was known as the legal right to redeem. If the borrower repaid the money but the property was not conveyed back to him or her, he or she could sue the mortgagee at common law for damages or in equity for an order of specific performance to have the property re-conveyed to him or her. After 1925 this method of creating a mortgage was abolished – a mortgage would take effect either by granting the mortgagee a long lease of property (typically 3,000 years) or by granting a charge by way of legal mortgage (LPA 1925, s 85(1) and s 86(1)).

10.5.3 Modern law

Section 85 of the LPA 1925 recognises only two ways to create a legal mortgage of a freehold:

(a)   demise for a term of years absolute; and

(b)   a charge by deed expressed to be by way of legal mortgage.

Either method can be used today to create a legal charge over unregistered land, although, in practice, the second method – a charge by deed expressed to be by way of legal mortgage – is the preferred form.

What is the difference between a mortgage and a charge?

The terms 'mortgage' and 'charge' tend to be used interchangeably. There is a technical difference between them, but now that virtually all mortgages are created by a charge by way of legal mortgage, this is largely irrelevant.

Table 10.2   'Mortgage' and 'charge'

Mortgage	Charge
Legal or equitable estate in land	Attaches to the land of the mortgagor and gives rights over it
Granted to mortgagee as security for payment of a debt	Does not grant a legal or equitable estate in land
Subject to the mortgagor's right of redemption	

Strictly speaking, a mortgagee has no estate in the land, only a charge, which is a legal interest (LPA 1925, s 1(2)). However, s 87(1) of the LPA 1925 gives the mortgagee under a charge by way of legal mortgage the same protections, powers and remedies as if an estate in the land had been granted.

A mortgage is still treated as a conveyance (LPA 1925, s 205(1)(ii)).

10.5.4 Methods of creating a mortgage over registered and unregistered land

In registered land, the only method of creating a mortgage is to create a charge by deed which is expressed to be by way of legal mortgage (Land Registration Act (LRA) 2002, s 23(1)). A mortgage by demise is no longer applicable to registered land.

Although it remains possible to create a mortgage over unregistered land by granting a long (3,000-year) lease to the mortgagee, this is very rare, and therefore, in practice, the only modern method of creating a mortgage is by a charge by way of legal mortgage.

10.6 Formalities and registration requirements for a legal charge

A legal charge is the best form of security. It is what a lender ideally wants. So how does it obtain this?

10.6.1 Deed

A charge by way of legal mortgage is required to be by deed under s 52(1) of the LPA 1925:

(1) All conveyances of land or of any interest therein are void for the purpose of conveying or creating a legal estate unless made by deed.

The deed must state that is it intended to take effect as a charge by legal mortgage (LPA 1925, ss 85(2), 86(2) and 87).

10.6.2 Registered land

In registered land, the mortgage will only take effect as a *legal* mortgage on registration in accordance with s 27(1) and s 27(2)(f) of the LRA 2002. There are two consequences of this:

(a) A registered legal charge will get the advantage of the special priority rule in s 29 of the LRA 2002 – it will take priority over any pre-existing interests in the land that are not protected at the time of registration. A pre-existing interest can be protected in one of the methods set out in s 29(2) of the LRA 2002: as a registered charge or the subject of a notice in the register, or as an overriding interest within Sch 3 to the LRA 2002 (for example an interest coupled with actual occupation under Sch 3, para 2 (see *Williams & Glyn's Bank v Boland* [1981] AC 487)).

(b) The registered legal charge will itself retain priority in the event of any subsequent dispositions of the registered estate (for example the grant of a second legal charge) as a registered charge under s 29(2)(a)(i) of the LRA 2002.

10.6.3 Unregistered land

The grant of a first legal mortgage over a qualifying estate will trigger the requirement of compulsory first registration of title (LRA 2002, s 4(1)(g)). A qualifying estate is an unregistered legal estate which is freehold or leasehold for a term which at the time of the transfer, grant or creation has more than seven years to run (LRA 2002, s 4(2)).

This means that the only time that the grant of a legal mortgage of unregistered land will *not* trigger first registration is when an unregistered title is already subject to an existing legal mortgage and the owner creates a second or further legal charge. As the grant of the existing first legal mortgage would generally need to have been created prior to 1997 in order not itself to have triggered first registration on its grant, this is likely to be increasingly rare. In such a case, the new legal charge is a 'puisne' mortgage, a second legal charge unprotected by holding the title deeds (which are held by the first mortgagee), and must be registered as a Class C(i) land charge under s 2(4)(i) of the Land Charges Act 1972 (see **3.5.3.2**).

10.7 Relationship between a mortgagee and third parties with rights in the mortgaged land

10.7.1 Overreaching

If capital monies are paid over to at least two trustees then the legal charge will take priority over any beneficial interests arising under a trust of the land (LPA 1925, s 2(1) and s 205(1)(ii); see also *City of London Building Society v Flegg* [1988] AC 54). Conversely, a lender who deals with only one trustee is at risk of taking subject to the interests of any such beneficiary who is in actual occupation of the relevant land (see LRA 2002, s 29(2)(a)(ii) and Sch 3, para 2). In practical terms, this means that if there are two or more co-owners of the legal title to the land (who must all enter into the mortgage deed) then trust interests will be overreached by the grant of the mortgage. If there is only one legal owner then the grant of the mortgage will not overreach trust interests and, if the beneficiary occupies the land, his or her interest will enjoy protected priority against the lender.

A lender who ensures that its legal charge is properly created (by deed executed by all legal owners who have received independent legal advice) and protected (by registration at the Land Registry under s 27(2)(f) of the LRA 2002) is in a privileged position.

10.7.2 Special priority rule

As discussed above, a legal charge over registered land that is completed by registration at the Land Registry within the period of a priority search will take priority over any pre-existing interest in land whose priority was unprotected at the date the charge was entered into. A priority search can be carried out at the Land Registry before completion of a registrable disposition to give that disposition priority for a period of 30 days to cover the 'registration gap' between actual completion and registration over other registrable dispositions, rights, interests or matters that have not been logged by the Land Registry or themselves protected by a priority search on the date the search is made (*Land Registry Practice Guide 12: official searches and outline applications*, HM Land Registry, updated 9 January 2017).

10.7.3 Occupiers

Any mortgagee who is aware of a person who is or may be in actual occupation of the land will want to ensure that any interest in the land held by that individual is postponed to the rights of the mortgagee. This means that the individual waives his or her rights in favour of the rights of the mortgagee. A mortgagee will want to obtain such a waiver as a precaution even if dealing with two trustees.

10.7.3.1 Express waiver

A mortgagee should obtain express confirmation of this by obtaining a signed waiver of rights in favour of the mortgagee by any person occupying or – if the mortgage is being used by the borrower to acquire the property – proposing to occupy property that it is taking security over. The bank should verify that such person has taken independent legal advice prior to signing the waiver to prevent a claim that it has been obtained by misrepresentation or undue influence (see 12.2 and 12.3). An express waiver should be taken whether the mortgage is being used to acquire property or to refinance a property already in the ownership of the borrower.

10.7.3.2 Implied waiver

Where the mortgage is being used to acquire property in circumstances where the potential occupier is aware that a mortgage will be required to meet the purchase price, it is possible that such a waiver will be implied. In the case of *Bristol & West Building Society v Henning* [1985] 1 WLR 778, Mrs Henning claimed an equitable interest under a constructive trust of property in which she lived, although not married, as husband and wife with Mr Henning. The property was acquired in the sole name of Mr Henning with the aid of a mortgage from the Bristol & West. Brown-Wilkinson LJ stated at 782:

> Mrs Henning knew of and supported the proposal to raise the purchase price of 'The Villa' on mortgage. In those circumstances, it is in my judgment impossible to impute to them any common intention other than that she authorised Mr Henning to raise the money by mortgage to the Society. In more technical terms, it was the common intention that Mr Henning as trustee should have power to grant the mortgage to the Society. Such power to mortgage must have extended to granting to the Society a mortgage having priority to any beneficial interests in the property.

10.7.4 Leases

10.7.4.1 Leases granted over the charged property before the grant of the charge

Another common interest that may affect a mortgagee is a lease of the property granted before the mortgage is entered into. Of course, in the case of commercial property, the rental income may be important to both the borrower and the mortgagee as a means of paying off the loan. The effect of the LRA 2002 priority rules is that a legal mortgagee will be bound by leases, granted out of the legal estate that is subject to the charge, which are already in existence at the date of completion of the charge:

(a) Provided that, where the lease is granted for a term of more than seven years, it must be substantively registered (LRA 2002, s 27(2)(b)(i)), in which case it will be protected by a notice on the superior title (LRA 2002, s 29(2)(a)(i)) and have protected priority against the charge.

(b) Legal leases of seven years or less will be an overriding interest (LRA 2002, s 29(2)(a)(ii) and Sch 3, para 1).

(c) Equitable leases should be protected by a notice in the register of the superior title (LRA 2002, s 29(2)(a)(i)) or may be protected as an overriding interest due to actual occupation (LRA 2002, s 29(2)(a)(ii) and Sch 3, para 2).

10.7.4.2 Leases granted over the charged property after the grant of the charge

A legal charge that is registered under s 27(2)(f) of the LRA 2002 will itself be protected against losing priority to subsequently created interests under s 29(2)(a)(i). This assumes that the mortgage has been completed by registration under s 27(2)(f), and, like all registrable dispositions, the mortgage is vulnerable to other interests unless and until this occurs.

As we have already seen at **5.6.1.2**, in *Barclays Bank Plc v Zaroovabli* [1997] Ch 321 a tenancy was granted in breach of a purported legal mortgage after the date of the mortgage but before its registration at the Land Registry. The mortgage was not registered during the priority period or indeed for some considerable time. Due to the lack of registration, at the time the tenancy was granted the bank merely had an unprotected equitable charge and therefore was subject to the unauthorised legal leasehold estate created by the tenancy. The same effect would occur under s 27(2)(f) and s 29(1) and (4) of the LRA 2002.

Under s 99 of the LPA 1925, the borrower, for so long as he or she remains in possession of the charged property, has a right to create certain leases that will bind the mortgagee. In general, the contractual terms of the mortgage will exclude the borrower's power to do so. An unauthorised lease is void against the legal mortgagee (*Dudley and District Building Society v Emerson* [1949] Ch 707) and the mortgagee is entitled to obtain possession against the unauthorised tenant.

In an effort to protect residential tenants during the last financial crisis, Parliament enacted the Mortgage Repossessions (Protection of Tenants etc) Act 2010, which provides that if a mortgagee is seeking possession of a property that includes a dwelling house and there is a tenancy of all or part of the property that is unauthorised by the lender or under the mortgage deed, the tenant can apply to the court for delay not exceeding two months in delivering possession (s 1).

Whether a postponement is granted will depend on a number of factors, including the circumstances of the tenant and the nature of any breaches of the unauthorised tenancy by the tenant (s 1(5)); the mortgagee can demand a payment for occupation from the tenant (s 1(6)). This gives the tenant the potential to obtain a two-month 'breathing space' before eviction to enable alternative accommodation to be found without prejudicing the mortgagee's right to possession after this period.

10.8 When might a lender want or end up with an equitable charge?

Now let us consider equitable mortgages. As we have explained above, in the standard situation where a lender is making a loan secured on real property, what they will want is a registered legal charge against the full legal and equitable ownership of the relevant estate. When we come to look at equitable charges, we are often looking at a situation where something has gone wrong in that process, and the lender, despite its intentions, has not ended up with a charge that is recognised by the common law. However, there are situations where a mortgage that does not meet the common law requirements will nevertheless be recognised in equity. An equitable charge may give some recourse for a lender, although it is more vulnerable against third parties and, depending on what has gone wrong in the process, may not be effective against all equitable interests in the relevant estate. A good example of a case where matters went wrong not once but twice (whether by the fraud or incompetence of conveyancers) is the case of *Halifax Plc v Curry Popeck (A Firm)* [2008] EWHC 1692 (Ch), which we discussed at 5.4 and which serves as a warning to all lenders and their solicitors.

A second scenario where an equitable mortgage is available is where the interest in land that is being charged is itself equitable, namely the interest of a beneficiary under a trust of land in a situation where the legal estate is not also being charged. Under the principle that persons may only grant rights that they themselves possess, an equitable owner of land cannot grant a legal interest (*Re North East Property Buyers Litigation* [2012] EWCA Civ 17). Therefore the charge will be equitable rather than legal.

There are still formality requirements and these are discussed below.

10.8.1 Creating an equitable charge

10.8.1.1 Attempted creation of legal mortgage has failed due to lack of a deed

A specifically enforceable contract or agreement to create a legal mortgage will, under the rule in *Walsh v Lonsdale* (1882) 21 Ch D 9, create an equitable mortgage. For this to occur, the contract must satisfy the requirements of s 2 of the Law of Property (Miscellaneous Provisions) Act (LPMPA) 1989. Where the parties intended to create a legal mortgage but have failed to comply with the necessary formalities of a deed, but the contract complies with s 2 of the LPMPA 1989, then equity will enforce such a contract and it will be an equitable mortgage. For specific performance to be available, the mortgage money must already be advanced because equity will not compel a person to make a loan (*Sichel v Mosenthal* 54 ER 932).

Prior to s 2 of the LPMPA 1989, it used to be possible to create an equitable mortgage by depositing title deeds with a lender with the intention to create a mortgage. This became an equitable mortgage once monies were advanced under the now repealed s 40 of the LPA 1925 and the doctrine of part performance. This method is no longer valid as it does not comply with s 2 of the LPMPA 1989 and would result in the lender simply having an unsecured debt (*United Bank of Kuwait v Sahib* [1997] Ch 107).

10.8.1.2 Attempted creation of legal mortgage has failed due to lack of compliance with registration requirements

Creation of a legal mortgage requires to be perfected by registration of the charge at the Land Registry under s 27(2)(f) of the LRA 2002, as a charge is a registrable disposition that is required to be completed by registration. Even though created by a deed, the charge will not operate at law until the relevant registration requirements are met (LRA 2002, s 27(1)) but will create an equitable charge.

If the charge is a first legal mortgage of unregistered land, as already explained, it will trigger a requirement for compulsory first registration under s 4(1)(g) of the LRA 2002. If the requirement of registration is not complied with in the two months from the date of the charge (LRA 2002, s 6(4)) then the grant of the mortgage has effect as a contract made for valuable consideration to grant or create a legal mortgage, and therefore the rule in *Walsh v Lonsdale* will apply where such contract has become specifically enforceable to create an equitable charge.

10.8.1.3 Mortgage by one of two or more co-owners

Where only one of two or more co-owners has entered into an effective charge then this takes effect only over the equitable interest of that co-owner. This can happen due to fraud (see *First National Securities Ltd v Hegerty* [1985] QB 850; *Edwards v Lloyds TSB Bank* [2004] EWHC 1745 (Ch)) or, as we explore further below, in cases where the innocent co-owner is entitled to have a charge set aside due to undue influence or misrepresentation. This can only be an equitable charge as it is effective over the equitable interest of the co-owner who is bound by it. This leads us on to our next category.

10.8.1.4 A mortgage of an equitable interest

The scenarios above concern the purported taking of a legal mortgage over the entire legal and equitable interest in the property, which has failed to be recognised at common law for one reason or other, whether through lack of formalities or failure to obtain a valid charge from all legal owners of the estate. As we describe above, it may nevertheless be recognised as an equitable mortgage. Our final category concerns a mortgage over an equitable interest in land (for example an interest under a trust of land). In fact the third example above (**10.8.1.3**) – the mortgage by one of two or more co-owners – is a version of this as it bites only on the equitable interest of one co-owner, even though the lender desired to take a full legal mortgage over the entire legal and beneficial interest.

In terms of formality requirements, although a deed would commonly be used in practice, the minimum requirements are those set out in s 53(1)(c) of the LPA 1925, which require the use of writing signed by the interest holder or his or her agent authorised in writing.

Section 53(1)(c) of the Law of Property Act 1925 provides:

> (c) a disposition of an equitable interest or trust subsisting at the time of the disposition, must be in writing signed by the person disposing of the same, or by his agent thereunto lawfully authorised in writing or by will.

10.8.2 Protecting an equitable charge

10.8.2.1 Registered land

An equitable mortgage must be registered as a notice on the mortgagor's register of title (LRA 2002, s 32). This will give it protection under s 29(2)(a)(i) of the LRA 2002 against later dispositions.

10.8.2.2 Unregistered land

An equitable mortgage does not trigger compulsory registration of the estate out of which it has been granted (LRA 2002 s 4(1)(g)). It should be protected by registration of a Class C(iii) land charge (Land Charges Act 1972, s 2(4)(iii)) or it will be void against a purchaser (including a second chargee) for valuable consideration of the charged land or any interest in it (LCA 1972, s 4(5) and s 17). If, of course, the equitable charge has resulted from the failure to register a purported legal charge then the correct route would be to seek an extension of time to register the legal charge.

10.8.2.3 Mortgage of the interest of a beneficiary under a trust of land

Where the charge is of the interest of a beneficiary under a trust of land then LRA 2002 does not apply due to the 'curtain' keeping trust interests off the title (see LRA 2002, s 33(a)(i)). In such an unusual case, then, the equitable charge will be unprotected unless the mortgagee also happens to be in actual occupation of the land and can claim an overriding interest (LRA 2002, s 29(2)(a)(ii) and Sch 3, para 3).

Notice of the charge should, however, be served on the legal owner of the land as trustee (*Dearle v Hall* 38 ER 475).

10.8.3 Practical implications of a protected equitable charge

An equitable charge should be protected by entry of a notice on the register (LRA 2002, s 32) in order to gain protection against later interests. In respect of earlier interests, an equitable chargee cannot take the benefit of overreaching or the special priority rule in s 29 of the LRA 2002 and will be subject to all prior created equitable interests, whether or not they are entered on the register. Under s 28 of the LRA 2002, competing equitable interests will take priority according to the order in which they were created; see *Halifax plc v Curry Popeck (A Firm)*, per Norris J at [25]:

> The effect of section 28 is to maintain the rule under the general law that the priority of competing equitable interests was determined by the order in which they were created. However, it removes the qualification that priorities might be changed if the holder of the prior equity was at fault.

If no notice is entered on the register in respect of the equitable charge, it will be unprotected and will be vulnerable to losing priority to a later registrable disposition that is completed by registration (LRA 2002, s 29(1)).

10.9 Further reading

C Hunter, 'Certainty rules in uncertain times!' (2016) 19(5) JHL 85–88.

What is a mortgage?

The mortgagee (lender) takes a proprietary interest in the property.

The lender is a secured creditor, and if the mortgagor (borrower) cannot pay the sum due, the lender can force the sale of the property and recover debt from sale proceeds.

The borrower has the right to redeem – to repay the loan and have the mortgage discharged.

Registered land

The *only* method of creating a mortgage is to create a charge by deed which is expressed to be by way of legal mortgage. This is required to be by deed (LPA 1925, s 52) and must be completed by registration (LRA 2002, s 27(2)(f)).

Section 87(1) of the LPA 1925 gives the mortgagee the same protection, powers and remedies as if an estate in the land had been granted.

A registered legal mortgage may take priority by overreaching trust interests if granted by two or more trustees. It will also take priority over all unprotected interests in the land under the special priority rule contained in s 29 of the LRA 2002.

An express waiver of rights should be obtained from occupiers; it may also be implied, especially for an acquisition mortgage where the occupier is aware that a mortgage is required to make up the purchase monies.

An equitable mortgage may be created if there is a defect in formalities and should be protected by entering a notice on the register (LRA 2002, s 32). A mortgage of an equitable interest in land can only be created in equity and must comply with s 53(1)(c) of the LPA 1925.

Revision point

How can you tell if a document is a contract or a deed or neither?

Deed	Contract	Neither
The document states on its face that it is a deed, is validly executed as a deed (for example in the case of an individual, his or her signature is witnessed) and is delivered.	All the expressly agreed terms of the contract are in writing and incorporated in a document (or, where contracts are exchanged, in each) that is signed by or on behalf of the parties.	If the document does not satisfy the requirements for a contract or a deed (eg it is not signed) then it does not create a legal or equitable mortgage. You will need to consider if the surrounding circumstances are such that there are grounds to assert that rights have been created informally.
Law of Property (Miscellaneous Provisions) Act 1989, s 1	Law of Property (Miscellaneous Provisions) Act 1989, s 2	This could happen, for example, by a proprietary estoppel for which the grant of a mortgage or charge may be given as a remedy (see *Halifax Plc v Curry Popeck (A Firm)* [2008] EWHC 1692 (Ch))

Revision point

How are mortgages treated in registered land?

A legal mortgage is a registrable disposition and must be registered in order to take effect at law (LRA 2002, s 27).

A mortgage that is intended to take effect in equity only should be protected by a notice on the register (LRA 2002, s 32). An equitable mortgage that has not been protected by a notice may be overriding, if protected by the occupation of the mortgagee (LRA 2002, s 29 and Sch 3, para 2).

Are the following mortgages legal or equitable?

Facts	What is it?	How to protect it?
Adam is borrowing £10,000 from his friend Bill. They prepare a document which creates a charge over Adam's house in favour of Bill. They both sign the document and Bill pays the money to Adam.	Equitable mortgage Why? Not legal because not created by deed (in writing, signed and witnessed). Complies with s 2 of the LPMPA 1989 and can be enforced by specific performance.	Registered land – notice on the register (LRA 2002, ss 29 and 34). Unregistered land – Class D(iii) land charge (Land Charges Act 1972, s 2(5)) assuming that Bill is not protected by a deposit of Adam's title deeds.
Charlotte borrows money from the bank. The charge is signed by Charlotte in a meeting with her solicitor, who signs also.	Legal mortgage Why? The mortgage has been granted by deed (LPA 1925, s 52). The requirements of a deed are set out in s 1 of the LPMPA 1989.	Registered land – substantive registration as a registrable disposition under s 27 of the LRA 2002. If it is not registered, it will only take effect in equity Unregistered land – as a legal mortgage the right is binding on the world. It acts as a trigger for first registration (LRA 2002, s 4).
Deborah contributes to the purchase of a property with a friend, but she is not registered as owner. She wants to raise some money so she borrows from her brother, Eddie. They draw up a document which purports to create a charge over the property. Eddie signs the documents.	No security created Why? This could only be an equitable mortgage because Deborah's interest is equitable. It is not necessary for Eddie to sign the document but Deborah must do so in order to satisfy s 53(1)(c) of the LPA 1925 – in writing and signed by Deborah as the person making the disposition.	No protection possible as it is not a proprietary right in land. If it had been properly created then notice should be served on the legal owner of the land as trustee (*Dearle v Hall* 38 ER 475).

Mortgages: Lender Enforcement Rights and Borrower Protection

After reading this chapter, you will be able to understand:

- the rights of the mortgagee
- what protection exists for the mortgagor
- how the law and practice of mortgages operate within a wider regulatory context.

11.1 Introduction to mortgagee enforcement rights

The principal remedy that a mortgagee wants to have is the ability to have its loan plus interest and costs repaid and to take possession of and sell the property if the borrower defaults. The Council for Mortgage Lenders (CML) is the main trade body representing UK mortgage lenders whose members are banks, building societies and other lenders who together, the CML states, account for around 97% of the nation's residential lending. The CML estimated in June 2015 that 'at any given time there are approximately 140,000 mortgage accounts where borrowers are failing to make the full payment due. This number is lower than historical trends and especially low in the context of the number of mortgages in the UK (currently just over 11 million)' (CML Policy Update: Arrears and possessions, 1 June 2015, <www.cml.org.uk>).

In this chapter we are really looking at the heart of the law of mortgages. It is frequently acknowledged by the courts that financial institutions would not be willing to lend money on the security of property if they did not consider themselves to be properly protected. A mortgagee has a variety of rights available to it, which can be used cumulatively (*Alliance & Leicester v Slayford* [2001] 1 All ER Comm 1) until there are no further liabilities outstanding from the borrower. These rights are:

(a) action on the borrower's covenant to pay;
(b) taking possession;
(c) sale;
(d) appointing a receiver;
(e) foreclosure.

We look first at the right to sue on the mortgagor's covenant. This will be of little value if the mortgagor is in financial difficulties; the mortgagee will want to force a sale of the property and take what is owed to it out of the proceeds of sale.

There are benefits to both parties if these rights are not dependent on long and expensive court proceedings, although whether the current balance is correct has been questioned. It is easy to see the benefit to the mortgagee from being able to look to the property to recover the money lent without going to court. There are benefits too for the borrower who, remember, is likely to pick up the cost of any proceedings, added to the amount which the lender seeks to recover.

There is a balance to be struck here. The effects of repossession on borrowers are stark. The law also needs to protect the interest of a borrower so that he or she is given an opportunity to put things right and that repossession is only available to a lender as a last resort. These competing principles are one of the continuing tensions in mortgage law. So, when considering what enforcement rights a mortgagee has, we will necessarily also look at what a borrower can do to prevent a lender from taking possession of and selling his or her property, which in many cases is also his or her home.

11.2 Right to payment

As the mortgage is a contract, the mortgagee can sue on the mortgagor's contractual promise to repay the amount borrowed. This remedy becomes important if the debt owed is greater than the value of the property (this is known as negative equity). The mortgagee may still be owed money even after the property is sold. Once the security (namely the property) is realised, the mortgagee is an unsecured creditor for any balance outstanding. In this case, the mortgagee can sue the borrower personally for the balance of the debt (*Rudge v Richens* (1873) 8 CP 358). This remedy is available to the mortgagee even if the mortgagee exercises its rights under another of the options open to it, although of course the mortgagee cannot be paid more than the total debt (including interest and costs) owed to it.

The right to sue on the mortgagor's covenant is subject to limitation periods: actions to recover interest arrears must be brought within six years (Limitation Act 1980, s 20(5)) and capital arrears within 12 years (s 20(1)). Under the Mortgage Conduct of Business Rules (MCOB), the customer must be notified of any decision taken to recover the sale shortfall within six years of the sale date (MCOB, r 13.6.4).

11.3 Taking possession

First let us remind ourselves what we mean by possession. Browne Wilkinson LJ stated in relation to adverse possession in *JA Pye (Oxford) Ltd v Graham* [2003] 1 AC 419 that

> there are two elements necessary for legal possession: (1) a sufficient degree of physical custody and control ('factual possession'); (2) an intention to exercise

such custody and control on one's own behalf and for one's own benefit ('intention to possess').

In short, possession means physically controlling the property for one's own benefit. It will mean the mortgagor giving up that control and, if he or she has not already done so, moving out of the property and the loss of the home, which may be home to a whole family.

There is therefore tension between two conflicting policy objectives that the law must resolve: the desire to encourage secured lending and certainty of property rights by allowing the mortgagee to take possession of the property, and the desire to avoid a family losing its home. It is important to analyse how the law resolves this conflict and to reflect on whether it strikes the right balance.

11.3.1 When will a mortgagee have the right to possession?

The traditional position is that a mortgagee has an immediate and unqualified right to possession as soon as the mortgage is granted. In the famous words of Harman J in *Four-Maids Ltd v Dudley Marshall (Properties) Ltd* [1957] Ch 317 (at 320), possession can be exercised 'before the ink is dry on the mortgage'. This will be the case even if the mortgagor is up to date with any payments required under the mortgage or if the legal date for redemption has not yet passed.

The reason for this is the way in which mortgages developed historically and that still shapes the law today. Until 1925, mortgages were structured as a transaction in which the mortgagor either transferred his or her entire title to the land to the mortgagee (subject to a right to redeem on paying all moneys due under the mortgage) or, from 1925 onwards, took the grant of a long lease of 3,000 years (Law of Property Act (LPA) 1925, s 85(2)(a)) which would be collapsed on paying back all moneys due. In the case of either a conveyance or a long lease, the purchaser would be entitled to take immediate possession of the land, and the same applied to mortgagees using these methods to take security. Note that whilst mortgages are no longer created by these methods (see 10.5.1), a mortgagee is still entitled to the rights of a mortgagee by sub-demise who has an immediate right to possession due to the leasehold term (LPA 1925, s 87(1)).

In practice, the mortgagee allows the mortgagor to remain in possession unless and until the mortgagor defaults in repaying the loan. The mortgagee will then take possession as a preliminary step to gain control of the property before exercising its power of sale.

In some cases, the mortgagee will voluntarily give up possession to the lender. If the property is vacant, the lender can obtain possession peaceably simply by changing the locks. If any person (whether or not they are the mortgagor) is living at the property, the mortgagee will seek a court order for possession. There are criminal penalties if it does not do so (see Protection from Eviction Act 1977, s 1 and Criminal Law Act 1977, s 6).

11.3.2 What protection does a mortgagor have against a mortgagee seeking possession?

11.3.2.1 Court's inherent jurisdiction to grant relief

The court has a limited inherent jurisdiction to grant relief (see *Birmingham Citizens Permanent Building Society v Caunt* [1962] Ch 883) but it is limited to a short time, not usually more than 28 days, for the mortgagor to pay off the entire debt. The court has no power to impose new terms:

> [W]here (as here) the legal mortgagee under an instalment mortgage under which by reason of default the whole money has become payable, is entitled to possession, the court has no jurisdiction to decline the order or to adjourn the hearing whether on terms of keeping up payments or paying arrears, if the mortgagee cannot be persuaded to agree to this course. To this the sole exception is that the application may be adjourned for a short time to afford to the mortgagor a chance of paying off the mortgagee in full or otherwise satisfying him; but this should not be done if there is no reasonable prospect of this occurring. (per Russell J at 912)

In reality this will be of little help to many mortgagors who will not be in a position to do this.

11.3.2.2 Section 36 of the Administration of Justice Act 1970

Section 36 of the Administration of Justice Act 1970 was introduced to give more realistic help:

> 36 **Additional powers of court in action by mortgagee for possession of dwelling-house**
>
> (1) Where the mortgagee under a mortgage of land which consists of or includes a dwelling-house brings an action in which he claims possession of the mortgaged property, not being an action for foreclosure in which a claim for possession of the mortgaged property is also made, the court may exercise any of the powers conferred on it by subsection (2) below if it appears to the court that in the event of its exercising the power the mortgagor is likely to be able within a reasonable period to pay any sums due under the mortgage or to remedy a default consisting of a breach of any other obligation arising under or by virtue of the mortgage.
>
> (2) The court—
>
> (a) may adjourn the proceedings, or
>
> (b) on giving judgment, or making an order, for delivery of possession of the mortgaged property, or at any time before the execution of such judgment or order, may—
>
> (i) stay or suspend execution of the judgment or order, or
>
> (ii) postpone the date for delivery of possession,

for such period or periods as the court thinks reasonable.

(3) Any such adjournment, stay, suspension or postponement as is referred to in subsection (2) above may be made subject to such conditions with regard to payment by the mortgagor of any sum secured by the mortgage or the remedying of any default as the court thinks fit.

The court has a wide discretion to adjourn proceedings or to make a possession order but suspend its operation. Read the section above carefully and note:

(a) *Dwelling-house.* The section applies where the mortgage of land consists of or includes a dwelling-house – it is therefore intended to protect residential occupiers and not commercial property (although if the 'dwelling-house' consists of a flat above a shop then the commercial property will indirectly be benefitted). It is not necessary for the dwelling-house to be the borrower's home (see *Bank of Scotland v Miller* [2001] EWCA Civ 344 in which the flat above a nightclub was occupied by the borrower's employee).

(b) *Action for possession.* The section applies where an action is brought for possession. In other words, it applies where a court order is sought. A mortgagee has a common law power to take possession without court proceedings. In practice, this would only be exercised if the property is unoccupied. Under s 6 of the Criminal Law Act 1977, it is a criminal offence for any person without lawful authority to use or threaten violence for the purpose of securing entry into any premises if that person knows that someone present on the premises is opposed to the entry. A right to possession is not lawful authority for this purpose. But it is an important limitation that s 36 does not apply if the mortgagee takes peaceable possession either because the occupying mortgagor vacates and gives it the keys or the property is vacant. A good example of this is given by the case of *Ropaigealach v Barclays Bank plc* [2000] QB 263, CA, where a property was vacant because renovation works were being carried out; the bank took possession peaceably by changing the locks and the borrower could not use s 36 to challenge that possession.

(c) *By the mortgagee.* The section applies where possession is being sought by the mortgagee. A worrying loophole was demonstrated by the case of *Horsham Properties Group Ltd v Clark and Beech* [2009] 1 WLR 1255, in which the property was sold whilst the borrowers remained in occupation. The purchaser then sought an order for possession against the borrowers, who were unable to use s 36 because the sale to the purchaser had overreached their equity of redemption. (See **3.3** for overreaching generally and **11.4.3** for overreaching on sale by a mortgagee.) The purchaser had bought a title free from the borrowers' interest in the land and was not acting as a mortgagee under a mortgage of land. Section 36 therefore did not apply. (The facts of the case were complicated by the fact that, unusually, the occupation of the borrower was in breach of the mortgage which was a 'buy-to-let' mortgage. It was treated by the mortgagee as a 'commercial' mortgage as it was a commercial investment by the borrower, albeit that it was a residential property.)

The Council of Mortgage Lenders (CML) recommends that its members seek possession prior to sale in residential, but not commercial, mortgages. This self-regulation would therefore not lead to a different outcome if the same facts as in *Horsham* were to arise but would do so in a standard residential mortgage held by an owner-occupier. Again, it is worth asking whether voluntary self-regulation (which in this case CML states applies to the 97% of UK mortgage lending that is carried out by its members) is satisfactory in a matter of such importance to borrowers, or if a clear statutory code should apply.

Similarly, it has been questioned whether the 'self-help' remedy for a lender of taking possession or selling without a court order is appropriate, or whether the court should have oversight in all cases. In December 2009, the Ministry of Justice consulted on whether mortgage lenders should be required to obtain a court order or the consent of the borrower before repossessing and selling residential owner-occupied homes. This is a strand in the wider tension as to whether the proper balance of rights between mortgagor and mortgagee has been found.

(d) *Pay any sums due under the mortgage.* The section requires that the borrower must be '... likely to be able within a reasonable period to pay any sums due under the mortgage ...'. This wording was initially interpreted in *Halifax Building Society v Clark* [1973] Ch 307 to mean the whole of the debt due, which limited its usefulness. Mortgages typically contain an acceleration clause that allows the lender to claim all monies outstanding under the mortgage in the event of a default. This problem led to the introduction of s 8 of the Administration of Justice Act 1973, which gave the court a discretion to ignore any clause in an instalment mortgage requiring the whole debt to be repaid in the event of a default:

> (1)   ... a court may treat as due under the mortgage on account of the principal sum secured and of interest on it only such amounts as the mortgagor would have expected to be required to pay if there had been no such provision for earlier payment.

The court has the right to look at whether the mortgagor would be able to pay off arrears of instalments in a reasonable period and meet any further instalments due within that reasonable period. Look at *Cheltenham and Gloucester BS v Norgan* [1996] 1 WLR 343, discussed below, for what is a reasonable period of time.

(e) *Powers of the court.* The court can adjourn proceedings, stay or suspend execution of a judgment or order for delivery of possession of the mortgaged property or postpone the date for delivery of possession. Proceedings cannot be adjourned indefinitely (*Royal Trust Co of Canada v Markham* [1975] 1 WLR 1416).

(f) *End of the power conferred by s 36.* The power ends when the judgment or order for delivery of possession has been executed. A mortgagee should therefore act quickly if it wishes to rely on s 36.

11.3.2.3 *Cheltenham and Gloucester BS v Norgan* [1996] 1 WLR 343

In this case, the reasonable period for repayment was examined in depth. On the facts of the case, the mortgage was for £90,000 under a 22-year repayment period with 13 years left to run. Possession proceedings were commenced when approximately £7,000 in arrears were outstanding. A possession order was obtained but not enforced pending a further application to suspend the warrant for possession, by which time the arrears were circa £20,000. A four-year period to clear the arrears was ordered, and the 'starting point' for the reasonable period was held to be the remaining term of the mortgage.

Per Waite LJ at 353:

> [T]he court should take as its starting point the full term of the mortgage and pose at the outset the question: would it be possible for the mortgagor to maintain payment-off of the arrears by instalments over that period?

Per Evans LJ at 357:

> [T]he following considerations are likely to be relevant …:
> (a) How much can the borrower reasonably afford to pay, both now and in the future?
> (b) If the borrower has a temporary difficulty in meeting his obligations, how long is the difficulty likely to last?
> (c) What was the reason for the arrears which have accumulated?
> (d) How much remains of the original term?
> (e) What are relevant contractual terms, and what type of mortgage is it i.e. when is the principal due to be repaid?
> (f) Is it a case where the Court should exercise its power to disregard accelerated payment provisions (section 8 of the 1973 Act)?
> (g) Is it reasonable to expect the lender, in the circumstances of the particular case, to recoup the arrears of interest (1) over the whole of the original term, or (2) within a shorter period, or even (3) within a longer period, i.e. by extending the repayment period? Is it reasonable to expect the lender to capitalise the interest, or not?
> (h) Are there any reasons affecting the security which should influence the length of the period for payment?

In the light of the answers to the above questions, the court can proceed to exercise its overall discretion, taking into account also any further factors that may arise in the particular case.

As a typical mortgage term is 25 years, on the face of it, using the full term of the mortgage gives great flexibility to a court to reschedule mortgage payments. However, it would be wise not to overstate this as, in *Norgan* itself, the mortgage was granted for a term of 22 years, of which 13 years were left. Although the 'starting point' for the reasonable period was the remaining term of the mortgage, a forbearance period of four years was ordered by the court.

Evidence suggests that it would be a mistake to overestimate the extent to which courts provide redress in practice. In practice, the court will not exercise the discretion unless there is a realistic likelihood that arrears and current instalments will be paid. The mortgagor must therefore show a realistic ability to meet the payments – current instalments, arrears, interest and any other sums due under the mortgage. If he or she can do so, the mortgagee will not get an order for immediate possession.

11.3.2.4 Is the mortgagor likely to be able within a reasonable period to pay any sums due under the mortgage?

It is important to understand that s 36 only comes into play *at all* '… if it appears to the court that in the event of its exercising the power the mortgagor is likely to be able within a reasonable period to pay any sums due under the mortgage …'. Any delay must be considered in the context that interest on the outstanding principal will continue to accrue. In a situation where there is negative equity (meaning that the debt is greater than the property value), or simply where the loan is a high proportion of the value of the property, then the ability of the mortgagor to use s 36 at all may be limited. Consider the case of *Bristol & West Building Society v Ellis* (1997) 73 P&CR 158, CA, in which Mrs Ellis had fallen into arrears after her husband left her. She was successful at first instance in obtaining a suspension of a warrant for possession on the basis that she would sell the property once her children had finished their education in three to five years' time. She produced as evidence estate agents' opinions that showed that in three to five years' time, the sale price of the property would discharge the mortgage debt. On appeal, Auld LJ held that uncertainty over the property market meant that this evidence was insufficient to demonstrate that Mrs Ellis would be able to pay any sums due under the mortgage 'within any reasonable period, and certainly not one of up to three to five years'.

A borrower can seek protection under s 36 of the AJA 1970 even if there are no arrears due under the mortgage. In *Western Bank Ltd v Schindler* [1977] Ch 1, which concerned an endowment mortgage, no capital payments were due for a period of 10 years after grant of the mortgage. There were no interest arrears but the borrower failed to make payments into the endowment policy, which was intended to repay the mortgage at the end of the mortgage term. The majority view of the court was that the mortgagor could use s 36 and that, in this circumstance, the 'reasonable period' for repayment would be the whole mortgage term.

11.3.2.5 Can s 36 be used for a postponement to allow sale by a mortgagor?

A borrower may wish to use s 36 to postpone an order for possession to allow a sale by the borrower to proceed. A borrower may argue that a sale by him or her will achieve a higher price than a distressed sale by a mortgagee. The courts have permitted some leeway here.

In *Target Home Loans Ltd v Clothier* (1992) 25 HLR 48, possession proceedings were postponed for three months where an offer had been made to purchase the property. And in *National and Provincial Building Society v Lloyd* (1996) 28 HLR 459, the court held that possession proceedings could be adjourned if there was 'clear evidence that the completion of the sale of a property, perhaps by piecemeal disposal, could take place in six or nine months or even a year' (per Neill LJ at 466) but that the prospect of sale must be realistic. In the case, the court did not feel that there was a realistic prospect of sale and it did not suspend possession.

The question that the court must answer is whether there is clear evidence that, through the sale, the 'mortgagor is likely to be able within a reasonable period to pay any sums due under the mortgage'. In line with the comments made above in relation to the *Ellis* case, if the evidence is not sufficient to allow the court to come to that conclusion, or indeed if the evidence points the other way, the court has no basis on which to suspend possession. The court affirmed in *Cheltenham and Gloucester BS v Krausz* [1997] 1 WLR 1558 that there is no power under s 36 to suspend possession to allow sale where the proceeds of sale would not discharge the mortgage debt unless the mortgagor has other funds available to make up the shortfall.

In *Krausz*, the court distinguished the case of *Palk v Mortgage Services Funding Plc* [1993] Ch 330. The facts of *Palk* were unusual; the mortgagee sought possession but intended to rent the property out to tenants until its value rose. (As we shall see at **11.4.4.2** and **11.4.4.3**, the lender is entitled to choose the timing of sale but is also subject to MCOB regulation concerning this.) The mortgagors wanted an immediate sale to prevent the debt from growing. You will recall that the mortgagor remains liable for any shortfall between the sale value and the debt, and therefore has an interest in preventing the shortfall from growing due to the continued accumulation of interest. The debt would continue to grow by circa £43,000 per annum. The court felt that the mortgagor was speculating on the property market at the expense of the borrower and ordered immediate sale under s 91(2) of the LPA 1925. The court noted in *Krausz* that *Palk* does not support the making of an order to suspend possession to allow the mortgagor time to sell

> where the mortgagee is taking active steps to obtain possession and enforce its security by sale. Still less does it support the giving of the conduct of the sale to

the mortgagor in a case where there is negative equity, so that it is the mortgagee who is likely to have the greater incentive to obtain the best price and the quickest sale. (per Millett LJ at 1567–8)

11.3.2.6 Who can use s 36 to defend possession proceedings?

First, and most obviously, the mortgagor can use s 36 to defend an action for possession taken by the mortgagee. However, reflecting the broader sweep of family law, other persons may also do so.

Under s 39 of the AJA 1970, any person deriving title from the mortgagor of a dwelling-house can ask the court to adjourn or suspend proceedings. This will include a spouse or civil partner of a mortgagor with rights of occupation ('home rights') under s 30 of the Family Law Act (FLA) 1996, as well as a person who has an equitable interest in the property under a trust of land. Moreover, under s 55 of the FLA 1996, any connected person can be made a party to possession proceeds if the court is satisfied that:

(a) the connected person is entitled under s 30 of the FLA 1996 to meet the mortgagor's mortgage commitments;

(b) the person has applied to the court before the possession action is finally disposed of in that court;

(c) there is no special reason against making the connected person a party; and

(d) the connected person may be expected to make payments or do such other things that might affect the outcome of the possession proceedings.

Under s 54(5) of the FLA 1996, a connected person includes a mortgagor's spouse, former spouse, civil partner, former civil partner, cohabitant or former cohabitant.

11.3.2.7 Pre-action Protocol

The Ministry of Justice publishes a pre-action protocol (current version 31 January 2017) which was developed in agreement with the CML. The Protocol recommends that mortgagees take certain steps prior to seeking possession, including:

(a) making initial contact providing information and seeking to agree repayments. This might result in no action if the borrower had a claim for mortgage interest with the Department for Work and Pensions or mortgage protection insurance, or if the borrower were already marketing the property;

(b) seeking to agree a repayment schedule in any letter before action; and

(c) even following the issue of court proceedings, giving more information, with the parties seeking to agree repayments and postpone proceedings.

Compliance with the Protocol is voluntary but is a matter that courts can take into account when exercising discretion under the Civil Procedure Rules relating to management of the action or costs.

The Law Society publishes a Practice Note to solicitors in relation to the Protocol which encourages solicitors to draw the attention of the court to the guidelines in *Norgan*.

11.3.2.8 Suggestions for reform

In many modern mortgages, the mortgagee contractually gives up the automatic right to possession. Martin Dixon has suggested that, in relation to residential property, possession

> should no longer be a right but a remedy. A lender seeking to take possession should be required to establish mortgage default *and* that the remedy of possession is required to ensure satisfaction of the debt. Of course, in most cases this would be straightforward and is already catered for in the [Mortgage Conduct of Business Rules] MCOB. However, by recasting possession as a remedy, not as a right, all contested possessions would require an order of the court. This would, in essence, reverse *Ropaigealach v Barclays Bank* ([2000] 1 QB 263) and channel all possession claims through the judicial process so that a mortgagor could take advantage of the provisions of s 36 of the Administration of Justice Act 1970. It would also mean that, in rare cases, possession might even be refused even though a borrower could not satisfy the conditions of s 36 – because possession would be a remedy not a right. For example if a lender had failed to observe the MCOB or a pre-action Protocol. ((2008) 6 Conv 473–81)

Research indicates that many borrowers are not legally represented at possession proceedings. Research published by the University of Cardiff based on a sample study on behalf of the Department of Constitutional Affairs showed that over 92% of defendants in the first hearing of mortgage possession cases were unrepresented (see R Moorhead and M Sefton, 'Litigants in person: unrepresented litigants in first instance proceedings', University of Cardiff, 2005). This is commented on by N Elphicke (see Further Reading), who counselled:

> If non-representation or lack of information is widespread for first hearings of mortgage repossession cases, the Civil Procedure Rules should more clearly include specific requirements for information on the legal position concerning the ability of the householder to repay arrears and reschedule mortgage payments over a lengthy period, up to the term of the loan; and to require official Protocols to include references to the scope of judicial discretion which is currently available.

11.3.3 Other restraints on a lender seeking possession

11.3.3.1 Human Rights Act 1998

We looked at this in **Chapter 1**. Article 1 of Protocol No 1 to the European Convention on Human Rights provides for a right to peaceful enjoyment of property, and Article 8 to a right to respect for family life. Both are now incorporated in the UK by the Human Rights Act 1998.

The Commission held in *Wood v UK* (1997) 24 EHRR CD 69 that there was no breach of Article 8 (right to respect for family life) by the law permitting repossession for default on mortgage payments. The mortgagee's right to possession was necessary for the protection and freedom of others, namely the mortgagee. And in *Birmingham Midshires Mortgage Services Ltd v Sabherwal* (1999) 80 P&CR 256, decided before the Human Rights Act 1998 came into force, it was stated that a possession made 'in accordance with the law and necessary for the protection of rights as a secured lender' would not breach the Protocol.

In *Horsham Properties Group Ltd v Clark and Beech* [2009] 1 WLR 1255, Beech claimed that exercise of the power of sale without a court order or without the mortgagee first obtaining an order for possession (in which proceedings the mortgagor could have claimed the benefit of s 36 of the AJA 1970) was a breach of Article 1 of Protocol No 1 – the right to peaceful enjoyment of possessions. Although the mortgage contract gave a right to possession, the court considered the wider question of the power given by s 101 of the LPA 1925 allowing a mortgagee to sell without obtaining possession or a court order, and which power amounted to State action.

The court held that the mortgagor's estate was always limited by the mortgage and therefore there was no deprivation of her possessions; Article 1 of Protocol No 1 was not engaged. Even if it had been engaged, the exercise of the mortgagee's remedies was justified in the public interest due to the critical importance of the mortgagee being able to realise its security.

11.3.3.2 Mortgage Conduct of Business Rules

We explained at 10.1(f) that mortgages are also subject to regulation by the Financial Conduct Authority (FCA) under the Mortgage Conduct of Business Rules (MCOB), which are based around the duty to treat customers fairly and have been amended to reflect the EU-wide Mortgage Credit Directive (MCD) which came into force on 21 March 2016. The MCOB apply to home finance transactions including regulated mortgage contracts under which a lender supplies credit to an individual or trustees that is secured on land of which at least 40% is used, or intended to be used, as, or in connection with, a dwelling.

Advising on, entering into or administering a regulated mortgage contract are regulated activities. Rule 13.3 of MCOB provides that a regulated firm must:

- deal fairly with any customer who has a payment shortfall under a regulated mortgage contract (MCOB, r 13.3.1);
- make reasonable efforts to reach agreement with the customer over the method of repaying the shortfall;
- allow a reasonable time over which the shortfall should be repaid;

- where no reasonable payment period can be made, allow the customer to remain in possession for a reasonable period to effect a sale; and
- not repossess the property unless all other reasonable attempts to resolve the position have failed (MCOB, r 13.3.2A).

In complying with the duty not to repossess unless all other reasonable attempts to resolve have failed, the firm must consider whether, given the individual circumstances of the customer, it is appropriate to do any one or more of the following in relation to the regulated mortgage contract (this list is not exhaustive) (MCOB, r 13.3.4A):

- extend its term;
- change its type;
- defer payment of interest;
- treat the payment shortfall as if it was part of the original amount provided (but a firm must not automatically capitalise a payment shortfall where the impact would be material); or
- make use of any Government forbearance initiatives in which the firm chooses to participate.

A firm must also give customers adequate information to understand the implications of any proposed arrangement.

In relation to adopting a reasonable approach to the time over which a payment shortfall should be repaid, the Financial Conduct Authority takes the view that the determination of the new period will depend upon the individual circumstances. In appropriate cases, this will mean that repayments are arranged over the remaining term.

11.3.4 Duties of mortgagee in possession

Once in possession, a mortgagee is under a duty to take reasonable care of the physical state of the property and to account strictly. It must account not merely for rent actually obtained but also for any notional benefit obtained from possession. In *White v City of London Brewery Co Ltd* (1899) 42 Ch D 237, a mortgagee, a brewery, chose to let the property as a tied house, meaning that the tenant was required to purchase beer from the mortgagee. The mortgagee had to account to the mortgagor during the period of possession for the higher rents that he would have received if the property had been let as a free house and not a tied house. These obligations on a mortgagee in possession are likely to dissuade a lender from taking possession lightly.

11.4 Sale

In practice, therefore, the right to possession will usually be used in conjunction with the power of sale, as the mortgagee wishes to sell the property and use the sale proceeds to recoup the money borrowed by the mortgagor. A legal mortgagee will usually have a contractual power of sale as well as a statutory power under ss 101 and 103 of the LPA 1925. Neither the contractual nor the statutory powers require the sanction of the court, although, as we have seen, a court order may be required in order to obtain possession as a pre-cursor to sale. In this section we are looking at the position of a legal mortgagee, and we shall consider the position of an equitable mortgagee at 11.8.

11.4.1 Power of sale arising and exercisable (LPA 1925, ss 101 and 103)

Sections 101 and 103 of the LPA 1925 give the power to sell. The mortgagee should ensure that the power to sell has both arisen and become exercisable.

Power of sale arising

101 **Powers incident to estate or interest of mortgagee**

(1)   A mortgagee, where the mortgage is made by deed, shall, by virtue of this Act, have the following powers, to the like extent as if they had been in terms conferred by the mortgage deed, but not further (namely):

(i)   A power, when the mortgage money has become due, to sell, or to concur with any other person in selling, the mortgaged property, or any part thereof, either subject to prior charges or not, and either together or in lots, by public auction or by private contract …

Power of sale exercisable

103 **Regulation of exercise of power of sale**

A mortgagee shall not exercise the power of sale conferred by this Act unless and until—

(i)   Notice requiring payment of the mortgage money has been served on the mortgagor or one of two or more mortgagors, and default has been made in payment of the mortgage money, or of part thereof, for three months after such service; or

(ii)   Some interest under the mortgage is in arrear and unpaid for two months after becoming due; or

(iii) There has been a breach of some provision contained in the mortgage deed or in this Act, or in an enactment replaced by this Act, and on the part of the mortgagor, or of some person concurring in making the mortgage, to be observed or performed, other than and besides a covenant for payment of the mortgage money or interest thereon.

The power of sale arises when the mortgage money becomes due. This means once the legal date of redemption has occurred. As explained in **Chapter 10**, the legal date for redemption has, for most practical purposes, become obsolete due to the willingness of the court to extend the equitable date for redemption. However, it retains a formal role under s 101 of the LPA 1925 in allowing the power of sale to arise. In a typical domestic mortgage, the legal date for redemption is set at six months after the date that the mortgage deed is entered into. Therefore the power of sale *arises* by virtue of the mortgage having been made by deed and the passing of the due date.

However, s 103 of the LPA 1925 states that the power of sale will not become *exercisable* until a default has occurred, namely:

(a) default for three months of payment of mortgage money after service of notice; or

(b) interest unpaid for two months; or

(c) other breach of the mortgage terms.

Once this situation has occurred, the power of sale can be exercised. There is no need for a legal mortgagee to seek the approval of the court, although if it is to sell with vacant possession, it may need a court order to obtain possession of the mortgaged property.

11.4.2 Purchaser protection

Given the importance within land law of certainty in the exercise of property rights, what protection is given to a purchaser from a mortgagee? This will be critical in situations where the sale is contested by the mortgagor.

Both the LPA 1925 and the Land Registration Act (LRA) 2002 give protection. Section 104 of the LPA 1925 provides:

104 Conveyance on sale

(1) A mortgagee exercising the power of sale conferred by this Act shall have power, by deed, to convey the property sold, for such estate and interest therein as he is by this Act authorised to sell or convey or may be the subject of the mortgage, freed from all estates, interests, and rights to which the mortgage has priority, but subject to all estates, interests and rights which have priority to the mortgage.

(2) Where a conveyance is made in exercise of the power of sale conferred by this Act, or any enactment replaced by this Act, the title of the purchaser shall not be impeachable on the ground—

(a) that no case had arisen to authorise the sale; or

(b) that due notice was not given; or

(c) where the mortgage is made after the commencement of this Act, that leave of the court, when so required, was not obtained; or

(d) whether the mortgage was made before or after such commencement, that the power was otherwise improperly or irregularly exercised;

and a purchaser is not, either before or on conveyance, concerned to see or inquire whether a case has arisen to authorise the sale, or due notice has been given, or the power is otherwise properly and regularly exercised; but any person damnified by an unauthorised, or improper, or irregular exercise of power shall have his remedy in damages against the person exercising the power.

...

Section 52 of the LRA 2002 provides:

52 Protection of disponees

(1) Subject to any entry in the register to the contrary, the proprietor of a registered charge is taken to have, in relation to the property subject to the charge, the powers of disposition conferred by law on the owner of a legal mortgage.

(2) Subsection (1) has effect only for the purpose of preventing the title of a disponee being questioned (and so does not affect the lawfulness of a disposition).

It is commonly accepted that protection under both provisions set out above only arises once the power of sale has arisen under s 101 of the LPA 1925; in other words that the date specified in the mortgage deed as the legal date for redemption has occurred.

A purchaser (or his or her solicitor) from a mortgagee in possession must, therefore, inspect the mortgage deed giving rise to the statutory power of sale under s 101 of the LPA 1925, in order to check that the power of sale has arisen. If the mortgagee purports to sell before the power of sale has arisen, the transaction will not operate as a transfer of the mortgagor's interest but of the mortgage itself. The prospective purchaser will therefore find him- or herself in the position of mortgagee, rather than as owner as he or she may have hoped!

However, once the purchaser has established that the power has arisen, he or she does not need to enquire whether the power has become exercisable (*Bailey v Barnes* [1894] 1 Ch 25). The purchaser therefore does not need to verify that the default required by s 103 of the LPA 1925 for the power to become exercisable has, in fact, occurred. There is a very practical reason for this, as it is relatively easy to check that the power of sale has arisen but difficult to verify that it has become exercisable.

11.4.3 Effect of sale

As stated above, a sale *before* the power of sale has arisen operates to transfer the mortgage. The purchaser will acquire the rights of the mortgagee and not the property.

Once the power of sale has arisen, the mortgagee can transfer good title to the purchaser, free from the mortgagor's rights (in essence, free from the equitable right to redeem).

Remember that conveyancing is usually a two-stage process:

(a) First, a contract is exchanged between the parties at which point the parties enter into a binding commitment to sell or buy, followed by completion when title is transferred. The borrower's equity of redemption is extinguished at the moment a contract for sale is made (*Lord Waring v London and Manchester Assurance Co Ltd* [1935] Ch 310). This means that the borrower cannot prevent completion by paying off the debt.

(b) Secondly, at completion, the freehold title that is being sold vests in the buyer under s 88(1) of the LPA 1925. In the case of leasehold property, the same occurs by virtue of s 89(1) of the LPA 1925. This is of course subject to completion of the disposition at law by registration in compliance with the relevant provisions of s 27 or (if the title is unregistered) s 4 of the LRA 2002. The conveyance of title overreaches the equitable rights of the borrower and all subsequent mortgages, in a similar manner to the overreaching that occurs on a conveyance by trustees, under a provision designed for sale by mortgagee and contained in s 2(1)(iii) of the LPA 1925.

Under s 104(2) of the LPA 1925, the mortgagee may be liable to the mortgagor in damages if the sale is 'unauthorised, or improper or irregular', and this can be used by the mortgagor to get a remedy in damages if the mortgagee sells after the power has arisen but before it becomes exercisable.

11.4.4 Duties of a selling mortgagee

11.4.4.1 Nature of selling mortgagee's duties

The selling mortgagee owes duties to the mortgagor. The power of sale is for the benefit of the lender to enable it to realise its security more efficiently than if it first had to get a court order. The mortgagee is not a trustee on behalf of the borrower; provided it acts in good faith and behaves fairly towards the borrower, it can put its own interests before those of the borrower.

It does, however, owe a duty of good faith and a duty of reasonable care towards the borrower. The duty of care is governed by equitable principles because of the relationship between the mortgagor and mortgagee. It is not a duty of care in tort. This means that the 'neighbour principle' does not apply; in other words, the duty is not extended to other people whom the mortgagee ought reasonably to know would be affected by the sale, such as a beneficiary under a trust of land (*Parker-Tweedale v Dunbar Bank Plc* [1991] Ch 12).

11.4.4.2 Duties

The case of *Cuckmere Brick Co Ltd v Mutual Finance Ltd* [1971] Ch 949 gives guidance on the duties owed by a selling mortgagee. It can choose the time of sale and does not need to wait for the market to improve. And in *China and South Sea Bank v Tan* [1990] AC 295, provided it acts in good faith, the mortgagee can sell at a time when the market for the mortgaged property is depressed. It may sell the property in its current condition and has no obligation to improve it, or it may delay sale to investigate the means of increasing value (for example by applying for planning consent), but it is also free to stop this investigation at any time and proceed with sale (*Silven Properties Ltd v Royal Bank of Scotland Plc* [2004] 1 WLR 997).

However, the mortgagee must take reasonable care to obtain a proper price for the property at the time that he does choose to sell, and it will be liable to account if it fails to achieve that price by not conducting the sale property. In *Cuckmere Brick Co Ltd*, the selling mortgagee failed to properly advertise the planning permissions for development that the mortgaged property had the benefit of, and in consequence failed to obtain the full market price. The mortgagee was liable to account to the borrower for the difference. The mortgagee must therefore give a full description of the property but it may sell at auction or by private treaty and, if selling by auction, can accept the best bid obtained even if the auction is poorly attended (*Cuckmere Brick Co Ltd*).

The morgagee's duty is 'to obtain "the fair" or "the true market" value of or the "proper price" for the mortgaged property at the date of the sale' (*Silven Properties Ltd*, per Lightman J at [19]). He continued:

> The mortgagee is not entitled to act in a way which unfairly prejudices the mortgagor by selling hastily at a knockdown price sufficient to pay off his debt: *Palk* [*v Mortgage Services Funding Plc* [1993] Ch 330] at 337-8 per Nicholls V-C. He must take proper care whether by fairly and properly exposing the property to the market or otherwise to obtain the best price reasonably obtainable at the date of sale. The remedy for breach of this equitable duty is not common law damages, but an order that the mortgagee account to the mortgagor and all others interested in the equity of redemption, not just for what he actually received, but for what he should have received: see *Standard Chartered* [*Bank Ltd v Walker* [1982] 1 WLR 1410] at 1416B.

The mortgagee must exercise informed judgement as to market conditions or market value or other matters affecting the sale, and it will be allowed 'a bracket – or a margin of error' when the court determines if that judgement has been exercised reasonably (*Michael v Miller* [2004] EWCA Civ 282, per Jonathan Parker LJ at [135]).

These duties are supplemented by the Mortgage Conduct of Business Rules.

11.4.4.3 Mortgage Conduct of Business Rules

The Mortgage Conduct of Business Rules (MCOB) provide that a firm must ensure that whenever a property is repossessed (whether voluntarily or though legal action), steps are taken to market the property for sale as soon as possible and obtain the best price that might reasonably be paid, taking account of factors such as market conditions, as well as the continuing increase in the amount owed by the customer (MCOB, r 13.6.1).

The Rules explicitly recognise that a balance has to be struck between the need to sell the property as soon as possible to reduce or remove the outstanding debt, and other factors which may prompt the delay of the sale. These might include market conditions but there may also be other legitimate reasons (eg the expiry of a period when a grant is payable on resale or the discovery of a title defect that needs to be remedied if the optimal selling price is to be achieved) (MCOB, r 13.6.2).

If the proceeds of sale are less than the amount due, then the firm must inform the customer of this (MCOB, r 13.6.3). If the decision is made to recover this shortfall, the firm must ensure that the customer is notified of this within six years of the date of sale (MCOB, r 13.6.4).

11.4.4.4 To whom may the mortgagee sell?

The mortgagee cannot sell to itself, a nominee in trust for itself or its agent (*Martinson v Clowes* (1882) 21 Ch D 857). If it sells to a company in which it has a substantial shareholding, the company is not debarred from purchasing the mortgaged property, but, in view of the close relationship between the company and the mortgagee, 'the sale must be closely examined and a heavy onus lies on the mortgagee to show that in all respects he acted fairly to the borrower and used his best endeavours to obtain the best price reasonably obtainable for the mortgaged property' (per Lord Templeman in *Tse Kwong Lam v Wong Chit Sen* [1983] 1 WLR 1349 at 1354).

11.5 Appointing a receiver

A legal mortgagee has a power under s 101 of the LPA 1925, once the mortgage money has become due, to appoint a receiver of the income of the mortgaged property or any part of it. This power will usually also be included in the mortgage deed. The receiver is only appointed once the power of sale has become exercisable under s 103 of the LPA 1925 (LPA 1925, s 109(1)). A receiver takes control of the mortgaged property and the receipt of any income relating to it, and the appointment of a receiver is therefore more appropriate to a commercial, income-producing property. A receiver must apply any monies received in the following order under s 109(8) of the LPA 1925:

(a) pay rents, rates etc with respect to the mortgaged property;

(b) pay interest on any mortgages that have priority to the mortgage under which he or she has been appointed;

(c) pay insurance premiums and, at the written direction of the appointing mortgagee, for any necessary or proper repairs on the property,

(d) pay interest to the appointing mortgagee;

(e) if the appointing mortgagee so directs, reduce the capital debt.

Any residue is paid to the mortgagor.

An important benefit for the mortgagee is that the receiver is deemed to be the agent of the mortgagor, rather than the mortgagee, and the mortgagor is solely responsible for his or her acts and defaults unless the mortgage deed provides otherwise (LPA 1925, s 109(2)). The receiver owes a duty of care to the mortgagor, including a duty of good faith. His or her primary duty is 'to try and bring about a situation in which interest on the secured debt can be paid and the debt itself repaid'. And, 'subject to that primary duty, the receiver owes a duty to manage the property with due diligence'. This does not require him or her to carry on the business on the mortgaged premises previously carried on by the mortgagor but, if he or she does so, 'due diligence requires reasonable steps to be taken in order to try to do so profitably' (*Medforth v Blake* [2000] Ch 86 per Sir Richard Scott V-C at 102).

11.6 Foreclosure

Traditionally this was the method by which mortgages were enforced. We have included it as our final option as it is all but obsolete today. Foreclosure is the process under which a mortgagee of land enforces its security by obtaining a court order which makes it outright owner of the mortgaged land – irrespective of the value of the land and the outstanding debt. The property is effectively 'swapped' for the debt.

In theory, a mortgagee could seek foreclosure of a property worth £1 million for an outstanding debt of £100,000. Unlike with the mortgagee's power of sale, the mortgagee keeps all the proceeds. In our example given above, the mortgagee would get a windfall of £900,000. Conversely, if the outstanding debt were £1 million and the value of the property £100,000, then the lender would have a shortfall of £900,000 for which the lender would have no recourse under the covenant to pay.

Foreclosure extinguishes both the debt and the borrower's equity of redemption. It is seen as draconian and in the case of *Palk v Mortgage Services Funding Plc* [1993] Ch 330 was referred to as 'almost unheard of today'. Foreclosure can only be obtained by court order and, if an application for foreclosure were made by the mortgagee, the court would be likely on the request of the mortgagor to make an order for sale under s 91(2) of the LPA 1925 to avoid the draconian implications of foreclosure. Following sale, rather than foreclosure, proceeds would be dealt with in accordance with s 105 of the LPA 1925.

11.7 Application of proceeds of sale

Section 105 of the LPA 1925 provides that sale proceeds must be applied in the following order:

(a) to discharge any prior incumbrances to which the sale is not made subject (for example, a prior charge);

(b) thereafter, in trust to be applied as follows:

    (i) to meet any costs of sale or any attempted sale;

    (ii) in discharge of the mortgage money, interest, costs and other money if any due under the mortgage;

    (iii) the residue to be paid to the person entitled to the mortgaged property (or authorised to give receipts for the proceeds of sale).

11.8 Powers of an equitable mortgagee

So far, we have looked at the powers of the holder of a charge by way of legal mortgage. We now turn to a mortgagee who has an equitable charge over a legal estate in land. These powers are as follows:

(a) *Right to payment.* An equitable mortgagee will be entitled to sue on the covenant to pay given by the mortgagor. If the mortgage has not been given by deed (for example by a specifically enforceable contract), the six-year limitation period applying to contracts will apply.

(b) *Possession.* A right to take possession may be contained in the mortgage deed. If not, an equitable mortgagee cannot claim possession as of right, unlike a legal mortgagee who can take the benefit of s 87(1) of the LPA 1925, but would need to apply to the court.

(c) *Power of sale.* Section 101 of the LPA 1925 applies to any mortgage created by deed, and therefore if the equitable mortgage were created by deed, the equitable mortgagee would have the same powers of sale as a legal mortgagee (*Swift 1st Ltd v Colin* [2012] Ch 206). If not made by deed, an equitable mortgagee would need to apply to the court for an order of sale under s 91(2) of the LPA 1925.

(d) *Receiver.* The same principle applies to the power to appoint a receiver, which is conferred by s 101(1)(iii) of the LPA 1925 on any mortgagee where the mortgage is made by deed.

(e) *Foreclosure.* Again, this remedy is considered obsolete, but an equitable mortgagee has the same power as a legal mortgagee to apply to the court for a foreclosure order.

An equitable mortgagee of a merely equitable interest in land would, however, need to apply to the court for an order of sale under s 14 of the Trusts of Land and Appointment of Trustees Act 1996, which would be considered in the light of the factors contained in s 15 of that Act, unless the mortgagor were bankrupt, in which case s 335A of the Insolvency Act 1996 would apply (see **Chapter 6**).

11.9 Further reading

N Elphicke, 'Save 100,000 homes from repossession', Centre for Policy Studies, February 2009.

'Does Article 8 broaden the court's powers under s 36 of the Administration of Justice Act 1970?' (2014) 17(1) JHL 9–15.

'Recovery of secured property by mortgagees: the balance of interests' (2005) 16(11) ICCLR 445–53.

S Evans, 'A scrutiny of powers of sale arising under an equitable mortgage: a case for reining these in' (2015) 2 Conv 123–32.

A legal mortgagee has the following rights:

- a right to payment of the mortgage debt, interest and costs;
- a right to immediate possession, although this is usually delayed until the mortgagee wishes to exercise its power of sale;
- right to sell;
- appointment of a receiver;
- foreclosure.

An equitable mortgagee may have the rights above depending on how the equitable charge is created and its terms.

The mortgagee's right to possession is subject to the mortgagor's right to apply for statutory relief under s 36 of the Administration of Justice Act 1970, as amended by s 8 of the Administration of Justice Act 1973, if:

- the property includes a dwelling-house; and
- the mortgagee is seeking possession by court order.

Section 36 of the AJA 1970 provides that if it appears to the court that the mortgagor is likely to be able within a reasonable period to pay any sums due or remedy a default, the court can adjourn proceedings, stay or suspend execution of judgment or order for delivery of possession or postpone the date for delivery of possession.

Cheltenham & Gloucester BS v Norgan provides that the starting point for a reasonable period is the remaining term of the mortgage, although in practice any order is usually made for a shorter period.

Power of sale:

- The statutory power of sale must arise (LPA 1925, s 101) and become exercisable on default (LPA 1925, s 103).
- A selling mortgagee has duties to the mortgagor to obtain the best price reasonably obtainable at the time of sale (*Cuckmere Brick Co Ltd v Mutual Finance Ltd*).
- The application of the proceeds of sale is set out in s 105 of the LPA 1925.

test your
knowledge

Possession and sale problems

1   Karen owns a property where she lives with her husband Dave. She decides to leave her job and go travelling. Dave stays at home. One morning he opens Karen's post and is shocked to find a letter from the bank stating that it intends to take proceedings to repossess the property. What can he do?

2   Bill buys a property as a development project. He does not live there. He falls behind with his mortgage payments. He opens his local paper one day to see that it is advertised for sale by auction. Can he challenge this?

3   The auction is poorly attended. The property sells for less than Bill thinks it is really worth. It is also less than the outstanding debt. What are the consequences of this?

chapter 12

Setting Aside a Mortgage for Undue Influence or Misrepresentation

study points

After reading this chapter, you will be able to understand:

- how and why the doctrines of undue influence and misrepresentation can be used to set aside a mortgage
- how a mortgagee can identify risks of undue influence or misrepresentation in mortgage transactions
- what steps a mortgagee should take to protect itself against the risk of its mortgage being set aside.

12.1 Introduction

Problems have arisen when a person provides security for a third party's debt while acting under undue influence or in reliance upon a misrepresentation. Whilst this can arise in a wide variety of situations, it is most common in relation to co-owned property. A typical example is a spouse agreeing to mortgage the family home as security for a loan for their husband or wife's business venture. The business venture fails and the mortgagee seeks to enforce its security. The concern is that the spouse was the subject of undue influence or misrepresentation from their husband or wife. A mortgage can be set aside or the terms modified where there is evidence of undue influence or misrepresentation. This principle is of general application to all contracts but it has had a particular impact in relation to mortgage contracts, in part due to the rise of co-ownership which expands the possibility of a co-owner agreeing to mortgage the jointly owned property as security for the debts of their fellow owner. In part it may also be due to the principle expressed by Lord Westbury in *Williams v Bayley* (1866) LR IHL 200 (at 218–19) that

> A contract to give security for the debt of another, which is a contract without consideration, is above all things, a contract that should be based on the free and voluntary agency of the individual who enters into it.

12.2 Misrepresentation

A party who is induced to grant security by a misrepresentation may be able to have that security set aside. For example, in *Barclays Bank Plc v O'Brien* [1994] 1 AC 180, a wife who consented to security being granted over the family home of which she was a co-owner was told by her husband that the security was limited to the sum of £60,000 and for a period of three weeks. The bank did not explain the mortgage to her or advise her to obtain independent legal advice. The bank was held to have constructive notice of the misrepresentation, and Mrs O'Brien was able to have the mortgage set aside in full.

Similarly, in *TSB Bank Plc v Camfield* [1995] 1 All ER 951, a husband told his wife that the security was limited to cover a loan of £15,000. In fact it was unlimited; the charge was set aside due to the misrepresentation. The court considered whether the mortgagee could enforce the charge up to the £15,000 limit to which Mrs Camfield had consented. Although it was considered that this might be just, there was no authority allowing a mortgagee to partially enforce a charge, so it was set aside in total.

12.3 Undue influence

Undue influence occurs when a mortgagor has been pressurised – perhaps by the mortgagee or perhaps by a third party – so that he or she is not entering into the transaction by his or her own free will. The court's intervention is justified by the defendant's influence or dominance over a claimant.

12.3.1 Actual undue influence

It may be possible to prove actual influence or pressure. In *Allcard v Skinner* (1887) 36 CLD 145, the gifts made by a member of a religious order could (subject to some exceptions due to laches or delay) be set aside. Although there appears to be some inconsistency between the judges as to whether the undue influence was actual or presumed, Lindley J concluded at 187:

> I believe that in this case there was in fact no unfair or undue influence brought to bear upon the Plaintiff other than such as inevitably resulted from the training that she had received, the promise she had made, the vows she had taken and the rules to which she had submitted herself. But her gifts were in fact made under a pressure which, while it lasted, the Plaintiff could not resist.

Although it is unlikely that an undue influence case will be brought where there is no disadvantage to the party seeking that the transaction be set aside, as a matter of law, it is not necessary to prove that the transaction causes a manifest disadvantage to that party (*CIBC Mortgages v Pitt* [1994] 1 AC 200). Evidential difficulties mean that in practice it is much more common for the influence to be presumed due to the relationship between the parties.

12.3.2 Presumed undue influence

There are specific relationships where the existence of undue influence will be automatically presumed. Examples include the relationship between a solicitor and his or her client, a medical adviser and patient, and a parent and child (*Royal Bank of Scotland plc v Etridge (No 2)* [2001] UKHL 44, per Nicholls LJ at [18]). It is worth noting that this does not include the relationship between spouses or civil partners.

However, where a case falls outside these categories, undue influence will be presumed to exist where it is proved that there is a relationship of trust and confidence between the parties, and that the nature of the transaction calls for explanation. If this can be shown to the satisfaction of the court, then a presumption of undue influence arises. The burden of proof then shifts to the other party to rebut the presumption. The presumption will most commonly be rebutted by demonstrating that the party alleging undue influence has been given independent legal advice and sufficient information about the transaction and its risks to enable a true choice to be made.

Table 12.1   Presumed undue influence

Relationship of trust and confidence	+ Nature of transaction calls for explanation	= Presumption of undue influence. Burden of proof shifts to other party to rebut

12.3.2.1   Relationship of trust and confidence

A relationship of trust and confidence can arise whatever the formal nature (or lack of) of the relationship. It could exist between a husband and wife (or a wife and husband) or civil partners but could also be between a brother and sister, friends, or an employer and employee.

It was not necessary to show in *Lloyds Bank v Bundy* [1975] QB 326 that the person exercising influence does so with wrongful intent or indeed is aware of the influence he or she is exercising; the bank employee who had attended on Mr Bundy 'failed to apprehend' the conflict between the bank (whose interests he represented) and Mr Bundy (per Sir Eric Sachs at 346) .

In *Royal Bank of Scotland plc v Etridge (No 2)* [2001] UKHL 44, Lord Nicholls (at [18]) stated that the examples given above of special relationships (such as solicitor and client) were simply cases where that relationship of trust and confidence was assumed to exist; in other cases it will need to be proven to exist as a question of fact.

12.3.2.2   Transaction that calls for explanation

Here, the court is considering whether the transaction can be readily explained by the parties' relationship. For example, in *Credit Lyonnais Bank Nederland NV v Burch* [1997] CLC 95, an employee guaranteed a loan to her employer; this transaction could not readily be explained by the employer–employee relationship and was set aside.

12.3.2.3 Rebutting a presumption of undue influence

Once the presumption has been established, the onus moves to the defendant to rebut the presumption. It is necessary to show that

> the gift was the spontaneous act of the donor acting under circumstances which enabled him to exercise an independent will and which justify the court in holding that the gift was the result of a free exercise of the donor's will. (*Allcard v Skinner*, per Cotton LJ at 171)

In *Re Estate of Brocklehurst (Deceased)* [1978] Ch 14, the gift of a valuable long lease of shooting rights over the deceased's estate was demonstrated to be 'motivated by a free and independent will'; it was clear that the character of the deceased, described as a 'strongwilled, autocratic and generous man' by Lawton LJ (at 36), was key to this.

In most cases, it is to be expected that the taking of independent legal advice will be required following *Royal Bank of Scotland plc v Etridge (No 2)*; see **12.3.4.4** below.

12.3.3 Undue influence exercised by a mortgagee against the mortgagor

This is relatively rare but an example is given by the case of *Lloyds Bank v Bundy* [1975] QB 326, which concerned an elderly farmer who banked with Lloyds Bank, as did his son. The son's business ran into trouble and the father, after taking independent legal advice, mortgaged his house to the bank to secure the company's overdraft. The charge was limited to £7,500; the house was worth £10,000 at the time. The company's troubles continued. A bank employee visited the father at home and stated that the bank would only continue to support the company if the father executed a second charge to the bank to a limit of £11,000. At this point no further independent advice was taken.

The court held that, before proceeding, Mr Bundy had needed 'careful independent advice', given in full knowledge of financial information known to the bank (per Sir Eric Sachs at 345). Had he received this, he would almost certainly have been advised not to proceed. The second charge merely delayed the collapse of the company whose problems were regarded as 'deep-seated'; no new money was advanced so the new charge was to protect the bank rather than to benefit the company.

However, the bank tried to argue that even if Mr Bundy had received advice, he would have proceeded anyway because he was so supportive of his son. The court commented that this was against public policy; the bank could not have the benefit of the transaction unless it had carried out its duty to the father properly.

There was a clear conflict of interest in the bank's position, and in the circumstances a special relationship existed between the bank and the father. The bank accepted that the father had relied on it implicitly as his bank too, to advise him about the further charge. The bank's employee had attended at the farm in good faith for the bank's purpose of taking the further charge, without appreciating the conflict of interests that meant Mr Bundy required independent legal advice. The second charge was set aside for undue influence; the father, without taking any benefit to himself, had signed away his sole significant asset without taking independent advice. It should be understood that if the father had received advice, even if this were against the transaction, and had proceeded, the bank would have satisfied its duty and the charge would not have been set aside.

12.3.4 Undue influence or misrepresentation exercised by a third party against the mortgagor

A more usual scenario is where a mortgagor stands surety for the debts of a third party, and the third party is accused of procuring the charge by undue influence or misrepresentation. This has been considered in many cases, but the leading case providing guidance on this is *Royal Bank of Scotland plc v Etridge (No 2)* [2001] UKHL 44.

This scenario reflects the fact that the family home is often used as a source of finance for small businesses that have insufficient assets to use as security. A common solution is to use the family home of the owner or majority shareholder. The family home will frequently be co-owned with a spouse, civil partner or cohabitee who is not involved in the business but nevertheless benefits from the profitability of the business. The wider picture here is that the law has to strike a balance between the need to enable small businesses to raise funds in this way and the interests of a spouse or partner. The borrower (the business owner) may be so keen to be advanced the loan that there is a risk that he or she may misrepresent the true financial position of the company or put pressure on his or her spouse or partner to agree to charge the property. The spouse or partner may be willing to take some risks to maintain the business; indeed, the business may be what makes it possible for the home to be owned in the first place. However, as the *Bundy* case demonstrated, if the business has reached a critical point such that it is likely to fail anyway, or the new security is to shore up existing borrowings rather than support new lending, the charge may merely delay the inevitable and bring little benefit but extensive liability.

12.3.4.1 Analysis of the relationships

The relationships form a triangle:

- the loan is between the lender (mortgagee) and the borrower;
- the charge is between the lender (mortgagee) and the mortgagors (often the borrower and his or her spouse or civil partner);
- the misrepresentation is between the borrower and the mortgagor being the spouse or civil partner.

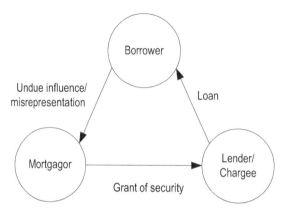

Figure 12.1 The triangle

The problems arise from the fact that the true financial position is known to the borrower and the lender but may not be known to the spouse or civil partner. The lender/mortgagee may be unaware that a misrepresentation or undue influence by the borrower to the spouse or civil partner has taken place.

12.3.4.2 When will a mortgagee be at risk of having its mortgage set aside for the actions of its borrower?

In the case of *Barclays Bank Plc v O'Brien* [1994] 1 AC 180 (which concerned misrepresentation, but the principles apply also to undue influence) the Court introduced the doctrine of notice; in other words the bank would be at risk of having its charge set aside against a mortgagor if it, the bank, had actual or constructive notice of the charge being procured by a misrepresentation or undue influence. This was simplified in *Etridge*: a lender will be put on inquiry in any non-commercial situation where one person provides security for the debts of another person. The formulation has the advantage of covering the classic case of a wife guaranteeing her husband's business debts but also the less common situation, such as the employee guaranteeing a loan to her employer (*Credit Lyonnais Bank Nederland NV v Burch* [1997] CLC 95).

Although this formulation is potentially wide, it is important to recognise its limits.

12.3.4.3 Debts of another person

A lender would not usually be put on inquiry where there is a joint loan, for example a couple mortgage their house for a loan granted to them jointly. In *CIBC Mortgages v Pitt* [1994] 1 AC 200, the loan appeared to be a joint venture for mutual benefit and the lender was not put on inquiry.

However, the mortgage of a couple's house for a loan to the company of one of them would call for explanation, even if the other party were a director or secretary or even a shareholder, as in a small private company the shareholdings are not a reliable guide as to who actually has control of the business (*Etridge*, see Lord Nicholls' comments at [49]).

12.3.4.4 How can a lender avoid constructive notice of the undue influence?

In *Etridge*, the House of Lords recognised the need to put in place procedures where the risk of undue influence could be reduced whilst at the same time providing certainty to lenders that their charges would be upheld. It proceeded to meet this need by setting out a clear checklist of what lenders must do to avoid being fixed with notice of undue influence.

The lender must either hold a private meeting with the mortgagor at which it brings home to him or her the risk that he or she is running, or it must make sure that the mortgagor receives independent legal advice. In practice, banks are reluctant to hold the private meeting, and the mandatory receipt by the mortgagor of independent legal advice prior to entering into the charge is the route that lenders have chosen to take. *Etridge* sets out the parameters of the instruction to the solicitor for independent advice and a core of advice that the solicitor must give. It is useful in setting a practical context to minimise the risk of undue influence.

in practice

***Etridge* guidelines**

- The mortgagor must nominate the solicitor to act on his or her behalf.
- A solicitor can act for more than one party, subject to professional conduct rules.
- The lender must supply the solicitor with all the financial information required to advise.
- The lender must inform the solicitor of any suspicions that it holds of pressure or misleading information having been given.
- The solicitor must explain the role of the legal advice – it is to explain the transaction and give advice so that the mortgagor can decide whether or not to proceed and, if the client's decision is to proceed, to allow the lender to rely on the security granted.
- The solicitor must obtain confirmation that the mortgagor wishes him or her to act.

Core advice

The solicitor must advise:

- in a private meeting;
- on the nature of the transaction and its implications;
- on the seriousness of the transaction;
- for example, that the mortgagor is putting his or her home at risk;
- on the fact that the mortgagor has a choice whether or not to proceed and on what terms (for example should a limit to the guarantee or mortgage be negotiated?);
- on some assessment of the commercial situation.

After the meeting

- The solicitor gives a certificate to the lender, with the client's authority, that the charge has been properly explained.

12.3.4.5 Is the certificate conclusive? What happens if the mortgagor proceeds against legal advice?

In almost all circumstances, yes, the security will still be valid.

Prior to *Etridge*, in *Credit Lyonnais*, the employee was asked to give a guarantee for a new loan of £20,000 but the security was for all outstanding borrowings up to £270,000. This would be likely to be a situation in which the solicitor should advise that the prospective mortgagor should seek to renegotiate the security. Millett LJ went further and stated that the solicitor should withdraw rather than continue to act. Lord Nicholls felt this went too far.

In *Etridge*, Lord Nicholls stated the general rule (at [61]) that it is for the client and not the solicitor to decide whether or not to proceed with the transaction, even if it is unwise to do so.

In *Thompson v Foy* [2009] EWHC 1076 (Ch), in which a mother asserted a claim of undue influence by her daughter, Lewison J (at [117]), after a detailed review of the evidence, found that Mrs Thompson was advised of the risks and insisted on going ahead; whilst it was unclear that she had fully understood the advice, there was evidence that she had understood that there was a risk in what she was doing.

However, in *Etridge*, Lord Nicholls stated (at [62]) that there could be exceptional circumstances where it is clearly obvious that a wife was being 'grievously wronged' where a solicitor should refuse to act. Moreover, if the bank had a belief or suspicion that the wife was not entering the transaction of her own free will or was being misled, it had a duty to inform the solicitor.

There was a warning for a bank which failed to act on its knowledge:

> Ordinarily it will be reasonable that a bank should be able to rely upon confirmation from a solicitor, acting for the wife, that he advised the wife appropriately. The position will be otherwise if the bank knows that the solicitor has not duly advised the wife or, I would add, if the bank knows facts from which it ought to have realised that the wife has not received the appropriate advice. In such circumstances, the bank will proceed at its own risk. (per Lord Nicholls at [56] and [57])

12.3.4.6 Remedies for mortgagor

In most cases, the lender can proceed secure in the knowledge that the existence of independent legal advice means that the charge will be valid, and the mortgagor will need to seek redress in professional negligence against the solicitor if he or she is unhappy about the advice received or the solicitor has failed to follow the *Etridge* steps correctly.

12.3.4.7 Is there any residual risk to the lender?

As we have seen, in *Etridge*, the Court held open the possibility that if the bank was aware of a problem with the advice, it could not rely on it. In *National Westminster Bank v Amin* [2002] UKHL 9, the bank could not rely on a solicitor's letter stating that a Mr and Mrs Amin had received independent advice when it was aware that the couple did not speak English and were vulnerable, the solicitor did not confirm that the couple had understood the advice received, and the bank had not made clear that the solicitor was to advise Mr and Mrs Amin. It was unclear whether the solicitor was acting for the bank or for Mr and Mrs Amin, and accordingly the matter should not be struck out on the basis that the bank had received a solicitor's certificate that independent advice had been received but should go to trial.

12.4 Does a mortgagee have other remedies?

In the cases that we have discussed above, where a mortgagor has been successful in establishing misrepresentation or undue influence of which a mortgagee has been put on inquiry or constructive notice, this means that the security given by the mortgagor will be voided completely. In *TSB Bank Plc v Camfield* [1995] 1 WLR 430, a wife believed on the basis of a misrepresentation that she was giving security up to a cap of £15,000; there was some discussion as to whether her security could be enforced partially up to that cap, but this was not adopted and the security was set aside completely as against her.

However, this does not mean that the security is voided completely. If, for example, a husband and wife are joint owners of the family home then the borrower will also have entered into the charge as joint estate owner. The setting aside of the mortgage insofar as the innocent wounded party does not avoid the security given by the borrower (who is usually the party culpable for the misrepresentation or undue influence).

This is where the links between different areas of property law become evident. As the security is entered into by one of two joint legal and beneficial owners, the bank is left with an equitable mortgage over the borrower's equitable interest in the property.

The grant of the mortgage effects a severance of the beneficial joint tenancy if one existed prior to the entry into the charge (*First National Securities Ltd v Hegerty* [1985] QB 850).

The mortgagee has a range of remedies still left in its arsenal.

12.4.1 Action under s 14 of the Trusts of Land and Appointment of Trustees Act 1996

The mortgagee, by virtue of its equitable charge over the borrower's equitable interest, is now a person with an interest in property subject to a trust of land, and it may apply to the court under s 14 of the Trusts of Land and Appointment of Trustees Act (TLATA 1996) for an order for sale of the property. The mortgagee successfully did so in *First National Bank v Achampong* [2003] EWCA Civ 487, with a view to recovering part of the money due to it from the borrower's share in the proceeds of sale.

12.4.2 Insolvency Act 1986, s 335A

This can be combined with an action to enforce the borrower's covenant to pay. Once a money judgment is obtained and goes unsatisfied, the lender will be entitled to petition for bankruptcy. An application under s 14 of the TLATA 1996 will then be heard using the stricter factors which apply on bankruptcy set out in s 335A of the Insolvency Act 1986, rather than the more balanced s 15 TLATA 1996 factors. There is more consideration of these factors in **Chapter 6**, but a key point is that, after one year, unless there are exceptional circumstances, the interests of the bankrupt's creditors outweigh all other considerations, and an order for sale will almost certainly be obtained (Insolvency Act 1986, s 335A(3)).

In *Alliance & Leicester v Slayford* [2001] 1 All ER Comm 1, it was held that the lender was entitled to pursue its rights for a debt judgment against the borrower in respect of the arrears. Such rights were in the nature of an unsecured creditor with a view to obtaining a bankruptcy order against the debtor. Alliance & Leicester was a secured creditor which had been unable to obtain possession because Mrs Slayford had successfully asserted her equitable interest. However, the lender was not limited to remedies relating to its security and was entitled to use its unsecured rights relating to Mr Slayford's covenant to pay. To do so was not an abuse of process. A well-protected mortgagee will usually have the benefit of a variety of rights ranging from procedural (such as a restriction on the mortgagor's registered title), to contractual (the borrower's covenant to pay), to security (the registered charge). Therefore if one method of enforcement, such as the right to possession, fails, there may be others that the lender can pursue. If so, it is proper for the mortgagee to use its other remedies, including an application for an order for sale as an equitable mortgagee or on bankruptcy of the borrower.

12.5 Further reading

E Mujih, 'Over ten years after *Royal Bank of Scotland Plc v Etridge (No 2)*: is the law of undue influence in guarantee cases any clearer?' (2013) 24(2) ICCLR 57–67.

G Andrews, 'Undue influence – where's the disadvantage?' [2002] Conv 2002 456–69.

A person who is induced by misrepresentation or undue influence to enter a mortgage to guarantee the debt of a third party is entitled to have the mortgage set aside against him or her.

There may be actual evidence of undue influence, or it may be presumed if there is a relationship of trust and confidence between the parties and the nature of the transaction calls for explanation. In such case, the onus of rebutting the presumption moves to the mortgagee.

Undue influence against the mortgagor may, unusually, be exercised by the mortgagee, but more commonly it is by a third party. The mortgagee will be put on inquiry for possible undue influence in any non-commercial case where a person stands surety for the debts of a third party.

To avoid notice of the undue influence, the mortgagee must either have a private meeting with the mortgagor or require the mortgagor to receive independent legal advice.

The mortgagor must nominate a solicitor. The solicitor giving independent legal advice can act for more than one party. The mortgagee must supply the solicitor with all the financial information required to advise and inform him or her of any suspicions of pressure or misleading information. The solicitor must explain the nature and risks of the transaction to the mortgagor and obtain his or her consent to confirm to the mortgagee that the solicitor has done so. The mortgagor has a possible remedy against the solicitor providing independent advice.

If a mortgage is set aside against one mortgagor, it remains valid against other mortgagors who are unaffected by the undue influence.

test your knowledge

Ed is the majority shareholder in a company operating a number of local newspapers. His girlfriend Catherine is a majority shareholder but is not involved in the day-to-day running of the business. The company recently launched a new paper that is not selling well, and the company has lost a significant amount of money in the new venture. Ed is concerned that he may need to close the business soon. He needs a new loan of £10,000 to tide the company over; the bank agrees to this provided that he supplies security over the home that Ed jointly owns with Catherine for all his outstanding borrowings of £250,000. Ed persuades Catherine to enter into the security, telling her that it is 'just for £10,000'. Catherine goes to see Ed's solicitor who tells her that it will 'all be ok'. Eight months later, Ed and Catherine receive a letter from the bank informing them that it is seeking possession of the property. Advise Ed and Catherine.

chapter

13 Easements

study
points

After reading this chapter, you will be able to:

- define easement rights and explain their role in land ownership
- explain how easements are created and protected
- have an understanding of some current problems with the operation of easements
- evaluate proposals for reform of the law.

13.1 What does an easement do?

An easement is a right to use or restrict the use of the land of another person. Common easements are:

- a right of way – which give a means of access to the benefitted land;
- a right to light – which give a right to receive light to a building through a window;
- a right to run water supply or drainage pipes through your neighbour's land.

All of the examples given above give a right to use land belonging to another person. These rights can be very valuable. If a valid easement is created and protected, it will bind all future owners of the land. See 13.3 for details of how easements are created and protected.

A further consequence of easements is that they restrict the use to which land may be put. For example, a landowner may not construct a new building on his land in such a way that it prevents use of a track over which rights of way exist, or that damages water supply pipes which a neighbour has an easement to use. An easement of light can be used to stop a landowner from building on his land if it would reduce the light received by neighbouring land with the benefit of the easement below the level necessary for its ordinary use.

The categories of easement are not closed, which means that new types of easement could – in theory – be developed. The courts have set out four essential characteristics that are required for an easement to exist (see 13.3).

13.2 Profits a prendre

There is a related class of rights over land known as profits a prendre. These are of much less practical significance in the modern law. They include rights over someone else's land, such as a right to extract minerals, to hunt or shoot over the land, to fish or to graze sheep or other livestock.

Like an easement or restrictive covenant, a profit must exist over specific 'servient land' that is burdened by it. Unlike an easement or a restrictive covenant, a profit need not benefit any dominant land but can exist 'in gross' as an independent right not attached to dominant land.

Profits fall within the definition of 'easement, right or privilege' in s 1(2)(a) of the Law of Property Act (LPA) 1925. If appurtenant to land, they function in the same way as easements. The requirements in *Re Ellenborough Park* [1956] Ch 131 apply to them and we turn to this now.

13.3 Four essential characteristics of an easement

Although the courts have said that the categories of easement are not closed, they have set out four essential requirements that a right or a claimed right must possess in order to qualify as an easement. If a right or claimed right does not possess all four of these qualities, it cannot be an easement, although it may be some other proprietary right in land, such as a lease. Alternatively it may be simply a licence or permission from a landowner which can be terminated at any time. It may even be a trespass and therefore an unlawful use of the land of another person.

The four requirements were set out in *Re Ellenborough Park* [1956] Ch 131:

(a) There must be a dominant and servient tenement.
(b) The easement must accommodate the dominant tenement.
(c) Dominant and servient owners must be different persons.
(d) The right must be capable of forming the subject matter of a grant.

Let us look at these in more detail.

13.3.1 There must be a dominant and servient tenement

This means that there must be two plots of land – the first, the dominant tenement, which has the benefit of the right, and the second, the servient tenement, which is burdened by the right.

If Charles lives next door to Sally, and Charles has a right to walk through Sally's land to reach the road then Charles's land – which has the benefit of the right – is the dominant tenement, and Sally's land – which is burdened by the right – is the servient tenement.

This is because an easement attaches to land and not to any person. In order to create an easement, both parties – the party whose land is benefitted and the party whose land is burdened – must have an estate in land for the right to attach to.

13.3.2 The easement must accommodate the dominant tenement

The right must benefit the land and not merely a person. Although the right may well increase the value of the benefitted land, this is not enough in itself. For a right to accommodate land, it must be connected with the 'normal enjoyment' of that property.

In the example above, where Charles uses Sally's land to get from his house to the road, it is clear to see that the right benefits Charles's land. Without it, his land might be landlocked or just less convenient to use.

There must be a close enough geographical tie between the two plots of land. For example, in the case of *Bailey v Stephens* (1862) 12 CB NS 91, it was famously said that it was impossible to have a right of way over land in Kent appurtenant to land in Northumberland.

One controversial question here is how far an easement can accommodate the business use of land. Compare the cases of *Hill v Tupper* (1863) 2 H & C 121 and *Moody v Steggles* (1879) 12 Ch D 261. It is fine for an easement to allow a right of way for business customers. In the case of *Moody v Steggles*, the law has also recognised the right to put up an advertising sign on the side of a property as an easement.

But in *Hill v Tupper*, the owner of a small piece of land next to a canal claimed that a contractual right to put boats on the canal was an easement. His claim was rejected as being unconnected with the use and enjoyment of the land. Putting boats on the canal had no normal connection with the ordinary use of his land but was merely an independent business enterprise.

13.3.3 Dominant and servient owners must be different persons

Put simply, an individual cannot have an easement over his or her own land.

A tenant can, however, have an easement over adjoining land owned by his landlord. This is very common in practice. For example, a tenant in a third-floor flat needs easement rights over the parts of the building that the landlord has retained in order to enter the building and use the lift or stairs to reach his flat.

Although this rule sounds innocuous, it is inconvenient for property developers who wish to set up a scheme of easements on a development and cannot do so until land has been transferred to separate ownership. There are practical implications to this in that the timing of sales off can affect the grant of easement rights. In its report, *Making Land Work: Easements, Covenants and Profits a Prendre* (Law Com No 327), 2011, para 4.44, the Law Commission has recommended that where title to benefitted and burdened land is registered, the fact that they are in common ownership should not prevent the creation or preservation of easements and profits. One very practical reason for this is that it will facilitate the Land Registry's services to developers by allowing them to plan in advance the grant of easements and covenants on individual units on a large-scale residential development to ensure that the correct rights are granted or reserved in respect of each plot.

13.3.4 The right must be capable of forming the subject matter of a grant

This fourth requirement is more difficult to apply. The key questions here are as follows.

13.3.4.1 Is the right clear enough to be capable of description in a deed?

An easement must be sufficiently definite. For example, a right to light through a particular window can be an easement. A general right to light or a right not to be overlooked by other buildings or to maintain a particular view is not.

13.3.4.2 Is the right of a kind that courts are willing to recognise as an easement?

An easement must also be of a kind that the courts are willing to recognise as an easement. A good example here is that the courts will not recognise as an easement a right whose effect is to give possession of the land to the person exercising it. That right may amount to a lease or a licence but it will not be an easement. The distinction is important because easement rights can be acquired by prescription or long use and are protected as legal rights against new owners of the land (in the case of unregistered land) or as an overriding interest in the case of registered land.

Imagine that Jane is using part of her neighbour William's land informally to store things or to park her car. If Jane has a licence to do so, William can withdraw his permission at any time; but if Jane has a prescriptive legal easement, she has a protected proprietary right in William's land which is binding on William and on anyone to whom William sells his land.

Controversial issue – parking

Storage and, in particular, car parking rights are a controversial topic where the boundaries of the law of easements are currently being tested. The law recognises that the right to store items or park cars on land belonging to another person can be an easement. However, the right must not be capable of being exercised in such a way that is excessive or that amounts to an ouster of the servient owner's rights so as to be incompatible with being an easement. If the right is excessive, it may be considered to be a claim to possession of the land or, at any rate, to a joint user with the owner. This cannot be an easement.

The courts have struggled to find a test which they can apply in these circumstances.

Table 13.1   Tests for recognition as an easement

Is servient owner left with any reasonable use of his or her land? *London & Blenheim Ltd v Ladbroke Retail Parks Ltd* [1992] 1 WLR 1278, applied by the CA in *Batchelor v Marlow* [2003] 1 WLR 764; *Virdi v Chana* [2008] EWHC 2901 (Ch); *Polo Woods Foundation v Shelton-Agar* [2010] 1 All ER 539	In *Batchelor v Marlow*, the Court of Appeal applied a test that had been formulated in the case of *London & Blenheim Ltd v Ladbroke Retail Parks Ltd*. If the right would leave the servient owner without any *reasonable use* of his or her land so that his or her ownership was rendered illusory, then the right could not be an easement, although it might be something else, such as a right to title to the land by adverse possession or a right to a lease.
Does the servient owner retain possession and control of his or her land? *Moncrieff v Jamieson* [2007] UKHL 42	The *Batchelor v Marlow* test was criticised by the House of Lords in *Moncrieff v Jamieson*. The criticism was obiter to the judgment and therefore is not binding as precedent although it is persuasive. Lord Scott rejected the reasonable user test and substituted for it a test which asks whether the servient owner retains possession and, subject to the reasonable exercise of the right in question, control of the servient land.
Does the right have the essential characteristics of an easement? Law Commission, *Making Land Work: Easements, Covenants and Profits a Prendre* (Law Com No 327)	The Law Commission has advocated a different approach still in its recent report No 327. It proposes that the 'best approach' is to consider the scope and extent of the right that is created and to ask whether it has the essential characteristics of an easement? If it has, it proposes that the right should not fail as an easement because it prevents the servient owner from making any reasonable use of his or her affected land. This would abolish the rule in *Batchelor v Marlow*.

Batchelor, as a Court of Appeal case, has not been overruled and is binding on lower courts despite the obiter comments in *Moncrieff*. As such, *Batchelor* has been followed in several more recent cases, such as the 2008 case of *Virdi v Chana* and the 2010 case of *Polo Woods Foundation v Shelton-Agar*. In the 2014 case of *Begley v Taylor* [2014] EWHC 1180 (Ch), *Batchelor* was accepted as binding but was distinguished: a continuing ability to drive along an access road and, in the case of a domestic property, alter the surface of the road for aesthetic reasons were sufficient to count as reasonable use of the servient land.

13.4 Creation of easements

13.4.1 Express creation

The most straightforward way to create an easement is to do so by an express grant. This must be by deed and, if the land out of which the easement is granted is registered, the easement is a registrable disposition which must be completed by registration under s 27(2) of the Land Registration Act (LRA) 2002.

It must also comply with s 1(2) of the LPA 1925 in order to take legal effect. This means that it must either be granted as a permanent easement or for a fixed term of years.

revision point

How are easements treated in registered land (see **Chapter 5**)?

- registrable – expressly created legal easements (LRA 2002, s 27)
- protect by notice – equitable easements (LRA 2002, s 34)
- overriding – informally created legal easements (LRA 2002, s 29 and Sch 3, para 2)
- protection of pre-LRA 2002 easements (LRA 2002, Sch 12, para 9)

However, the law also recognises easements that are created impliedly or by prescription. Both are recognised as legal easements, despite the fact that the formalities set out above have not been followed on their creation.

Let us look at these in more detail.

13.4.2 Implied

When land is sold, sometimes the seller retains neighbouring land. For example, a homeowner sells part of his garden to a developer to build new houses on. In this situation, even though the contract and conveyance may be silent on the issue, the purchaser might acquire an easement (for example, a right of way) over any land that the seller is retaining. (It is important to recognise that easements will not be implied over unrelated land. For example, if that same homeowner sells all of his property to the same developer, there is no scope for easements to be implied over any other land that was not in the homeowner's ownership.)

To analyse this, we have to look at how and when easements will be implied.

The first question we have to ask is whether the easement claimed is a grant or a reservation? As we have said, easements may be implied when land is sold or leased, if the seller or lessor retains some land. If the easement is to be implied for the benefit of the land that has been sold or leased, this is a grant of an easement. The law here is relatively generous to allow a purchaser to get what he or she thought he or she was getting as part of the deal. If the easement is claimed for the land that was retained by the seller, this is known as a reservation, and the law is much stricter because a seller may not derogate from his or her grant; he or she should be clear about the rights that he or she requires. Although this rule makes sense, it causes difficulty when a seller is disposing of several plots of land close together, as the order in which the plots are sold can affect any implied rights that the eventual buyers end up with. Of course, the ideal is for all rights to be granted and reserved expressly, but the case law shows us that this ideal does not always occur in practice. Such implied rights are:

- legal, if implied into a deed (usually a transfer deed or lease); and
- overriding under s 29 of and Sch 3, para 3 to the LRA 2002 and therefore binding even if not registered.

There are three ways that an easement might be impliedly granted to a purchaser or tenant of land:

(a) necessity;

(b) the rule in *Wheeldon v Burrows* (1879) 12 Ch D 31; and

(c) statutory implication under s 62 of the LPA 1925.

Of these three ways, only the first, necessity, is available to a seller or lessor of land.

Table 13.2   Implied grant of easement

Grant (land sold)	Reservation (land retained)
Necessity/common intention	Necessity/common intention
Rule in *Wheeldon v Burrows*	
LPA 1925, s 62	

13.4.2.1   Necessity

The second question then is whether the grant or reservation is necessary. The law uses necessity here in two ways.

Necessary to use the land – otherwise 'landlocked'

The first is that the law will imply the grant or reservation of an easement when it is necessary to do so for land to be used at all (*Union Lighterage Co v London Graving Dock Co* [1902] 2 Ch 557). This is limited to a right of way to land to which there is no other access. If there is another access, no matter how inconvenient, no right of way will be implied. It also, of course, requires there to be a transaction into which the right can be implied – in other words a sale or a lease. A right of way will not be implied for all landlocked land.

Necessary for the use and enjoyment of the land in the way contemplated by the parties

The second use is that the law will imply the grant or reservation of an easement if it is necessary for the use and enjoyment of the sold land or the retained land, in the way contemplated by the parties. As Lord Parker stated in *Pwllback Colliery Co Ltd v Woodman* [1915] AC 634 (at 647), it is '… essential for this purpose that the parties should intend that the subject of the grant or the land retained by the grantor should be used in some definite and particular manner'. See also *Wong v Beaumont Property Trust Ltd* [1965] 1 QB 173 where an easement for a ventilation duct on the landlord's retained land was implied where it was necessary for the intended use of the property by the tenant as a restaurant.

Necessity, whether it is to prevent land being landlocked or to give effect to the common intention of the parties, is restrictive. Necessity is construed strictly. It will not be enough that the grant or reservation of an easement would be convenient or usual or reasonable. However, it is potentially available whether the right claimed is a grant to benefit the land sold or leased, or whether it is by way of reservation to benefit the land retained by the seller.

The next two classes are more generous but will only benefit a buyer or lessee. They cannot be used by a seller or lessor of land.

13.4.2.2 The rule in *Wheeldon v Burrows*

The requirements under the rule in *Wheeldon v Burrows* are as follows:

* quasi-easement used for the benefit of 'dominant' land;
* continuous and apparent; and
* necessary for the reasonable enjoyment of the 'dominant' land.

According to Thesiger LJ:

> [O]n the grant by the owner of a tenement of part of that tenement as it is then used and enjoyed, there will pass to the grantee all those continuous and apparent easements (by which, of course, I mean *quasi* easements), or, in other words, all those easements which are necessary to the reasonable enjoyment of the property granted, and which have been and are at the time of the grant used by the owners of the entirety for the benefit of the part granted.

What is a quasi-easement?

It is the term used when the two plots of land are in common ownership. Immediately prior to the sale or lease, both plots – the land to be sold and the land to be retained – are owned by the seller.

If the common owner – the seller – exercises over one plot for the benefit of the other a right which, if they had been in separate ownership, could have been an easement, this is a quasi-easement. For example, let us say that James owns a field at the back of his house. He gets access to the field by going down a track – which he also owns – which runs from the road, down the side of his house, alongside his back garden and then into the field. If his field were separately owned, this right would be capable of being an easement – a right of way. It cannot be an easement as things stand as both plots of land – the track through his garden and the field – are owned by James. The dominant and servient owners are not different people. It is a quasi-easement.

If James sells the field without granting a right to way to the buyer, the buyer could almost certainly obtain an implied right of way by necessity over this track. Without it, his field is landlocked. But let us imagine that there *is* an alternative access to the field that the buyer does have an express right to use. It is not particularly convenient – perhaps it crosses other fields and can only be used on foot. The track through James's garden is much better because it can be used by a vehicle. But the right to use the path would be fatal to any claim by the buyer to use the track based on necessity. The rule in *Wheeldon v Burrows* gives the buyer another opportunity to get the easement right that he should have negotiated for in the transfer deed.

If he can show, as he probably could in this case, that use of the track to access the field satisfies the next two tests, then he will be entitled to an implied easement under the rule in *Wheeldon v Burrows*.

Continuous and apparent

Continuous and apparent means that the right is regularly used and there is physical evidence of the right on the land (ie the existence of the track itself).

Necessary for reasonable enjoyment

Use of the right will be necessary for the reasonable use and enjoyment of the land if it is necessary for its reasonable or convenient enjoyment. It is not the strict test of necessity that we saw earlier.

If the buyer can show both that the easement is continuous and apparent and necessary for the reasonable enjoyment of his land then he will get his implied easement. It has never been satisfactorily resolved whether the quasi-easement must satisfy both tests, ie it must be both continuous and apparent *and* necessary for the reasonable enjoyment. The better view seems to be that both tests must be met.

13.4.2.3 Section 62 of the LPA 1925

The third rule, again, will only benefit a buyer or lessee and cannot be used by a seller or lessor of land. On the sale or leasing of land, easements can be statutorily implied under s 62 of the LPA 1925.

A conveyance of land shall be deemed to include … all … liberties, privileges, easements, rights and advantages whatsoever, appertaining or reputed to appertain to the land …

It is likely that this wording was never intended to allow new easements to be created but was merely to confirm the common law rule that, when land has the benefit of an existing easement or profit, a conveyance of that dominant land includes the benefit of the right to enjoy that easement or profit.

But the courts have used it as a way of converting an existing informal right into a full-blown legal easement.

Wright v Macadam [1949] KB 744

A good example is *Wright v Macadam*. Mrs Wright had a lease of a flat. Her landlord gave her an informal right to store coal in a coal shed in the garden. There was no mention of this in the lease. Later she renewed her lease. Again, the lease was silent on the ability to store coal. Later, the landlord tried to charge her a weekly sum for use of the coal house. Mrs Wright refused and the Court of Appeal held that, on the renewal of the lease, there was implied into that lease an easement to store coal in the coal shed by virtue of s 62 of the LPA 1925. The effect of s 62 is so strong that, if when Mrs Wright's lease had ended the landlord had let the flat to a new party, the new tenant would also have had the benefit of an implied easement to store coal, by virtue of s 62.

For s 62 to operate there must be a conveyance of the land. Remember that under s 205(1)(ii) of the LPA 1925, a conveyance includes a lease and mortgage as well as a transfer of the land. Section 62 only works in favour of rights that are being exercised at the date of the conveyance, and it only comes into play if there has been a prior diversity of occupation – this is most likely to have happened when the dominant land has previously been occupied by a third party under a lease or a licence.

Let us look again at our example of a field at the back of James's house. As before, it has been sold without granting an express right of way over the access track. But let us change the facts and assume that, before the sale, a tenant occupied the field under a lease, using it to graze his horses. His lease gives him an express right of way over the access track. James agrees to sell the land to the tenant but no right of way is included in the transfer deed. Section 62 will operate to incorporate the right of way into the transfer deed and upgrade it from a leasehold easement into a freehold one.

In fact, s 62 goes even further. Let us assume that the tenant's lease gave no right of way over the access track, but, as a matter of practice, James had allowed the tenant to use the track with vehicles to get to the field. When the tenant's lease ends and he vacates, James decides to sell the field to an unconnected buyer. Although the lease gave no right of way over the track, s 62 applies not only to 'easements' but also to 'liberties' and 'privileges'. When James later sells the field, s 62 of the LPA 1925 will allow that licence informally granted to the previous tenant to be converted into an easement which the later buyer can take advantage of.

The wide wording of s 62 means that it can be difficult to predict its effects, and it is standard practice to exclude it from land transactions.

13.4.2.4 What conclusions can we draw about the creation of implied easements?

First, it is a reflection of the importance of easements to enable the full use of land that the law permits legal easements to be created impliedly. Remember that if an easement is implied into a deed (generally a transfer deed or lease), it will take effect at law and will bind the world (unregistered land). The same result is achieved in registered land by the overriding status of implied legal easements if not placed on the register (see LRA 2002, s 29 and Sch 3).

Secondly, it emphasises that parties should think very carefully about easements when dealing with land that forms part of a larger parcel of land or estate. A party that fails to incorporate the easements that he or she needs into the transfer deed risks being unable to enjoy land effectively or, even if the circumstances are such that a court may be willing to imply an easement, the uncertainty and cost of litigation. Conversely, a party may find that an easement is implied against him or her in a manner that he or she objects to.

The Law Commission has made proposals for reform of the rules relating to implied easements. It accepts their importance but recommends that the distinction between grant and reservation should be removed and the same rules should be applied to both. It has recommend replacing the existing tests – necessity and the rule in *Wheeldon v Burrows* – by focusing on what is 'necessary for the reasonable use of the land', taking into account a number of factors including:

(a) the use of the land at the time of grant;

(b) the presence on the servient land of any relevant physical features;

(c) any intentions for the future use of the land known to both parties at the time of grant;

(d) so far as relevant, the potential routes for the easement sought; and

(e) the interference with the servient land and inconvenience to the servient owner.

As now, parties to a transaction should be able to provide expressly that easements will not be implied into their transaction documents. The Law Commission recommends that s 62 should continue to apply, subject to the right of parties to exclude the operation of the section. The Commission recommends that s 62 should continue to apply to convert easements that are enjoyed by a tenant into freehold easements if the land is transferred (such as in our first example above where the tenant has a leasehold easement to use the track). However, it recommends that it should no longer convert informal rights (such as the licence to use the track in our second example) into legal easements. The Commission refers to these as 'precarious benefits' and recommends that they are removed from the ambit of s 62 of the Law of Property Act 1925. It also recommends that it should no longer be possible to create a profit by implication, but only by express grant or by statute.

13.4.3 Prescription

easements by prescription – requirements

- legal
- overriding under s 29 of and Sch 3, para 3 to the LRA 2002 and therefore binding even if not registered
- easement acquired by use of claimed right over a long period of time
- user must be 'as of right':
  - without force
  - without secrecy
  - without permission
- user must be continuous
- user must be by or on behalf of a fee simple against a fee simple – a prescriptive easement will only be granted in fee simple
- user must be against a servient owner capable of granting an easement

User as of right means user which is open and is neither with the servient owner's express consent nor against his or her expressed objections.

There are three methods by which an easement can arise by prescription:

(a) common law;

(b) lost modern grant; and

(c) Prescription Act 1832.

13.4.3.1 Common law

Under prescription at common law, this is presumptively established if the claimant can show 20 years' user as of right. In practice that can usually be rebutted by showing that the user has not been continuous since 1189. This date is taken to be the origin of legal memory. If it can be shown that an easement could not have existed in 1189 – perhaps because it relates to a building that was only built in 1800 – then it will fail.

13.4.3.2 Lost modern grant

The user must show 20 years' user as of right. It can only be rebutted by showing that the grant was legally impossible, for example because the owner was a minor. It relies on the fiction that if a right has been used for at least 20 years (which need not be the last 20 years) then the courts are willing to presume that an easement has been granted but that the deed of grant has been lost.

13.4.3.3 Prescription Act 1832

The claimant must show 20 or 40 years' user as of right without interruption which is 'next before action'. Remember that user must be without the landowner's permission: the difference between the two time periods is that a claim based on 40 years' user can only be defeated by evidence that it has been enjoyed with the permission of the landowner in writing or by deed. It will not be defeated if permission was granted orally. If the exercise is interrupted (eg because the owner of the servient land stops exercise of the right) then legal proceedings must be brought within 12 months of the interruption of the right. If the interruption is longer then the claim will fail.

As you can immediately see, the law in this area is complex and archaic. The Law Commission has recommended that it be simplified but believes that the benefits of recognising long-standing land use mean that prescription should be retained.

in practice

Reform proposals – Law Commission Report No 327

- single scheme
- 20 years' continuous qualifying use
- qualifying use – without force, stealth or permission

The Law Commission recognises the importance of prescription as a way of 'bringing the legal position into line with practical reality'.

It recommends abolishing all three current methods and replacing them with a single new statutory scheme based on 20 years' continuous qualifying use.

It also recommends that it should no longer be possible to create a profit by prescription but only by express grant or by statute.

13.5 Scope of easements

13.5.1 Changes in use

Once the grant of an easement has been established – whether by express grant, implication or prescription – what exactly does this allow the owner or occupier of the benefitted land, or his or her visitors, to do?

What if the use of the land changes? For example, what if a developer buys agricultural barns which have the benefit of a right of way for access and creates a busy distribution centre? Can the new owners continue to rely on the easement right or can the servient owner prevent use for the new purpose?

A different approach is taken depending on whether the easement was expressly granted or arose by implication or prescription.

13.5.1.1 Express easement

The precise scope of the easement will depend on the construction of the document that created it, if there is one. When construing the document, the courts tend to interpret any ambiguity against the person granting the easement (although this rule is applied less strictly where an easement is reserved in favour of a seller of land and therefore the person granting the easement is technically the buyer).

Where the right was expressly granted, the courts will look first at the construction of the particular easement. If there is no limitation in the wording of the easement then a change of use will not invalidate the easement.

If the change of use of the dominant land intensifies the use of the easement then this will not invalidate the easement *unless* the use becomes excessive so that it unreasonably interferes with the rights of the servient owner or of others who have rights to use the land (see *Rosling v Pinnegar* [1987] 54 P&CR 124).

13.5.1.2 Implied easement

Where the grant was acquired by implication then the courts look to the use that was contemplated at the date of the conveyance or transfer. This may often just be the actual use at that date, but a change in use will not be excessive if it is clear that it was contemplated by the parties. See *Stafford v Lee* (1965) P&CR 172, where although current user was as woodland, conveyancing plans showed that the common intention was that a house would be built on the land.

13.5.1.3 Prescriptive easement

And where it was acquired by prescription then the scope is limited to the user by which the easement was acquired. An increase in the extent of use may not be excessive, but use for a different use (eg if the dominant land is converted from agricultural to industrial, as happened in *Williams v James* (1867) LR 2 CP 577, or from a small private house into a large hotel as in *British Railways Board v Glass* [1965] Ch 538) will not be permitted under the prescriptive easement that has been acquired.

13.5.2 Use for other land

As an easement benefits land, rather than an individual, it cannot be extended to benefit other land even if it is also owned by that individual. So if the access to a development site is via a right of way over a neighbouring owner's track, the developer cannot buy further land at the back of the existing site and extend the easement to use it to access the new land. See *Harris v Flower* (1904) 74 LJ Ch 127. However, this may be possible if the additional land is merely ancillary to the original use of the easement (*Peacock v Custins* [2001] 2 All ER 827) or the secondary user is insubstantial or non-profit-making (*Massey v Boulden* [2002] 2 All ER 87). In practice, this rule causes difficulty for developers who are piecing together a development site from various parcels of land, although if new easements are being negotiated, this can be mitigated by enabling land to be acquired simultaneously.

The Law Commission (Consultation Paper No 186, *Easements, Covenants and Profits a Prendre*, para 5.70) proposed reform of this rule that the guiding principle should always be the effect on the servient land. Extending the easement to new land would not be permitted if it would cause excessive user of the servient land. However, extension of the rule was opposed by responders to the consultation and no recommendation was included in the Law Commission's final report, *Making Land Work: Easements, Covenants and Profits a Prendre* (Law Com No 327).

The converse question must also be asked: once the grant of an easement has been established – whether by express grant, implication or prescription – what exactly does this allow the owner or occupier of the burdened or servient land, or his or her visitors, to continue to do?

You will remember from our discussion of parking rights that questions of what the servient owner can continue to do go to the heart of whether a claimed right is recognised as an easement or not.

If the servient owner wrongfully interferes with the exercise of the easement, the dominant owner has a remedy in nuisance. The remedies for interference are an injunction (to remove the interference) and damages. If damages are considered adequate and an injunction would be oppressive to the servient owner, damages in lieu of an injunction can be awarded.

The leading case is *Celsteel Ltd v Alton House Holdings Ltd* [1985] 1 WLR 204. Scott J held that interference will be wrongful if it is substantial. An interference will not be substantial if it does not interfere with the reasonable use of right of way.

Most cases will therefore turn on their facts. What is the extent of the easement and what is the interference or proposed interference? In the *Celsteel* case, the servient owner wanted to construct a building which would have affected a driveway over which a right of way was exercisable. The proposed narrowing of the driveway from 9 metres to 4 metres was substantial, and therefore wrongful, as it was reasonable for commercial vans and lorries to use the driveway in the exercise of the easement. However if the narrowing had been more modest and had merely meant that some easy manoeuvring was necessary to use the roadway, this would have been acceptable.

13.5.3 Rights to light

There are different rules for rights to light, which are usually obtained by prescription. They:

- apply to windows in buildings;
- entitle the dominant owner to sufficient light for the ordinary use and enjoyment of the building, depending on its purpose and potential purposes to which the building could reasonably be put.

13.6 Abandonment of an easement

An easement can be extinguished where there has been an act or omission on the part of the estate owner of the dominant tenement with intention to abandon the right. This is a question of fact. It may occur, for example, if the owner of the dominant tenement carries out alterations to his or her property that render the easement impossible or unnecessary to enjoy. In practice, this can be difficult to prove and will not be inferred by the court lightly because

> Owners of property do not normally wish to divest themselves of it unless it is to their advantage to do so, notwithstanding that they may have no present use for it. (*Gotobed v Pridmore* (1971) 217 EG 759, 760, per Buckley LJ, cited with approval in *Benn v Hardinge* (1993) 66 P&CR 246, 257–61, per Dillan LJ)

In *Benn v Hardinge*, lack of use for 175 years was insufficient evidence of intent to abandon because the right 'might be of significant importance in the future' (per Hirst LJ at 262).

In its 2011 report, the Law Commission recommends (at para 3.230) a rebuttable presumption that an easement has been abandoned after a continuous period of 20 years' non-use.

13.7 Commercial issues

As we have seen through the cases, easements give rights to use land that benefit the dominant land but also can restrict the use to which the servient or burdened land can be put. This can be seen most acutely when land is being developed and new rights are needed to support that development, or existing rights are proposed to be used in a manner that is more intense or to support a change of use. This can apply to a development of either the dominant or the servient land. Where rights are expressly reserved or granted, the drafting of the underlying documents can be critical.

This is something that practitioners need to be wary of when working on the sale or purchase of land for development. This is illustrated by the case of *Donovan v Rana* [2014] EWCA Civ 99. Land was sold at auction, with the particulars making clear that the buyer was expected to develop a house on the plot. In the transfer, an express right of way was granted over a roadway with or without vehicles for all purposes. There was a specific limitation that no rights other than those set out in the transfer were deemed to be granted either expressly or impliedly. The developer dug up the surface of the roadway in order to lay essential services to connect into public utilities. The Court of Appeal held that, despite the limiting words in the transfer, a 'common intention' easement existed as it was obvious that the development would require services to be available.

As a commercial point, the need for easements should always be anticipated so far as possible and rights included in the documents. When acting for developers, there is a clear message here that it is also important to get express agreement to the proposed development when purchasing land. In this case, because of the underlying agreement that the development of the house was permitted, easements of necessity or 'common intention' to support that development were implied.

A case involving the proposed development of the servient land was *Kettel v Bloomfold Ltd* [2012] EWHC 1422 (Ch). The case concerned the nature of rights to park in a communal car park serving a block of flats. Leaseholders had been granted in their leases rights to use the communal car park to park a car or motorbike, and, in practice, each had been allocated a particular parking space. The freeholder wanted to build a new block of flats on part of the car park and allocated the leaseholders alternative parking spaces on other parts of the site. When the leaseholders objected and sought an injunction, the court held that although the leaseholders did not have rights to specific car parking spaces, their right was to use the car park area. General wording in the lease allowing the freeholder to develop its neighbouring land did not permit it to interfere with the leaseholders' proprietorial easement rights over the car park. Clear wording might have achieved this, and this is something to be wary of when planning a phased development or developing an existing site more intensively. In this case, the injunction was granted in favour of the leaseholders, and, ultimately, it is likely that in order to carry out its proposed development, the freeholder will need to try to negotiate a financial settlement with those leaseholders to persuade them to accept alternative parking spaces. There is some discussion in the case of the basis on which the judge would have awarded damages had he refused to grant the injunction, and this is likely to give the parties a starting point for that negotiation!

13.8 Restrictive covenants

Before we finish, a quick word about restrictive covenants, which we will look at in more detail in **Chapter 14**. A covenant is a promise made in a deed. Negative or restrictive covenants (but not positive covenants) can run with the land and be enforced by and against future owners of the land.

As we have seen, the existence of an easement allows the dominant owner to prevent use of the servient land in a way which substantially interferes with the exercise of the easement. This may allow the dominant owner to prevent an otherwise lawful development of the servient land. This is most strikingly seen in the exercise of rights to light, which can be used to block development that interferes with the access of light to windows, but other rights such as rights of way or to drainage can also affect the servient owner's ability to develop or use his or her land. In the *Celsteel* case, the existence of the right of way meant that a development of the servient land could not go ahead as planned.

In this way, easements can play a role in the private control of development. The public control of development is dealt with by planning and building regulation controls.

A landowner can also exercise control over neighbouring land if he or she obtains a covenant against development. These are commonly extracted when a landowner sells part of his or her land and wants to prevent the new owner acting in a way which compromises his or her retained land. For example, the seller may require the buyer to covenant to use the sold land only for residential purposes or not to build on it unless the seller approves the plans.

The covenant will be binding between the original contracting parties but may also bind future owners of land.

A negative covenant (for example not to build) is capable of running with the land so as to potentially bind successors in title to the original covenanting parties.

However the burden of a positive covenant (such as a covenant *to* build or to pay money) cannot be enforced against a successor in title to the person who made the promise. The Law Commission has also made proposals to reform this area of the law.

13.9 Further reading

S Douglas, 'Reforming implied easements' (2015) 131 LQR 251–74.

G Spark, 'Easements of parking and storage: are easements non-possessory interests in land?' (2012) 1 Conv 6–18.

A Lyall, 'What are easements attached or appurtenant to?' (2010) 4 Conv 300–07.

P Kenny, 'Vanishing Easements in registered land' [2003] Conv 304–13.

S Pulleyn, 'Equitable easements revisited' (2012) 5 Conv 387–404.

Law Commission, *Making Land Work: Easements, Covenants and Profits a Prendre* (Law Com No 327), 2011.

An easement is capable of being a legal interest in land if granted for the equivalent of a freehold or leasehold estate in land (LPA 1925, s 1(2)(a)).

An easement must meet the four requirements set out in *Re Ellenborough Park*:

(1) dominant and servient tenement;

(2) right must accommodate dominant tenement;

(3) owners must be different persons;

(4) capable of grant.

An easement may be created expressly, in which case it should be created by deed and, if land is registered, registered under s 27(2)(d) of the LRA 2002.

An easement may also be created impliedly when part of a larger parcel of land is disposed of and the appropriate easements are not granted or reserved in the transfer deed. The methods of implication available to the buyer in whose favour an easement is to be granted are necessity, common intention, the rule in *Wheeldon v Burrows* and s 62 of the LPA 1925.

Only necessity and common intention are available if a seller of land seeks easements reserved in his or her favour.

Easements may also be obtained informally by prescription if user has existed as of right, without force, without secrecy and without permission for a continuous period of at least 20 years. User must be exercised by fee simple owner against fee simple owner, and the servient owner must have capacity to grant the easement. There are a variety of methods of prescription:

(a) common law prescription – that the user has operated from 1189; this is easily rebutted;

(b) lost modern grant – strong evidence of 20 years' user;

(c) Prescription Act 1832 – 20 or 40 years' user.

The Law Commission has recommended that future easements should be granted using a new 'land obligation' right.

test your
knowledge

1 Quick quiz

Facts	What is it?	How to protect it?
Annie grants Bal a right by deed to drive over a track on her land for the rest of her life.	Equitable easement Why? Although made by deed, it is for Bal's life and therefore not for an interest equivalent to an estate in fee simple absolute in possession or a term of years absolute, as required for a legal easement by s 1(2) of the LPA 1925.	Registered land – notice on the register (LRA 2002, ss 29 and 34). Unregistered land – Class D(iii) land charge (Land Charges Act 1972, s 2(5)).
Chris's new house is connected to the public water supply via a length of private pipe that runs from his property, underneath his neighbour's drive, and then under the public road to the water supply connection point. The neighbour has entered into a document setting out the right which he has signed in the presence of a third neighbour, who has also signed the document.	Legal easement Why? The document has been granted by deed (LPA 1925, s 52). The requirements of a deed are set out in s 1 of the Law of Property (Miscellaneous Provisions) Act 1989.	Registered land – substantive registration as a registrable disposition under s 27 of the LRA 2002. Unregistered land – as a legal easement the right is binding on the world. It does not act as a trigger for first registration (LRA 2002, s 4).
Rajesh, who lives on the main road, tells his neighbour, who lives up a steep lane behind Rajesh's property, that when it is icy, he can park in his driveway.	Licence Why? No formalities have been used to create valid legal or equitable rights. It is also unlikely that the right is sufficiently certain to be an easement as it will only apply when it is icy.	No protection possible as it is not a proprietary right in land. It is therefore not binding on third parties. There is a line of authority where a licence may be binding on a third party if, exceptionally, he or she has agreed to be bound by it and a constructive trust is imposed to ensure this (*Ashburn Anstalt v Arnold* [1989] Ch 1).

Facts	What is it?	How to protect it?
David agrees with his next-door neighbour to grant him a right of way on foot over a path in his back garden as a short cut to the train station in return for a payment of £10,000. David and his neighbour draw up a short written document and sign it.	Equitable easement Why? The document appears to be a specifically enforceable contract to enter into the easement, which complies with s 2 of the Law of Property (Miscellaneous Provisions) Act 1989. It will be treated as an equitable easement under the rule in *Walsh v Lonsdale* (1882) 21 Ch D 9.	Registered land – notice on the register (LRA 2002, ss 29 and 34). Unregistered land – Class D(iii) land charge (Land Charges Act 1972, s 2(5)).

2   Madeleine is buying business premises from Donald to use as an art gallery and discovers that he has agreed with the adjoining café owner, Della, that Della and her customers can park in the drive 'whenever there is space to do so'. The pair have signed a document recording this agreement. Madeleine needs full use of the drive for parking for her gallery business. Does she have to honour the agreement?

chapter 14

Covenants

study points

After reading this chapter, you will be able to understand:

- the nature of a covenant
- the circumstances in which a covenant will be considered a proprietary right in land
- how and to what extent the benefit and burden of covenants pass with the title to land in relation to positive and negative covenants
- the Law Commission's proposals for reform of restrictive covenants.

14.1 What is a covenant?

14.1.1 Freehold titles

A covenant is a promise contained in a deed. It will be enforceable between the parties to the deed itself. Imagine that A sells off part of his garden to B, to build a new house in the grounds. In the transfer deed, A takes a promise or covenant from B that the land will only be used for one dwelling. If B tries to build two houses on the land then A can enforce that promise against B. Provided that he does so in a timely manner, A should be able to obtain an injunction to prevent B building more than one house. (We will look in more detail at remedies in 14.9.) In this situation, B is the covenantor (because he gives the covenant or promise) and A is the covenantee.

This is a benefit to A but it is a limited benefit. Due to the doctrine of privity of contract, A can enforce the contract against B but cannot enforce it against any person who is not a party to the original contract or has not agreed to become bound by it. A is likely to have two questions. What if B sells his land – or part of it – to a new owner, C, who proposes to build more houses? And, if the development of B's land affects the value of A's retained land, can A make sure that anyone to whom he sells his retained land (D) can also enforce the covenant that B has given against the owner of B's land from time to time?

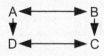

The two questions are illustrated by the diagram above:

(1) Has the *burden* of B's covenant passed from B to C?
(2) Has the *benefit* of B's covenant passed from A to D?

It is tempting to view this as one problem, namely, 'Can D enforce the covenant against C?' However, to solve the problem it is necessary to answer both questions (1) and (2).

The general answer to both questions is 'no'. However, land law is willing to recognise that the benefit and burden of certain promises or covenants can become attached to the land itself. If certain conditions are satisfied, that benefit can be enjoyed or the burden shouldered not just by the owners of the land at one point in time who made or received the original promise or covenant, but by the future owners of the land and people who derive title from them, such as mortgagees or tenants.

This means that a personal contractual right can be recognised as a proprietary right. The dangers of converting a personal right into a proprietary right that may permanently burden the land are recognised in the case law. For example, Pollock CB stated in *Hill v Tupper* (1863) 2 H & C 121 at 127–28:

> A new species of incorporeal hereditament cannot be created at the will and please of the owner of property; but he must be content to accept the estate and the right to dispose of it subject to the law as settled by decisions or controlled by Act of Parliament.

The remainder of this chapter focuses on the conditions required for such a covenant to attach to the land in order for this contractual arrangement to become binding upon successors in title. We will examine the conditions for the passing of the benefit and burden of a covenant at law and in equity. These two sets of rules may not be mixed: a person who holds the benefit of a covenant at law may only enforce it against a person who is subject to its burden at law (namely the original covenantor or an individual who is subject to it at law under the doctrine of mutual benefit and burden, see **14.2** below); a person with the benefit of a covenant in equity may enforce it against the wider range of persons who may be subject to its burden in equity (see **14.3** below). We are looking at freehold land, but note first the position regarding leasehold and commonhold titles.

14.1.2 Leasehold and commonhold titles

It is possible to enforce positive and negative covenants relating to leasehold land, due to the privity of estate between landlord and tenant (see **Chapter 9**), and commonhold, a new arrangement created by the Commonhold and Leasehold Reform Act 2002 (see **1.3.1.3**).

14.2 Burden of covenants at law

14.2.1 General rule

The doctrine of privity of contract applies so that, at common law, a person cannot be made liable on a contract unless he or she is a party to it (*Cox v Bishop* (1857) 8 De GM & G 815). Therefore the burden of a covenant does not run with the land so as to bind a successor in title (*Austerberry v Corporation of Oldham* [1884] A 4096).

To apply this to our covenant example at **14.1**, there is no privity of contract or contractual nexus between the incoming owner, C, and the party claiming to have the benefit of the covenant or promise, whether that is the original owner of the neighbouring land, A, or, after A's sale, his transferee D. Therefore, at law, neither A or D can enforce the covenant against C.

14.2.2 Mutual benefit and burden

This principle is an exception to the general rule stated above. A claimant who is not a party to a contract but who wants to make use of its benefits must also meet its burdens. The leading case is *Halsall v Brizell* [1957] Ch 169 in which persons who wanted to use a road to access their property were obliged to pay for its maintenance. This was described by Upjohn J (at 182) as an 'ancient law', and he cited Coke on Littleton 230b (published 1628), and applied in *Elliston v Reacher* [1908] 2 Ch 665 at 669, that 'a man who takes the benefit of a deed is bound by a condition contained in it though he does not execute it'.

The principle has been refined by the House of Lords in *Rhone v Stephens* [1994] 2 AC 310 to be limited to a benefit that is relevant to the burden that is sought to be enforced; in other words, taking a benefit granted by a deed will not mean that *every* burden in the deed becomes enforceable. The Court of Appeal clarified in *Wilkinson v Kerdene* [2013] EWCA Civ 44 that the benefit need not be expressed to be conditional upon compliance with the burden. It is enough if, for example, a payment for use of a private road is intended to ensure that a right to use that private road is capable of being exercised because the road is maintained. The requirements can be summarised as follows:

(a)   the benefit and burden must be conferred in and by the same transaction, and in relation to land, this will be by a deed or deeds;

(b)   the benefit must be relevant to the burden; and

(c) the person on whom the burden is imposed must have had the opportunity to reject or disclaim the benefit.

The Court of Appeal emphasised in *Davies v Jones* [2009] EWCA Civ 1164 that there must be a burden imposed for the doctrine to apply. In relation to land, this will usually be by a deed. Jones contracted to buy land and entered into a subsale with Lidl supermarket. Jones's purchase contract required him to carry out works after completion at the joint cost of Jones and the sellers, covered by a retention of £100,000 from the purchase price, with the balance of the retention to be paid to the sellers on completion of the works. Lidl took the benefit of the contract in a deed of assignment and, at completion, a transfer deed. Neither deed imposed a burden relating to the works or the retention. The principle of 'benefit and burden' was irrelevant and Lidl was under no obligation in relation to the personal obligations of Jones.

As to whether the principle of mutual benefit and burden exists at law or in equity, in *Tito v Waddell (No 2)* [1977] 1 Ch 106 at 308, Megarry V-C took the view that this would depend on the nature of the burden; if the burden existed at law then the liability would also operate at law; if the burden were merely equitable then the liability would exist in equity only.

14.3 Burden of covenants in equity

Equity makes a distinction between positive covenants (which require the covenantor to do something or to lay out money – for example to carry out repairs or to contribute to the cost of repairs) and negative covenants (which prevent the covenantor from doing something – such as in our example at **14.1** where B promises not to build on his land).

A court will look at the impact of the covenant to determine whether it is positive or negative. A covenant expressed in negative terms may still impose a positive obligation (for example an obligation 'not to allow a roof to fall into disrepair' is framed as a negative covenant but in reality imposes a positive obligation to repair the roof).

Like the common law, equity will not enforce a positive covenant against a successor or a person deriving title from the original covenantee. A positive covenant does not run with the land and therefore will not bind a successor in title. This position was upheld by the Court of Appeal in 1881 in *Haywood v The Brunswick Permanent Benefit Building Society* (1882) 8 QBD 403 and confirmed more recently by the House of Lords in *Rhone v Stephens* [1994] 2 AC 310. The argument against enforcing a positive covenant is that to do so would require an assignee to be compelled to expend money, when he or she has not accepted an obligation to do so.

However, equity will enforce a restrictive covenant or an obligation *not* to do something against a successor to the original covenantee, where that successor had notice of the covenant. The argument for this is that the conscience of the successor is affected by his or her prior notice of the covenant. As Lord Cottenham stated in the leading case of *Tulk v Moxhay* [1848] 2 Ph 774 at 778: 'if an equity is attached to the property by the owner, no one purchasing with notice of that equity can stand in a different situation from the party from whom he purchased.'

case example

Tulk v Moxhay [1848] 2 Ph 774

In 1808 Tulk owned the vacant piece of ground in Leicester Square in London as well as several of the houses forming the Square. He sold the vacant piece of land to Elms who covenanted in the conveyance

> that Elms, his heirs and assigns should, and would from time to time, and at all times thereafter at his and their own costs and charges, keep and maintain the said piece of ground and square garden, and the iron railing round the same in its then form, and in sufficient and proper repair as a square garden and pleasure ground, in an open state, uncovered with any buildings, in neat and ornamental order …

The piece of land passed by various conveyances to Moxhay. His purchase deed did not refer to the covenant, but he admitted that he purchased with notice of the 1808 covenant. Moxhay asserted a right to build on the land, and Tulk obtained an injunction restraining him from doing so. Moxhay sought to have the injunction discharged.

It was accepted that the burden of a covenant does not run with the land at law. However, the court held that equity would act to prevent a purchaser with notice of the covenant from acting in breach of it:

> It is said that, the covenant being one which does not run with the land, this Court cannot enforce it; but the question is, not whether the covenant runs with the land, but whether a party shall be permitted to use the land in a manner inconsistent with the contract entered into by his vendor, and with notice of which he purchased. Of course, the price would be affected by the covenant, and nothing could be more inequitable than that the original purchaser should be able to sell the property the next day for a greater price, in consideration of the assignee being allowed to escape from the liability which he had himself undertaken. (per Lord Cottenham at [778])

The courts have only been willing to apply this argument to restrictive covenants *not to do* something rather than to positive covenants *to do* something. The reason for this is expanded upon by Templeman LJ in *Rhone v Stephens* at 317–18:

> Equity does not contradict the common law by enforcing a restrictive covenant against a successor in title of the covenantor but prevents the successor from exercising a right which he never acquired.… Equity can thus prevent or punish the breach of a negative covenant which restricts the user of land or the exercise of other rights in connection with land. Restrictive covenants deprive an owner of a right which he could otherwise exercise. Equity cannot compel an owner to comply with a positive covenant entered into by his predecessors in title without flatly contradicting the common law

rule that a person cannot be made liable on a contract unless he was a party to it. Enforcement of a positive covenant lies in contract; a positive covenant compels an owner to exercise his rights. Enforcement of a negative covenant lies in property; a negative covenant deprives the owner of a right over property.

And later, at 321, more bluntly:

To enforce a positive covenant would be to enforce a personal obligation against a person who has not covenanted. To enforce negative covenants is only to treat the land as subject to a restriction.

This rule has been subject to criticism and various proposals for reform of the law have been made, which we consider further at **14.13**. However Templeman LJ made it clear (at 321) that 'judicial legislation' (by overruling the decision in *Austerberry*) would create difficulties and 'affect the rights and liabilities of people who have for over 100 years bought and sold land in the knowledge, imparted at an elementary stage to every student of the law of real property, that positive covenants affecting freehold land are not directly enforceable except against the original covenantor'. Parliamentary legislation would require 'careful consideration of the consequences'.

The Law Commission's proposals for reform are aimed at future covenants only, and existing covenants would be unaffected (*Making Land Work: Easements, Covenants and Profits a Prendre* (Law Com No 327), 2011, para 6.36).

14.4 Tests to determine if a restrictive covenant runs with the land

The judgment in *Tulk v Moxhay* itself is brief but it is now accepted that, as well as the requirement that the covenant be negative in nature, the following tests apply to determine whether the burden of a restrictive covenant will bind successors of the original covenantee.

14.4.1 The burden must be intended to run with the land

Intention to run with the land is now implied by s 79 of the LPA 1925, unless a contrary intention is expressed. This saves the need for additional wording in the deed imposing the covenant referring to successors in title (eg purchasers) and persons deriving title under the covenantor (eg lessees).

Section 79 of the LPA 1925 provides:

(1) A covenant relating to any land of a covenantor of capable of being bound by him, shall, unless a contrary intention is expressed, be deemed to be made by the covenantor on behalf of himself his successors in title and the persons deriving title under him or them, and, subject as aforesaid, shall have effect as if such successors and other persons were expressed.

...

(2) For the purposes of this section in connexion with covenants restrictive of the user of land 'successors in title' shall be deemed to include the owners and occupiers for the time being of such land.

(3) This section only applies to covenants made after the commencement of this Act.

14.4.2 There must be dominant land

A covenant must benefit land held by the covenantee (and, if enforced by a successor to him, that continues to be held by his or her successors) (*Formby v Barker* [1903] 2 Ch 539). In our example at 14.1, if A had disposed of all his property to B, then any covenant given by B to A would simply be personal as there is no land retained by A to which it can attach.

14.4.3 The covenant must benefit the dominant land

Restrictive covenants usually relate to the manner in which land is used or developed. In *Keppell v Bailey* 39 ER 1042, covenants to buy limestone from a certain quarry and to transport it via a railway were not covenants capable of being attached to land. Whilst the current owner of land may be free to choose to contractually bind him- or herself in such a way, such stipulations were not recognised by the law as being of a nature where they could be used to control the future use of the land in the hands of another party.

To be enforceable against successors in title to the original covenantor:

(a) The burden must have been intended to and have been capable of benefitting the dominant land of the covenantee, rather than the covenantee personally. Intention might be shown by the wording of the document (for example: 'The Covenantee covenants on behalf of himself and his successors in title'). After 1 January 1926, statutory implication under s 79 of the LPA 1925 makes such wording unnecessary as it will be presumed that covenants relating to land are made not just by the original covenantor but also his or her successors unless a contrary intention is shown. At one stage it was suggested that s 79 was sufficient by itself to make the burden of a covenant run with the servient land, but this was rejected in *Morrells of Oxford Ltd v Oxford United Football Club* [2000] WL 1084374.

(b) The covenant must continue to benefit that land at the time that its enforcement is sought (*Dano Ltd v Earl Cadogan* [2003] EWHC 239 (Ch)).

(c) Benefit will be presumed unless it can be shown that the covenant cannot reasonably be considered to confer a benefit on the dominant land (*Marten v Flight Refuelling Ltd* [1962] Ch 116; *Wrotham Park Estate Co Ltd v Parkside Homes Ltd* [1974] 1 WLR 798, Ch D). In *Wrotham Park*, Brightman J (at 808) explained the reasons for this as follows:

> If a restriction is bargained for at the time of sale with the intention of giving the vendor a protection which he desires for the land he retains, and the restriction is expressed to be imposed for the benefit of the estate so that both sides are apparently accepting that the restriction is of value to the retained land, I think that the validity of the restriction should be upheld so long as an estate owner may reasonably take the view that the restriction remains of value to his estate, and that the restriction should not be discarded merely because others may argue that the restriction is spent.

In *Marten*, Wilberforce J (at 136) said that a court would normally assume that a restriction imposed to benefit retained land was capable of doing so, but there might be 'exceptional cases where the covenant was, on the face of it, taken capriciously or not bona fide …'.

In *Dano Ltd v Earl Cadogan*, adopting the *Wrotham Park* approach, the Cadogan Estate did not have to prove that the covenant to restrict use of burdened land to affordable housing benefitted its neighbouring land; it was 'sufficient that an estate owner could reasonably take that view, even though others may reasonably argue to the contrary' (per Etherton J at para 68). It was a reasonable view that people might be attracted to the Cadogan Estate's neighbouring land by the social mix and the provision of local services made possible by the availability of affordable housing.

This was examined in *Cosmichome Ltd v Southampton City Council* [2013] EWHC 1378 (Ch), where a covenant restricted use of the site to occupation by the BBC, subject to a proviso that if the restriction were to be lifted and planning permission granted for a use other than radio television studios, payment of 50% of any enhanced value would become due. The court held that the covenant did not benefit the Council's adjoining land at the date it was imposed or the date that it was sought to be enforced, for two reasons. The dual purpose of the covenant was believed to be to seek to maintain the BBC at the site and to extract a payment if the BBC were to leave and dispose of the site. Whilst the court could see the benefit of both to the Council, neither benefitted the Council's adjoining or adjacent land. The court adopted the working test used in *P & A Swift Investment v Combined English Stores Group Plc* [1989] 1 AC 632 at 642 (which concerned a leasehold covenant) whether the covenant 'affected the nature, quality, amenity and value' of the Council's land. The court found no convincing evidence that the BBC's continued presence would impact on the nature or the value of Council-owned land in the immediate vicinity of the property. In doing so it looked at the nature of the BBC's property (which was solely for broadcasting use and not open to the public) and considered that a change of its use would have no impact on the Council's adjoining multi-storey carpark or even on public-attracting uses in the area which included a theatre, museum, library and retail uses.

14.4.4 The restriction must not be personal

In *Cosmichome*, although the covenant was expressed to be for the benefit of the Council's land, its substance was to confer personal or quasi-personal benefit, intended to secure a payment. The Council's general desire to retain the BBC on the site and to extract a payment if that came to an end did not benefit the Council's retained land, rather than the Council itself, and therefore the covenant was personal in nature.

If the Council had been able to show that the covenant protected the value of its retained land then it would have fallen within the *P & A Swift Investment* test set out above: that the covenant 'affected the nature, quality, amenity and value' of the Council's land. The fact that the Council was financially motivated was not the problem; the problem was that the covenant was a mechanism to secure a financial payment, unrelated to its retained land.

In *Newton Abbott Co-operative Society v Williamson & Treadgold Ltd* [1952] Ch 286, HC, a restrictive covenant not to use a property as an ironmongery was held to benefit the seller's retained land, on which she carried on business as an ironmonger. The court rejected an argument that the covenant was a personal, anti-competition covenant solely designed to protect the ironmongery business, as there was an additional purpose to protect the value of the seller's retained land if the seller ultimately chose to sell her land, business and the benefit of the covenant in one transaction.

14.4.5 There must be proximity between the servient and dominant land

This is another facet of the requirement set out at **14.4.1** and **14.4.2** above that the covenant must be capable of benefitting the covenantee's land. To take an extreme example, a covenant burdening land in Central London could not benefit land in Yorkshire. The problem has been seen in less extreme form in *Re Ballard's Conveyance* [1937] Ch 473, where a covenant was taken for the benefit of a large landed estate. It was held ineffective as it could not 'touch and concern' the whole of the land comprised in the estate, only those parts closest to the burdened property. In practice, this difficulty is worked around by drafting: a reference to 'the estate' will be interpreted to mean the whole or at least substantially the whole of the land, which means that the covenant may fail because it cannot benefit the whole area. However, a reference to 'any part or parts' of it or 'all or any' of an estate means that the covenant can be valid over those parts that are benefitted by it, whilst not affecting the remainder. See *Marquess of Zetland v Driver* [1929] Ch1 and *Rogers v Hosegood* [1900] 2 Ch 388.

14.5　Benefit of covenants

At common law, a person who is not a party to a contract or deed cannot enforce it, even if it is made for his or her benefit (*Hohler v Aston* [1920] 2 Ch 420). There are limited statutory rights for a person to take a benefit:

(a) Section 56 of the LPA 1925 relates to agreements relating to land or other property that are expressly made for the benefit of a person who is not a party to it, and allows that person to enforce the agreement despite not being a party. To take a benefit, an individual must be identifiable and in existence at the time of creation of the covenant, even though he or she is not a party to the document (*Re Ecclesiastical Commissioners for England's Conveyance* [1936] Ch 430). This means that it will not usually assist a successor in title, as a successor is not individually identifiable at the time that the covenant is made.

(b) The Contracts (Rights of Third Parties) Act 1999 provides for a person who is not a party to a contract to enforce a term in his or her own right if the contract expressly provides that he or she, or a class of which he or she is a member, may do so. In theory, therefore, the Act could be used to pass the benefit of a covenant on to future owners of a property. Unlike s 56(1) of the LPA 1925, it can apply to a class of persons (eg future owners of a property) and not merely to identifiable individuals. In practice, the Act is not routinely used for restrictive covenants, and the fear of unwittingly benefitting a party means that it is excluded from property contracts as standard. The Law Society's Standard Conditions of Sale (5th edn) and Standard Commercial Property Conditions (3rd edn) both exclude the Act.

Section 1 of the Contracts (Rights of Third Parties) Act 1999 provides:

1　**Right of third party to enforce contractual term**

(1) Subject to the provisions of this Act, a person who is not a party to a contract (a 'third party') may in his own right enforce a term of the contract if—

  (a) the contract expressly provides that he may, or

  (b) subject to subsection (2), the term purports to confer a benefit on him.

(2) Subsection (1)(b) does not apply if on a proper construction of the contract it appears that the parties did not intend the term to be enforceable by the third party.

(3) The third party must be expressly identified in the contract by name, as a member of a class or as answering a particular description but need not be in existence when the contract is entered into.

. . .

(5)   For the purpose of exercising his right to enforce a term of the contract, there shall be available to the third party any remedy that would have been available to him in an action for breach of contract if he had been a party to the contract (and the rules relating to damages, injunctions, specific performance and other relief shall apply accordingly).

...

The Act deals only with the benefit of a contract and not the burden. Therefore, even if it were to be adopted, it would be only a partial solution to the transmissibility of covenants.

14.6   Exceptions to the non-transmissibility of the benefit of a covenant

Despite the rules on privity of contract, the law recognises certain cases where the benefit of a covenant can be passed on to a successor in title of the original covenantee. Many of these rules are very technical and for the purposes of this book we need only outline them.

14.6.1   Annexation

Annexation means that the covenant has become part of the land. It will then pass automatically when the land is transferred. Annexation may occur at law and in equity; for the benefit to pass at law the transferee must hold a legal estate in the benefitted land (*Smith and Snipes Hall Farm Ltd v River Douglas Catchment Board* [1949] 2 KB 500). For covenants entered into after 1925, covenants relating to land will automatically be annexed by s 78 of the LPA 1925:

78   **Benefit of covenants relating to land**

(1)   A covenant relating to any land of the covenantee shall be deemed to be made with the covenantee and his successors in title and the persons deriving title under him or them, and shall have effect as if such successors and other persons were expressed.

For the purposes of this subsection in connexion with covenants restrictive of the user of land 'successors in title' shall be deemed to include the owners and occupiers for the time being of the land of the covenantee intended to be benefited.

(2)   This section applies to covenants made after the commencement of this Act ...

Section 78 only applies to covenants 'relating to any land of the covenantee'. Using more old-fashioned language found in many of the cases, it must 'touch and concern' the land, rather than being for the personal benefit of the particular owner of the land at the time that the covenant was taken. We have looked at this distinction at 14.4 above.

14.6.2 Assignment

Even if the benefit of a restrictive covenant relating to land has not been annexed to the land, it can be expressly assigned to successors in title of the original covenantee and persons deriving title from him or her or them. In other words, when the benefitted land is transferred to a new owner, the exiting owner can also transfer the benefit of any covenants that benefit the land to the new owner. This would need to be done expressly on each occasion that the benefitted land changes hands. This would require an unbroken chain of assignments from the original covenantee via each intervening owner to the present owner of the benefitted land. In *Re Union of London and Smith's Bank's Limited's Conveyance* [1933] Ch 611, CA, it was held that a successor of the original covenantee must show that:

(a) the covenant was taken for the benefit of ascertainable land of the covenantee capable of being benefitted by the covenant; and

(b) he or she (the covenantee's assignee) has had the benefit of the covenant expressly assigned to him or her.

Like annexation, assignment can occur at law and in equity; to operate at law the assignee must hold a legal estate in the benefitted land.

***

case example

Federated Homes Ltd v Mill Lodge Properties Ltd [1980] 1 WLR 594

The difference between annexation and assignment can be seen in *Federated Homes Ltd v Mill Lodge Properties Ltd* [1980] 1 WLR 594.

A property owner, M Ltd, bought four equal sized areas of land (described as the 'red, green, pink and blue land'). It obtained outline planning permission for construction of approximately 1,250 dwellings in total on the four areas and entered into a phasing agreement with the planning authority to control the rate of development. M Ltd subsequently sold the blue land to the defendant (D) and imposed a covenant preventing D from building more than 300 dwellings, so as not to reduce the number of dwellings that M Ltd could build on its retained land. M Ltd then sold the red and green land to B Ltd. B Ltd sold the green land to the plaintiff (P) and the red land to another purchaser. In the conveyances to and from B Ltd, the benefit of the covenant by D to restrict development to 300 dwellings was expressly assigned. P subsequently bought the red land but, in the conveyance to him, no assignment of the benefit of the covenant was made. At the time of the action, P owned the red and green land, and D owned the blue land.

M Ltd

Red land	Green land ·	Pink land	Blue land
B Ltd (with express assignment of benefit of D's covenant)	B Ltd (with express assignment of benefit of D's covenant)		
Another party (with express assignment of benefit of D's covenant)			
P (**without** express assignment of benefit of D's covenant)	P (**with** express assignment of benefit of D's covenant)		D (land subjected to covenant restricting building to 300 dwellings)

Having built 300 dwellings on the blue land, D obtained planning permission for a further 32 dwellings. Due to the overall limit of approximately 1,250 dwellings on the whole of the red, green, pink and blue land, this planning permission, if implemented, would reduce the number of dwellings that P could build on the red and green land. P obtained an injunction preventing D from implementing the permission, which D appealed to the Court of Appeal.

The Court dismissed D's appeal and held that P had the benefit of the covenant in respect of both the red and the green land because:

(1) as the covenant related to land, the benefit was annexed to the red and green land by virtue of s 78 of the LPA 1925.

(2) in addition, it had been validly assigned for the benefit of the green land by the unbroken chain of assignments from M Ltd to B Ltd and from B Ltd to P.

Although both annexation and assignment had occurred, either one of them would have entitled P (as owner of the red and green land in the case of annexation or as owner of the green land in the case of assignment) to enforce the covenant and to obtain an injunction preventing D from building the additional 32 dwellings.

14.6.3 Building schemes

A building scheme is recognised in equity where the benefit and burden of mutually enforceable covenants fall on the owners of plots within an estate, as part of a scheme of development. The requirements for a scheme were looked at by the Court of Appeal in 2016 in the case of *Birdlip v Hunter* [2016] EWCA Civ 603. Lewison LJ set out the characteristics of a building scheme as follows:

(a) it applies to a defined area;

(b) owners of properties within that area have purchased their properties from a common owner;

(c) each of the properties is burdened by covenants which were intended to be mutually enforceable between the several owners;

(d) the limits of the defined area are known to each of the purchasers;

(e) the common owner is him- or herself bound by the scheme. The scheme crystallises on the first sale of a plot within the defined area; following that the estate owner is not able to dispose of plots within that area otherwise than on the terms of the scheme; and

(f) the effect of the scheme will bind future purchasers of land falling within the area, potentially for ever.

It is clear from the list above that it is onerous to establish that a scheme has been created. The mere fact that a series of conveyances contains similar covenants is not enough to establish that a scheme of mutual covenants exists (*Re Wembley Park Estate Co's Transfer* [1968] 1 Ch 491). The identification of the area of land affected by the scheme is vital to establish that a scheme exists; usually this will require a map to be attached to the document containing the covenants, although a verbal description can suffice if the area can be established by extrinsic evidence. The reason for this strict requirement is explained by Sir Herbert Cozens-Hardy MR in *Reid v Bickerstaff* [1909] 2 Ch 305, at 319, cited with approval in *Birdlip*:

> Reciprocity is the foundation of the idea of the scheme. A purchaser of one parcel cannot be subject to an implied obligation to purchasers of an undefined and unknown area. He must know both the extent of his burden and the extent of his benefit.

In *Birdlip*, the court undertook two steps:

Step 1

The Court reviewed the conveyances that were said to establish the scheme to see if they had the characteristics set out above. Unfortunately for the claimant, the conveyances that imposed the covenants did not refer verbally or by a map to any estate of which the land sold formed part, there was no reference to other plots in an estate, and the covenants were not expressed to be mutually enforceable between any such plot owners. This indicated that the conveyances did not establish a building scheme.

Step 2

The Court considered whether any evidence extrinsic to the conveyances could be relied upon; in this case, contracts for sale of other plots in 1908 and 1914, which contained plans showing the estate boundaries. The Court had two concerns in doing so; first, a doubt that a building scheme could be established on extrinsic evidence alone, and, secondly, the age of the extrinsic evidence. Lewisham LJ stated (at 42) that, unless cogent, it would be very 'unsatisfactory' to rely on extrinsic evidence 'now over a century old ... given that the existence of enforceable restrictive covenants is potentially a perpetual interference with the right of successive property owners to do as they please with their own property'. In this case the plans attached to the contracts for other lots showed different boundaries for the estate. This went against the requirement that all buyers of land affected by the scheme must know what area of land is within the scheme. Lewisham LJ noted that the point went further: if a scheme had been established, the common owner would have had no power to exclude land from the scheme completely, as was the case here with the different estate boundaries shown on the 1908 and 1914 plans. The purpose of the plans was to identify the plot for sale and not to delineate an area affected by a building scheme.

Answering problem questions

Reading cases is a good way to understand how to use the 'IRAC' method of answering problem questions. We recommend that you adopt this in your own answers.

Table 14.1   The 'IRAC' method

Issue	Rule	Application	Conclusion
Has a building scheme been created?	The rules are set out at **14.6.3(a)** to **(f)** above.	Step 1: The Court applied the rules to the conveyances that contained the covenants. They did not satisfy the rules. Step 2: The Court considered extrinsic evidence to see if this indicated that the rules had been satisfied. The extrinsic evidence did not satisfy the rules either.	Both Steps 1 and 2 showed evidence that pointed against a scheme having been created. The rules had not been satisfied and the Court concluded that no building scheme existed.

reflection

Where the *benefit* of a restrictive covenant is held by an owner of benefitted land, whether he or she is the original covenantee or a successor who has the benefit through annexation or express assignment, at law the owner of the benefitted land can only sue the original covenantee, because of privity of contract. However, as we have already seen from *Tulk v Moxhay*, if a new owner of the burdened land had notice of a restrictive covenant at the time of his or her purchase, then the *burden* will be enforceable against him or her in equity.

However, if the covenant falls within a building scheme, the benefit and burden of restrictive covenants will pass.

Similarly, if there is a mutual benefit and burden, both the benefit and the burden of restrictive and positive covenants will pass at law.

14.7 Limits of covenants or has there been a breach?

A restrictive covenant applies only to the land that is burdened by it. Whilst this might seem obvious, it has caused difficulties where the land subject to a covenant is developed or used as part of a wider scheme that also includes land that is not subject to the same restrictions.

In *Co-operative Retail Services Ltd v Tesco Stores Ltd* (1998) 76 P&CR 328, Tesco had developed a new supermarket on a site which included a parcel of land subject to a restrictive covenant in favour of the Co-op, preventing it being used for food retailing. Tesco took care to ensure that the area in question was used for landscaped green space (which was required under the planning permission) and that no part of the store, petrol station or car park was situated on the burdened land. The Court of Appeal held that there was no breach of the covenant because the burdened land was not being used for food retailing but as a landscaped area, open to the public at large and not merely Tesco customers. It was irrelevant that it formed part of a larger scheme, and in fact it was required under the planning consent to be landscaped in order to allow the scheme to go ahead.

The Court of Appeal followed a similar approach in *Coventry School Foundation Trustees v Whitehouse* [2013] EWCA Civ 885. In this case a new school was proposed to be built on land that was subject to a restrictive covenant that prevented use in a manner that would be a nuisance, annoyance or disturbance or tend to lessen the value of the benefitting land. The Court held that increased traffic caused by the twice daily school run could not breach the covenant as the activity took place on the public highway and not on the burdened land. The covenant was restricted to activities that took place on the burdened land. The case was distinguished from the much older case of *Tod-Heatly v Benham* (1888) 40 Ch D 80, where a similar covenant could prevent use as a hospital as the act complained of (the treatment of out-patients with infectious diseases) took place on the land affected by the covenant. This use would breach the covenant if sensible people felt a reasonable apprehension of risk and interference with the pleasurable enjoyment of their houses for ordinary purposes.

14.8 Protection

At **14.3** above, we explained that under *Tulk v Moxhay* the burden of a covenant will pass in equity to a successor in title or person deriving title to property for value if he or she has notice of the covenant. This has become more formalised by registration requirements that apply to both registered and unregistered titles.

A volunteer (someone who has acquired title to the land otherwise than for valuable consideration) will not be in any better position than his or her predecessor in title and therefore will be deemed to have notice of the covenant.

14.8.1 Registered land

In order to be protected against a purchaser for valuable consideration, the restrictive covenant should be protected by registration as a notice on the charges register of the servient land (Land Registration Act 2002, s 32). If not protected by a notice at the time of a disposition then it will not bind a purchaser of a registered estate in the servient land for valuable consideration.

14.8.2 Unregistered land

A restrictive covenant entered into from 1 January 1926 is registrable as a land charge under Class D(ii) (Land Charges Act 1972). Registration acts as notice to a purchaser (LPA 1925, s 198(1)). If unregistered then it will be void against a purchaser of a legal estate for money or money's worth (Land Charges Act 1972, s 4(6)).

Pre-1926 restrictive covenants are governed by the doctrine of notice (actual, constructive or imputed notice).

See **Chapters 3** and **5** for further information.

14.9 Remedies

The prima facie remedy for breach of restrictive covenants is an injunction to restrain the defendant from future breach. This equitable relief is available because the common law remedy of damages based on the claimant's loss is inadequate. As the remedy is equitable, it can be defeated if an equitable defence (including laches (delay), acquiescence or estoppel) is established.

Where the court has power to award an injunction or specific performance, it also has a statutory power under s 50 of the Senior Courts Act 1981 to award damages 'in addition to or in substitution for such injunction or specific performance'. (This power was original given by s 2 of the Chancery Amendment Act 1858, also known as Lord Cairn's Act. You will find such damages referred to in the older case law as being given under Lord Cairn's Act.)

Millett LJ explained the difference between common law damages and damages under s 50 as follows in *Jaggard v Sawyer and Another* [1995] 1 WLR 269 at 284:

> Damages at common law are recoverable only in respect of causes of action which are complete at the date of the writ; damages for future or repeated wrongs must be made the subject of fresh proceedings. Damages in substitution for an injunction, however, relate to the future, not the past. They inevitably extend beyond the damages to which the plaintiff may be entitled at law.

He continued to explain that the 'practical result' of withholding injunctive relief is that the defendant is permitted to continue to act in breach of the restrictive covenant (or other proprietary right) and cannot be prevented from doing so. Therefore, when awarding damages in substitution under s 50,

> The court can in my judgment properly award damages 'once and for all' in respect of future wrongs because it awards them in substitution for an injunction and to compensate for those future wrongs which an injunction would have prevented. (at 286)

On a number of occasions, the court has considered what approach it should take to the question whether to impose an injunction and/or damages, and, if damages are awarded, how these should be assessed.

In *Coventry (t/a RDC Promotions) v Lawrence* [2014] UKSC 13, the Supreme Court considered remedies in relation to a nuisance claim. Although a claim in nuisance, it has relevance to a restrictive covenant claim because it considers use of the s 50 discretion to award damages in lieu. The Court confirmed that injunction should prima facie be the primary remedy but the court should always consider damages.

In the 1885 case of *Shelfer v City of London Electric Lighting Co* [1895] 1 Ch 287, CA, at 322–33, AL Smith LJ set out the following four tests for when damages in substitution for an injunction may be given:

(1) If the injury to the plaintiff's legal rights is small,
(2) And is one which is capable of being estimated in money,
(3) And is one which can be adequately compensated by a small money payment,
(4) And the case is one in which it would be oppressive to the defendant to grant an injunction.

And in 2014, in *Lawrence*, the Supreme Court affirmed that:

(a) The prima facie position is that an injunction should be granted so the legal burden is on the defendant to show why it should not.
(b) When a judge is called on to decide whether to award damages in lieu of an injunction, he or she should not incline either way (subject to the legal burden at (a) above); the outcome should depend on all the evidence and arguments.
(c) The *Shelfer* tests should be considered only as a general guide rather than as creating a firm rule or to be applied mechanically; in other words, the court's discretion is unfettered. Lord Neuberger stated at 120 that it is a 'classic exercise of discretion, which should not, as a matter of principle, be fettered … And … each case is likely to be so fact-sensitive that any firm guidance is likely to do more harm than good'. It would, in the absence of relevant circumstances pointing the other way, normally be right to refuse an injunction if those four tests are satisfied. However, the fact that those tests are not all satisfied does not mean that an injunction should be granted.

When damages are awarded, conventionally these are based on the reduction in the value of the claimant's property as a result of the continuation of the breach. However, the court is not confined to nominal damages (*Wrotham Park Estate Co Ltd v Parkside Homes Ltd* [1974] 1 WLR 798, followed by the Court of Appeal in *Jaggard v Sawyer*). Both cases concerned construction of a house or houses in breach of a restrictive covenant, and, in both cases, the claimant had objected to the construction but had not sought an injunction to restrain building until the houses were complete or nearly compete. Whilst this did not mean that an injunction could never be issued, the court was not willing to grant an injunction on the facts because of the waste of housing and the oppression to the defendant.

However, in both cases, the loss to the claimant was nominal; the development breached the covenant but did not affect the value of its property in any material way. The court concluded that a just substitute for an injunction was to award damages for a sum that the claimant might reasonably have demanded as a quid pro quo for relaxing the covenant, if the defendant had applied to it for relaxation. In *Wrotham*, the court calculated that a relevant factor to that demand would be the expected profit from the venture, and it set damages at 5% of that profit.

14.10 Discharge and modification of restrictive covenants

A person interested in land subject to a restrictive covenant can apply to the Upper Tribunal to discharge or modify that covenant in whole or part if it no longer serves a useful social purpose.

Application can be made by any person interested in any freehold land that is affected by a restriction on its user or the building upon it arising under a covenant or otherwise. The Lands Chamber of the Upper Tribunal has a discretion to modify or discharge the restriction in whole or part if:

(1) the restriction ought to be deemed obsolete due to changes in the character of the property or the neighbourhood or other circumstances of the case which the Upper Tribunal deems material (LPA 1925, s 84(1)(a)); or

(2) the continued existence of the restriction impedes some reasonable user of the land for public or private purposes (s 84(1)(aa)) and the restriction either:

    (i) does not secure any practical benefits of substantial value or advantage to the persons entitled to it; or

    (ii) is contrary to the public interest, and money will be an adequate compensation for the loss or disadvantage (if any) which any such person will suffer from the discharge or modification (s 84(1A)); or

(3) the persons of full age and capacity entitled to the benefit of the restriction have agreed either expressly or by implication by their acts or omissions, to the restriction being discharge or modified (s 84(1)(b)); or

(4) the proposed discharge or modification will not injure the persons entitled to the benefit of the restriction (s 84(1)(c)).

If the Tribunal does make an order to modify or discharge the restriction, it has a further discretion whether to award compensation under one, but not both, of the following heads (LPA 1925, s 84(1)(i) and (ii)):

(i)   to make up for any loss or disadvantage suffered by that person in consequence of the discharge or modification; or

(ii) to make up for any effect which the restriction had, at the time imposed, in reducing the consideration received for the land affected by it.

Obsolescence under s 84(1)(a) will be considered in relation to the original purpose of the covenant at the date when it was imposed. Whether the restriction impedes reasonable user without providing practical benefits of substantial value under s 84(1)(aa) will be considered at the time of application under s 84, and may well be different from the original purpose. This distinction was considered in *Re Kennet Properties' Application* (1996) 72 P&CR 353 which concerned a 1953 restrictive covenant that prevented building on land set aside for paddock use in connection with adjoining building lots. A developer, Kennet Properties, obtained planning permission to build 27 houses on the paddock land and applied for the discharge or modification of the restrictive covenants. Twenty-eight local residents of land with the benefit of the covenants objected to the application. The tribunal found that modifying the covenant to allow the 27 houses to be built would injure the owners of the building lots adjacent to the paddock area in providing an attractive recreational area and a view from some of the lots. This meant that the tribunal had no grounds to make an order under s 84(1)(aa) or (c) above. However, the tribunal considered that the original purpose of the covenant was to procure an open view for the owners of each of the building lots. This purpose was no longer achievable because other developments already impinged on the view. Some of that development was outside the estate and some was on other parts of the original paddock land, itself in breach of the covenant. The finding that the original purpose of the covenant could no longer be achieved meant that it was obsolete, and therefore, under the ground in s 84(1)(a), the tribunal had a discretion to modify or discharge it. In considering whether to exercise the discretion under that ground, the tribunal was required under s 84(1B) to

> take into account the development plan and any declared or ascertainable pattern for the grant or refusal or planning permission in the relevant areas, as well as the period at which and the context in which the restriction was created … and any other material circumstances.

This allows the restrictive covenant to be viewed alongside the public control of development as evidenced by the local planning authority's development plan. Rich J placed some weight on the fact that Haringey Council, as the local planning authority, had agreed in principle to the residential development of the paddock site, and he discharged the principal covenant and modified other covenants so as to enable the proposed development to proceed. Some compensation was payable under the ground in s 84(1)(a), that the discharge would cause loss of amenity to some of the objectors. No or reduced compensation was payable where the objector occupied land on which a breach of the covenant had already taken place (eg the earlier developments on other parts of the paddock land and individual summerhouses built on the paddock).

14.11 Reflection

The law setting out the conditions required for a covenant to attach to the land so that the benefit and burden pass to future owners is, it has to be said, imperfect and over-complicated. Reform has been recommended by the Law Commission (see 14.12). The proposed reforms are forward-looking and leave the current system in place for existing covenants. This is because of the many arrangements that have been put in place in reliance on the current law (see Templeman LJ's comments at 14.3).

However, one critical discussion that needs to be had is in what circumstances will it be right that a landowner can make commitments that not only bind him or her or bind the land for a finite period of time, such as a lease, but that bind the land permanently? This is the true purpose behind the conditions relating to enforceability of covenants that are set out above. Are those conditions fit for purpose? And is it still appropriate to allow such private controls on land use in an era where, through the Town and Country Planning Acts amongst other legislation, there is comprehensive public control of the uses to which land can be put?

The leading case on the enforceability of covenants in equity is *Tulk v Moxhay* [1848] 2 Ph 774 (see more below). One of the concerns of Cottenham LJ was that if a restrictive covenant could be ignored by a subsequent purchaser, '... it would be impossible for an owner of land to sell part of it without incurring the risk of rendering what he retains worthless' (at 777–78).

Also, a landowner would likely have accepted a lower price because of the restrictions that he wished to impose on land he was selling. Nothing, in Lord Cottenham's view, 'could be more inequitable than that the original purchaser should be able to sell the property the next day for a greater price, in consideration of the assignee being allowed to escape from the liability which he had himself undertaken'.

These arguments are persuasive. *Tulk v Moxhay* came to court over 150 years ago. It is presumably the reason why Leicester Square, a prime piece of Central London real estate, still exists as an open square, with a statue and railings surrounding the gardens, today. The effect of the Square on the values of surrounding properties (what was once Mr Tulk's retained land) also, presumably, continues.

It is now difficult to carry an argument based on the inequity to Mr Tulk, who accepted a lower price when selling the land over 200 years ago in 1808. It is true that Mr Tulk's successors in title purchased, and continue to purchase, land surrounding Leicester Square in the knowledge that Leicester Square cannot be built upon without their consent. And that Mr Moxhay and his successors have bought land in the knowledge that its use was restricted. This does not answer the question whether it is right that the actions of private individuals over 200 years ago should continue to affect land use today.

14.12 Private law and public law

A common use for covenants is to restrict the development of land. Covenants are a private law means of doing so, by creating rights between two individuals. Today, we also have extensive public law restrictions contained principally in the series of Town and Country Planning Acts, notably the Town and Country Planning Act 1990. The private law of covenants operates independently of the public system of planning control. To go back to our example at **14.1**, it is immaterial to the enforceability of B's promise to A whether B has obtained planning permission (in other words, a public or State permission) to build two or more houses. Even if B has obtained such permission, A would still be able to enforce B's private promise to him.

Many of the leading cases on restrictive covenants date from the 19th century, in an age when public controls on development were much weaker. The role for private controls (which is wider than merely restrictive covenants but also encompasses nuisance and rights to light) has begun to be questioned in the light of the considerably stronger 21st century public regulation. In a private law case on nuisance, Lord Neuberger, giving judgment in the Supreme Court (*Coventry (t/a RDC Promotions) v Lawrence* [2014] UKSC 13), indicated that the fact that planning permission had been granted for an activity could be taken into account when considering whether it was a nuisance.

14.13 Reform

In its 2011 report *Making Land Work: Easements, Covenants and Profits a Prendre* (Law Com No 327), 2011, the Law Commission proposed a new way to attach obligations to land, replacing, for the future, the law relating to restrictive covenants and enabling positive as well as negative obligations to be directly enforceable against successors in title. As well as simplifying the law and minimising litigation, its aim is stated to be to 'maximise the effective use of land … Obligations can protect the character of land and enhance its amenity or financial value.'

It proposes a new legal interest in land known as a land obligation. It would be registrable in the same way as an easement, with the benefit registrable against the registered title to the dominant land and the burden registrable against the servient land title. Unlike the current system, which is based on contract, the original parties to the land obligation would not be liable for breaches occurring after they have parted with the land.

The land obligation could be negative (restricting the burdened owner from doing something on his land) or positive (obliging the burdened owner to do something in relation to his land). There would therefore be no need for conveyancing devices such as a chain of indemnity covenants or rentcharges.

The Law Commission believes that this would facilitate sharing of facilities between neighbours, such as a shared driveway. However, for 'truly interdependent properties such as flats where a management arrangement is needed', leasehold or commonhold structures will continue to be more suitable.

The existing jurisdiction of the Lands Chamber of the Upper Tribunal under s 84 of the LPA 1925 to discharge and modify restrictive covenants would be expanded to cover positive and negative land obligations.

Existing restrictive covenants would be unaffected by the reform. The current status of the proposed reforms is that on 18 May 2016, following the Queen's Speech, it was announced that the Government would bring forward proposals to respond to the Law Commission's recommendations in a draft Law of Property Bill.

14.14 Alternatives to covenants

The non-transmissibility of positive covenants and technicalities of restrictive covenants means that, in practice, there are a number of 'work-arounds' that are used when a covenant is not suitable or is not suitable on its own to create an effective obligation.

14.14.1 Practical means of enforcing obligations

One of the problems with the unenforceability of positive covenants is that essential repairs may be left undone. This was seen in *Rhone v Stephens* where the unenforceability of a positive covenant to repair a roof, coupled with the defendant's refusal to allow access to the plaintiff to carry out the repairs at the plaintiff's own cost, caused damage to the plaintiff's property. Under s 1 of the Access to Neighbouring Land Act 1992, an applicant would now be able to apply for an 'access order' to get access to adjoining or neighbouring land to do works that are reasonably necessary for the preservation of his or her land if the works cannot be carried out (or would be substantially more difficult to be carried out) without access. Works would be at the applicant's costs.

14.14.2 Chain of indemnity covenants

In theory, positive covenants could be enforced indirectly (or at least a breach compensated for) by a chain of indemnity covenants. As covenants are based in contract, the original covenantor remains liable on the covenant even after he or she has disposed of his or her interest in the servient land. The covenantor's conveyancer will usually require the new owner to enter into a covenant in the transfer deed indemnifying the original covenantor against future breach. In turn, the new owner will seek an indemnity to protect him or her when he or she sells on. If this is done on each occasion that the property is disposed of without fail, then the dominant land owner who has the benefit of the covenant could sue the original covenantor, who sues the next link in the chain, until the current owner who is responsible for the breach is joined in to the legal action. In practice, this can be broken if a conveyancer fails to get an indemnity covenant, or if a former owner who was a link in the chain has died or cannot be traced. It may therefore fail to remedy the breach complained of.

14.14.3 Restriction on registered title to servient land

Restrictive covenants can also be used by the seller of land as a method to try to secure overage (a payment which is additional to the original sale price and which will become payable in specified circumstances in the future, for example if planning permission for development which increases the value of the site is obtained) or a payment in order to relax the restriction. A restrictive covenant will only be appropriate to achieve such a payment if the seller imposing the overage retains neighbouring land that is capable of benefitting from the covenant. Even if the seller does retain land, as we have seen in the case of *Cosmichome Ltd v Southampton City Council*, the burden of a covenant will not pass to successors if the restriction is construed as a personal benefit to the covenantee designed to secure a payment rather than a covenant that actually benefits the dominant land. For this reason, a common method of securing overage is to register a restriction at the Land Registry against the title to the servient land preventing registration of a dealing with it unless a direct covenant is given by the new registered owner. In this way, it does not matter whether the burden of the covenant passes on disposal of the servient land as the new owner will have given a direct obligation to the covenantee. Entering a restriction against the registered servient title could also be used as a means of obtaining a direct covenant to comply with positive obligations, such as payment of money for a shared roadway.

14.14.4 Estate rentcharge

This method is used in relation to freehold land where there is a need to enforce positive obligations, such as payment of a maintenance sum, but use of a full leasehold or commonhold management scheme is not considered necessary.

14.14.5 Leasehold/commonhold

These are alternative structures that can be used to enforce positive covenants. Because of their more complex structure, they are more suitable where there are significant ongoing responsibilities. We deal with leasehold land in Chapters 7, 8 and 9.

14.15 Further reading

C Hunter, A Brookes and G Peaker, 'Airbnb – issues for housing lawyers' (2017) 20(2) JHL 39–46.

T Sutton, 'On the brink of land obligations again' (2003) 1 Conv 17–29.

Law Commission, *Making Land Work: Easements, Covenants and Profits a Prendre* (Law Com No 327), 2011.

Enforceability of covenants

	Burden		Benefit
Common law	**Positive covenants – NO** (*Austerberry v Oldham Corporation*) Exceptions • mutual benefit and burden (*Halsall v Brizell; Wilkinson v Kerdine Ltd*) • commonhold • indemnity covenants • estate rentcharges	**Negative covenants – NO** (*Austerberry v Oldham Corporation*)	**Positive or negative covenants – YES if:** 1. covenant touches and concerns the land; 2. original covenantee held a legal estate in the land; 3. benefit must have been intended to run with the land (now occurs under s 78(1) of the LPA 1925)
Equity	**Positive covenants – NO** (*Haywood v Brunswick Permanent Building Society; Rhone v Stephens*)	**Negative covenants – YES, if:** • successor is not a purchaser of a legal estate for value without notice; • the covenant touches and concerns the covenantee's land; and • covenant was intended to run with the covenantor's land (*Tulk v Moxhay*)	**Negative covenants** Express assignment Annexation Building scheme

test your
knowledge

1   What do you consider to be the main difficulties with the current law of covenants?

2   Review the Law Commission's proposals for reform at **14.13**.

3   Do you consider that the proposed 'land obligation' should be introduced?

INDEX